Word breaks are the orphan of orthography development, with the challenges they present tending to be overlooked, deprioritized or ignored altogether. Practitioners seeking guidelines, models and inspiration have hitherto been limited by a sparse repertoire of research. This welcome volume brings ten new contributions from around the world, single-handedly increasing the extant literature by about 50% by my calculations: a giant leap forward in a neglected subdomain.

David Roberts
Independent Scholar

What is a WORD?

We think we all know. We can pronounce it in isolation. We can write it in isolation. But how to establish the boundaries of a WRITTEN WORD in languages which are in the process of developing a writing system is not always an easy task.

In addition to making the best choices for vowels, consonants, tones or other features that need to be represented in a new orthography, choices concerning word boundaries are important to help beginning readers become fluent readers.

This book contains chapters pertaining to languages from Africa, India, Mexico, and Southeast Asia. Different authors have written about their experiences and struggles in this domain. They have weighted different linguistic and other factors and tried to set priorities among these criteria. The chapters in this book may provide orthography developers with new ideas for treating problems in the domain of word-boundary choices.

Constance Kutsch Lojenga
Senior Linguistics Consultant, SIL Global

This eye-opening volume brings together insights from research in multiple disciplines across multiple continents addressing one of the foundational issues in written language—the concept of a word and its written representation. This unique collection of studies from a range of underrepresented languages and orthographies offers the reader a vastly broader non-Eurocentric view of this topic, one that will enrich theory and practice around the globe.

David Share
University of Haifa

The Orthographic Word in Languages of the World

SIL Global
Publications in Language Use and Education 8

Publications in Language Use and Education is a peer-reviewed series published by SIL Global. The series is a venue for works concerned with mother tongue literacy, multilingual education, educational anthropology, and other issues related to language and education. While most volumes are authored by members of SIL, suitable works by others will also form part of the series.

Series Editor
Susan McQuay

Editorial Staff
Eugene C. Burnham, Volume Editor
Eleanor J. McAlpine, Proofreader

Production Staff
Priscilla Higby, Production Manager
Judy Benjamin, Compositor
Barbara Alber, Graphic Designer

The Orthographic Word in Languages of the World

Edited by Helen Eaton

SIL Global
Dallas, Texas

Library of Congress Catalog No: 2025941956
ISBN: 978-1-55671-575-4 (pkb)
ISBN: 978-1-55671-576-1 (ePub)
ISSN: 1545-0074

Copies of this and other publications of SIL Global may be obtained through distributors such as Amazon, Barnes & Noble, other worldwide distributors and, for select volumes, publications.sil.org:

SIL Global Publishing Services
7500 W Camp Wisdom Road
Dallas, TX 75236-5629 USA
publications@sil.org

Contents

Map

Figures

Tables

Preface

Helen Eaton

Words are often assumed to be an intuitive concept which can be clearly defined in crosslinguistic terms. However, for some years now linguists have challenged this assumption, defining different kinds of words by different, potentially conflicting criteria. In recognising different kinds of "words", the orthographic word is often set aside as the one type whose definition is uncontroversial. In many languages an orthographic word is simply a character or sequence of characters typically separated from other orthographic words by spaces, and is therefore considered instantly recognisable. However, leaving aside languages which do not use spaces to separate words, this, of course, assumes that a language has an accepted and standardised orthography, which many languages in the world do not have.[1] In languages where orthographies are in the early stages of development, the question of how to decide on the units which will constitute orthographic words is one which must pay attention to the potentially conflicting linguistic criteria, as well as to sociolinguistic factors, such as the acceptability of the orthography to its users. As such, these decisions are complex, involving the interplay of multiple factors.

The number of written languages in the world has risen over the past few decades and orthography developers have much experience to share with

[1] The *Ethnologue* (Eberhard et al. 2024) currently lists 7,164 living languages, of which 4,153 are reported to have a developed writing system. However, it is not always known whether these writing systems are widely used.

linguists in other subdisciplines concerning the reasoning behind decisions relating to the orthographic word. Orthography developers are also able to contribute to our understanding of the concept of the word with insights from practical orthography development and the research which underpins it. This volume has collected together a series of case studies from lesser-known languages[2] around the world which highlight the complexity of the orthographic word, and it is our hope that together these case studies will be of value both to those who are involved in orthography development and also to those whose interest is in the concept of the word, in its many forms.

Chapter 1, by Bartram and Eaton ("The Orthographic Word") sets the scene for the rest of the volume by discussing the concept of the word in linguistics and reviewing research into the word in literacy. They show how in linguistics, attempts to define a "word" have encountered challenges, even when the concept is divided into subtypes of word, such as phonological or grammatical, in an effort to come up with crosslinguistically valid definitions. Research into reading shows that for all the difficulty of defining words, the practice of word spacing in text has value in facilitating reading and comprehension. Bartram and Eaton also discuss some practical approaches which have been suggested for making decisions concerning the word in the development of orthographies for languages without standardised writing systems. These approaches have in many cases been followed by those developing orthographies for the languages discussed in the following chapters.

Chapter 2, by Bartram ("Orthographic Words in Lamkang Noun Phrases: Linguistic and Participatory Approaches") shows how with respect to some orthographic decisions for Lamkang [lmk], a Tibeto-Burman language of India, a facilitated participatory approach was followed. Linguistic analysis and community input together informed the decision-making process. Bartram presents data from written material showing the orthographic choices Lamkang writers made for three particular morphemes before discussions were held on how to standardise these choices and then considers the reasoning behind the eventual decisions made by the community. Interestingly, native speaker intuitions generally lined up with the decisions suggested by linguistic analysis. Bartram also notes how some decisions changed over a relatively short period of time as the orthography stakeholders within the community began to rank conflicting criteria differently, feeling more able to deviate from English spelling norms and coming to accept that it was possible to have consistency without uniformity.

Chapter 3, by Eaton, Gray, Mészároš and Walker ("Orthographic Word Boundary Challenges Posed by Nouns and Clitics in Eighteen Tanzanian Bantu Languages") also reports on orthography development where final decisions have been made by language communities. Put simply, the

---

[2] Three-letter ISO 639-3 language codes are given [in square brackets] for all languages.

phonological behaviour of the clitics in this chapter argues for writing them attached to nouns and their grammatical status argues for writing them as independent words. However, the authors show that microvariation in morphophonological behaviour across the languages means that factors in the conflict between phonology and grammar can be weighted differently for different languages, resulting in diverse compromise solutions in the orthographies, despite many apparent surface similarities between the languages. Eaton et al. show clearly how the complexity and interrelatedness of the behaviour of nouns with different clitics can mean that making a word boundary decision about one clitic in isolation can have undesirable consequences for other clitics. Therefore keeping the wider system in mind is important when helping a community to make informed choices.

Chapter 4, by Roberts and Soulokadi ("The Orthographic Treatment of Clitics in Musey") also deals with clitics and the difficulties they pose for word boundary choices in an orthography. The authors begin by providing a detailed phonological and morphosyntactic description of two common clitics in Musey [mse], a Chadic language. They then discuss the different ways these clitics have been written in the extant literature. As there are currently no guides for how to write the clitics, the way they have been written in the literature can be argued to reflect the intuitions of the speakers. Roberts and Soulokadi note the similarities and differences in current practice and suggest that some differences may be due to differing degrees of cliticisation in the morphemes under discussion.

Chapter 5, by Norton ("Participatory Word Spacing in Acheron Preverbal and Prenominal Inflection") describes participatory research in Acheron [acz], a Niger-Congo language of the Republic of Sudan. As part of the research, four word boundary criteria were chosen and presented to participants as questions. Examples were then discussed orally in order to minimise interference from familiarity with spacing practices in equivalent English forms. Participants' judgements were consistent and matched the results of other language-internal evidence, but the complexity of the prenominal inflections discussed showed the importance of the latter kind of evidence in interpreting the participants' judgements. Norton argues for the importance of language community members assessing word boundary criteria themselves. In particular, he advocates for a focus on oral data rather than written data during participatory research on word boundaries, in order to minimise the impact of interference from other language orthographies on speaker intuitions.

Chapter 6, by Yee and Boyd ("Orthographic Word Difficulties in Central Chadic Languages") looks at four languages in Cameroon which have highly mutable vowels. These vowels change according to phonological processes, such as palatalisation and labialisation, and also according to other factors, such as whether the word in question occurs before a pause or is followed by a suffix, clitic, or another word. Yee and Boyd show how this mutability has consequences for decisions about word boundaries and how to maintain a consistent word image. However, they conclude that word boundary issues are less dependent on whether a following element is a clitic or a suffix, but rather on whether a morpheme is cohesive and whether there are restrictions on the syntactic category of its host.

Chapter 7, by Solomiac ("Different Types of Nasality as Orthographic Word Issues: The Case of the Samogo Languages in Burkina Faso and Mali") takes a similar approach to the previous chapter in focussing on phonological issues which occur at the edges of words and have implications for orthographic word boundary decisions. He presents an autosegmental analysis of two types of nasality (associated vowel nasality and a floating nasal). The similarities and differences in how these types of nasality are realised in the four languages under discussion have various consequences for the writing of word boundaries and the resulting orthographies show varying levels of ambiguity, explicitness and redundancy regarding how the nasality is written.

Chapter 8, by Schwab ("Linguistics, Politics, and Native Speaker Perception: The Analysis and Orthography of Pronominal Enclitics in Amoltepec Mixtec") looks at some grammatical and phonological features of pronominal enclitics in Amoltepec Mixtec [mbz], an Oto-Manguean language of Mexico. These features argue both for and against separating the enclitics from their hosts in the orthography. Schwab discusses how to resolve this conflict by reference to various orthographic word boundary criteria and then balances these considerations with the intuitions of language users and the political background of orthography choice in the country. A compromise solution is then presented which allows different rules for enclitics with particular syllabic structures and takes into account potential orthographic ambiguities. This solution makes use of the hyphen as a middle way between disjunctive and conjunctive writing and has proved to be acceptable to all stakeholders.

Chapter 9, by Benítez and Benítez-Torres ("The Orthographic Word in the Tagdal Verb Phrase") considers data from Tagdal [tda], a Northern Songhay language spoken in the Republic of Niger and parts of Mali. The authors show how the grammatical, phonological, and morphological processes and structures of the verb phrase in Tagdal provide a good starting point for considering what constitutes an orthographic word in the language as a whole. Orthography development in Tagdal is at a very early stage and there are not currently many readers or writers, so Benítez and Benítez-Torres recognise that the word boundary recommendations they put forward need further discussion and testing with the language community. It is already clear, however, that issues such as vowel elision and vowel length need to be considered when deciding on orthographic word boundaries.

Chapter 10, by van den Berg ("When Is Long Too Long? Word Length and Readability: A Case Study from Muna [Indonesia]") takes a different perspective from the preceding chapters by focussing on the issue of word length as it relates to readability. Can an orthographic word which otherwise meets good criteria for wordhood be so long that it negatively impacts its readability, particular for new readers of developing orthographies? Van den Berg presents a case study using data from the Western Austronesian language of Muna [mnb] and compares the length of orthographic words in this language with orthographic words in other languages of the area and further afield. He concludes with the exhortation that orthography developers should pay attention to the issue of word length and the recommendation that testing on the relationship between word length and readability is undertaken in order to understand this area better.

Chapter 11, by Manson ("The Orthographic Word as a Social Construct: A Perspective from Karen Languages") moves the focus away from the orthographic word in writing systems using the Latin alphabet and starts by looking at different scripts in use in Greater Mainland Southeast Asia. Manson then goes on to look at some recently developed Latin-based orthographies for the Karen languages and shows how certain types of grammatical words and phrases present challenges for word boundary decisions, resulting in different decisions for similar phenomena across the languages. Manson proposes that we should not think of the orthographic word as a linguistic object but rather as a social one, which develops out of the language community's use of an orthography.

This focus on the importance of the language community itself in the development of orthographic word boundary decisions is a common thread running through all the chapters of this volume. Although the linguistic issues involved in representing words in writing are complex and worth studying for their own sake, the final decision about orthographic word boundaries is up to the users of the language. Since an orthographic word is what is written on a page in a certain way, it is ultimately defined by use, which may change over time. It does not matter what a linguist may recommend, or even what might have been decided officially and written in an orthography guide, it is actual practice by language users which shows us what an orthographic word is.

In this volume the following conventions are used in chapters where multiple types of data transcription occur together: [a] for phonetic representation, /a/ for phonemic representation and <a> for orthographic representation. IPA is followed for phonemic and phonetic representation, unless otherwise noted by an author. In addition, a hyphen is commonly used to represent affixes and an equals sign (=) to represent clitics.

Reference

Eberhard, David M., Gary F. Simons, and Charles D. Fennig, eds. 2024. *Ethnologue: Languages of the world.* Twenty-seventh edition. Dallas, TX: SIL International. www.ethnologue.com.

1
The Orthographic Word

Cathryn Bartram and Helen Eaton

1.1 Introduction

Linguists and nonlinguists alike tend to proceed through life with the assumption that we all know, and agree on, what a word is. For the linguist, the word is what makes it possible to separate morphology and syntax as areas of study. For the nonlinguist, words are the pieces of language we learn to speak and understand as children and – for those of us growing up with languages with a particular kind of orthography – words are what we learn to write surrounded by blank spaces on a page. However, once we look more closely at these assumptions, we discover that it is hard to define what constitutes a word even in one language, let alone crosslinguistically. Moreover, once we attempt to formulate criteria to arrive at a definition, we realise that different criteria – semantic, phonological, grammatical or orthographic – can lead to competing definitions which do not line up with what we may feel intuitively should be a single concept.

In this introductory chapter, we consider briefly first the concept of the word in linguistics (§ 1.2) and research into the word in literacy (§ 1.3), before turning to the practical approaches which have been suggested for making decisions concerning the word in orthography development (§ 1.4).

1.2 The word in linguistics

1.2.1 Introduction to words

For some time now linguists have recognised the difficulties of defining the word. It is not our intention here to go into these challenges in detail, but it is helpful to begin with an overview of the discussion of this topic as many of the orthographic challenges concerning writing words stem directly from the difficulties of defining the word. The reader who is interested in an in-depth discussion of wordhood is directed to excellent treatments in Haspelmath (2011), Wray (2015) and Aikhenvald, Dixon and White (2020), and a historical overview of the topic in Dixon and Aikhenvald (2002).

Of the potentially competing criteria for determining wordhood, often the main conflict is between phonological and grammatical criteria, as will be exemplified in § 1.2.4. A semantic definition of a word may be in evidence in everyday language, but linguistics has given us the term *lexeme* to keep this meaning separate from other types of words. The concept of a lexeme, or semantic word, enables us to treat different grammatical words as instances of the same lexeme (Saeed 2016:53). The lexeme *WRITE* in English [eng], for example, can be realised as <write>, <writes>, <wrote>, <written> and <writing>. In nontechnical language, a "word" can refer to a lexeme, and therefore we can say that the five forms listed in the example are all forms of the "same word". It would be acceptable to list these forms under the same headword in a dictionary as in a certain sense they have the "same meaning". Dixon and Aikhenvald (2002:7) point out that adopting the term lexeme allows us to easily talk about lexemes which are made of more than one (grammatical) word, as in phrasal verbs in English, for example. Thus *WRITE OFF* is a single lexeme consisting of two words, each free to occupy its own syntactic slot in the sentence.

1.2.2 Phonological and grammatical words

In their review of earlier linguistic research into the concept of the word, Dixon and Aikhenvald (2002:13) note that often both phonological and grammatical criteria are used to define a word and no explicit provision is made for how to deal with the many conflicts between these criteria which occur. They conclude that it is therefore better to keep separate both the two types of criteria and the units which they define. Thus they favour defining a phonological word in phonological terms and a grammatical word in grammatical terms. The former type of word is defined by Dixon and Aikhenvald (2002:13) as follows:

> A phonological word is a phonological unit larger than the syllable (in some languages it may minimally be just

one syllable) which has at least one (and generally more than one) phonological defining property chosen from the following areas:

(a) Segmental features – internal syllabic and segmental structure; phonetic realisations in terms of this; word boundary phenomena; pause phenomena.
(b) Prosodic features – stress (or accent) and/or tone assignment; prosodic features such as nasalisation, retroflexion, vowel harmony.
(c) Phonological rules – some rules apply only within a phonological word; others (external sandhi rules) apply specifically across a phonological word boundary.

The case studies in this volume provide many examples of such properties. For example, a segmental feature marking out the boundaries of a phonological word is seen in Acheron (Norton, § 5.3.2), where there is the possibility of pausing between two elements of a progressive structure. The prosodic feature of vowel harmony is restricted to the phonological word in Malila (Eaton et al., § 3.2.4).

As Haspelmath (2011:37) points out, the phonological defining properties need not necessarily converge in a language, leading to an analysis of different kinds of phonological words. In Walungge [ola] (Tibeto-Burman; Nepal) for example, segmental features and prosodic features across a negative morpheme plus verb root do not converge for phonological wordhood. The underlying tone of the verb root surfaces on the negative morpheme (/ma-kʰúr/ → [mákʰur] 'NEG-carry'), indicating a single phonological word. However, aspiration is retained, indicating a phonological word boundary (Bartram 2011:252–254).

Dixon and Aikhenvald (2002:19) go on to define a grammatical word in the following way:

A grammatical word consists of a number of grammatical elements which:

(a) always occur together, rather than scattered through the clause (the criterion of cohesiveness);
(b) occur in a fixed order;
(c) have a conventionalised coherence and meaning.

They consider the criterion of cohesiveness a particularly strong one for grammatical wordhood, but exceptions can be found to the second requirement of a fixed order of grammatical elements. To use an example from a language included in this volume, the relative order of the subject prefix and the negative prefix in some Bena verbs is not fixed (Morrison 2011:283–284), but in other ways these verbs are strong candidates for being analysed as grammatical words.

Haspelmath (2011:38) presents ten criteria for morphosyntactic wordhood:

1. Potential pauses
2. Free occurrence
3. External mobility and internal fixedness
4. Uninterruptibility
5. Nonselectivity
6. Noncoordinatability
7. Anaphoric islandhood
8. Nonextractability
9. Morphophonological idiosyncrasies
10. Derivations from biuniqueness

His conclusion after examining each criterion is that "none of them is necessary and sufficient for wordhood, and that many are problematic in one way or another". For example, in relation to the fourth criterion of uninterruptibility, Haspelmath notes that it is not possible to place anything between <very> and <good> in <very good food>, but we do not consider <very good> a complex word in English (2011:45).

In the light of such difficulties, Haspelmath concludes that although applying the criteria to different languages can result in interesting insights into the structure of these languages, it does not provide convincing support for a crosslinguistically valid notion of a morphosyntactic word defined in nonfuzzy terms (2011:60). Morphosyntactic words can more easily be defined in language-specific ways or by means of a fuzzy or prototypical definition using multiple criteria. This, as Haspelmath goes on to argue, has serious implications for the traditional linguistic division between morphology and syntax, and for theories and typologies which are based upon this division (2011:66).

Another recent author to express doubt as to the validity of the grammatical or morphosyntactic word is Wray (2015). She presents a case for the word as "an inherently vague phenomenon, one that looks more solid and more clear-cut than it is because of the domination of a strong prototype (the noun) and of a cultural practice (writing)" (2015:725–726). She also questions the assumption of the universal discreteness of words, commenting that it "may be that much of language is not really words at all" (2015:750).

1.2.3 Orthographic words

In addition to semantic, phonological and grammatical criteria for wordhood, it is possible to define a word in orthographic terms.[1] Many languages have

[1] Other types of words and further subdivisions have been identified as well, such as those listed in Packard 2000:7–14, where eight types are given and discussed:

orthographies which use spaces between words and in such languages an orthographic word is simply that which is written between spaces (with the possibility of certain punctuation marks intervening before or after those spaces). Complications can ensue with the status of hyphenated words (<meeting face to face> versus <a face-to-face meeting>) and it is not hard to find examples where different word boundary choices for the same item exist (<houseplant> or <house plant>?) or for apparently comparable items (<flowerpot> but <plant pot>). There may also be minimal pairs for word spacing which convey distinct meanings and represent different pronunciations (<blackboard> versus <black board>). However, in the main, defining and recognising an orthographic word in print is simple for a language with an established orthography. Deciding where to mark the word boundaries in languages where no standard yet exists, however, is a complex process, as many of the case studies in this volume attest.

1.2.4 Conflicts between types of words

Often semantic, phonological, grammatical and orthographic criteria for wordhood match up without conflict and this is one reason why at first glance the concept of the word feels simple and intuitive. However, the possibility for conflict exists and is evident in many languages. Often the most interesting conflicts are between the phonological word and the grammatical word. Aikhenvald et al. (2020:7) give three possible conflicts. First, two or more phonological words may correspond to a single grammatical word, as seen in the example they give from Yidiñ [yii] (Australian). Second, two or more grammatical words may correspond to a single phonological word, as seen in Lamkang (Bartram, § 2.2.2). And finally, there is the possibility that "one type of word does not necessarily consist of a whole number of instances of the other type" (Dixon 2010b:24–25). Dixon illustrates this in reference to Fijian [fij] (Austronesian).

Mismatches between phonological and grammatical words are features of several linguistic phenomena, including compounds, clitics and reduplications. Compound words, such as <sunflower> or <sometimes>, comprise two or more roots which together form a single grammatical word. This grammatical word may be a single phonological word or may consist of more than one phonological word (see the examples summarised in Aikhenvald et al. (2020:9) and discussed in that volume). A clitic is partway between a word and an affix. The term typically refers to a morpheme which is a grammatical word but not a phonological word (Dixon 2010a:221 and Dixon 2010b:20). Thus clitics attach to a preceding or following word in order to create a phonological word with the host. Acheron (Norton, § 5.4.4) provides us with an example of a proclitic in the form of the comitative

---

orthographic word, sociological word, lexical word, semantic word, phonological word, morphological word, syntactic word and psycholinguistic word.

preposition /əŋ/ 'with'. Amoltepec Mixtec (Schwab, § 8.2) has a set of enclitic pronouns. Reduplication is a morphological process which results in a single grammatical word and may form either a single phonological word (cohering reduplication) or more than one phonological word (noncohering reduplication) (Aikhenvald et al. 2020:8). Muna (van den Berg, § 10.4.5) provides examples of full and partial reduplications in verbs, which are being handled differently in the orthography. Full disyllabic reduplications are written with a hyphen, but using a hyphen for a partial reduplication would mean the element before the hyphen was not a viable phonological word, so such reduplications are written conjunctively, without a hyphen.

The preceding discussion has highlighted the potential conflicts and complicating factors which can come into play when deciding on the boundaries of the orthographic word. Such decisions can therefore be complex and require thorough linguistic investigation. Given the effort needed to make well-informed, principled decisions about what will constitute the set of orthographic words in a language, it is appropriate to question the value of this effort in practical terms for the orthography users. That is, how important are orthographic words for the reader? It is to this question which we now turn.

1.3 The word in reading

1.3.1 Introduction to reading

Is there evidence that reading is easier with spaces between words, and if so, what is the evidence and what are the reasons? Do spaces facilitate or hinder the reading process for constructions such as compound words? What differences are there for scripts which do not have spaces between words? Although ease of reading may mean different things to different people, arguably reading is about the identification of meaning and not merely the identification of sounds. Whilst there are multiple factors which can affect access to meaning (see, for example, Rayner et al. 2013, Pollatsek and Treiman 2015, and Schwanenflugel and Knapp 2016), this section is particularly focused on the relationship between access to meaning and word-spaced text. Our discussion, therefore, focuses on one particular facet of the reading process which is relevant to this relationship, and that is eye movements.

1.3.2 Eye movements

When we read, our eyes do not move in a smooth continuous manner across the text. Rather, they make rapid movements (*saccades*), separated by periods when the eyes are relatively still (*fixations*) and new visual information is obtained. Whilst most of the time saccades move forwards, sometimes they move backwards (*regressions*). Saccade length, fixation duration and number of regressions vary according to various factors, including reading ability, text complexity and oral versus silent reading. Further, some words are skipped over without any fixation. Function words are more likely to be skipped over than content words, and shorter words are more likely to be skipped over than longer words (Rayner 1998:375). The basic characteristics of eye moments are the same across different languages and writing systems, including those without spaces between words, but with differences in the specific details (Rayner et al. 2013:97–98). For spaced text, the greatest influence on where the eyes move comes from word length and spaces (Schotter and Rayner 2015:51).

The *gaze duration* of a word (the sum of the fixation durations) is influenced by many factors including word frequency, word predictability, number of meanings, phonological properties, semantic relations with prior words, and word familiarity (Schotter and Rayner 2015:52). Importantly, it reflects more than simply the time taken for identifying the orthographic and phonological forms of the word, but also the time taken for accessing its meaning and whether this meaning agrees with the prior context (Rayner et al. 2013:139–143).

Because of the influence of spaces on eye movements, and because of the relationship between eye movements and access to meaning, comparing eye movements for spaced and unspaced text can give an indication of the relative ease of meaning identification.

1.3.3 Spaces and ease of reading

One particularly significant study looking at the effect of removing spaces from English text is that of Rayner et al. (1998), who found that reading rate for unspaced English was reduced by approximately 40–50 percent. From their analysis of eye movements, they argue that the largest contributor to this dramatic decrease in reading rate, is a decrease in ease of word identification. Perea and Acha (2009) found a similar decrease in reading rate for unspaced Spanish [spa]. Sheridan et al. (2013) investigated the relationship between spacing and word identification in English by means of an eye movement study, concluding that their results provide further evidence that removing spaces interferes with word identification.

It is important to consider not only the effect of removing spaces from spaced text, but also the effect of adding spaces to unspaced text. If there is a similarly disruptive effect by adding spaces to text which is normally unspaced, the above results could be attributed to lack of familiarity with unspaced text. If, however, the disruption caused by adding spaces is minimal, or if the spaces have a positive effect, this strengthens the argument that spaces aid word identification.

There have been various eye movement studies on the effects of adding word spaces to standard unspaced text. These include Thai [tha] (e.g., Kohsom and Gobet 1997, Winskel et al. 2009, and Kasisopa et al. 2013), Chinese [cmn] (e.g., Inhoff et al. 1997, Bai et al. 2008, and Bassetti 2009), and Japanese [jpn] (e.g., Sainio et al. 2007). Typically, in each of these, any difference in overall reading rate was either not significant, or only marginally significant.

For Thai, Winskel et al. (2009) found that fixations were shorter for spaced text but fewer words were skipped over, resulting in an overall reading rate which was slightly slower but with only marginal significance. They suggest that the increased visual distinctiveness of words in spaced text caused fixations on words which would normally be skipped over. Kohsom and Gobet (1997) give the reading rate for spaced Thai as slightly faster, but again with only marginal significance.

Bai et al. (2008) found a similar effect for Chinese as Winskel et al. (2009) did for Thai. Although they found no significant difference in overall reading rate comparing word-spaced and unspaced Chinese text, they did find that fixation times were shorter for word-spaced text, but there were more fixations. They make the point that despite the unfamiliarity of spaces, Chinese readers could read word-spaced text as easily as normal Chinese unspaced text. They argue that word spaces do have a facilitative effect on reading, which was being balanced out by the disruptive effect of unfamiliarity.

Japanese writing contains a mixture of *kanji* and *hiragana* characters, with the kanji frequently appearing at the beginning of words. Similarly to the above studies, Sainio et al. (2007) found no significant difference in overall reading rate for spaced and unspaced kanji-hiragana text. Whilst the unfamiliarity argument might also apply to Japanese, it is important to note the role of the kanji in indicating word boundaries. By comparing eye movements for kanji-hiragana text and purely hiragana text, Sainio et al. (2007) argue that the kanji are giving cues to signal word boundaries, and thus spaces provide no additional help.

Another way in which a writing system may indicate words is by connecting the characters. For example, in Arabic [arb] script the characters within a word are typically connected cursively, and in Devanagari script the characters within a word are typically connected with a horizonal line. It is beyond the scope of this section to look further at this, and very little research appears to have been done on teasing apart the intertwining effects of interword spaces and other mechanisms (although see, for example, Leung et al. 2021 on the removal of spaces in Arabic).

A further type of spacing or separation which is beyond the scope of this section, is that of syllables. In Tibetan [bod], for example, word boundaries are not indicated, but syllables are separated with a dot. In Vietnamese [vie], syllables are separated by spaces. Very little research appears to have been done on syllable versus word spacing (although see, for example, Vitrano-Wilson 2016 for Hmong Daw [mww]). Our discussion will therefore move on to looking at compound words.

1.3.4 Compound words

There have been a variety of studies of eye movements across compound words. The following are a small selection which compare spaced/hyphenated/unspaced compounds in sentence context. Whilst there are differences in the studies, they each illustrate the trade-off between ease of identification of the components (particularly the first component), and identification of the meaning as a whole.

Inhoff et al. (2000) analysed fixation and gaze durations for spaced and unspaced compounds in German [deu], concluding that whilst spaces make it easier to identify the components, they make it harder to identify the meaning as a whole. A similar result was found for spaced versus unspaced compound words in English by Juhasz et al. (2005). They concluded that spaces were facilitating identification of the first constituent, but hindering access to the full compound meaning. This disruptive effect was greater for adjective-noun compounds than for noun-noun compounds.

Comparisons of hyphenated versus unspaced compounds in Dutch [nld] and in Finnish [fin] gave similar results to the above (Bertram et al. 2011). In both languages compounds are typically written unspaced. Hyphens facilitated processing of the first component but hindered processing of the whole word. Interestingly in both studies, as the experiment progressed, overall gaze durations for hyphenated compounds became shorter. By the end of the experiment, compounds with a hyphen at a major component boundary were processed as fast as (Dutch) or faster than (Finnish) unspaced compounds.

Bertram and Hyönä (2012) compared eye movements across unspaced and hyphenated Finnish compounds of differing length. Short compounds potentially only need one fixation, whereas long compounds potentially need multiple fixations. They concluded that a hyphen in shorter compounds is disruptive because it encourages sequential processing of components in words where simultaneous processing is possible. In longer words, however, the hyphen facilitates the processing because of the need for multiple fixations.

Whereas the above studies compared unspaced versus spaced/hyphenated compounds, Kuperman and Deutsch (2020) compared spaced versus hyphenated compounds in Hebrew [heb]. The compounds were transparent noun-noun constructions (e.g., <salt crystal>), normally written with spaces. The results suggested that rather than being an aid, a hyphen was a hindrance. Further, processing times for hyphenated compounds did not decrease as the experiment progressed. Kuperman and Deutsch also considered compounds where the first noun was linguistically marked for compounding. In this instance hyphens appeared to be neither an aid nor a hinderance. They suggest that the presence of a linguistic cue makes the same information coming from a hyphen unnecessary.

A few overall points can be drawn from the above studies. First, when considering unspaced versus separated (by space or by hyphen) compounds, there is a trade-off between ease of identification of the first component versus hindrance to identification of the meaning as a whole. For shorter compounds in particular, the benefit of holistic processing seems to outweigh ease of identification of the first component. Second, the use of a hyphen may be something that at least in some situations may be advantageous, and which readers may adapt to. Finally, some languages may have linguistic cues which facilitate ease of processing without need for additional orthographic cues.

1.3.5 Summary

The studies outlined above illustrate ways in which spaces can affect ease of reading. All of the studies demonstrate, at least to some extent, that spaces appear to aid identification of individual words or morphemes. However, the effect of spaces on identification of overall meaning depends on a variety of factors, including the nature of the spaces (e.g., spaces between words, spaces within words but between morphemes), the linguistic structure and the writing system. This may result in a trade-off between ease of identification of individual morphemes or components versus ease of identification of overall meaning. Keeping this in mind, we will now turn to the issue of how to decide where to put spaces.

1.4 The word in orthography development

In § 1.3, we saw how word-spaced text can aid word identification. We also saw ways in which spaces may aid, hinder or have a neutral effect on accessing overall meaning. Section 1.2 gives linguistic criteria for words, but also outlines the complexities of defining a word and the kinds of mismatches that might occur between the criteria. Taking this picture as a whole, how do we make decisions about orthographic words?

1.4.1 Alignment of grammatical and phonological criteria

As a starting point, if a particular morpheme or group of morphemes is both a grammatical and a phonological word, or neither, an initial decision would generally be to write that morpheme (or group of morphemes) spaced or unspaced accordingly. For example, the Lamkang plural morpheme <rek>, which is both a grammatical and a phonological word, as in <skool rek> 'horses' and <skool kvom rek> 'black horses' (Bartram, § 2.2.2), is written as a separate word. Writing morphemes in this way not only matches the linguistic alignment, but also fits with various research presented above on spaces aiding or hindering reading. This general principle would include writing grammatical morphemes either as separate orthographic words or as affixes according to their grammatical and phonological alignment. It would include writing multiple roots as separate orthographic words if they do not form a single grammatical word. And for compound words which are a single phonological word as well as being a single grammatical word, an initial decision might be to write the roots unspaced.

1.4.2 Conflicting linguistic criteria

In each of the cases in the previous section, there is no conflict between the linguistic criteria and therefore the word boundary decision is simple. But what should orthography developers do when the criteria do not align?

One early treatment of this question focused on Bantu languages, where writers divided into "conjunctivists" and "disjunctivists" according to how they felt it was best to write orthographic words (Guthrie 1948). Guthrie notes that writing sentences in a way which represented an unbroken stream of speech would "not only make reading impossible, but would also obscure the structure of the language" (1948:5). He offers various principles for determining whether segments of a sentence should be written as distinct words, such as whether they can be isolated, omitted or substituted. Guthrie notes several times the difficulties with applying the principles and the inadequacy of any principle taken by itself.

Pike and Pike (1982:98–101)[2] give guidance on word division for as yet unwritten languages of any family based on similar principles to those in Guthrie and drawing on earlier discussion on how to identify the word by Bloomfield (1933:178–183). Pike and Pike begin by admitting that with respect to word division, there is no "fail-safe mechanically applicable set of steps for arriving at one correct result" and that "one set of criteria will identify many words, but other sets of criteria are needed to identify other words" (1982:98).

More recently, Kutsch Lojenga (2014:91–98) gives the following criteria for aiding decisions about orthographic word boundaries:

Grammatical:
- Mobility
- Separability
- Substitutability

Phonological:
- Pronounceability in isolation
- Phonological unity
- Phonological bridging

[2] The word division section of Pike and Pike (1982:98–101) is reproduced in the appendix.

Semantic:
- Referential independence
- Conceptual unity
- Minimal ambiguities

These criteria were originally given in Van Dyken and Kutsch Lojenga (1993), where the semantic criteria were presented first, followed by grammatical and phonological. Kutsch Lojenga (2014) comments that since then many situations have convinced her that grammatical criteria should be used first, followed by phonological, and finally semantic. This is due to the importance she places on determining the morphosyntactic status of grammatical morphemes.

1.4.3 Grammatical morphemes

Kutsch Lojenga (2014) uses the grammatical criterion of *mobility* to refer to the ability of a morpheme to occur in different places in a sentence, giving an example from Lendu [led], a Nilo-Saharan language, where negative particles are written as separate words because they can take different places in the clause (Kutsch Lojenga 2014:92). Haspelmath (2011:40–44) also discusses the use of mobility as a criterion for grammatical wordhood, noting how it needs to be a different word ordering (e.g., <yesterday I saw her> versus <I saw her yesterday>) rather than different constructions. In Jimjimən [jim] (Yee and Boyd, § 6.3.2.3) demonstrative morphemes are written as separate orthographic words from the noun they refer to. One of the reasons for this is the ability to swap the order of a number and a demonstrative depending on the focus. For example, in the following phrase <bik> 'two' and the demonstrative <ətə> can appear in either order; <jəhunyini ətə bik> and <jəhunyini bik ətə> 'my two aforementioned horses' are both grammatical.

The criterion of *separability* is used by Kutsch Lojenga to refer to the possibility of a morpheme being separated from a neighbouring lexical morpheme by the insertion of another lexical morpheme. In Lamkang (Bartram, § 2.2.1), one of the reasons why the nonsingular enclitic /=in/ is written disjunctively is its separability from a noun by other words (e.g., <m'skool in> 'their horse', <m'skool klin soom in> 'their ten large horses'.

Substitutability refers to the ability to substitute the grammatical morpheme under consideration for a lexeme in the same syntactic position. For example, in the Nilo-Saharan language Lendu, a grammatical morpheme representing the subject may be substituted by a nominal subject and is thus considered a true pronoun and written disjunctively (Kutsch Lojenga 2014:94). In other languages, such as the Bantu language Swahili [swh], a grammatical morpheme representing the subject remains with the verb when a nominal subject is added and is not substituted by it (Kutsch Lojenga 2014:94). Thus writing the morpheme conjunctively with the verb is recommended.

Pronounceability in isolation has parallels to, but is not synonymous with phonological wordhood, which is relevant to decisions regarding clitics. An example is the English indefinite and definite articles, "a" and "the". Their normal, unstressed forms [ə] and [ðə] are clitics.[3] These forms do not typically occur on their own without the lexical morpheme to which they associate. However, in a contrived situation (e.g., in answer to the question "Did you say 'a' or 'the'?") it is possible in English to pronounce them in isolation, which is one of the reasons in favour of writing them disjunctively. On the other hand the clitic form of the English auxiliary "is" ([s]/[z]) would not be pronounced in isolation, which is a reason for writing it conjunctively.

Kutsch Lojenga uses the term *phonological unity* to describe the influence of one morpheme on another morpheme by phonological processes. This can be seen in the gender markers <na> (masculine) and <ra> (feminine) within the noun phrase of the Chadic language Musey (Roberts and Soulokadi, §§ 4.2.1–4.2.2). The initial /n/ and /r/ of these markers undergo phonological changes triggered by the final consonant of the previous word, which serves as the host of these clitics. In addition, the gender markers are toneless at the underlying level, and their surface tone is wholly determined by the last tone of the host word. The consonant changes in the gender markers, and the surface tone they exhibit, indicate that there is strong phonological unity between these clitics and the host word to which they attach.

When considering the issue of phonological unity, it is important to determine the phonological domain of a particular phonological process, as some processes have as their domain a phrase or an utterance, rather than a phonological word. An example of this would be English nasal place of articulation assimilation, which occurs both within words and across word boundaries. Even though the <n> might be pronounced as a velar in the phrase <Susan goes>, this is not indicating that the two morphemes are forming one phonological word and thus is not indicating that the two words should be written conjunctively.

Phonological bridging refers to how to divide words which are blended with other words in a phrase. Kutsch Lojenga (2014:97) relates this to whether or not the observed phonological processes are postlexical rules which occur as an automatic consequence of blending words together in speech. If this is the case, the process should not be represented orthographically; each word should retain a constant orthographic image. The implication of this in the context of word division is that they should be written disjunctively. Van Dyken and Kutsch Lojenga (1993:14) give the example of vowel elision across word boundaries in Sabaot [spy] (Nilotic). The elision is not represented orthographically and the words are written disjunctively. Solomiac (§ 7.1) uses the phonological bridging criterion to address the issue of different types of nasality in four languages of Burkina Faso and Mali.

[3] See Spencer and Luís (2012) for further discussion on English clitics.

Referential independence refers to a morpheme communicating meaning, even when seen or heard in isolation (Van Dyken and Kutsch Lojenga 1993:7). Van Dyken and Kutsch Lojenga rank this as the first criterion, arguing that readers need to recall to mind the item, event, etc. that a given word refers to. This criterion implies that grammatical morphemes should be written conjunctively. However, they note the discrepancy between this criterion and the fact that many languages write various function words separately. In the ranking of Kutsch Lojenga (2014), referential independence is lower than grammatical and phonological criteria. This later ranking takes into account that the balance of grammatical and phonological criteria may favour writing a grammatical morpheme disjunctively even though it is not referentially independent. An example of this is the locative proclitic in several of the Bantu languages discussed in Eaton et al. (§ 3.3.2.1), which is written as a separate word or joined to the following word with a hyphen. Grammatical criteria argue for writing the locative disjunctively and have been taken as the deciding factor for some languages, even though phonological criteria and the locative's lack of referential independence argue instead for conjunctive writing.

1.4.4 Compound words

Semantic criteria are particularly relevant to decisions about the writing of compound words. Kutsch Lojenga uses *conceptual unity* in the case of opaque and semitransparent compound words, and *minimal ambiguities* when the components may occur both as a compound and as a phrase (e.g., <lighthouse> versus <light house>; <blackbird> versus <black bird>). For these various types of compounds, she suggests writing unspaced. Writing such compounds unspaced is supported by the body of research presented above on eye movements, suggesting that whilst spaces might aid identification of the first component they hinder identification of the meaning of the compound as a whole.

The decision on whether to write transparent compounds spaced or unspaced is often not as straightforward. For a particular compound in a particular language there might not be minimal ambiguities such as <blackbird> and <black bird>. Further conceptual unity might be difficult to decide (for example, is <rubbish bin> one concept or two concepts?), particularly in instances where what is one concept in one language might not be one concept in another language (for example, <bai> 'younger brother' (Nepali) is one word in Nepali [npi] but two words each with its own concept in English).

Although Kutsch Lojenga relates the use of phonological criteria specifically to grammatical morphemes, phonological unity can be a reason to write transparent compounds unspaced. For example, in Walungge (Bartram 2011:232–234), the components of compounds form a single phonological word, as evidenced by a) loss of tone on noninitial syllables and b) loss of aspiration word-medially, for example /lùk-ʈ^{h}úk/ → [lùkʈuʔ] 'lamb' (2011:275). In such instances, the appropriate decision might be to write the compound unspaced.

Kutsch Lojenga suggests ascertaining if there is a distinction between transparent compound nouns and inalienable possessive constructions, and if there is no clear difference then to write both the same way in order to avoid confusion when writing.

1.4.5 The challenge of conflicting criteria

One of the challenges in deciding on orthographic words is weighing the above criteria when they do not align. For clitics, which are typically grammatical but not phonological words (Dixon 2010a:221), there are likely to be conflicts between the grammatical and phonological criteria for orthographic words. An example of this is found in the Northern Songhay language Tagdal (Benítez and Benítez-Torres, this volume). Tagdal pronominal clitics are syntactically free (§ 9.1.3), which argues for writing them as separate orthographic words, but they are unstressed and phonologically bound (§ 9.2.1.1), which supports writing them joined to the verb. In this case the phonological criteria were taken as decisive and therefore the conjunctive writing is currently favoured in the orthography.

It is important to remember that the above criteria are only an aid, and speakers of the language may weigh them differently from how an outsider may weigh them, and may have other considerations to be taken into account. Eaton et al. (§ 3.5.2) give an example from Kabwa [cwa] where an exception was made to the rule of writing locative proclitics conjunctively, in order to maintain constant word image of proper nouns, yet avoid word-medial capitalisation (e.g., write <ku Masige> rather than <kuMasige> or <Kumasige> 'at Masige's place'). They also give an example from Jita [jit], where the decision was made to separate a copula from a noun with a space rather than the hyphen originally proposed, due to the influence of Swahili. In Lamkang (Bartram, § 2.4.2), there was a general desire to avoid writing three grammatical morphemes conjunctively (e.g., for the construction /m-k^{h}ut rek=in=ŋi/ 'with their hands', avoid writing <mkhut rekinni>). In Ikoma [ntk] (Eaton et al., § 3.3.1.1), a proclitic comprising a single nasal consonant is written hyphenated, e.g., <n-omutëmi> 'is the king'. A hyphen is used due to a desire to give greater prominence to the proclitic. Word length may also be a consideration in word boundary decisions. In Muna (van den Berg, § 10.4.1), for example, certain object suffixes are written as separate words in order to reduce word length in verbs.

It is also important to be aware that orthographic decisions dealing with word boundaries may change over time. An example of this can be found in Kayan [pdu], a Karen language of Burma (Manson, § 11.3.2.1), where negative elaborate expressions were originally written without spaces and are now showing a tendency to be written with spaces. In cases like this it may be that as language communities become more used to reading and writing their language, they begin to weigh conflicting criteria concerning word boundaries differently.

The case studies in this volume illustrate different challenges and different decision-making processes regarding orthographic word divisions. Whilst there may be challenges, and the solutions may be different for different language communities, the above criteria provide a useful tool to aid the decision-making process.

1.5 Conclusion

In this introductory chapter we have looked at the word in linguistics, the word in reading and the word in orthography development. In linguistics, the concept of the word is a useful one, but a problematic one, as care must be taken to define what kind of word is meant and different kinds of words do not necessarily align. In reading, research shows that the use of spaces to signify orthographic word boundaries can affect reading ease and comprehension, which means the choice of where to put those boundaries in developing orthographies is an important one. Various linguistic criteria have been suggested to inform this choice, but the very existence of multiple criteria shows that the matter is not a simple one. Linguistic criteria are also not the only criteria to be considered and may be in conflict with nonlinguistic considerations, such as politics and aesthetics, as well as with each other.

References

Aikhenvald, Alexandra Y., R. M. W. Dixon, and Nathan M. White. 2020. The essence of "word." In Alexandra Y. Aikhenvald, R. M. W. Dixon and Nathan M. White (eds.), *Phonological word and grammatical word: A cross-linguistic typology*, 1–24. Explorations in Linguistic Typology 10. Oxford: Oxford University Press.

Bai, Xuejan, Guoli Yan, Simon P. Liversedge, Chuanli Zang, and Keith Rayner. 2008. Reading spaced and unspaced Chinese text: Evidence from eye movements. *Journal of Experimental Psychology: Human Perception and Performance* 34(5):1277–1287.

Bartram, Cathryn. 2011. An investigation of tone in Walungge. PhD dissertation. SOAS, University of London.

Bassetti, Benedetta. 2009. Effects of adding interword spacing on Chinese reading: A comparison of Chinese native readers and English readers of Chinese as a second language. *Applied Psycholinguistics* 30:757–775.

Bertram, Raymond, and Jukka Hyönä. 2012. The role of hyphens at the constituent boundary in compound word identification: Facilitative for long, detrimental for short compound words. *Experimental Psychology* 60(3):1–7.

Bertram, Raymond, Victor Kuperman, R. Harald Baayen, and Jukka Hyönä. 2011. The hyphen as a segmentation cue in triconstituent compound processing: It's getting better all the time. *Scandinavian Journal of Psychology* 52:530–544.

Bloomfield, Leonard. 1933. *Language*. New York: Holt.

Dixon, R. M. W. 2010a. *Basic linguistic theory. Vol. 1: Methodology*. Oxford: Oxford University Press.

Dixon, R. M. W. 2010b. *Basic linguistic theory. Vol. 2: Grammatical topics*. Oxford: Oxford University Press.

Dixon, R. M. W., and Alexandra Y. Aikhenvald. 2002. Word: A typological framework. In R. M. W. Dixon and Alexandra Y. Aikhenvald (eds.), Word: A cross-linguistic typology, 1–41. Cambridge: Cambridge University Press.

Guthrie, Malcolm. 1948. *Bantu word division: A new study of an old problem*. London: Oxford University Press.

Haspelmath, Martin. 2011. The indeterminacy of word segmentation and the nature of morphology and syntax. *Folia Linguistica* 45(1):31–80.

Inhoff, Albrecht W., Weimin Liu, Jian Wang, and D. J. Fu. 1997. Use of spatial information during the reading of Chinese text. In Danling Peng, Hua Shu, and Xuanzhi Chen (eds.), *Cognitive research on Chinese language*, 296–329. Jinan, China: Shan Dong Educational Publishing.

Inhoff, Albrecht W., Ralph Radach, and Dieter Heller. 2000. Complex compounds in German: Interword spaces facilitate segmentation but hinder assignment of meaning. *Journal of Memory and Language* 42(1):23–50.

Juhasz, Barbara J., Albrecht W. Inhoff, and Keith Rayner. 2005. The role of interword spaces in the processing of English compound words. *Language and Cognitive Processes* 20(1):291–316.

Kasisopa, Benjawan, Ronan G. Reilly, Sudaporn Luksaneeyanawin, and Denis Burnham. 2013. Eye movements while reading an unspaced writing system: The case of Thai. *Vision Research* 86:71–80.

Kohsom, Chananda, and Fernand Gobet. 1997. Adding spaces to Thai and English: Effects on reading. *Proceedings of the Cognitive Science Society* 19:383–393.

Kuperman, Victor, and Avital Deutsch. 2020. Morphological and visual cues in compound word reading: Eye-tracking evidence from Hebrew. *Quarterly Journal of Experimental Psychology* 73(12):2177–2187.

Kutsch Lojenga, Constance. 2014. Basic principles for establishing word boundaries. In Michael Cahill and Keren Rice (eds.), *Developing orthographies for unwritten languages*, 73–106. Publications in Language Use and Education 6. Dallas, TX: SIL International.

Leung, Tommi, Farima Boush, Qiang Chen, and Meera Al Kaabi. 2021. Eye movements when reading spaced and unspaced texts in Arabic. *Proceedings of the Annual Meeting of the Cognitive Science Society* 43:439–444.

Morrison, Michelle. 2011. A reference grammar of Bena. PhD dissertation. Rice University, Houston.

Packard, Jerome L. 2000. *The morphology of Chinese: A linguistic and cognitive approach.* Cambridge: Cambridge University Press.

Perea, Manuel, and Joana Acha. 2009. Space information is important for reading. *Vision Research* 49:1994–2000.

Pike, Kenneth. L., and Evelyn G. Pike. 1982. *Grammatical analysis.* Second edition. Summer Institute of Linguistics Publications in Linguistics 53. Dallas, TX: Summer Institute of Linguistics and University of Texas at Arlington.

Pollatsek, Alexander, and Rebecca Treiman, eds. 2015. *The Oxford handbook of reading.* Oxford: Oxford University Press.

Rayner, Keith. 1998. Eye movements in reading and information processing: 20 years of research. *Psychological Bulletin* 124(3):372–422.

Rayner, Keith, Martin H. Fischer, and Alexander Pollatsek. 1998. Unspaced text interferes with both word identification and eye movement control. *Vision Research* 38(8):1129–1144.

Rayner, Keith, Alexander Pollatsek, Jane Ashby, and Charles Clifton Jr. 2013. *Psychology of reading.* Second edition. New York: Routledge.

Saeed, John I. 2016. *Semantics.* Fourth edition. Chichester, UK: Wiley-Blackwell.

Sainio, Miia, Jukka Hyönä, Kazuo Bingushi, and Raymond Bertram. 2007. The role of interword spacing in reading Japanese: An eye movement study. *Vision Research* 47:2575–2584.

Schotter, Elizabeth, and Keith Rayner. 2015. The work of the eyes during reading. In Alexander Pollatsek and Rebecca Treiman (eds.), *The Oxford handbook of reading.* Oxford: Oxford University Press.

Schwanenflugel, Paula J., and Nancy Flanigan Knapp. 2016. *The psychology of reading: Theory and applications.* New York: Guilford.

Sheridan, Heather, Keith Rayner, and Eyal M. Reingold. 2013. Unsegmented text delays word identification: Evidence from a survival analysis of fixation durations. *Visual Cognition* 21(1):38–60.

Spencer, Andrew, and Ana R. Luís. 2012. *Clitics: An introduction.* Cambridge: Cambridge University Press.

Van Dyken, Julia R., and Constance Kutsch Lojenga. 1993. Word boundaries: Key factors in orthography development. In Rhonda L. Hartell (ed.), *Alphabets of Africa.* 3–22. Dakar: UNESCO and SIL.

Vitrano-Wilson, Seth. 2016. Reading syllable-spaced versus word-spaced text in Hmong Daw: Breaking up isn't so hard to do. *Writing Systems Research* 8(2):234–256.

Winskel, Heather, Ralph Radach, and Sudaporn Luksaneeyanawin. 2009. Eye movements when reading spaced and unspaced Thai and English: A comparison of Thai-English bilinguals and English monolinguals. *Journal of Memory and Language* 61(3):339–351.

Wray, Alison. 2015. Why are we so sure we know what a word is? In John R. Taylor (ed.), *The Oxford handbook of the word*, 725–750. Oxford: Oxford University Press.

2
Orthographic Words in Lamkang Noun Phrases: Linguistic and Participatory Approaches

Cathryn Bartram

Abstract

Noun phrases in Lamkang (Tibeto-Burman, India) have various grammatical morphemes which have posed a challenge for orthography developers, particularly regarding whether or not to write them as separate orthographic words. With no standardised orthography, the small amount of published material in the language is not consistent in this respect. The three morphemes which are discussed in this chapter each have different grammatical and phonological properties. These properties, together with considerations from orthography stakeholders within the language community, including length of words, consistency of writing, and perceived naturalness, need to be balanced when making orthographic decisions. Community participation, and a trial and revision process, are shown to be crucial to the acceptability and usability of the resulting orthographic strategy for these morphemes. Furthermore, decisions based on native speaker intuitions are shown to generally match those based on linguistic analysis.

Abbreviations

=	clitic
1	1st person
2	2nd person
3	3rd person
ABL	ablative
ERG	ergative
FOC	focus
LOC	locative
NEG	negative
NMLZ	nominalizer
NSG	nonsingular
PFV	perfective
PL	plural
SG	singular
TOP	topic

2.1 Introduction

2.1.1 Context

Lamkang [lmk] is a Tibeto-Burman language primarily spoken in the Chandel District of Manipur, India, with a population of approximately 10,000 speakers (Eberhard et al. 2024). The district is approximately ninety percent Christian, with a literacy rate of just over sixty percent in English (Census of India 2011). The language uses Roman script for its orthography due to the high prevalence of English-medium formal education. There is currently no education, formal or otherwise, in Lamkang. People typically learn to read Lamkang by transfer from English.

The language has two versions of the New Testament, one published by Bibles International in 2001 (henceforth BIV[1]) and the other by The Bible Society of India in 2002 (henceforth BSIV). They use different orthographic

[1] Scripture portions marked "BIV" are taken from *Pautum Ren Kchiir Laika*, Lamkang New Testament, copyright © 2001 by Bibles International, the Bible Society of Baptist Mid-Missions. Used by permission. All rights reserved.

Scripture portions marked "BSIV" are taken from *Ren Paurina* (Alt. *Ren Pauriina*), Lamkang New Testament, copyright © 2002 by The Bible Society of India. Used by permission. All rights reserved.

conventions from each other. Apart from these, currently there is only a relatively small amount of published material in the language. This includes hymn books, a few primer booklets, and a small variety of other booklets. The orthography is not standardised and each of these publications follows different orthographic strategies.

2.1.2 Focus of chapter

This chapter focuses on just one of the issues relating to orthographic words in Lamkang, that of three particular grammatical morphemes in noun phrases: the plural morpheme /rek/, the ergative/ablative[2] case marker /=ŋi/ and the nonsingular morpheme /=in/. These morphemes have been chosen because of the different challenges that they present for decisions about orthographic word divisions, individually, and in their various combinations. This chapter considers linguistic and orthographic criteria relating to the wordhood of these morphemes. It outlines various conventions which have been used for writing them, and illustrates the balancing of different linguistic and nonlinguistic criteria. It discusses the process which has led to current orthographic strategies, which centres around a participatory approach with community-based decision making. Importantly, it demonstrates the match between native speaker intuitions and arguments based on linguistic analysis concerning word divisions.

Whilst the scope of this chapter is restricted to noun phrases, some references to verb phrases will be made for comparative purposes. It should also be noted that the research methodology is qualitative not quantitative.

2.1.3 Orthography development and workshops

Since the mid-1980s there have been several orthography development efforts, both from within the community, and with the assistance of external organisations including Bibles International and SIL International (Lamkang Language Resource 2022). Until relatively recently, most of these efforts appear to have been primarily focused on the phoneme-grapheme correspondences. In 2016 the author was invited to a workshop organised by the Lamkang Literature Society (henceforth LLS), to assist the language community in resolving various orthography issues. LLS is the community body responsible for Lamkang literature matters. Membership of its general body is open to all stakeholders within the community. Its committee is elected by the general body and has the authority to make orthography decisions, with the expectation that Lamkang literature should only be published with its approval (LLS 2002).

2 In many Tibeto-Burman languages, roles which are generally considered different may be marked by the same form, with ergative (or agentive) and ablative being a common pairing (LaPolla 2004: 56). Following Noonan (2009:263), /=ŋi/ has been analysed as displaying syncretism, which Noonan describes as the "situation where a given relational marker is used to mark more than one relational function".

The number and scope of the orthography issues, combined with a process of trialling and revising decisions, resulted in further workshops being held in 2017 and 2018. Participants had been invited to these workshops from each of the main Lamkang areas, with each workshop attracting approximately twenty to thirty adults, both male and female, with a variety of ages, levels of education, and professions. Lamkang organisations represented included the Lamkang General Tribal Organisation, Baptist Association, Catholic Association, Students' Union and Women's Union. Decisions were taken by consensus and ratified by the LLS committee.

2.1.4 Data

Much of the data in this chapter is drawn from the published materials mentioned above, with additional data from a collection of stories written by participants at a writers' workshop in the language area in 2015. Uncited data was collected by the author during the 2016–2018 orthography workshops and by subsequent communication with the LLS.

The orthographic form of language data cited below retains the spelling, including spaces, which was used in the material. This means that the same morpheme may appear with different orthographic representations (indicated by <chevrons>). Consonantal phoneme-grapheme correspondences are generally predictable and consistent (e.g., /k^h/-<kh>, /k/-<k>, /ŋ/-<ng>, etc.).[3] Vowel length has not been consistently represented by authors. In the instances when it has been represented, this is generally by doubling the letter (e.g., <aa> for /aː/).[4]

Interlinearised language data is written with spaces according to the linguistic status of the morphemes (i.e., affix, clitic, or word). The language is tonal. However, tone has a light functional load and is only occasionally represented in the orthography.[5] Tone, therefore, has been omitted from the interlinearised data.

2.1.5 Outline of chapter

The chapter is structured as follows. Section 2.2 discusses the linguistic status of the morphemes /rek/, /=ŋi/ and /=in/ with regard to grammatical and phonological wordhood, and considers linguistic criteria for making decisions about orthographic word divisions. It outlines the intertwining of orthographic depth and word divisions. It also presents nonlinguistic criteria and the reasons for choosing a participatory approach. Sections 2.3, 2.4 and 2.5

3 /ʋ/ is represented by <w> in earlier materials and <v> in later materials, /s/ is generally represented by <s> but occasionally some authors use <sh>, and /j/ is represented by <y> or <j> depending on author.

4 Earlier materials use <uw> for /uː/ and <ow> for /oː/

5 The orthography currently uses an accent representing high tone to disambiguate tonal minimal pairs, for example <rúu> 'bone' and <ruu> 'bamboo'.

discuss /rek/, /=ŋi/ and /=in/ respectively. Each of these sections has a similar structure, presenting examples of how these morphemes have been written previously, outlining the decision-making process, and discussing the decisions made. Section 2.6 is a general discussion that draws together the key points of the chapter.

2.2 Linguistic properties of the morphemes /rek/, /=ŋi/, /=in/

2.2.1 Grammatical wordhood

Bartram and Eaton (§ 1.2.2) discuss linguistic wordhood, including criteria which various authors have proposed as being salient for determining the linguistic status of a morpheme. In particular, they present criteria from Haspelmath (2011:38) and Dixon and Aikhenvald (2002:19), which relate to grammatical words, and criteria from Dixon and Aikhenvald (2002:3–5), which relate to phonological words.

Among Haspelmath's criteria, those which are particularly applicable to demonstrating the grammatical wordhood of /rek/, /=ŋi/ and /=in/ are *uninterruptibility*, and *nonselectivity*, with the former being equivalent to Dixon and Aikhenvald's criterion of *cohesiveness*. If two adjacent morphemes form a single grammatical word it should not be possible to interrupt them by adding another word between them (uninterruptibility). If a particular grammatical morpheme is not highly selective with the kinds of hosts it can combine with, that morpheme is likely to be a separate grammatical word rather than an affix (nonselectivity). Consider examples (1)–(5):

(1) a. /iːn rek/
house PL
'houses'

b. /iːn k-poːl rek/
house NMLZ-be.white PL
'white houses'

(2) a. /m-skoːl=in/
3-horse=NSG
'their horse'

b. /m-skoːl k-lin=in/
3-horse NMLZ-enlarge=NSG
'their large horse'

(3) a. /nau=ŋi/
child=ERG
'child'

b. /nau k-ʈaː=ŋi/
child NMLZ-be.good=ERG
'good child'

(4) a. /m-sko:l = in/
3-horse = NSG
'their horse'

b. /m-sko:l k-lin so:m = in/
3-horse NMLZ-enlarge ten = NSG
'their ten large horses'

(5) a. /nau = ŋi/
child = ERG
'child'

b. /nau k-ʈa: so:m = ŋi/
child NMLZ-be.good ten = ERG
'ten good children'

Example (1) shows /i:n rek/ 'houses' being interrupted by /kpo:l/ 'white'. This suggests that /i:n rek/ is two grammatical words. Similarly examples (2)–(5) point in favour of / = in/ and / = ŋi/ being separate grammatical words. In addition, the examples above illustrate the nonselectivity of /rek/, / = in/ and / = ŋi/, because in addition to nouns, they can occur following adjectives and, for / = ŋi/ and / = in/, numbers.[6] This further supports the grammatical wordhood of /rek/, / = ŋi/ and / = in/.

2.2.2 Phonological wordhood

Whilst /rek/, / = ŋi/ and / = in/ can all be analysed as grammatical words, they differ with regard to phonological wordhood. Of the properties relating to phonological words presented by Dixon and Aikhenvald (2002:3–5), two will be discussed here: *segmental features* and *phonological rules.* The property of *segmental features* includes internal syllabic and segmental structure. *Phonological rules* refers to some rules applying only within a phonological word but others applying across a phonological word boundary.

Phonological words in Lamkang have a minimum size requirement, which can be analysed as two moras, with a monosyllabic structure being monomoraic if it comprises a single short vowel and no coda.[7] The morpheme /rek/ thus fulfils this property of phonological wordhood, but / = ŋi/ [= ŋɪ] does not. Further, when / = ŋi/ follows a consonant there is complete assimilation to that consonant,[8] a process which does not occur across phonological word boundaries, as example (6) illustrates:

---

[6] Following Dixon (2004:9, 2004:14–22, 2010:77–91), constructions such as /k-po:l/ in example (1) are analysed as adjectives. More on the prefix **gV-* in Tibeto-Burman languages, particularly its analysis as a nominalizer whose functional range includes adjectival marking, is found in Konnerth (2016).

[7] The orthographic forms cited in this chapter retain the spellings used by the particular writer being cited. As vowel length has not been consistently represented in the orthography in the past, and thus is still sometimes missed by local editors, the orthographic forms do not necessarily reflect the moraic structure of the words (e.g., <nu> /nu:/ 'mother').

[8] For borrowed words (e.g., names) ending with consonants which do not occur syllable-finally in Lamkang, there is partial assimilation.

(6) a. /t^{h}eipaː = ŋi/ → [t^{h}eipɑːŋɪ] ‘squirrel’
squirrel = ERG

b. /kruːŋ = ŋi/ → [kruːŋŋɪ] ‘king’
king = ERG

c. /plap = ŋi/ → [plɜppɪ] ‘friend’
friend = ERG

d. /plap rek = ŋi/ → [plɜprekkɪ] ‘friends’
friend PL = ERG

e. /m-plap rek = in = ŋi/ → [məplɜprekɪnnɪ] ‘their friends’
3-friend PL = NSG = ERG

As for / = in/ [= ɪn], whilst it meets the minimum phonological word requirements, it, too, undergoes a phonological process which does not occur across phonological word boundaries. This can be analysed as elision of /i/ when / = in/ is immediately preceded by a vowel, as illustrated by examples (7) and (8).

(7) a. /a-paː = in/ → [ɜpɑːn] ‘your (PL) father’
2-father = NSG

b. /m-nuː = in/ → [m^{ə}nuːn] ‘their mother’
3-mother = NSG

(8) [ʋɑːntɜmsiːŋɪ m^{ə}hinɪnnɪ t^{h}eːdɜ ʈiː mɑːn]
/ʋaːntamsiː = ŋi m-hin = in = ŋi t^{h}eː = da ʈiː ma = in/
angel = ERG 3-direction = NSG = ABL speak = PFV fear NEG = NSG
‘The angel said to them “Do not fear.”’ (Luke 2:10 BSIV)

Example (7) demonstrates the elision when / = in/ follows a long vowel. When following an underlying short vowel as in example (8), there is compensatory lengthening of that vowel. It can also be noted from examples (7) and (8) that / = in/ may occur in a verb phrase as well as a noun phrase.

This is important when making orthographic decisions and will be returned to in § 2.5 when discussing /=in/ in greater detail.

In summary, then, /rek/ is a both a grammatical and a phonological word, whereas /=ŋi/ and /=in/ are clitics because they are grammatical but not phonological words.

2.2.3 Orthographic words

Bartram and Eaton (§§ 1.2.3–1.2.4) introduce the concept of an orthographic word, and discuss how grammatical and phonological properties of morphemes can feed into decisions about orthographic words. If the grammatical and phonological properties of a morpheme align with regard to wordhood, an initial decision would generally be to write that morpheme accordingly. Thus an appropriate initial orthographic decision for /rek/ would be to consider writing it separated from the preceding morpheme. Of course, orthography stakeholders in the language community might bring up other considerations, and this is indeed the case with /rek/ due to the influence of English (see § 2.3).

With regard to orthographic word divisions for clitics, Bartram and Eaton (§ 1.4.2) present and discuss the criteria listed in Kutsch Lojenga (2014:91–98). Grammatical and phonological criteria are as follows:

Grammatical:
- Mobility
- Separability
- Substitutability

Phonological:
- Pronounceability in isolation
- Phonological unity
- Phonological bridging

In addition to these criteria, Kutsch Lojenga (2014:92) also lists semantic criteria, which are of particular relevance for compound constructions and thus will not be discussed here.

Kutsch Lojenga defines *mobility* as being the ability of a morpheme to occupy different slots in a sentence, which would then be an argument in favour of writing the morpheme as a separate orthographic word. This relates to the criterion of *external mobility and internal fixedness* presented in Haspelmath (2011:40–44). Neither /=ŋi/ nor /=in/ can occupy different slots within the construction in which they occur. The case marker /=ŋi/ only occurs phrase-finally, and whilst the clitic /=in/ occurs in both noun phrases and verb phrases, its syntactic position within a phrase is fixed.

The criterion of *separability* is the opposite of Haspelmath's criterion of *uninterruptibility* (see § 2.2.1). This criterion supports the possibility of writing /=ŋi/ and/or /=in/ as separate orthographic words. However, this needs to be weighed against other criteria.

Kutsch Lojenga presents the criterion of *substitutability* as being the ability to substitute the morpheme for a lexeme in the same syntactic position. It is not possible to do this for either /=ŋi/ or /=in/.

The criterion of *pronounceability in isolation*, whilst being similar to phonological wordhood, is not synonymous with this. Bartram and Eaton (§ 1.4.3) give the example of the English indefinite and definite articles "a" [ə] and "the" [ðə] which may be pronounced in isolation in a contrived situation, compared with the clitic form of English auxiliary "is" ([s]/[z]) which would not be pronounced in isolation. In the case of Lamkang /=ŋi/, there appears to be no situation where [=ŋɪ] (or any of the other allomorphs of /=ŋi/) might be pronounced in isolation. Further, during the orthography workshops when participants responded to questions specifically about /=ŋi/, they mostly answered by giving the relevant allophone of /=ŋi/ together with whatever morpheme came before it. If they responded with /=ŋi/ by itself, they would modify the vowel so that what they pronounced matched minimum phonological word requirements, for example by saying [ŋiː] rather than [ŋɪ]. This criterion, therefore, supports writing /=ŋi/ joined to the preceding morpheme. Kutsch Lojenga (2014:95) expresses this even more strongly: "this criterion applies to those grammatical morphemes which cannot be pronounced in isolation and which must therefore automatically be written together with the main lexical morpheme." As concerns the morpheme /=in/, whilst the form [=ɪn] is pronounceable in isolation in Lamkang, the form [=n] is not. This raises the related issue of which phonological level should be represented orthographically. For further discussion, see § 2.2.4.

The criterion of *phonological unity* refers to the presence of phonological processes which might indicate that two (or more) morphemes are a single phonological word. Section 2.2.2 outlines phonological processes for both /=ŋi/ and /=in/ which do not occur across Lamkang phonological word boundaries. These processes support the possibility of writing /=ŋi/ and/or /=in/ attached to a preceding morpheme.

The criterion of *phonological bridging* refers to postlexical phonological processes which are an automatic consequence of blending words together in speech (Kutsch Lojenga 2014:97). This criterion is not relevant to /=ŋi/ and /=in/ because the phonological processes outlined in § 2.2.2 are not ones which occur automatically across phonological word boundaries when blending words together in speech.

Even though *separability* supports writing /=ŋi/ as a separate orthographic word, lack of *pronounceability in isolation*, combined with *phonological unity* would be strong arguments for writing it joined to the preceding morpheme. For /=in/, arguments presented in § 2.2.4 combined with the above suggest that this, too, might be best written joined. However, as will be discussed in the following sections, community stakeholders might bring up other considerations which weigh heavily upon the decision and the approach by which the decision is reached.

2.2.4 Lexical orthography hypothesis

Examples (6)–(8) illustrate phonological processes undergone by /=ŋi/ and /=in/. Part of the orthographic decision for these morphemes is whether to transparently represent the allomorphic alternation. Although this is a separate issue from that of word divisions, they are intertwined, particularly in the case of /=in/. A different word-division decision might be reached depending on whether or not the elided vowel is represented orthographically (for example, whether in (7) [ɜpɑːn] 'your (PL) father' is written <apaan>, <apaain> or <apaa in>).

The issue of whether to write the elided vowel is illustrative of the wider debate that exists about which phonological level should be represented orthographically, in other words, what orthographic depth to choose (Frost et al. 1987; Katz and Frost 1992). Historically, the debate has centred around whether to represent the classic phonemic form (e.g., Pike 1947) or the underlying form (e.g., Chomsky and Halle 1968, Venezky 1970). More recently, Snider (2014) has contributed to the debate by proposing the *Lexical Orthography Hypothesis* (*LOH*), which he articulates as "what works best from a practical viewpoint is an orthography that consistently represents the output of the lexical level of Lexical Phonology" (2014:29–30). This hypothesis is situated within the theoretical framework of Lexical Phonology (Mohanan 1982, 1986; Kiparsky 1982), which distinguishes between two overarching types of phonological process: lexical and postlexical, with the *lexical representation* being the level between these processes. Concerning this level, Mohanan (1982:29) comments "The judgements of native speakers of a language on sameness and distinctness of sounds appear to be based on this level, not on the underlying or the phonetic."

The vowel elision undergone by /=in/ can be analysed as a lexical process. It is not a process occurring automatically across phonological word boundaries; if it were, it could be analysed as postlexical. Whilst this does not necessarily point towards it being a lexical process, it is also important to note that the process operates to avoid a disallowed syllable structure. Syllable formation can be analysed as occurring at the lexical rather than postlexical level (see Mohanan 1982 and 1986 for treatment of syllables). Further, the process operates slightly differently for nouns and verbs when the stem ends with /ŋ/. For verbs, /ŋ/ deletes before /=in/, for example /arvaŋ=in/ [ɜrvɑːn] 'come down'. For nouns it does not, for example /a-pluŋ=in/ [ɜplʊŋɪn] 'your hearts'. This, too, suggests that the process is lexical.

Applying the LOH, an initial orthographic decision for /=in/ would be to transparently represent the vowel elision, for example, writing <apaan> for /a-pa:=in/ [ɜpɑ:n] 'your (PL) father'. As a consequence of this, an initial decision for, e.g., /a-sko:l=in/ [ɜsko:lɪn] 'your (PL) horse' might be to write <askoolin> rather than <askool in> for consistency in whether or not to divide before /=in/. However, as mentioned in § 2.2.3, community stakeholders may bring up other considerations which need to be taken into account.

2.2.5 Participatory approach

The above sections outline linguistic properties of the three morphemes /rek/, /=ŋi/ and /=in/ and the orthographic decisions that might be made on the basis of these properties. However, the acceptability of an orthography depends on nonlinguistic factors at least as much as, if not more than, linguistic ones (see, for example, Smalley 1959, Cahill 2014, Hinton 2014), with social and cultural considerations nearly always involved (Sebba 2009:36). For Lamkang orthography stakeholders, such factors include attitudes (both positive and negative) towards existing materials, loyalties, dialects, and considerations relating to perceived ease of reading and writing.

Furthermore, acceptance of an orthography "is most often promoted when speakers of the language are key participants in a decision-making process" (Casquite and Young 2017). Various approaches to community participation in orthography development are discussed in the literature (e.g., Kutsch Lojenga 1996, Easton and Wroge 2002, Bow 2012, Page 2013, Jones and Mooney 2017, Lew 2019). Through her experience of orthography development in hierarchical Asian societies, Lew (2019:73) suggests a *facilitated participatory approach* combining linguistically and educationally sound orthography design through varying levels of external academic involvement, with participatory methods. This facilitated participatory approach is similar to the approach taken by the present author in the Lamkang orthography workshops, with the goal of enabling not just consensus but ownership of the decision by the participants, and ultimately acceptability by the wider community. For word divisions, the facilitation centred around enabling participants to consider the implications of their preferences for the spelling of a particular morpheme in one context, for other morphosyntactic contexts.

The sections that follow discuss the approaches taken for each morpheme. Of particular note is that almost all the decisions made through a participatory approach based on native speaker intuitions match those which may be argued from linguistic criteria alone.

2.3 The morpheme /rek/

2.3.1 Introduction

The plural morpheme /rek/ is the first of the morphemes to be considered in this chapter, and the most straightforward, due to alignment of grammatical and phonological criteria. Nevertheless it has still caused confusion for writers, which can be attributed to the mismatch between the linguistic structure of English and Lamkang plural morphemes. Whereas the English plural morpheme is a suffix on the noun, the Lamkang plural morpheme may be separated from the noun by another word, as can be seen in example (1). What follows gives an overview of how different Lamkang writers and publications have written /rek/, and how the stakeholders reached agreement on an orthographic decision.

2.3.2 Spelling practices

One of the earliest publications in Lamkang is a small primer booklet from 1965 by Tholung, in which /rek/ is written joined to a preceding noun. This is illustrated in example (9):

(9)	<wakrek>	/ʋak	rek/	(Tholung 1965:10)
		pig	PL	
		‘pigs’		

Tholung (1965) contains no examples of /rek/ immediately following any word other than the noun it is pluralising, so it is not possible to know whether he would have continued to join /rek/ when separated from the noun by an intervening word.

In contrast to Tholung, both versions of the New Testament typically write /rek/ as a separate orthographic word, as in (10) and (11):

(10)	<plap rek>	/plap	rek/	(John 15:5 BIV)
		friend	PL	
		‘friends’		
(11)	<pauna rek>	/pauna	rek/	(Matthew 12:37 BSIV)
		word	PL	
		‘words’		

Participants at the 2015 writers’ workshop made different orthographic choices with regard to /rek/, and some inconsistently. One writer, for example, switched between separate and joined for /serkit rek/ 'porcupines' in the same sentence. Examples (12)–(14) are from a participant who chose to write /rek/ joined when it immediately follows the noun it is pluralising, but otherwise separated from the preceding word:

(12)	<yongrekki>	/joːŋ	rek = ŋi/	
		monkey	PL = ERG	
		'monkeys'		
(13)	<yong mlung rekki>	/joːŋ	m-luːŋ	rek = ŋi/
		monkey	3-group	PL = ERG
		'group of monkeys'		
(14)	<yong kver rekki>	/joːŋ	k-ver	rek = ŋi/
		monkey	NMLZ-become.older	PL = ERG
		'older monkeys'		

Arguably Tholung (1965) and the writer of examples (12)–(14) were choosing to follow the English orthography, even if, as in (12)–(14), this resulted in inconsistency when writing /rek/ in different syntactic contexts.

2.3.3 Orthographic decision for /rek/

Because both versions of the New Testament write /rek/ separated from the preceding word, which matches its linguistic status, most of the participants at the 2016 workshop were already in favour of writing it this way. Upon discussion, it became apparent that those writers who were joining /rek/ to the preceding word were indeed doing so out of a perceived need to imitate English. The focus of the workshop discussion was on examples such as (12)–(14), with participants generating language examples, exploring how their language differed from English, and discussing whether or not it was necessary to follow English. As they started to appreciate the difference between Lamkang and English and realise that it was not necessary for Lamkang orthography to follow English, agreement on writing /rek/ separately rapidly followed.

A booklet of Lamkang stories (LLS 2017a) was produced shortly after the workshop, reflecting the decisions of the workshop, including the decision to write /rek/ separated from the preceding word. Follow-up workshops in 2017 and 2018 confirmed that the language community were happy with this decision and that it was being implemented.

The main point to draw out of the decision for /rek/ is that the decision made through community participation matches linguistic analysis. In particular, participants appeared to be intuitively responding to the grammatical criterion of separability (see § 2.2.3), with perceptions of naturalness aligning with what may be argued linguistically.

2.4 The clitic /=ŋi/

2.4.1 Introduction

Section 2.2.3 outlines how orthographic word criteria for / = ŋi/ 'ERG/ABL' do not all align in favour of a particular decision. Further, the prevailing opinion in the language community was to avoid joining multiple grammatical morphemes to a preceding word, which affects the decision for/ = ŋi/ because it may be preceded by one or more grammatical morphemes. Section 2.2.2 describes how the initial consonant of / = ŋi/ completely assimilates to a preceding consonant. This raises the additional issue of whether to write the morpheme as <ngi> throughout, or whether to write each allomorph. The one orthographic issue about / = ŋi/ that writers appear to be consistent on, is to represent each allomorph transparently.

The following sections illustrate how different writers have dealt with / = ŋi/, and discuss the more recent decisions which the community stakeholders have made about it.

2.4.2 Spelling practices

As is the case for the morpheme /rek/ discussed in § 2.3, different writers have employed different strategies for writing / = ŋi/. Tholung (1965) typically writes it joined to the preceding word, as in (15):

(15) <kumikhatti> /ku:-mi:-k^{h}at = ŋi/ (Tholung 1965:9)
who-person-one = ERG
'whoever'

Tholung's primer contains only one example of / = ŋi/ following either /rek/ or / = in/, which is given in (16). In this example he wrote / = ŋi/ separately possibly because, having made the decision to join /rek/ to the preceding morpheme, he wanted to avoid joining a further morpheme.

(16) <shiliingrek ki> /siliŋ rek = ŋi/ (Tholung 1965:6)
ant PL = ERG
'ants'

With only one example of /=ŋi/ following /rek/ or /=in/, it is not possible to know whether Tholung applied this strategy consistently. However, this apparent avoidance of attaching multiple grammatical morphemes to the one stem is in evidence in both New Testaments and in the various texts produced during the writers' workshop, as can be seen in examples (18), (19), (22) and (23).

Like Tholung, the BSIV typically writes /=ŋi/ joined to the preceding word. However, unlike Tholung, because the BSIV typically separates /rek/ and /=in/ from the preceding word, it is able to join /=ŋi/ when following either of these morphemes, without resulting in multiple morphemes joined to the one word. Examples (17)–(19) illustrate this:

(17) <dultipaammi> /dulti:-pa:m=ŋi/ (John 17:21 BSIV)
earth-land=ERG
'the world'

(18) <mii rekki> /mi: rek=ŋi/ (John 7:32 BSIV)
person PL=ERG
'people'

(19) <mkhut rek inni> /m-k^hut rek=in=ŋi/ (Luke 4:11 BSIV)
3-hand PL=NSG=ABL
'in their hands'

However, the BSIV does not follow this system consistently, particularly with proper nouns (for example, /iso:r=ŋi/ 'God=ERG' is written as <Isowrri> in Matthew 22:31 and Matthew 27:43, but as <Isowr ri> in Philippians 2:13 and Romans 5:8). Further, the BSIV typically writes the allomorph [=ŋɪ] separately, as in example (20):

(20) < diibiing ngi > /di:-bi:ŋ=ŋi/ (Matthew 14:14 BSIV)
water-bank=ABL
'on the shore'

In contrast, the BIV typically writes /=ŋi/ as a separate orthographic word. This decision is arguably interlinked with a decision to join /=in/ 'NSG' to the preceding word (see 2.5.3) and a desire to avoid joining multiple grammatical morphemes, as in examples (21) and (22):

(21) <dultipaam mih>[9] /dulti:-pa:m = ŋi/ (John 17:21 BIV)
earth-land = ERG
'the world'

(22) <mmikin ni> /m-mik = in = ŋi/ (Matthew 13:15 BIV)
3-eye = NSG = ABL
'with their eyes'

Interestingly, when / = ŋi/ is immediately preceded by /rek/, the BIV chooses to join / = ŋi/ to /rek/ despite writing it separately in most other situations. Example (23) illustrates this. The preference to write <rekki> over <rek ki> is picked up in § 2.4.3 and § 2.5.3.

(23) <pauna rekki> /pauna rek = ŋi/ (1 Corinthians 1:17 BIV)
word PL = ABL
'with words'

Given that both New Testaments follow different strategies for / = ŋi/, it is unsurprising that these differences exist in the writings of others. Khullar (2006) typically joins / = ŋi/ to whatever precedes it, whereas Bepol (2002) tends to separate it. Participants at the 2015 writers' workshop followed different strategies from each other. Most either followed the BIV or the BSIV, or a mixture of the two. However, all except one avoided attaching multiple grammatical morphemes to a preceding word.

2.4.3 Orthographic decision for /=ŋi/

When the issue of how to represent / = ŋi/ was discussed at the 2016 orthography workshop, the main desire of those present was to have a totally consistent system with regard to word divisions. They agreed that they wanted to avoid the kind of orthographic inconsistencies found in the two New Testaments and other materials.

Participants voiced several concerns about writing / = ŋi/ joined, the primary one being that they felt the potential orthographic sequence <ngng> was ungainly. Because /ŋŋ/ only occurs at morpheme boundaries, writers tend to avoid <ngng> by separating the morphemes. The BSIV, for example, uses a space to separate the two occurrences of <ng>, as in (20). Tholung (1965) tends to use a hyphen, for example <nang-ngi> '2SG = ERG' (1965:4). Other concerns included the desire to avoid long words for the

[9] <h> following a vowel is used by some authors to represent high pitch (not necessarily contrastive tone).

sake of less confident readers, and not to join morphemes to proper nouns, especially in the case of less familiar biblical names.

Because of these concerns, and because of the desire for total consistency, the community, as represented at the workshop, made the tentative decision to write /=ŋi/ separately. A booklet of Lamkang stories (LLS 2017a) was produced, as a trial of the decisions made at the workshop.

By the time of the workshop in mid-2017, preferences were swinging. There were comments that writing separately sometimes made the reading process stilted, particularly in the case of frequent constructions such as /=ŋi/ preceded by /rek/ or /=in/ (i.e., <rek ki> or <in ni>), temporal constructions (e.g., <tún ni> 'now', <audil li> 'after that'), and locative constructions (e.g., <léen ni> 'on'). In general, an orthographic word of two or three letters followed by a space and then /=ŋi/ was said to make reading feel stilted.

The 2017 workshop participants considered retaining the 2016 decision to write /=ŋi/ separately, but introducing a list of exceptions which would be written joined. However, as the potential list of exceptions grew, the decision was revisited. The main concern was still the sequence <ngng>, but the other concerns from 2016 were now ranked as being less important than rectifying the stiltedness. Alternatives to writing <ngng> were discussed but rejected, including the use of a single character such as <ŋ> to represent /ŋ/. Eventually the decision was reached to write <ngi> separately (e.g., <nang ngi>), but join all the other allomorphs of /=ŋi/ (e.g writing <rekki>, <túnni>, <audilli>, etc.). A second booklet of Lamkang stories was subsequently produced (LLS 2017b). During the 2018 workshop this decision was discussed and reaffirmed.

2.4.4 Discussion

A number of points can be noted about the above process and decision. The above subsections have been focused specifically on /=ŋi/. However, /=ŋi/ is one of a small number of phrase-final enclitics, which have the same phonological properties of being monomoraic and displaying complete assimilation to a preceding consonant. The orthography workshops considered each of these enclitics. Indeed, part of the facilitation aspect of the participatory approach was to guide participants to consider each of these morphemes and contexts, and the implications of one decision upon another. The ultimate decision for each of these enclitics was to join them to the preceding word.

Section 2.2.3 discusses orthographic word criteria, with (lack of) *pronounceability in isolation* and *phonological unity* being two criteria in support of writing /=ŋi/ joined to the preceding morpheme. However, as can be seen from the above, the orthography stakeholders from within the community had other criteria which ranked higher in the decision-making process.

Interestingly, the final outcome did match the decision that might have been made on the basis of linguistic considerations alone (with the possible exception of avoiding <ngng>). But the process by which the decision was made was crucial to its ownership by the wider language community, particularly because of the divergent spellings in the two New Testaments and the possibility of individual preferences being influenced by this.

The perceived stiltedness resulting from separating /=ŋi/ may be due to several factors. First, it might, at least in part, be traced to the lack of phonological wordhood of /=ŋi/, resulting in it feeling unnatural to write /=ŋi/ as a separate word. Second, from a semantic point of view, constructions such as <audil li> 'after that' or <tún ni> 'now' may be being perceived as being single words. Kutsch Lojenga (2014:99) lists *conceptual unity* as a semantic criterion for deciding word divisions particularly for compound words. However, in this instance it may be appropriate to implement this criterion even though these are not compound constructions. Third, some constructions are likely to be subject to a familiarity effect. If readers are used to seeing, for example, <rekki> written as one orthographic word, it might feel unnatural to see it written separately as <rek ki>.

Joining /=ŋi/ has made orthographic words slightly longer, and has meant proper nouns may have a morpheme joined to them, both of which were initial concerns about joining. However, the allomorphic alternation serves to mitigate these concerns. Because sequences of identical consonants only occur at morpheme boundaries, they serve as a cue to the morpheme break, thus reducing need for the additional orthographic cue of a space.

2.5 The morpheme /=in/

2.5.1 Introduction

The nonsingular morpheme /=in/ is the final morpheme to be discussed in this chapter. Section 2.2.2 outlines the vowel elision which occurs when /=in/ follows a morpheme which ends with a vowel. Thus /=in/ involves a two-fold decision about whether to write it separated from or joined to the preceding morpheme, and whether or not to write the elided vowel. Any decision about whether to write, for example, <aplap in> or <aplapin> 'your (PL) friend' is intertwined with the decision about whether to write, for example, <apaa in> or <apaain> or <apaan> 'your (PL) father'. This issue is in evidence in both versions of the New Testament (see § 2.5.2) and is discussed in further detail in § 2.5.3 and § 2.5.4.

Another factor is the position of /=in/ within a noun phrase. Specifically, /=in/ follows /rek/ and precedes /=ŋi/ as illustrated by (24):

(24) /m-k^{h}ut rek=in=ŋi/
3-hand PL=NSG=ABL
'in their hands'

Participants at each of the 2016–2018 workshops were unanimous in their desire not to join all three morphemes (i.e., <rekinni>), and this appears to be a prevalent desire throughout the community. Taking account of this, it would be possible to write the combination of all three morphemes either as <rek in ni>, <rekin ni> or <rek inni>. The two New Testaments differ in their approach to this issue (see § 2.5.2).

Yet a further factor is that /=in/ occurs in verb phrases as well as in noun phrases, as in (25). Although the primary focus of this chapter is noun phrases, any decision about /=in/ needs to take its presence in verb phrases into account.

(25) /kni:=ŋi mi: plum=in=da/
sun=ERG person warm=NSG=PFV
'the sun warmed the people'

2.5.2 Spelling practices

The two New Testaments have divergent spellings for /=in/. The BIV writes the allomorphy transparently and writes both <in> [=ɪn] and <n> [=n] joined to the preceding word. Arguably, the decision to write <in> joined is at least in part influenced by a desire to treat both <in> and <n> the same way. Examples (26) and (27) illustrate this.

(26) <aplungrilin> /a-pluŋril=in/ (2 Thessalonians 2:2 BIV)
2-heart=NSG
'your (PL) heart'

(27) <apaan> /a-pa:=in/ (Matthew 6:1 BIV)
2-father=NSG
'your (PL) father'

In contrast, the BSIV writes <in> separated from the preceding word, as in (28), which is from the same verse as (26):

(28) <aplungbin in> /a-plungbin = in/ (2 Thessalonians 2:2 BSIV)
2-heart = NSG
'your (PL) heart'

Of particular note is the difference between the BIV and BSIV in writing / = in/ when following a vowel. Whereas the BIV writes the allomorphy transparently (for example <apaan> [ɜpɑːn] 'your (PL) father' in [27]), the BSIV often does not, choosing instead to write the elided vowel as in (29), which is from the same verse as (27):

(29) <apah in> /a-paː = in/ (Matthew 6:1 BSIV)
2-father = NSG
'your (PL) father'

Neither New Testament follows its prevailing strategy consistently. In the BSIV, the elided vowel tends to be written in the case of a noun phrase as in (29), but not in the case of a verb phrase, as in (30):

(30) <arvaan ungu suwn> /arvaː = in ungu suː = in/ (John 1:39 BSIV)
come = NSG and see = NSG
'come and see'

In the BIV, on the other hand, the issue is whether there is an enclitic following / = in/. If / = in/ is joined to the preceding word, and if the joining of multiple morphemes is to be avoided, as many in the language community desire, then any enclitic following / = in/ would need to be written separately. Indeed, this is what the BIV often does, for example:

(31) <naan ahinin nih> /naːn a-hin = in = ŋi/ (Ephesians 1:1 BIV)
2PL 2-direction = NSG = ABL
'to you (PL)'

However, in other places the BIV separates / = in/ from the preceding word, enabling the final enclitic to be joined to / = in/, as in (32):

(32) <adak inni> /a-dak = in = ŋi/ (1 Peter 1:14 BIV)
2-body = NSG-ABL
'in your (PL) body'

Given that the two New Testaments adopt different strategies for / = in/, and given the intertwining factors which need balancing, it is unsurprising that participants at the 2015 writers' workshop took different approaches to / = in/.

2.5.3 Orthographic decision for /=in/

The concerns voiced at the 2016 workshop about / = in/ were predominantly the same as those expressed for / = ŋi/ (see § 2.4.3). There was a strong desire for consistency, and also for avoiding long words. There was also anecdotal evidence that less confident readers struggled when <in> was joined to a preceding word. In addition, there was a desire to have one rule which worked for all the grammatical morphemes discussed at the workshop. Participants felt that it would be easier to teach learners to write them either all joined or all separately, than when to join and when to separate. Thus they made a tentative decision to write / = in/ separately, which included writing <in> for both [= ɪn] and [= n], both after nouns and after verbs (for example, writing <apaa in> rather than <apaan> 'your (PL) father' and <che in> rather than <cheen> 'walk.NSG'). This is different from both the BIV (which typically joins / = in/, as in examples [26] and [27]) and the BSIV (which tends to treat noun phrases and verb phrases differently, as in examples [29] and [30]).

As with / = ŋi/, the decision for / = in/ was included in the trial booklet of Lamkang stories (LLS 2017a), and was revisited at subsequent workshops.

2.5.3.1 Whether or not to write the elided vowel

In 2017 participants spent time reflecting on the choices made in 2016. Two of the phrases in the trial booklet which they found particularly problematic were <m'nu in> [mᵊnu:n] 'their mother' (LLS 2017a:3) and <m'dei in> [mᵊde:n] 'they see' (LLS 2017a:2). Comments were that less confident readers struggled with comprehension when trying to read these because they were too different from the pronunciation.

Furthermore, even though the 2016 decision had been to write the elided vowel after both nouns and verbs for consistency, there were places in the booklet where this was not followed, for example <dei man> /dei ma = in/ [dei mɑ:n] 'see NEG = NSG' (LLS 2017a:2). The reason given was that it felt too unnatural to separate the negative auxiliary <man> into <ma in>. Participants were of the opinion that learners would not understand what was written if <man> was changed to <ma in>. In the case of <luun> /luu = in/ 'enter = NSG' (LLS 2017a:13), local editors apparently did not notice that it could be separated as <luu in> and perceived the joined form as being more natural.

Discussion thus revolved around issues of naturalness and consistency. Workshop participants clearly found it more natural to represent the pronunciation. A minority felt it to be "more correct" to write <in> even when they did not pronounce the vowel (e.g., writing <luu in> [lu:n] 'enter.NSG'), whilst still agreeing that it felt more natural to write it as pronounced (e.g., <luun>). The main reason for the 2016 decision had been a desire for consistency. However, the experience of the trial booklet served to illustrate the difficulties with a consistent rule that did not feel natural. What followed was a discussion about different ways in which it is possible to be consistent, and that consistency does not necessarily mean writing both <n> and <in> joined, or writing /=in/ as <in> to represent [=n]. Consistency might mean, for example, writing <n> joined and <in> separated but following this rule consistently. The general feeling at the 2018 workshop was that it would be best to write <n> to represent [=n]. However, because of the question of how this might affect the joining or separating of <in>, the decision was not finalised until the issue of whether to write <in> joined or separated had been addressed.

2.5.3.2 Whether to write <in> joined or separately

As discussed in § 2.4.3, there was a general opinion that reading the trial booklet felt stilted when common constructions were written as a series of separate orthographic words, particularly when the latter were short. This included when <in> was followed by another grammatical morpheme, for example <m'khut in ni> 'with their hand(s)' (LLS 2017a:14), or <m'nu in va> 'their mother FOC' (LLS 2017a:4).

Because the decision about writing /=in/ separately or joined was intertwined with decisions about other morphemes, participants spent time adding various morphological combinations to different root words, and discussing which orthographic option felt more natural. Table 2.1 shows the root word <skool> 'horse' with different combinations of /rek/, /=ŋi/ and /=in/. The prefix /m-/ '3' was included because without it /skool=in/ would be ungrammatical. In column 4, the initial majority preference is indicated in italics; the decided form in bold.

Table 2.1. <skool> 'horse' with various morpheme combinations

Morpheme combination	Morphemic glosses	English gloss	Orthographic options
/m-skool=ŋi/	3-horse=ERG	'his horse'	<m'skool li>, ***<m'skoolli>***
/m-skool=in/	3-horse=NSG	'their horse'	**<m'skool in>**, <m'skoolin>
/m-skool rek=ŋi/	3-horse PL=ERG	'his horses'	<m'skool rek ki>, ***<m'skool rekki>***

Table 2.1 (*continued*)

Morpheme combination	Morphemic glosses	English gloss	Orthographic options
/m-skool rek=in/	3-horse PL=NSG	'their horses'	**<m'skool rek in>**, *<m'skool rekin>*
/m-skool=in=ŋi/	3-horse=NSG=ERG	'their horse'	<m'skool in ni>, ***<m'skool inni>***, <m'skoolin ni>, <m'skoolinni>
/m-skool rek=in=ŋi/	3-horse PL=NSG=ERG	'their horses'	<m'skool rek in ni>, ***<m'skool rek inni>***, <m'skool rekin ni>, <m'skool rekinni>

Whilst majority preferences were consistent with repect to /=ŋi/, this was not the case for /=in/. Although the majority wished to join /=in/ when it was phrase-final and preceded by /rek/ (e.g., <m'skool rekin>), participants were roughly equally split over whether it felt more natural to join or separate /=in/ when directly following a root word. If the root was short (e.g., /sil/ 'cow') a slightly higher percentage wanted to join; as the root length increased, the percentage of people wanting to join /=in/ decreased.

In the case of /m-skool rek=in=ŋi/, nobody wanted to write <m'skool rek in ni> or <m'skool rekinni>. There was considerable discussion about <m'skool rek inni> versus <m'skool rekin ni> because of the implications of the decision for /m-skool rek=in/ and /m-skool rek=ŋi/. The difficulty was that majority preference was for <m'skool rekki> and <m'skool rekin> but not <m'skool rekinni>. To write a single morpheme consistently with regard to being joined or separated, there needed to be some compromise. Writing <m'skool rek inni> would mean writing <m'skool rek in> rather than <m'skool rekin>; writing <m'skool rekin ni> would mean writing <m'skool rek ki>.

As the discussion progressed, it became apparent that the minority wanting to write <m'skool rekin ni> rather than <m'skool rek inni>, felt that <m'skool rek inni> was more natural. Their reason for preferring <skool rekin ni> was because they did not want to compromise on writing <m'skool rekin>. This in turn appeared to be motivated by a desire for total consistency regarding both allomorphs of /=in/. If /=in/ was to be written joined when it was spelled <n> participants felt it should also be written joined when it was spelled <in>. Because they did not want to write <rekinni>, that meant compromising by writing the less natural <rekin ni>. In the end the group decided that providing they were able to consistently apply whatever strategy they settled upon, they were willing to follow the majority opinion. Thus they opted for what was felt to be overall the more natural option, that is to write a) /=ŋi/ joined to whatever precedes it, b) /=in/ joined to whatever precedes it when it is written <n>, c) /=in/ separated from whatever precedes it when it is written <in>. For the above combinations this gives <m'skoolli>, <m'skool in>, <m'skool inni>, <m'skool rekki>, <m'skool rek in>, and <m'skook rek inni>. For a construction such as /a-pa:=in=ni/ '2-father=NSG=ERG' this would give <apaanni>.

2.5.4 Discussion

Regarding the question of whether to write /=in/ as <n> or <in> when the vowel is elided, § 2.2.4 analyses the vowel elision as a lexical process, suggesting that under the Lexical Orthography Hypothesis (LOH) /=in/ [=n] might best be written as <n>. It was noted in § 2.5.3 that some workshop participants felt it "more correct" to write <in>, whilst others struggled with this spelling. However, even those who felt it more correct to write <in> agreed that it felt more natural to write <n>, and local editors appeared to have missed spelling amendments (e.g., re-writing <luun> as <luu in>) due to the naturalness of what had been written. These observations add further weight to the hypothesis that the output of the lexical level is a preferable level of orthographic depth than the underlying form. However, given that in this particular instance representing the output of the lexical level is equivalent to representing the phonemic form, it is not possible to go as far as saying that the data supports the LOH.

Regarding the question of joining or separating <in>, particularly in the case of multiple morphemes, three points can be made.

First, for the different combinations of morphemes given in table 2.1, the preference was typically to join the final two morphemes of the phrase. This was observed for other combinations of morphemes as well. The process was repeated with other phrase-final morphemes besides /=ŋi/, (for example /m-sil rek=in=va/ '3-cow PL=NSG=FOC'), and also for sequences of grammatical morphemes in verb phrases as well as for noun phrases. For every combination explored, and in both types of phrases, the typical preference was for joining the final two morphemes. It can also be noted that when some of the participants were exploring this preference they would say a phrase aloud, changing the rhythm and intonation as they went back and forth between orthographic options to determine which they found the most natural. A topic for further research would be to further investigate such native speaker intuitions in the light of the phonological foot structure.

Second, there is undoubtedly a familiarity effect on decision making. For example, the BSIV (typically) and the BIV (sometimes) write <inni> as an orthographic word, e.g., (19) and (32). If people are used to seeing <inni> as an orthographic word, it is likely influencing their preferences.

Finally, from a linguistic perspective, the LOH combined with the lack of pronounceability in isolation of the form [n] would suggest that /=in/ when pronounced [=n] should be written as <n> attached to the preceding morpheme. The need for consistency would suggest writing /=in/ [=ɪn] <in> attached as well. However, this does not factor in the desire to avoid writing both /=in/ and /=ŋi/ attached. It is possible to take account of this by way of the minimum phonological word requirement of two moras, which is fulfilled by [=ɪn] but not by [=ŋɪ]/[=nɪ]/[=lɪ]/ etc. (the allomorphs of /=ŋi/). Thus, if it is a choice between writing <ni>/<li>/etc. separately or writing <in> separately, it is arguably preferable to write <in> separately, even if <n> is written joined. This is the conclusion the participants came to based on their own perception of naturalness as they explored their language.

2.6 General discussion

The preceding sections discuss the orthographic decisions made for /rek/, /=ŋi/ and /=in/, and the process by which these were made, which included initial decisions, trialling, and subsequent revision. At all stages of the process there was a heavy focus on community participation, with people exploring their language, discussing their intuitions, balancing the considerations they felt to be important, and being the ones to make the decision. External facilitation was primarily by way of helping participants to consider the implications of a particular spelling preference in a particular context, for other contexts and other morphemes.

For each of the morphemes /rek/, /=ŋi/ and /=in/, the decisions which were ultimately made are those which might have been made by an approach based primarily on linguistic argument. However, the participatory approach was crucial to the ownership of the decision by those involved in the process, and acceptance by the wider language community, as was the cyclical process of initial decision, trial, and revision. The match between native speaker perceptions of naturalness and what may be argued from linguistic criteria is particularly notable and serves to strengthen the arguments in favour of a participatory approach to orthography development.

This chapter has focused on three specific noun phrase morphemes. However, any decision for one morpheme and one type of construction has potential implications for other morphemes and other constructions. This needs to be taken into account as part of the decision-making process. Only a very small amount of this wider context has been touched on in the preceding sections, due to the scope of the chapter. It was, however, an important part of the workshops.

The research and analysis presented above is qualitative in nature. Whilst the decisions about word divisions have undergone trialling in the community, and are currently in use, there is only anecdotal evidence of the positive impact of the decisions. A recommendation for further research would be to quantitatively test the effect on reading and writing of word divisions with regard to these morphemes.

Finally, Bartram and Eaton (§ 1.4.5) note that decisions may change as people become more used to reading and writing their language, and therefore weigh criteria differently. This was manifest in some of the decisions made and reconsidered across the series of 2016–2018 Lamkang orthography workshops. It might be that in the future the language community again revisits the decisions outlined above, as orthographic priorities evolve.

References

Bepol, Michael. 2002. *System of spelling in Lamkang.* Kakching: Lamkang Literature Society.

BIV. 2001. *Pautum Ren ki Kchir Laika* [Lamkang New Testament]. Grand Rapids, MI: Bibles International.

Bow, Catherine. 2012. Community-based orthography development in four western Zambian languages. *Writing Systems Research* 5(1):73–87.

BSIV. 2002. *Ren Paurina* (Alt. *Ren Pauriina*) [Lamkang New Testament]. Bangalore, India: The Bible Society of India.

Cahill, Michael. 2014. Non-linguistic factors in orthographies. In Michael Cahill and Keren Rice (eds.), *Developing orthographies for unwritten languages*, 9–25. Publications in Language Use and Education 6. Dallas, TX: SIL International.

Casquite, Mansueto, and Catherine Young. 2017. Hearing local voices, creating local content: Participatory approaches in orthography development for non-dominant language communities. In Mari C. Jones and Damien Mooney (eds.), *Creating orthographies for endangered languages,* 54–68. Cambridge: Cambridge University Press.

Chomsky, Noam, and Morris Halle. 1968. *The sound patterns of English.* New York: Harper and Row.

Dixon, R. M. W. 2004. Adjective classes in typological perspective. In R. M. W. Dixon and Alexandra Y. Aikhenvald (eds.), *Adjective classes: A cross-linguistic typology*, 1–49. Oxford: Oxford University Press.

Dixon, R. M. W. 2010. *Basic linguistic theory. Vol. 2: Grammatical topics.* Oxford: Oxford University Press.

Dixon, R. M. W., and Alexandra Y. Aikhenvald. 2002. Word: A typological framework. In R. M. W. Dixon and Alexandra Y. Aikhenvald (eds.), *Word: A cross-linguistic typology*, 1–41. Cambridge: Cambridge University Press.

Easton, Catherine, and Dianne Wroge. 2002. *Manual for alphabet design through community interaction.* Ukarumpa, Papua New Guinea: SIL. www.sil.org/resources/archives/51482.

Eberhard, David M., Gary F. Simons, and Charles D. Fennig, eds. 2024. *Ethnologue: Languages of the world.* Twenty-seventh edition. Dallas, TX: SIL International. www.ethnologue.com.

Frost, Ram, Leonard Katz, and Shlomo Bentin. 1987. Strategies for visual word recognition and orthographical depth: A multilingual comparison. *Journal of Experimental Psychology: Human Perception and Performance* 13:104–115.

Haspelmath, Martin. 2011. The indeterminacy of word segmentation and the nature of morphology and syntax. *Folia Linguistica* 45(1):31–80.

Hinton, Leanne. 2014. Orthography wars. In Michael Cahill and Keren Rice (eds.), *Developing orthographies for unwritten languages*, 139–168. Publications in Language Use and Education 6. Dallas, TX: SIL International.

Jones, Mari C., and Damien Mooney. 2017. *Creating orthographies for endangered languages.* Cambridge: Cambridge University Press.

Katz, Leonard, and Ram Frost. 1992. The reading process is different for different orthographies: The orthographic depth hypothesis. In Ram Frost and Leonard Katz (eds.), *Orthography, phonology, morphology and meaning,* 67–84. Amsterdam: Elsevier Science Publishers B.V.

Khullar, Beshot. 2006. *The first Lamkang book on old Lamkang proverbs, sayings and quiz.* Nagaland: D. Edenrei Family.

Kiparsky, Paul. 1982. Lexical morphology and phonology. In The Linguistic Society of Korea (ed.), *Linguistics in the morning calm: Selected papers from SICOL-1981,* 3–91. Seoul: Hanshin.

Konnerth, Linda. 2016. The Proto-Tibeto-Burman *gV- nominalizing prefix. *Linguistics of the Tibeto-Burman Area* 39(1):3–32.

Kutsch Lojenga, Constance. 1996. Participatory research in linguistics. *Notes on Linguistics* 73(2):13–27. www.sil.org/sites/default/files/kutschlojcommuninvolv1996.pdf.

Kutsch Lojenga, Constance. 2014. Basic principles for establishing word boundaries. In Michael Cahill and Keren Rice (eds.), *Developing orthographies for unwritten languages*, 73–106. Publications in Language Use and Education 6. Dallas, TX: SIL International.

Lamkang Language Resource. n.d. The ongoing story of Lamkang (Lamkaang) language revitalization. Accessed February 25, 2022. https://lamkanglanguageresource.weebly.com/the-ongoing-story-of-lamkang-language-revitalization.html.

Lamkang Literature Society (LLS). 2002. *Regulation of the Lamkang Literature Committee.* New Chayang Village, India: Lamkang Literature Committee.

Lamkang Literature Society (LLS). 2017a. *Lamkaang Paumin: Laika 1* [Lamkang stories: Book 1]. Chandel, India: Lamkang Literature Society.

Lamkang Literature Society (LLS). 2017b. *Lamkaang Paumin: Laika 2* [Lamkang stories: Book 2]. Chandel, India: Lamkang Literature Society.

LaPolla, Randy J. 2004. On nominal relational morphology in Tibeto-Burman. In Ying-chin Lin, Fang-min Hsu, Chun-chih Lee, Jackson T.-S.

Sun, Hsiu-fang Yang, and Dah-an Ho (eds.), *Studies on Sino-Tibetan languages,* 43–73. Taipei, Taiwan: Academia Sinica.

Lew, Sigrid. 2019. Proposing a facilitated participatory approach for Southeast Asian minority language design. *Journal of the Southeast Asian Linguistics Society* 12(1):67–75.

Mohanan, Karuvannur P. 1982. Lexical phonology. PhD dissertation. Massachusetts Institute of Technology, Boston.

Mohanan, Karuvannur P. 1986. *The theory of lexical phonology.* Dordrecht: Reidel.

Noonan, Michael. 2009. Patterns of development, patterns of syncretism of relational morphology in the Bodic languages. In Jóhanna Barðdal and Shobhana L. Chelliah (eds.), *The role of semantic, pragmatic, and discourse factors in the development of case,* 261–282.

Page, Christina J. 2013. A new orthography in an unfamiliar script: A case study in participatory engagement strategies. *Journal of Multilingual and Multicultural Development* 34(5):459–474.

Pike, Kenneth L. 1947. *Phonemics: A technique for reducing languages to writing.* Ann Arbor: The University of Michigan Press.

Registrar General and Census Commissioner India. 2011. *Census of India.* Ministry of Home Affairs, Government of India. https://censusindia.gov.in/census.website/data/census-tables.

Sebba, Mark. 2009. Sociolinguistic approaches to writing systems research. *Writing Systems Research* 1(1):35–49. Doi:10.1093/wsr/wsp002.

Smalley, William. 1959. How shall I write this language? *The Bible Translator* 10(2):49–69.

Snider, Keith. 2014. Orthography and phonological depth. In Michael Cahill and Keren Rice (eds.), *Developing orthographies for unwritten languages,* 27–48. Publications in Language Use and Education 6. Dallas, TX: SIL International.

Tholung, Bedok. 1965. *The first primer of Hero Lamkang.* Thamlapokpi, India: Executive Committee of Lamkang Literature.

Venezky, Richard L. 1970. Principles for the design of practical writing systems. *Anthropological Linguistics* 12:256–270.

3
Orthographic Word Boundary Challenges Posed by Nouns and Clitics in Eighteen Tanzanian Bantu Languages

Helen Eaton, Hazel Gray, Rebekah Mészároš and John B. Walker

Abstract

The eighteen Tanzanian Bantu languages in the current study exhibit a great variety of morphophonological interactions between nouns and clitics. This poses a challenge for the orthographies of these languages. Should the clitics be written attached to the noun or not? How should morphophonological changes at the word boundary, such as vowel elision or vowel harmony, be written? Phonological, grammatical and aesthetic factors play a part in the different orthography decisions made by the language speakers. Often these factors are in conflict, and in the absence of an ideal spelling rule, the decision made is a compromise which is deemed acceptable by the language community.

Abbreviations

*	reconstructed or incorrect/ ungrammatical	LOC	locative
1, 2, etc.	noun class or person number	LWC	language of wider communication
A	any augment vowel	N	nasal unspecified for place of articulation
ANT	anterior	NAR	narrative
AUG	augment	NP	noun phrase
C	consonant	PL	plural
CAUS	causative	PP	pronominal prefix (e.g., PP7, pronominal prefix of class 7)
CNJ	conjunction	PRO	pronoun
CON	connective	PROX	proximal
COP	copula	PRS	present
DEM	demonstrative	PST	past
EP	numeral prefix (e.g., EP7, numeral prefix of class 7)	RECP	reciprocal
FOC	focus	REF	referential
FV	final vowel	SG	singular
IND	indicative	SP	subject prefix (e.g., SP7, subject prefix of class 7)
L1	first language	V	vowel

3.1 Introduction

Defining the concept of the "word" is not as simple as it first seems (Haspelmath 2011), since there may be competing views from phonology, grammar, semantics, or even the orthography itself. Even when restricting the discussion to the "orthographic word," challenges arise within languages that do not have established orthographies and therefore no firm conventions for what constitutes a written word.

Throughout the process of orthography development, it is common to encounter various challenges regarding the marking of word boundaries. This is the case for the eighteen Bantu languages that are the focus of this chapter, especially because these languages are highly agglutinative, concatenating multiple morphemes to form a complex word. Verbs can be particularly long because they may take various affixes on the verbal root, such as ones indicating subject, object, tense, aspect and negation. In addition to affixes, there are also clitics in these languages, which must be considered separately for the orthography. The term clitic is "typically used of something which is a grammatical word, but not a phonological word in its own right" (Dixon 2010:20).

This chapter specifically looks at the interaction between nouns and clitics (mainly evidenced as proclitics in the languages under discussion) and the implications for the orthography. As the current study shows, there are a number of valid ways to write nouns and the clitics that combine with them. The first is to write the clitic conjunctively with the noun so that they form a single orthographic word. The second is to write them disjunctively as two separate orthographic words. The third is to join the clitic and the noun with a punctuation mark (e.g., a hyphen for the languages in the current study) so that they form a single orthographic word while still indicating some separation between the two parts.

One of the underlying principles that informs the choice between these three options is the desire to preserve a constant word image. This makes it easier for readers to quickly decipher what they are reading, as mature readers do not sound out familiar words they read, but recognise them at a glance (Venezky 1977:12). Another important principle is that orthographic words should not be word fragments. That is, a lexical morpheme should be written together with any obligatory affixes and not broken up (Kutsch Lojenga 2014:82). A third principle which will be relevant to the discussions below is that words should be written as they are pronounced in slow speech (Schroeder 2010:6). In normal or rapid speech, native speakers frequently omit certain sounds or blend two or more sounds together so that they sound quite different from the underlying units of which they are composed.[1]

The remainder of this section looks at the context of the languages referred to in this study and the data used. Then § 3.2 introduces the main clitics which will be discussed in the following sections. Sections 3.3–3.5 take a look at how phonology, grammar and aesthetic factors respectively have influenced the writing of clitic-noun combinations in the sample languages. The final section provides some discussions based on the lessons learned during the development of the orthographies in these languages.

[1] See Van Dyken and Kutsch Lojenga (1993) and Kutsch Lojenga (2014) for further criteria which can be used to determine word boundaries and Eaton and Schroeder (2012) for a discussion of these criteria in relation to data from Bantu languages.

3.1.1 Language context

All of the languages referenced in this current study (hereafter "the sample languages") are from the Bantu language family and are spoken in the East African country of Tanzania,[2] in the regions indicated in table 3.1. This table also gives some specific data for each language, including their ISO 639-3 codes, Guthrie classification, the number of speakers in Tanzania (Eberhard et al. 2024), the start date for SIL's involvement in each of the projects and the current status of community approval of the language's orthography.

Table 3.1. Sample languages

Language name	ISO 639-3 code	Guthrie classification	Main region where it is spoken	Estimated number of speakers	SIL project start date	Community approval status
Bena	bez	G63	Njombe	592,000	2003	Approved
Bungu	wun	F25	Songwe	30,000	2003	In testing
Ikizu	ikz	JE402	Mara	48,900	2006	Approved
Ikoma	ntk	JE45	Mara	19,400	2007	Approved
Jita	jit	JE25	Mara	365,000	2007	Approved
Kabwa	cwa	JE405	Mara	14,000	2007	Approved
Kinga	zga	G65	Njombe	217,000	2003	Approved
Kisi	kiz	G67	Njombe	11,000	2012	In testing
Kwaya	kya	JE251	Mara	70,000	2006	Approved
Malila	mgq	M24	Mbeya	78,000	2003	Approved
Ndali	ndh	M301	Songwe	193,000	2003	Approved
Nyiha	nih	M23	Songwe	276,000	2003	Approved
Safwa	sbk	M25	Mbeya	300,000	2003	Approved
Sangu	sbp	G61	Mbeya	119,000	1998	Approved
Simbiti	ssc	JE431	Mara	33,000	2006	Approved
Vwanji	wbi	G66	Njombe	41,800	2003	Approved
Zanaki	zak	JE44	Mara	97,400	2007	Approved
Zinza	zin	JE23	Geita	187,000	1991	Approved

Swahili is a Language of Wider Communication (LWC) in Tanzania and, due to the language policies in the country, it is widely used in the domains

[2] Ndali and Nyiha are cross-border languages that are also spoken in Malawi.

of education, religion, politics and other social spheres where Tanzanians from multiple language groups are interacting. The Swahili orthography (with Roman script) is the most well-known in Tanzania, and any orthography development in local languages has to take this sociolinguistic environment into account. English, while the official language of education, administration and business in Tanzania, is less widely understood and used than Swahili, so has less influence on orthography development.

Orthography development in these sample languages has taken place as a partnership between SIL Tanzania and representatives from each of the local language communities. While the linguists working for SIL Tanzania have been the ones to put forward options for orthographic decisions, the final decision has always been made by a representative group of first language (L1) speakers of the language. These groups have largely worked independently of other groups and have therefore sometimes made different decisions on similar issues. No attempt has been made by the SIL linguists to harmonise spelling rules across languages simply for the sake of consistency, since speakers of one language are unlikely to ever want to use the orthography of another. Nevertheless, many decisions across languages are the same, as will be seen, simply because the same reasoning has been applied to similar issues and has resulted in comparable orthographic decisions.

As the orthographies for the sample languages have been developed during the process of translating the New Testament into the local languages, there have been many opportunities to evaluate orthography decisions and receive feedback from L1 orthography users. This informal feedback forms the basis for comments made throughout this chapter relating to L1 speaker intuitions and attitudes to certain decisions.

3.1.2 Language data

The data in this chapter come from published and unpublished sources produced by SIL Tanzania in partnership with the language communities. Our thanks go to the many current and former colleagues who provided examples and helped to check data. Examples come from multiple sources and original transcription decisions on issues such as the representation of vowel length, aspiration and glides have been followed. With respect to tone transcription, original sources have also been followed where tone was transcribed and speakers have been consulted where tonal information was missing. Tone is shown for surface forms only, not underlying forms. Only high tones and contour tones are marked; low tones are unmarked. Downstep (ꜜ) and upstep (ꜛ) are marked where they occur. Kisi and Vwanji are not tone languages.

With regard to the orthographies, vowel length has generally been represented by doubling the vowel symbol, e.g., Ikoma [aβasaːni] 'friends' is written <abhasaani>. Compensatory lengthening and automatic lengthening of the penultimate vowel of a prosodic unit are usually not represented orthographically, e.g., Malila [aβâː^{n}t^{h}ʊ] 'people' <abhantu>; however some languages are exceptions to this, e.g., Zinza [aβaː^{n}t^{h}u] 'people' <abaantu>. Sound-symbol correspondences are not identical from one orthography to another. One notable difference is the representation of vowels (particularly mid vowels), e.g., Simbiti /i e ɛ a ɔ o u/ <i ë e a o ö u>; Ikizu /i e ɛ a ɔ o u/ <i ɨ e a o ʉ u>; Vwanji /i ɪ ɛ a ɔ ʊ u/ <i ɨ e a o ʉ u>; Bena /i e a o u/ <i e a o u>; Kabwa /i ɛ a ɔ u/ <i e a o u>. Another difference is the voiced bilabial fricative consonant /β/ which is written as a digraph <bh> in most of the languages, but as <b> in Zinza.

In the examples, bold type is used to indicate clitics which are relevant to the point being made in the underlying form, surface form and morpheme gloss. Nouns are shown with augments (a particular kind of prefix, see § 3.2.1) in the underlying transcription when the augment is in evidence in the surface form. In order to simplify the transcription of examples, not all parts of all examples are given a morpheme-by-morpheme analysis.

In Swahili, an apostrophe is used in the grapheme <ng'> which represents the velar nasal /ŋ/. Since L1 speakers of local languages are familiar with this convention, it has also been used in their orthographies for the same phoneme. In some of the sample languages, an apostrophe has also been used to represent other phenomena, such as syllabic nasals, e.g., Kisi [m̩bu^{w}at^{h}u] 'in the canoe' <m'bwatu>. As such, an apostrophe is considered unsuitable for marking word boundaries, leaving the hyphen as the only available punctuation symbol to mark a word boundary.

3.2 Linguistic preliminaries

This section first presents a brief summary of the basic features of nouns in Bantu languages (§ 3.2.1). Then it goes on to consider some key formal and functional properties of the four main clitics which are discussed in relation to orthographic decisions in §§ 3.3–3.5. These are the connective (§ 3.2.2), the coordinating conjunction (§ 3.2.3), the locative (§ 3.2.4) and the copula (§ 3.2.5).

3.2.1 Bantu nouns

A Bantu noun typically consists of a stem which is preceded by a prefix signalling its membership of a noun class associated with a particular grammatical agreement pattern. The same stem may fit into multiple classes in order to express singular or plural number, or to create different lexical items. So, for instance, in Swahili the stem <tu> with a class 1 prefix expresses the singular form <mtu> 'person', but with a class 2 prefix it expresses the plural form <watu> 'people'. This same stem can also take a prefix from another noun class, in order to express a distinct lexical item (e.g., class 7 <kitu> 'thing', class 14 <utu> 'humanity/humanness'). In many of the languages in the current study, an additional vowel, referred to in Bantu studies as an augment, can occur in front of the noun class prefix in certain grammatical contexts (and also sometimes on certain other words, such as connectives and adjectives). For instance, the Kabwa word for 'person' is <o-mu-ntu> where <mu-> is the noun class prefix and <o-> is the augment. The function of the augment exhibits great variation across the Bantu family (Van de Velde 2019:249–255). For example, its presence on a noun may mark referentiality or may be determined by the syntactic environment. The shape of the augment also varies. In some of the sample languages, vowel harmony driven by the quality of the vowels of the noun class prefix or noun root affects the augment vowel. Augments pose a challenge for orthographic word boundary decisions because they occur at the beginning of the noun and therefore interact with any vowel-final clitics that precede them, as will be shown below.

3.2.2 Connective

The Bantu connective (also called an "associative") relates two nominal constituents in a relationship of dependency, such as possession (Van de Velde 2013). The connective is preceded by the head nominal constituent and followed by the dependent nominal constituent. The segmental form of the connective stem has been reconstructed as **-a*, with the same tone as its prefix (Meeussen 1967:106). The connective stem typically takes a prefix agreeing with the noun class of the head and may also bear an augment.

In the sample languages, there is variety in the vowel which surfaces at the juncture of the clitic and following noun, both across languages and within individual languages (according to the noun class of the dependent nominal constituent). The underlying vowel of the connective may surface as in Bena (1a) or it may be replaced by the initial vowel of the following noun as in Nyiha (1b) or by another vowel as in Safwa (1c).

(1) a. [líse:la **l**^{j}**a**mô:t^{h}o] (Bena)

/li-se:la **li-a** = mu-ot^{h}o/

5-lake PP**5**-CON = 3-fire

'lake of fire'

b. [ama^{n}t^{h}onǒː^{ŋ}g^{w}a **ágiːk^{hw}i**] (Nyiha)
/a-ma-^{n}t^{h}ono^{ŋ}g^{w}a **a-ga-a** = i-k^{hw}i/[3]
AUG-6-fruit **AUG-PP6-CON** = 5-tree
'fruits of the tree'

c. [ɪʃip^{h}ɛ́l^{w}a **ɪʃɪ^{m}bːílɪ**] (Safwa)
/ɪ-ʃi-p^{h}ɛl^{w}a **ɪ-ʃi-a** = mu-βɪlɪ/
AUG-7-organ **AUG-PP7-CON** = 3-body
'organ of the body'

Both the underlying connective vowel and the augment vowel may surface, without assimilation, as in Bungu (2a). The vowel at the juncture may also be lengthened as in Ikizu (2b) and the tone of the connective may be determined by the tone pattern of the following noun, such as the high tone on the augment of the connective in Nyiha in (1b). Assimilation of the agreement prefix and the connective may result in the connective surfacing as a single vowel as in Ikoma (2c).

(2) a. [etʃet^{h}âbu **étʃaʔ**emilêmɔ jaːt^{h}wâlɛ] (Bungu)
/e-tʃe-t^{h}abu **e-tʃe-a** = e-mi-lemɔ je-a = a-t^{h}walɛ/
AUG-7-book **AUG-PP7-CON** = AUG-4-work PP4-CON = 2-apostle
'the book of Acts (lit., works of apostles)'

b. [zǐːs^{w}é **zúː**múɾimi] (Ikizu)
/zi-is^{w}e **za** = u-mu-ɾimi/
10-fish **PP10.CON** = AUG-1-farmer
'fish of the farmer'

[3] In Bungu, Ndali, Nyiha and Safwa, the class 5 noun prefix is analysed as having the underlying form /li-/ and in Malila it is analysed as /lɪ-/. The consonant of this prefix is elided in many grammatical contexts, and it could be argued that the vowel which remains is at least in some contexts a fusion of the augment vowel and the prefix vowel. We have chosen to gloss vowels in such debatable contexts with a noun class number only, without AUG, as in /i-k^{hw}i/ 5-tree 'tree' here. In Bungu, two other noun class prefixes, namely 2 and 14, show a similar reduction from /CV-/ to /V-/ and are similarly glossed, as in /a-t^{h}walɛ/ 2-apostle 'apostles' in (2a).

c. [omó:ná ꜜ**ʔó**muɣaβo] (Ikoma)
/o-mo-ona **o** = mu-ɣaβo/
AUG-1-child PP**1**.CON = 1-doctor
'child of the doctor'

Phonological behaviour of the kind seen in examples (1–3),[4] coupled with the phrasal status of the following constituent, characterises the connective as a clitic which is phonologically dependent on a host while connecting phrases rather than words. Example (3) from Kinga illustrates how the constituent following the clitic can be a NP ('that crowd').

(3) [aʋâ:nu **ʋa**xíp^{h}ʊka íx^{j}ɔ] (Kinga)
/a-ʋa-nu **ʋa-a** = xɪ-p^{h}ʊka ɪx^{j}ɔ/
AUG-2-person PP**2**-CON = 7-crowd EP7.REF.DEM
'people of that crowd'

3.2.3 Coordinating conjunction

The underlying form of the coordinating conjunction is <na> in all the sample languages, as can be seen when it precedes a consonant-initial word, as in Ikizu (4a). For nouns with augments, the vowel of the conjunction is replaced with the augment vowel in most environments, as in Vwanji (4b), or with the pre-root vowel, as in Malila (4c), depending on the class. In Kisi (4d), a language where nouns do not have augments in any environment, the vowel of the conjunction is replaced with what we analyse as a historical augment (i.e., a vowel which matches the prefix in vowel quality and is [i] in the case of the class 9 and 10 nouns where the prefix has no vowel), shown here in brackets in the underlying form.

(4) a. [**na**ɲǎ:mu] (Ikizu)
/**na** = ɲa:mu/
CNJ = 1A.cat
'and cat'

[4] This behaviour can also be observed when the clitic is a coordinating conjunction, locative or copula, as shown in § 3.3.

b. [**nɪ**k^{h}ɪt^{h}ɛː^{ŋ}gɔ] (Vwanji)
/**na** = ɪ-k^{h}ɪ-t^{h}ɛ^{ŋ}gɔ/
CNJ = AUG-7-chair
'and chair'

c. [**nî**ːzʊβa] (Malila)
/**na** = ɪ-zʊβa/
CNJ = 5-sun
'and sun'

d. [**ni**soː^{m}ba] (Kisi)
/**na** = (i-)so^{m}ba/
CNJ = AUG-10.fish
'and fish'

The coordinating conjunction also functions as a comitative preposition, depending on the grammatical context. For one sample language, Sangu, the phonological behaviour of the conjunction depends on whether it conjoins phrases (5a) or clauses (5b). The underlying vowel of the conjunction is replaced by the augment of the following noun when it is part of a phrase and not when it is part of a clause.

(5) a. [iʃílo **ni**lísik^{h}u] (Sangu)
/i-ʃi-lo **na** = i-li-sik^{h}u/
AUG-7-night CNJ = AUG-5-day
'night and day'

b. [iʃílo ʃǎːsila **na** ilísik^{h}u lijâː^{n}sa] (Sangu)
/i-ʃi-lo ʃi-a-sil-a **na** i-li-sik^{h}u li-ja^{n}s-a/
AUG-7-night SP7-PST-end-FV CNJ AUG-5-day SP5.PRS-begin-FV
'the night has ended and the day begins'

3.2.4 Locative

Two patterns of locative formation tend to be found in Bantu languages: locative nouns in classes 16–18, and prepositions (Nurse and Philippson 2003:7). Locative nouns are typically formed by adding a locative nominal prefix to a noun which already has a noun class prefix. The resulting locative noun behaves as an ordinary noun with respect to agreement and not as a prepositional phrase (Schadeberg and Bostoen 2019:191).

The sample languages have locative morphemes which are formally the same as the class 16–18 noun prefixes[5] (reconstructed as **pà-*, **kʊ̀-* and **mʊ̀-* respectively, Meeussen 1967:97), but act as phrasal prefixes, i.e., clitics, rather than locative nominal prefixes, and do not control agreement within the NP. The Malila example in (6a) shows the class 16 noun prefix controlling agreement on the numeral, whereas in (6b) the class 16 locative clitic does not control agreement on the connective.

(6) a. [a**pʰâː**^{n}tʰʊ **pʰá**mu] (Malila)
/a-**pʰa**-^{n}tʰʊ **pʰa**-mu/
AUG-**16**-place EP**16**-one
'a certain place'

b. [**pʰâː**^{m}pʰʊga **ja**βâː^{n}tʰʊ] (Malila)
/**pʰa**=N-pʰʊga jɪ-**a**=βa-^{n}tʰʊ/
LOC**16**=9-crowd PP**9**-CON=2-person
'at the crowd of people'

In (6a), [apʰâː^{n}tʰʊ] is a noun in class 16 with the nominative prefix [pʰa-] and an augment [a-]. The modifier [pʰamu] therefore takes class 16 agreement. In contrast, in (6b) a class 9 noun [îː^{m}pʰʊga] controls the agreement of the connective [ja] and the class 16 locative clitic [pʰa] has scope over the NP 'crowd of people' as a whole, without affecting agreement within the NP. In (6b), the locative clitic retains its underlying vowel and the noun to which the clitic attaches occurs in a form (full noun prefix but no augment) which is found in other grammatical structures. In certain noun classes in other languages, further changes take place. For example, in Nyiha, the locative vowel of classes 17 and 18 is desyllabified when the following noun is from class 5 and has a consonant-initial stem (7a). In Malila, the locative clitics /kʰʊ/ and /mʊ/ become [kʰu] and [mu] through vowel harmony when the noun root contains /u/ or /i/ (7b). In Kisi, the class 18 locative clitic may be reduced to [m̩] before certain nouns from

[5] The southern languages in the sample (Bena, Bungu, Kinga, Kisi, Malila, Ndali, Nyiha, Safwa, Sangu, Vwanji) freely use all three locative clitics, whereas the northern languages (Ikizu, Ikoma, Jita, Kabwa, Kwaya, Simbiti, Zanaki and Zinza) are more restricted, with some languages using (or mainly using) only one or two of the three clitics.

classes 4, 5, 6 and 14 (7c). Bungu has an additional locative, class 18a [eN] (7d) which can surface as [eː-] before a nasal-initial class prefix.

(7) a. [**mʷĭː**zina] (Nyiha)
/**mu** = i-zina/
LOC**18** = 5-name
'in the name'

b. [**kʰu**lʲîːna] (Malila)
/**kʰʊ** = lɪ-ina/
LOC**17** = 5-hole
'at the hole'

c. [m̩buʷatʰu] (Kisi)
/**mu** = βu-atʰu/
LOC**18** = 14-canoe
'in the canoe'

d. [**eː**mí↓kʰɔ́↑nɔ̂] (Bungu)
/**eN** = mi-kʰɔnɔ/
LOC**18a** = 4-hand
'in the hands'

3.2.5 Copula

Meeussen (1967:115) proposes **ní* as a reconstructed Eastern Bantu copula, which is invariable for person and tense. Gibson et al. (2019:217) note that this copula may become segmentally reduced in some Bantu languages and appear as a clitic. The languages in our sample which have an invariable copula do not all show segmental reduction, but the copula has been analysed as a clitic in all cases. This copula may surface in an underlying form, such as [ni] in Jita (8a), or may undergo vowel harmony with the word to which it attaches, as in Ikizu (8b). In Simbiti, the copula is [N] which may attach to a following augment (8c), or the augment may elide and the copula [N] then assimilates to the place of articulation of the following consonant and is lengthened (8d).

(8) a. [unu **ni**mút^h^ɛgi] (Jita)
/unu **ni** = mu-t^h^ɛgi/
EP1.PROX.DEM COP = 1-fisherman
'this is a fisherman'

b. [gono **ní**muɾi] (Ikizu)
/gono **ne** = mu-ɾi/
EP3.PROX.DEM COP = 3-root
'this is a root'

c. [ɔnɔ **nɔ**mɔ́:na] (Simbiti)
/ɔnɔ **N** = ɔ-mɔ:na/
EP1.PROX.DEM COP = AUG-1.child
'this is a child'

d. [ɔnɔ **m:**ɔ́:na] (Simbiti)
/ɔnɔ **N** = mɔ:na/
EP1.PROX.DEM COP = 1.child
'this is a child'

3.3 Phonological factors affecting orthography decisions

As mentioned in § 3.2.1, augment vowels pose a particular challenge for orthographic word boundary decisions because they may interact with the vowel of a proclitic attaching to the noun. Where a noun has no augment, and a CV-shaped clitic interacts with this noun, phonological merging of the clitic with the noun occurs infrequently and therefore the options for writing clitic and noun are quite simple: to write the clitic together with the noun as one word, separate it from the word by a punctuation mark such as a hyphen, or write it as an entirely separate word. In the latter two options, the clitic vowel would remain with the consonant of the clitic. Grammatical factors (see § 3.4) may also feed into the decision; however, preserving a constant word image for both clitic and noun is much simpler if the disjunctive option is chosen. This is particularly important as a joined clitic would obscure the shape of the start of the word, which is the most salient part of a word in the reading process (Jordan et al. 2003). For example:

(9) a. <na kʉsʉmba> [**na**k^{h}ʊsʊ̂ː^{m}ba] /**na**=k^{h}ʊsʊ^{m}ba/ 'and throwing' (Malila)
<kʉsʉmba> [k^{h}ʊsʊ̂ː^{m}ba] 'to throw'

b. <ku nyumba> [**k^{h}u**ɲuː^{m}ba] /**k^{h}u**=ɲu^{m}ba/ 'at the house' (Kisi)
<nyumba> [ɲuː^{m}ba] 'house'

c. <gwa nyaamu> [**g^{w}aː**ɲǎːmu] /**g^{w}a**=ɲaːmu/ 'of the cat' (Ikizu)
<nyaamu> [ɲǎːmu] 'cat'

Vowel harmony between the root vowels of the noun and the vowel of the clitic may complicate this picture by requiring a decision to be made between writing the clitic vowel in its underlying form or its surface form. Simbiti locatives are written in their surface form, (10).

(10) a. <kö bhëënyu> [**k^{h}ó**βeːɲu] /**k^{h}ɔ**=βeːɲu/ 'as for you' (Simbiti)

b. <ko bhoora> [**k^{h}ɔ**βɔ́ːɾa] /**k^{h}ɔ**=βɔːɾa/ 'for the reason' (Simbiti)

When the underlying form of a clitic can be heard in slow speech, even if it is not pronounced in rapid speech, speaker awareness of the underlying form makes it a viable option in writing. This can be demonstrated in the interaction of locatives with class 5 nouns in Bena (class 16 [11a], class 17 [11b], class 18 [11c]), where the unelided form is used in writing.

(11) a. <pa lifunde> [**p^{h}iː**fûː^{n}de ~ **p^{h}ali**fûː^{n}de] /**p^{h}a**=lifu^{n}de/ 'at the cloud' (Bena)

b. <ku litaawa> [**k^{hw}í**taːwa ~ **k^{h}ulí**t^{h}aːwa] /**k^{h}u**=lit^{h}aːwa/ 'in the name' (Bena)

c. <mu liwoko> [**m^{w}í**wok^{h}o ~ **mulí**wok^{h}o] /**mu**=liwok^{h}o/ 'in the hand' (Bena)

As soon as an augment is part of the picture, it becomes harder to disentangle the clitic from the noun while preserving the ideal of a constant word image. Two scenarios will be discussed separately: the consonant-final clitic (§ 3.3.1) and the vowel-final clitic (§ 3.3.2).

In order to discuss the outcome of clitic and noun interactions as observed in the sample languages, we use the following notation: [A] and <A> represent any augment vowel (phonetic and orthographic representations, respectively), [C] and <C> represent any consonant, and [V] and <V> represent any vowel. [Noun] and <Noun> represent the noun stem plus its noun class prefix. Thus, a noun with its augment is represented phonetically as [ANoun] and orthographically as <ANoun>. Using this notation, a consonant-final clitic will be represented as <C> (thus including both C and VC clitics, such as /eN/ 'in' [class 18a locative] in Bungu), and a vowel-final clitic will be represented as <CV> (thus including both CV and VCV clitics, such as /a^{n}za/ 'like' in Malila). The first vowel in clitics of the shape /VC/ or /VCV/ is unlikely to be affected in the interaction with the following noun and therefore /C/ and /VC/ clitics and /CV/ and /VCV/ clitics can be grouped together based on their final segments for the purposes of our discussion. /C/ and /CV/ clitics are by far the most common of their respective groupings and have therefore been chosen to represent these groupings for the sake of simplicity. Section 3.3.3 discusses further complicating factors that have been observed.

3.3.1 Clitic is consonant-final

In the sample languages, the final consonant of the clitic is always a nasal, and in many cases only a nasal (without a preceding vowel). Included in this section is the class 18 locative clitic (underlyingly /mu/, /mʊ/, or /mo/, depending on the language) when it loses its vowel and interacts directly with the consonant of the noun prefix. Interactions of clitic and noun result in the two outcomes described in § 3.3.1.1 and § 3.3.1.2.

3.3.1.1 Clitic attaches to noun plus augment ([CANoun])

With this outcome, a few spelling options can be considered. Writing the combination conjunctively as <CANoun> is a possibility. However, in the interests of preserving a constant word image, and from a desire to give greater prominence to the clitic, this is less preferable and so has not been chosen in any of the sample languages. Separating the single consonant by itself (<C ANoun>) is also unlikely to give sufficient prominence to the clitic, as an isolated consonant may easily be missed in reading, and so this option has not been used either. The only remaining option of disjunctive spelling is <CA Noun>. This has also not been chosen for any of the sample languages, often due to a desire to differentiate one clitic from another which behaves in a similar way, as discussed in § 3.4.2. Instead, hyphenation is the preferred strategy, with the hyphen either preceding the augment, <C-ANoun> as in the Ikoma copula (12) or following it, <CA-Noun> as in the Simbiti copula, (13).

<C-ANoun>

(12) a. <n-omutëmi> [**n**omut^{h}ɛ́mi] /**N**=omut^{h}ɛmi/ 'is the king' (Ikoma)
<omutëmi> [omut^{h}ɛ́mi] 'king'

b. <n-abhasaani> [**n**aβasaːní] /**N**=aβasaːni/ 'are the friends' (Ikoma)
<abhasaani> [aβasaːní] 'friends'

<CA-Noun>

(13) a. <nö-möntö> [**n**omóː^{n}t^{h}o] /**N**=omo^{n}t^{h}o/ 'is the person' (Simbiti)
<ömöntö> [omoː^{n}t^{h}o] 'person'

b. <nu-muki> [**n**umúk^{h}i] /**N**=umuk^{h}i/ 'is the vein' (Simbiti)
<umuki> [umuk^{h}i] 'vein'

3.3.1.2 Clitic attaches to noun minus augment ([CNoun])

In this scenario, there may be consonant interaction effects to consider. While <C Noun, C-Noun> or <CNoun> are all possible spelling options, <C Noun> is dispreferred in the orthographies of all the languages concerned, as the interaction of the clitic consonant and prefix consonant makes the clitic and noun an inseparable unit in the speaker's mind, as in Kabwa (14), where the lengthened nasal resulting from the interaction of the copula and nasal-initial noun prefix is represented as <C-Noun>.

(14) <m-murimi> [**m**ːúɾimi] /**N**=muɾimi/ 'is the farmer' (Kabwa)
(not *<m murimi>)

Likewise, writing <CNoun> (i.e., *<mmurimi>) would not give due prominence to the clitic, but it has been found to be an appropriate choice for exceptions to a normal spelling rule. An example of this is when the class 18 locative clitic attaches to certain nouns in Kisi (15). In this language, the class 18 locative is normally written disjunctively, <CV Noun> (15a), but for some noun classes the vowel of the locative clitic elides and the resulting nasal becomes syllabic noun-initially. These exceptions are written conjunctively, <CNoun> (15b, c), as in this context the unelided form is not an acceptable pronunciation. The apostrophe in the Kisi orthography indicates that the preceding nasal is syllabic and so is not a marker specific to showing a clitic boundary.

(15) a. <mu nyanja> [**mu**ɲaː^{ɲ}ɟa] /**mu**=ɲa^{ɲ}ɟa/ 'in the lake' (Kisi)

b. <m'bwatu> [**m̩**bu^{w}at^{h}u] /**mu**=βu^{w}at^{h}u/ 'in the canoe' (Kisi)

c. <m'mwojho> [**m̩**mu^{w}oʝo] /**mu**=mu^{w}oʝo/ 'in the heart' (Kisi)

Hyphenation is the preferred choice for representing [CNoun] for the sample languages, as shown for the Simbiti (16a) and Kabwa (16b) copula plus noun combinations.

<C-Noun>

(16) a. <n-ditamboka> [^{n}**d**it^{h}á:^{m}bɔk^{h}a] /**N**=ɾit^{h}a^{m}bɔk^{h}a/ 'is a step' (Simbiti)
<ritamboka> [ɾit^{h}á:^{m}bɔk^{h}a] 'step'
b. <m-barimi> [^{m}**b**aɾími] /**N**=βaɾimi/ 'are the farmers' (Kabwa)
<abharimi> [aβaɾími] 'farmers'

Bungu has a VC-shaped locative clitic, which is also written with a hyphen, though the hyphen is not placed between the clitic consonant and noun but between the vowel and consonant of the clitic, <V-CNoun> (17). This positioning of the hyphen is due to the way the consonant interacts with the noun prefix consonant; it becomes part of the same syllable as the prefix, as prenasalisation of the noun prefix consonant, thus it is illogical to separate it visually.

<V-CNoun>

(17) <ɨ-ndʉkʉwa> [**e:**^{n}**d**ók^{h}owa] /**eN**=lok^{h}owa/ 'in the lake' (Bungu)
<ʉlʉkʉwa> [olók^{h}owa] 'lake'

Splitting the clitic from the noun by means of a hyphen (<C-Noun>) leaves open the option of writing the noun in its underlying form in order to aid recognition. The underlying form of the noun is written in Ikoma (18), but not in Simbiti (16a) or Kabwa (16b).

(18) a. <m-bhoheene> [^{m}**b**ohê:ne] /**N**=βohe:ne/ 'is good' (Ikoma)
<bhoheene> [βohê:ne] 'good'
b. <n-ghaare> [^{ŋ}**g**â:ɾe] /**N**=ɣa:ɾe/ 'is those' (Ikoma)
<ghaare> [ɣâ:ɾe] 'those'

Writing the underlying form of the clitic rather than its surface form may also be a possibility, but not in any of the languages represented in this chapter, as in most cases it is impossible to know what the underlying form of the clitic is.

3.3.2 Clitic is vowel-final

For vowel-final clitics, the interaction of clitic plus noun results in a variety of different outcomes, depending on the language, each opening up different spelling options.

3.3.2.1 Augment vowel is absent in surface form; clitic vowel remains ([CVNoun])

Given that the augment is no longer present in the resulting form in this scenario, it is counterintuitive to L1 speakers to reintroduce it in writing and represent two vowels where only one is pronounced.

When deciding on conjunctive or disjunctive spelling of such clitics for each language, it is important to consider whether the noun could appear in any other context without its augment. When the answer to this is no, conjunctive (<CVNoun>) or hyphenated (<CV-Noun>) options are often preferable to writing the noun in a form in which it otherwise never appears (e.g., <Noun> in <CV Noun>), in order to avoid having two representations of the same noun. When a noun is commonly found without its augment in other contexts, such as when used vocatively or in predicate nominal constructions, then readers are used to seeing it written both with (<ANoun>) and without its augment (<Noun>), and have no problem with there being two word images for the noun. Examples (19–22) illustrate how several languages have dealt with the [CVNoun] scenario orthographically. <CVNoun> is exemplified by the Zinza locative (19a), Ikizu locative (19b) and Kinga negative (19c). Note that for the Ikizu locative (19b), vowel harmony affecting the clitic vowel had to be taken into consideration. This Ikizu clitic is written transparently, that is, the vowel changes are represented.

<CVNoun>

(19)	a.	<omubaantu>	[**omu**βaː^{n}t^{h}u]	/**omu** = βa^{n}t^{h}u/	‘among the people’	(Zinza)
		<abaantu>	[aβaː^{n}t^{h}u]		‘people’	
	b.	<kokereesa>	[**k^{h}ɔ**k^{h}ɛ́ɾɛːsa]	/**k^{h}o** = k^{h}ɛɾɛːsa/	‘at the beard’	(Ikizu)
		<ekereesa>	[ɛk^{h}ɛ́ɾɛːsa]		‘beard’	
	c.	<nanyumba>	[**ná**ɲuː^{m}ba]	/**na** = ɲu^{m}ba/	‘not the house’	(Kinga)
		<ɨnyumba>	[íɲuː^{m}ba]		‘house’	

<CV Noun> is exemplified by the Bena connective (20a), Malila locative (20b) and Sangu connective (20c). As with the Ikizu locative (19b), vowel harmony affecting the Malila locative vowel (20b) had to be considered. These vowel alternations are written transparently.

<CV Noun>

(20)	a.	<lya mooto>	[**l^{j}a**:mô:t^{h}o]	/**l^{j}a**=mo:t^{h}o/	'of the fire'	(Bena)
		<umooto>	[umô:t^{h}o]		'fire'	
	b.	<mu lyina>	[**mu**l^{j}î:na]	/**mʊ**=l^{j}ina/	'in the hole'	(Malila)
		<ilyina>	[il^{j}î:na]		'hole'	
	c.	<uwa wutasi>	[**úwa**wút^{h}asi]	/**uwa**=wut^{h}asi/	'the first (lit., of beginning)'	(Sangu)
		<uwutasi>	[uwút^{h}asi]		'beginning'	

Also in this category of <(C)V Noun>, Ikoma provides a rare example of the clitic as a single vowel (21). In this case, the connective is a single vowel when it agrees with a head noun from class 1, 3 or 9.

(21) <omutëmi o ghetumbe> (Ikoma)
[omut^{h}ɛ́mi **o**ɣet^{h}û:^{m}be]
/o-mu-t^{h}ɛmi **o**=ɣe-t^{h}u^{m}be/
AUG-1-king PP1.CON=7-chair
'king of the chair'

The spelling <CV-Noun> is exemplified by the Bungu locative (22a), Ikizu copula (22b) and Jita locative (22c).

<CV-Noun>

(22)	a.	<pa-mbana>	[**p^{h}a:**^{m}bâna]	/**p^{h}a**=^{m}bana/	'on the river'	(Bungu)
		<ʉmbana>	[o:^{m}bâna]		'river'	
	b.	<nɨ-mʉʉtʉ>	[**né**mo:t^{h}o]	/**ne**=mo:t^{h}o/	'is the person'	(Ikizu)
		<ʉmʉʉtʉ>	[ómo:t^{h}o]		'person'	
	c.	<ku-bhategi>	[**k^{h}u**βat^{h}ɛ́gi]	/**k^{h}u**=βat^{h}ɛgi/	'at the fishermen'	(Jita)
		<abhategi>	[aβat^{h}ɛ́gi]		'fisherman'	

3.3.2.2 Augment vowel is absent in surface form; clitic vowel changes ([CV$_2$Noun])

Although this scenario is infrequent among the sample languages, it should also be mentioned. Since the resultant vowel (represented here as V$_2$) is different from both the underlying clitic vowel and the augment vowel, L1 orthography stakeholders found it counterintuitive to write both clitic and noun in their underlying forms (<CV ANoun, CV Noun>). The remaining options are therefore <CV$_2$Noun, CV$_2$-Noun, CV$_2$ Noun>. In this context, only disjunctive spelling has been used in the orthographies of the sample languages.

The Safwa connective is an example of [CV$_2$Noun] which is written <CV$_2$ Noun>, (23). Safwa connectives will be treated in greater depth in § 3.4.1, which considers the situation where a clitic behaves differently according to the class of the noun to which it is attached.

(23) <gɨ wʉʉmi> [gɪwʊ̂:mi] /**ga**=wʊ:mi/ 'of the life' (Safwa)
(not *<ga ʉwʉʉmi>)
<ʉwʉʉmi> [ʊwʊ̂:mi] 'life'

Kisi provides a second example of [CV$_2$Noun], but for a different reason to Safwa. Kisi no longer has an augment as part of its nominal system, yet the vowel of the coordinating conjunction /na/ still changes to match the form of this historical augment (24). On the one hand, it is counterintuitive to write the augment before the noun (<CV ANoun> *<na isomba>), as this form of the noun no longer exists. On the other hand, the historical augment vowel could not be omitted entirely from the written form (<CV Noun> *<na somba>), as this does not reflect present-day pronunciation. Instead, the most natural solution is to represent the vowel change on the clitic.

(24) <ni somba> [**ni**so:^{m}ba] /**na**=(i)so^{m}ba/ 'and the fish' (Kisi)
<somba> [so:^{m}ba] 'fish'

3.3.2.3 Clitic vowel elides; short augment vowel remains ([CANoun])

In the previous scenarios, the L1 orthography development stakeholders preferred not to write the augment before the noun as it did not appear in the surface form. However, in the scenario considered in this section, the augment is retained in the surface form so it is necessary to consider whether or not to write it before the noun. This leaves many options open: write the augment vowel only once (<CANoun, CA Noun, CA-Noun>), write the underlying clitic vowel and the augment before the noun (<CV ANoun, CV-ANoun>), or write the augment vowel as part of the clitic and also before the noun (<CA ANoun, CA-ANoun>).

As has been mentioned before, <CANoun> is close in structure to the noun without the clitic, <ANoun>, and does not give due prominence to the clitic. Note that in several of the sample languages, writing the noun without the augment vowel (<CA Noun, CA-Noun>) leaves a word fragment, if the augment vowel and prefix have merged together (e.g., Bungu [ɪ́ꜜt^{h}áwa] /i-li-t^{h}awa/ AUG-5-name 'name'; *[t^{h}awa] has no identifiable meaning). Ideally, writing word fragments should be avoided.

For Kinga (25a), Bena (25b) and Nyiha (25c), the coordinating conjunction /na/ is written with the altered vowel, and the following noun is represented without its augment vowel.

<CA Noun>

(25)	a.	<nʉ mwana>	[**nʊ́**m^{w}a:na]	/**na**=ʊm^{w}ana/	'and the child'	(Kinga)
		<ʉmwana>	[ʊ́m^{w}a:na]		'child'	
	b.	<ni numbula>	[**ni**nu:^{m}búla]	/**na**=inu^{m}bula/	'and the heart'	(Bena)
		<inumbula>	[inu:^{m}búla]		'heart'	
	c.	<nu mupaafi>	[**nu**mup^{h}â:fi]	/**na**=umup^{h}a:fi/	'and the parent'	(Nyiha)
		<umupaafi>	[**u**mup^{h}â:fi]		'parent'	

For the Nyiha connective plus class 5 noun (26), the underlying vowel of the clitic is written as well as the augment represented before the noun, <CV ANoun>. This solution has been chosen in order to avoid the meaningless word fragment left by removing the combined augment plus class prefix /i-/ (e.g., *<kwi>).

<CV ANoun>

(26)	<aga ikwi>	[**ági:**k^{hw}i]	/**aga**=ik^{hw}i/	'of the tree'	(Nyiha)
	<ikwi>	[**î:**k^{hw}i]		'tree'	

The regular spelling rule for Nyiha connectives is to write <CV Noun> (27).

(27)	<aga muntu>	[**aga**mû:^{n}t^{h}u]	/**aga**=mu^{n}t^{h}u/	'of the person'	(Nyiha)
	<umuntu>	[**u**mû:^{n}t^{h}u]		'person'	

For the Nyiha orthography stakeholders, writing the underlying form of the connective vowel is acceptable here because before all other noun classes the same connective retains its underlying shape /aga/, thus making the underlying vowel easily discernible, even though it never surfaces in its underlying form before class 5 nouns, even in slow speech.

The same decision to write the underlying form of the clitic vowel (<CV ANoun>) has not been made for the coordinating conjunction /na/ plus class 5 noun, [nî:k^{hw}i] 'and tree' <ni ikwi> (not *<na ikwi>), as class 5 is not unique in affecting the underlying vowel of the conjunction (25c), making <CV Noun> the more logical regular rule for spelling this clitic. Class 5 nouns are still written exceptionally in this context compared to other classes, <CA ANoun> rather than <CA Noun>, in order to avoid writing the noun without its initial vowel (*<kwi>), which is a word fragment.

In Sangu, writing the coordinating conjunction plus noun as <CV ANoun> instead of <CA Noun> actually distinguishes between conjoined phrases (pronounced [CANoun]) and conjoined clauses (pronounced [CVʔANoun]), as shown in example (5) in § 3.2.3. This makes <CV ANoun> unsuitable for writing [CANoun], thus serving as a reminder that writing the underlying form of a clitic might not always be the ideal solution.

<CA ANoun> is exemplified by Bungu connective (28a), Bungu coordinating conjunction (28b), Nyiha coordinating conjunction (28c), all with class 5 nouns; as well as the Ikoma coordinating conjunction (28d). The class 5 examples (28a–c) are exceptions to the regular spelling rule for these clitics, which in all three cases is to write <CA Noun>. These exceptions are required to avoid writing <Noun>, which for class 5 is an unidentifiable word fragment. Example (28d) illustrates the regular spelling rule for the Ikoma coordinating conjunction. Writing the vowel twice (once on the clitic and once before the noun prefix) when it is pronounced short is not acceptable to some L1 speakers, and so writing a vowel twice is often a compromise for class 5 words. Some L1 speakers object to two vowels on the grounds that they will be incorrectly read, either as two separate vowels or as one long vowel, rather than as the intended short vowel.

<CA ANoun>

(28)	a.	<gi itawa>	[**gí**$^{\downarrow}$t^{h}áwa]	/**ga** = it^{h}awa/	'of the name'	(Bungu)
		<itawa>	[**í**$^{\downarrow}$t^{h}áwa]		'name'	
	b.	<ni itawa>	[**ní**$^{\downarrow}$t^{h}áwa]	/**na** = it^{h}awa/	'and the name'	(Bungu)
	c.	<ni ikwi>	[**nî:**k^{hw}i]	/**na** = ik^{hw}i/	'and the tree'	(Nyiha)
		<ikwi>	[**î:**k^{hw}i]		'tree'	
	d.	<no omote>	[**no**mot^{h}é]	/**na** = omot^{h}e/	'and the tree'	(Ikoma)
		<omote>	[**o**mot^{h}é]		'tree'	

The Safwa coordinating conjunction (29a), connective (29b) and locative (29c) with class 5 or class 15 nouns all have hyphenation as an aid to avoiding mispronunciations as a long vowel or as two separate vowels. Writing <CA-ANoun> is a compromise on the one hand between word fragments being written (which would happen following the regular <CA Noun> spelling rule for these clitics, e.g., *<na jelwe>, *<gi booma>, *<pi booma>), and on the other hand the vowel being written as part of the clitic and also before the noun <CA ANoun> (e.g., *<na ajelwe>, *<gi ibooma>, *<pi ibooma>). The Safwa orthography stakeholders object to the vowel being written twice without the hyphen as <CA ANoun> on the grounds that readers would mispronounce this.

<CA-ANoun>

(29) a. <na-ajelwe> [**ná**ɟɛlʷɛ] /**na**=aɟɛlʷɛ/ 'and the temptation' (Safwa)
<ajelwe> [**á**ɟɛlʷɛ] 'temptation'

b. <gi-ibooma> [**gi**bɔ̂ːma] /**ga**=ibɔːma/ 'of the town' (Safwa)
<ibooma> [ibɔ̂ːma] 'town'

c. <pi-ibooma> [**pʰi**bɔ̂ːma] /**pʰa**=ibɔːma/ 'at the town' (Safwa)

In contrast to the Safwa examples where hyphenation is used as a pronunciation aid, using hyphenation is part of the regular Bungu spelling rule for locatives, <CV-Noun> (30a). The difference for class 5 nouns is that the vowel is written before the noun and also as part of the clitic to avoid a word fragment following the hyphen, <CA-ANoun> (30b).

(30) a. <pa-mbana> [**pʰa**ːᵐbâna] /**pʰa**=ᵐbana/ 'on the river' (Bungu)
<ʉmbana> [**o**ːᵐbâna] 'river'

b. <pi-ikwi> [**pʰí**kʰwi] /**pʰa**=ikʰwi/ 'at the tree' (Bungu)
<ikwi> [**í**kʰwi] 'tree'

The remaining spelling possibilities, <CV-ANoun, CA-Noun>, are not used in the orthographies of the sample languages. The first of these is perhaps never likely to be an option; if representatives of a language community have accepted writing the underlying form of a clitic, it is hard to see why they would then require hyphenation, rather than writing the clitic disjunctively.

3.3.2.4 *Clitic vowel elides; augment vowel is lengthened ([CA:Noun])*

In some languages, elision of the clitic vowel results in compensatory lengthening of the remaining vowel. In this context, writing a vowel on both clitic and augment is often acceptable to L1 speakers (since they pronounce the resulting vowel long anyway), but the choice of whether to write the clitic vowel in the same way as the augment vowel <CA ANoun> or as the underlying vowel <CV ANoun> varies between language communities. Once again, for languages where the underlying vowels of both clitic and noun resurface in slow pronunciation, L1 speakers are often more accepting of writing the underlying structure <CV ANoun>. <CV-ANoun> is not being used to represent [CA:Noun] in the sample languages for the same reasons mentioned in § 3.3.2.3. Example (31a) shows the Zanaki connective, and (31b) the Zanaki coordinating conjunction, both of which are written <CA ANoun>.

<CA ANoun>

(31)	a.	<gwe ebhiguru>	[**gʷɛː**βɪgʊ́rʊ]	/**gʷa** = ɛβɪgʊrʊ/	‘of the mountains’	(Zanaki)
		<ebhiguru>	[ɛβɪgʊ́rʊ]		‘mountains’	
	b.	<no omwiisi>	[**noː**mʷíːsi]	/**na** = ɔmʷisi/	‘and the day’	(Zanaki)
		<omwiisi>	[omʷíːsi]		‘day’	

Although the Bungu orthography represents [CA:Noun] as <CA ANoun>, e.g., class 2 (32a) and class 14 (32b), and although the noun in isolation has a long vowel in this position created by the elision of the prefix vowel ([A:Noun]), this length in the isolation form is not represented orthographically. Instead it is written as <ANoun>, so Bungu is slightly different from the other sample languages in this respect.

(32)	a.	<wa alɨmi>	[**waː**lêmi]	/**wa** = aːlemi/	‘of the farmers’	(Bungu)
		<alɨmi>	[**a**ːlêmi]		‘farmers’	
	b.	<nʉ ukʉwɨ>	[**noː**kʰôwe]	/**na** = oːkʰowe/	‘and the adultery’	(Bungu)
		<ukʉwɨ>	[**o**ːkʰôwe]		‘adultery’	

In Simbiti, since pronunciation of the underlying vowels is possible in slow speech, the connective (33a) and coordinating conjunction (33b) are written in their underlying forms, <CV ANoun>.

<CV ANoun>

(33)	a.	<uwa umukungu>	[**uwuː**mukʰúːᵑgu] ~ [**uwaʔu**mukʰúːᵑgu]	/**uwa** = umukʰuᵑgu/	‘of the old woman’	(Simbiti)
		<umukungu>	[**u**mukʰúːᵑgu]		‘old woman’	
	b.	<na omobhohe>	[**nɔː**mɔβɔ́hɛ́] ~ [**naʔ**ɔmɔβɔ́hɛ́]	/**na** = ɔmɔβɔhɛ/	‘and the prisoner’	(Simbiti)
		<omobhohe>	[ɔmɔβɔ́hɛ́]		‘prisoner’	

As mentioned before (and shown in [30a]), the regular spelling rule for Bungu locatives is hyphenation <CV-Noun>. The exception for writing class 5 locatives as <CA-ANoun> to represent [CANoun] is mentioned in § 3.3.2.3 and shown in example (30b). Although the spelling rule is the same, the exception shown in (34) for writing class 14 locatives as <CA-ANoun> represents the surface form [CA:Noun], not [CANoun].

<CA-ANoun>

(34) <kʉ-ʉfumɨlo> [**k^{h}ó:**ꜜfúꜛmélɔ] /**k^{h}o** = o:fumelɔ/ 'from the source' (Bungu)

<ʉfumɨlo> [**ó:**ꜜfúꜛmélɔ] 'source'

3.3.2.5 Clitic vowel and augment vowel both remain ([CVANoun])

Although this is quite a rare scenario in the sample languages, it is easy to resolve orthographically, as both underlying vowels are pronounced and so writing them is acceptable to L1 speakers, either as <CV ANoun> or <CV-ANoun>.

In Zanaki, this scenario occurs as a matter of free variation where some L1 speakers pronounce the augment before the noun following the copula, while others do not (35). The orthography permits both spellings, according to individual speaker preference.

(35) <ni abhaatu> [**niʔa**βá:t^{h}ʊ] /**ni** = (a)βa:t^{h}ʊ/ 'are the people' (Zanaki)
~ <ni bhaatu> ~ [**ni**βá:t^{h}ʊ]

In Bungu, an augment can be found in certain contexts where normally it is absent, such as in book names which in isolation begin with an augment (36).

(36) a. <ɨchɨtabu ɨcha Ɨmilɨmo ya Atwale> (Bungu)
[etʃct^{h}âbu **étʃa**ʔemilêmɔ ɟa:t^{h}wâlɛ]
/etʃet^{h}abu **e-tʃe-a** = e-mi-lemɔ ja:t^{h}wâlɛ/
AUG.7.book AUG-PP7-CON = AUG-4-work PP4.CON.2.apostle
'the book of Acts (lit., the book of works of the apostles)'

b. <ɨchɨtabu ɨcha milɨmo ya ndʉ> (Bungu)
[etʃet^{h}âbu **étʃa**milêmɔ já^{n}do]
/etʃet^{h}abu **e-tʃe-a** = mi-lemɔ já^{n}do/
AUG.7.book AUG-PP7-CON = 4-work PP4.CON.1.person
'the book of a person's deeds (lit. book of works of the person)'

Finally, Bungu class 14 nouns with their reduced augment plus prefix (/o-wo-/ becomes /o:-/) are exceptions to the regular spelling rules for writing the locative clitic and connective clitic (which are <CV-Noun> and <CV Noun> respectively). For class 14 nouns, the locative is written <CV-ANoun> (37a) and the connective <CV ANoun> (37b). Note that the glide which is heard between the clitic and prefix vowels is not written, as it is not part of the isolation form of the noun, and is inserted automatically in pronunciation.

(37)	a.	<pa-ʉdamu>	[**pʰawo**dâmu]	/**pʰa**=o:damu/	'the area of the sitting room'	(Bungu)
		<ʉdamu>	[o:dâmu]		'sitting room'	
	b.	<ɨzya ʉkʉwɨ>	[**ézjawo**kʰôwe]	/**ezja**=o:kʰowe/	'of the adultery'	(Bungu)
		<ʉkʉwɨ>	[o:kʰôwe]		'adultery'	

3.3.3 Further complicating factors

Several additional phonological factors may complicate orthographic choices. Vowel harmony, which may result in three surface forms of a clitic for seven-vowel languages, has already been mentioned (example [10], § 3.3). The copula plus NP examples from Ikizu in (38) exemplify writing the surface form.

(38)	a.	<nɨ-mʉʉtʉ>	[**né**mo:tʰo]	/**ne**=mo:tʰo/	'is the person'	(Ikizu)
	b.	<ni-muri>	[**ní**muɾi]	/**ne**=muɾi/	'is the root'	(Ikizu)
	c.	<ne-ngoko>	[**nɛ**:ᵑgɔ́kʰɔ]	/**ne**=ᵑgɔkʰɔ/	'is the chicken'	(Ikizu)

In many languages where a noun has word-initial high tone and where the interaction of clitic and augment vowels result in a single short vowel, this short vowel will receive the high tone in place of the augment. Separating the clitic in writing as <CV Noun, CV-Noun, CV_2 Noun, CV_2-Noun, CA-Noun> or <CA Noun> means that the high tone is then visually separated from the noun it belongs to phonologically, as for the Safwa connective in (39a) where in <ga mwana> the high tone is on the vowel of the clitic [gá] (see also examples of the Kinga coordinating conjunction [39b] and Bungu locative [39c]). This may cause problems for readers and writers, but the advantages outweigh the disadvantages.

(39)	a.	<ga mwana>	[gámʷa:na]	/**ga**=mʷana/	'of the child'	(Safwa)
	b.	<ni samba>	[nísa:ᵐba]	/**na**=isaᵐba/	'and the branches'	(Kinga)
	c.	<pa-ntwe>	[pʰá:^{n}tʰwɛ]	/**pʰa**=^{n}tʰwɛ/	'on the head'	(Bungu)

Finally, in many Bantu languages compensatory lengthening may occur word-initially in certain environments. As this length is automatic and non-contrastive, it may not be necessary to represent it orthographically. However, when a clitic attaches to such nouns and the compensatory lengthening occurs on the clitic vowel instead, a decision needs to be made regarding how to represent this length. In Ndali, the clitic vowel on a noun with a non-canonical (non-CV or zero) shaped prefix is lengthened for words which would otherwise contain three morae or fewer (40). The issue of whether the length should be written or not has been avoided in this context as the clitic is written disjunctively from the noun.

(40) a. <mu sila> (Ndali)
[**muː**síla]
/**mu** = N-sila/
LOC**18** = 9-path
'on the path'

b. <nu nyoko> (Ndali)
[**nuː**ɲók^{h}o]
/**na** = u-ɲok^{h}o/
CNJ = AUG-1A.your.mother
'and your mother'

3.4 Grammatical factors affecting orthography decisions

Orthography decisions can also be affected by a variety of grammatical factors, such as different noun classes exhibiting different phonological behaviour for the same grammatical clitic (§ 3.4.1), different grammatical morphemes being homophones in certain contexts (§ 3.4.2), semantic exceptions for grammatically identical constructions (§ 3.4.3), or particular contexts causing an unusual word order which influences the desirability of certain orthographic choices (§ 3.4.4).

3.4.1 Noun classes behaving differently for the same clitic

In some languages, certain clitics show different phonological behaviour between different noun classes. In Safwa, the vowel resulting from the cliticisation of a connective to a noun (the noun always has an augment vowel in isolation) does not depend on the interaction of the clitic vowel and augment, but on the class of the following noun. That is, the outcome is driven by grammar rather than phonology. Thus, although class 1 and class 3 nouns both have the augment vowel /ʊ/ in isolation, the surface vowel resulting from the clitic plus noun is different for these two classes, as shown in (41a) and (41b) which show class 1 and class 3 respectively. Examples (41c) and (41d) show respectively the class 6 augment /a/ and class 9 augment /ɪ/ interacting with the connective vowel /a/ and both resulting in the vowel /ɪ/. The resulting forms are written disjunctively, with the surface vowel written as part of the connective (<CV$_2$ Noun>, see § 3.3.2.2), since the surface quality of the vowel is phonologically unpredictable.

(41)	a.	<sha mwana>	[ʃ**á**m^{w}a:na]	/ʃ**a** = m^{w}ana/	‘of the child’	(Safwa)
		<ʉmwana>	[ʊ́m^{w}a:na]		‘child’	
	b.	<shɨ m’bɨlɨ>	[ʃ**ɪ**^{m}b:ílɪ]	/ʃ**a** = ^{m}b:ɪlɪ/	‘of the body’	(Safwa)
		<ʉm’bɨlɨ>	[ʊ^{m}b:ílɪ]		‘body’	
	c.	<shɨ manama>	[ʃ**ɪ**mánama]	/ʃ**a** = manama/	‘of the legs’	(Safwa)
		<amanama>	[**a**mánama]		‘legs’	
	d.	<shɨ ntondwe>	[ʃ**ɪ**^{n}t^{h}ɔ̌:^{n}d^{w}ɛ]	/ʃ**a** = ɪ^{n}t^{h}ɔ^{n}d^{w}ɛ/	‘of the star’	(Safwa)
		<ɨntondwe>	[**ɪ**^{n}t^{h}ɔ̌:^{n}d^{w}ɛ]		‘star’	

Clitics frequently exhibit unusual phonological behaviour with class 5 nouns. In many of the sample languages the consonant of the class 5 prefix either elides on attachment of the clitic, as for the Ikizu locative (42a), or is absent both when the noun follows the locative and also when it is pronounced in isolation, as for the Ndali locative (42b). In languages where the augment and prefix combine in the surface form as a single vowel, e.g., Ndali <ibhingu> ‘cloud’, removing this vowel from the noun in disjunctive (or hyphenated) writing of the clitic would leave a word fragment, e.g., *<mu bhingu>, where *<bhingu> is not a meaningful word. Thus, when the regular spelling rule for a clitic involves not writing the augment before the noun, e.g., <CV Noun>, an exception should be made to this rule for class 5 nouns in order to avoid writing a word fragment. The options for this exception are to write the augment before the noun, e.g., *<mwi ibhingu> or <mu ibhingu> (as was chosen, see [42b]), or to write the clitic plus noun conjunctively, *<mwibhingu>.

(42)	a.	<kwibhigi>	[**k**^{hw}**i**:βígi]	/**k^{h}o** = ɾiβigi/	‘at the place with the cave’	(Ikizu)
		<ribhigi>	[**ɾi**βígi]		‘cave’	
	b.	<mu ibhingu>	[**m**^{w}**i**βî:^{ŋ}gu]	/**mu** = iβi^{ŋ}gu/	‘in the cloud’	(Ndali)
		<ibhingu>	[**i**βî:^{ŋ}gu]		‘cloud’	
	c.	<mu miishi>	[**mú**ꜜmí:ʃi]	/**mu** = mi:ʃi/	‘in the water’	(Ndali)
		<amiishi>	[**á**ꜜmí:ʃi]		‘water’	

In Malila and Nyiha, class 5 noun prefixes interact with the vowel of a preceding connective by causing it to elide. In both of these languages, the vowel of the connective usually remains unaltered by the following noun,[6] and so the regular orthographic rule for these clitics is disjunctive spelling, <CV Noun> as in Malila (43a), and Nyiha (43c). The orthographies of these two languages represent the combination of connective and class 5 noun differently. In Malila (43b), the vowel [ɪ], originally from the noun class prefix, is written as part of the connective rather than before the noun (<CA Noun>), leaving a word fragment, whereas in Nyiha (43d), the underlying vowels are written on both connective and noun (<CV ANoun>).

(43) a. <ʉwa mupaafi> [**ʊ́wa**mup^{h}â:fi] /**ʊwa**=mup^{h}a:fi/ 'of the parent' (Malila)
<umupaafi> [**u**mup^{h}â:fi] 'parent'
b. <ʉwɨ taawa> [**ʊw**ɪ́t^{h}a:wa] /**ʊwa**=ɪt^{h}a:wa/ 'of the name' (Malila)
<ɨtaawa> [ɪ́t^{h}a:wa] 'name'
c. <izya muntu> [**iz^{j}a**mû:^{n}t^{h}u] /**iz^{j}a**=mu^{n}t^{h}u/ 'of the person' (Nyiha)
<umuntu> [**u**mû:^{n}t^{h}u] 'person'
d. <uwa ɨlenga> [**uw**ɪlê:^{ŋ}ga] /**uwa**=ɪle:^{ŋ}ga/ 'of the lies' (Nyiha)
<ɨlenga> [ɪlê:^{ŋ}ga] 'lies'

For languages where different noun classes exhibit different behaviour for the same clitic, it can be necessary to make a choice between (i) allowing a less than ideal outcome to result from applying a spelling rule to certain classes (as in the Malila connective, [43b]); (ii) adding a class-specific exception in order to keep a spelling rule which works well for most classes (as in the Nyiha connective, [43d]); and (iii) choosing a spelling rule which works for all noun classes without exception even when a more desirable rule would work for some classes (such as would be the case if all connectives in Malila and Nyiha were written conjunctively with the preceding noun).

3.4.2 Distinguishing different grammatical morphemes

In some cases it might be desirable to distinguish homophonous grammatical morphemes orthographically. In many languages of the Mara region, this is the case for the copula attaching to class 9 and 10 nouns, as the class 10 prefix elides following the copula, leading to the singular and plural forms being homophonous. In the orthographies of some languages, such as Jita (class 9 [44a], class 10 [44b]) and Kwaya (class 9 [44c], class 10 [44d]),

[6] This is not true for Malila classes 9 and 10, e.g., [ʊ́l^{w}ɪ^{m}p^{h}ɛ̆:^{ŋ}ga] /ʊl^{w}a=ɪ^{m}p^{h}ɛ^{ŋ}ga/ 'of the rat (class 9)', where the connective vowel is affected. These are written <CA Noun>, <ulwɨ mpenga>.

only one pronunciation is possible for these forms, even in slow speech, and these forms are written as pronounced, not distinguishing between singular and plural. However, in other languages such as Kabwa (class 9 [44e], class 10 [44f]) the full form of the underlying class 10 prefix is written when this is an acceptable slow pronunciation.[7]

(44)	a.	<ni nyumba>	[**ni**ɲúː^{m}ba]	/**ni** = iɲu^{m}ba/	'is the house'	(Jita)
		<inyumba>	[iɲúː^{m}ba]		'house'	
	b.	<ni nyumba>	[**ni**ɲúː^{m}ba]	/**ni** = dʒiɲu^{m}ba/	'are the houses'	(Jita)
		<jinyumba>	[**dʒi**ɲúː^{m}ba]		'houses'	
	c.	<ni ntungwa>	[**niː**^{n}t^{h}úː^{ŋ}gwa]	/**ni** = i^{n}t^{h}u^{ŋ}gwa/	'is the tradition'	(Kwaya)
		<intungwa>	[iː^{n}t^{h}úː^{ŋ}gwa]		'tradition'	
	d.	<ni ntungwa>	[**niː**^{n}t^{h}úː^{ŋ}gwa]	/**ni** = gi^{n}t^{h}u^{ŋ}gwa/	'are the traditions'	(Kwaya)
		<gintungwa>	[**giː**^{n}t^{h}úː^{ŋ}gwa]		'traditions'	
	e.	<ni-nkoko>	[**níː**^{ŋ}k^{h}ɔk^{h}ɔ]	/**ni** = ɛ^{ŋ}k^{h}ɔk^{h}ɔ/	'is the chicken'	(Kabwa)
		<enkoko>	[ɛ́^{ŋ}k^{h}ɔk^{h}ɔ]		'chicken'	
	f.	<ni-ginkoko>	[**níː**^{ŋ}k^{h}ɔk^{h}ɔ] ~ [**nigíː**^{ŋ}k^{h}ɔk^{h}ɔ]	/**ni** = ɛgi^{ŋ}k^{h}ɔk^{h}ɔ/	'are the chickens'	(Kabwa)
		<eginkoko>	[**ɛgíː**^{ŋ}k^{h}ɔk^{h}ɔ]		'chickens'	

In Kwaya, for the second person singular pronoun, the pronunciation of the coordinating conjunction plus pronoun (45a) is homophonic with the copula plus pronoun (45b). These two constructions were originally distinguished orthographically by writing the elided clitic vowels as shown in (45) since it was thought that there was a third homophonous form, the emphatic pronoun, which was in turn written distinctly as a single word, <naawe>.

(45)	a.	<na awe>	[**náː**wɛ]	/**na** awɛ/	'and you (SG)'	(Kwaya)
	b.	<ni awe>	[**náː**wɛ]	/**ni** awɛ/	'is you (SG)'	(Kwaya)

Kwaya speakers now feel that the copula plus pronoun and emphatic pronoun are not two distinct forms (unlike in Swahili), and so do not need to be distinguished orthographically. The choice of how to write the copula plus pronoun/emphatic pronoun is therefore currently under review, with differing opinions about whether to favour conjunctive spelling or the disjunctive spelling shown in (45).

[7] Occasionally only the reduced form is acceptable (for reasons unknown), in which case the reduced form is written.

In Ikizu, the copula (which is underlyingly /ne/) can be pronounced as [ni, ne, nɛ] depending on the vowel height of the following noun, the augment of which elides. When the augment of the noun following a coordinating conjunction (underlyingly /na/) is a front vowel (i.e., [i, e, ɛ] in classes 4, 5, 7, 8, 9 and 10) the copula and conjunction become homophones, because the vowel of the coordinating conjunction elides before the augment of the following noun. In order to disambiguate these homophones, it has been decided to distinguish the copula and coordinating conjunction orthographically for all noun classes. The copula is separated from the following word by a hyphen (<CA-Noun>), whereas the conjunction is written disjunctively (with the augment vowel written as part of the noun, <CA ANoun>). The Ikizu orthography stakeholders strongly prefer writing phrase-level pronunciation in all contexts.[8] Concerning this specific context with the coordinating conjunction, the Ikizu orthography statement comments that stakeholders "... are not bothered by the numerous forms of a single word and instead believe that it actually increases comprehension and is a better representation of their language" (Robinson and Gray 2016:49). The Ikizu examples in (46) show how the copula and conjunction may be heterographic homophones for class 4 (copula [46a], conjunction [46b]), class 8 (copula [46c], conjunction [46d]) and class 9 (copula [46e], conjunction [46f]).

(46)	a.	<ni-miri>	[**ni**miɾi]	/**ne** = imiɾi/	'are the roots'	(Ikizu)
		<imiri>	[**i**miɾi]		'roots'	
	b.	<ni imiri>	[**ni**miɾi]	/**na** = imiɾi/	'and the roots'	(Ikizu)
		<imiri>	[**i**miɾi]		'roots'	
	c.	<nɨ-bhɨsʉbhɨ>	[**ne**βésóβe]	/**ne** = eβesoβe/	'are the corn kernels'	(Ikizu)
		<ɨbhɨsʉbhɨ>	[**e**βésóβe]		'corn kernels'	
	d.	<nɨ ɨbhɨsʉbhɨ>	[**ne**βésóβe]	/**na** = eβesoβe/	'and the corn kernels'	(Ikizu)
		<ɨbhɨsʉbhɨ>	[**e**βésóβe]		'corn kernels'	
	e.	<ne-ngoko>	[**nɛː**^{ŋ}gɔ́k^{h}ɔ]	/**ne** = ɛ^{ŋ}gɔk^{h}ɔ/	'is the chicken'	(Ikizu)
		<engoko>	[**ɛː**^{ŋ}gɔ́k^{h}ɔ]		'chicken'	
	f.	<ne engoko>	[**nɛː**^{ŋ}gɔ́k^{h}ɔ]	/**na** = ɛ^{ŋ}gɔk^{h}ɔ/	'and the chicken'	(Ikizu)
		<engoko>	[**ɛː**^{ŋ}gɔ́k^{h}ɔ]		'chicken'	

[8] Ikizu has extensive vowel harmony, such that even verb stems can have multiple surface forms which are represented orthographically, for example: <ʉkagega> [okagɛ́ga] /o-ka-gɛg-a/ SP2SG-NAR-carry-FV 'you carried' and <ʉgɨgirɨ> [ogégire] /o-gɛg-ire/ SP2SG-carry-ANT 'you have carried'.

In Nyiha, certain locative clitics are homophonous with other morphemes, and so may also create homophonous (or near homophonous) word pairs. For example, the class 17 locative clitic (47a) resembles the class 15 noun prefix (used for infinitives) (47b), and the class 18 locative clitic (47c) resembles the class 3 noun prefix (without its preceding augment) (47d). As these are noun class prefixes rather than clitics, and thus are written conjunctively, there is additional support for writing the clitics disjunctively (<CV Noun>), and therefore distinctively from the prefixes.

(47) a. <ku maha> [**k^{h}uː**máha] /**k^{h}u**=maha/ 'by the strength' (Nyiha)
b. <kumala> [k^{h}ǔːmala] /k^{h}u-mala/ 'to finish' (Nyiha)
c. <mu nsi> [**mûː**^{n}si] /**mu**=^{n}si/ 'in the country' (Nyiha)
d. <munsi> [mûː^{n}si] /mu-^{n}si/ 'pestle' (Nyiha)

In Malila, certain person-marking clitics on nouns are written conjunctively (<CVNoun>) and thus distinguished orthographically from homophonous clitic and noun combinations, which are written disjunctively (<CV Noun>). First person marking (48a) is distinguished from the coordinating conjunction (48b).

(48) a. <ɨne numufinjile> (Malila)
[ǐːnɛ **nú**mufiː^{ɲ}dʒile]
/ɪnɛ **nʊ**=mʊ-fi^{ɲ}dʒile/
PRO1SG 1SG=1-holy
'I the holy one'

b. <ɨne nu mufinjile> (Malila)
[ǐːnɛ **nú**mufiː^{ɲ}dʒile]
/ɪnɛ **na**=ʊ-mʊ-fiː^{ɲ}dʒile/
PRO1SG CNJ=AUG-1-holy
'I and the holy one'

Second person singular marking (49a) is distinguished from the class 1a copula (49b).

(49) a. <ɨwe wʉkalʉlʉ> (Malila)
[ĭ:wɛ **wʊk^{h}álʊlʊ**]
/ɪwɛ **wʊ**=k^{h}alʊlʊ/
PRO2SG 2SG=1A.hare
'you hare'

b. <ʉnʉ wʉ kalʉlʉ> (Malila)
[ʊ̂:nʊ **wʊk^{h}álʊlʊ**]
/ʊnʊ **wʊ**=k^{h}alʊlʊ/
EP1.PROX.DEM COP1A=1A.hare
'this one is the hare'

Second person plural marking (50a) is distinguished from the class 18 locative (50b).

(50) a. <ɨmwe mubhalandati> (Malila)
[ĭ:m^{w}ɛ **mu**βalǎ:^{n}dat^{h}i]
/ɪm^{w}ɛ **mʊ**=βa-la^{n}dat^{h}i/
PRO2PL 2PL=2-follower
'you (PL) followers'

b. <ʉmo mu bhalandati> (Malila)
[ʊ́mɔ **mu**βalǎ:^{n}dat^{h}i]
/ʊ-mɔ **mʊ**=βa-la^{n}dat^{h}i/
EP1-one LOC18=2-follower
'one among the followers'

In Kinga and Vwanji, the negative morpheme[9] and the coordinating conjunction are homophones when combined with [a]-initial nouns and therefore they are distinguished orthographically. It was first decided that the conjunction should be written disjunctively (<CA Noun>, [51b] and [51d]). Because of this, the negative morpheme could not also be written disjunctively without causing ambiguity, leaving the options of either hyphenation (<CA-Noun>) or conjunctive spelling (<CANoun>). Conjunctive spelling was chosen (51a, 51c) and this has the added benefit

9 The negative morpheme is analysed as a clitic when it attaches to nouns as it has scope over the following NP.

of consistency with the decision for verbs, where the negative morpheme <na> is a prefix and written joined to the verb. The negative and coordinating conjunction are also distinguished orthographically before nouns which are non-[a]-initial, but they are homophones only before a noun whose augment is [a], as shown by the Vwanji class 9 examples (51e, 51f).

(51) a. <namasaago> [**na**masâːkɔ] /**na**=masaːkɔ/ 'not the thoughts' (Kinga)
b. <na masaago> [**na**masâːkɔ] /**na**=amasaːkɔ/ 'and the thoughts' (Kinga)
c. <namalenga> [**nama**lɛː^{ŋ}ga] /**na**=malɛ^{ŋ}ga/ 'not the water' (Vwanji)
d. <na malenga> [**nama**lɛː^{ŋ}ga] /**na**=amalɛ^{ŋ}ga/ 'and the water' (Vwanji)
e. <nambombo> [**na**^{m}bɔː^{m}bɔ] /**na**=^{m}bɔ^{m}bɔ/ 'not the work' (Vwanji)
f. <nɨ mbombo> [**nɪ**^{m}bɔː^{m}bɔ] /**na**=ɪ^{m}bɔ^{m}bɔ/ 'and the work' (Vwanji)

In Ikoma, the connective is always written disjunctively (<(C)V Noun>). This is particularly important in classes 1 and 3, since the connective for these classes can be the same as the augment vowel of the second noun, but because the augment vowel is written conjunctively with the noun, it is distinguished orthographically from the connective.

(52) a. <omoona omughabho> (Ikoma)
[omóːnomuɣaβo]
/o-moːna o-mu-ɣaβo/
AUG-1.child AUG-1-doctor
'child doctor'
(i.e., a child who is a doctor, not a paediatrician)

b. <omoona o mughabho> (Ikoma)
[omóːn**á** ꜜʔómuɣaβo]
/o-moːna **o**=mu-ɣaβo/
AUG-1.child PP**1**.CON=1-doctor
'child of the doctor'

These phrases are slightly different phonetically; the final vowel of <omoona> usually elides in (52a), whereas in (52b) a break is inserted before the connective. This final vowel is written in (52a) even though it is not usually pronounced in normal speech, as it is present when the phrase is pronounced slowly. Including it in the written form thus follows both the principle of writing words according to slow or careful pronunciation and also the principle of maintaining a constant word image.

3.4.3 Semantic exceptions

In the previous section, different spelling rules distinguished different grammatical constructions, but it may also be desirable to have different spelling rules for the same grammatical construction when semantic factors are taken into consideration. For many of the languages in our sample, the application of a regular rule to write a clitic and noun disjunctively is suspended when doing so would violate Kutsch Lojenga's (2014) principle of "conceptual unity". This states that "if two independent words acquire a new meaning when put together, they are conceptually a unit and there should be a closer link on the page than if they were two independent units" (2014:99). This can be illustrated with the examples in (53) and (54) from Vwanji. Normally in this language, a connective and a locative are written disjunctively (<CV Noun>), but when the resulting construction is considered a complete conceptual unit by speakers, as in (53a) and (53b), it is written conjunctively.

(53) a. <kyakʉlia> (Vwanji)
[**k^{hj}a**k^{h}ʊlia]
/**k^{h}i-a**=k^{h}u-li-a/
PP**7**-CON=15-eat-FV
'food (lit., of + eating)'

b. <kʉnsana> (Vwanji)
[**k^{h}ʊ**n̩sana]
/**k^{h}ʊ**=mʊ-sana/
LOC**18**=3-back
'behind (lit., at + back)'

Speaker intuition in such cases is perhaps a consequence of the agreement properties of the resulting construction, as shown in (54a, b). The possessive modifier in (54a) agrees with the class 7 morpheme attached to the connective and not with the class 15 prefix of <kʉlia> 'eating', thus showing that <kyakʉlia> has lexicalised and is being treated as a class 7 noun rather than as a connective plus a class 15 noun. Similarly, in (54b), the connective <kwa> agrees with the class 17 locative in <kʉnsana> 'behind'. In contrast, if the connective instead agrees with the class 3 noun <ʉnsana> 'back', as in (54c), a literal meaning of the locative plus noun is understood and the normal spelling rule of separating the locative clitic from the host noun is followed.

(54) a. <kyakʉlia kyango> (Vwanji)

[**kʰʲa**kʰʊlia **kʰʲ**aːᵑgɔ]

/**kʰi-a** = kʰu-li-a **kʰi**-aᵑgɔ/

PP**7-**CON = 15-eat-FV PP**7**-POSS1SG

'my food'

b. <kʉnsana kwa Yoona> (Vwanji)

[**kʰ**ʊn̩sana **kʰʷa**jɔːna]

/**kʰʊ** = mʊ-sana **kʰʊ-a** = jɔːna/

LOC**18** = 3-back PP**18-**CON = Jonah

'behind Jonah'

c. <kʉ nsana ghwa Yoona> (Vwanji)

[kʰʊ**n̩**sana **ɣʷa**jɔːna]

/kʰʊ = **mʊ**-sana **ɣʊ-a** = jɔːna/

LOC18 = **3**-back PP**3-**CON = Jonah

'on Jonah's back'

Another example of an orthographic exception for semantic reasons is the Simbiti locative. Usually, locative clitics are written with a hyphen before the noun (<CV-Noun>, [55a, b]). However, in contexts where the meaning is not strictly locative but rather abstract, Simbiti speakers felt that this should be written in a different manner than the normal locatives; therefore, in such contexts the locative clitic is written disjunctively, (55c–e).

(55)	a.	<ko-bhantö>	[**kʰ**ɔβáːⁿto]	/**kʰɔ** = aβaⁿto/	'in the area of people'	(Simbiti)
	b.	<mö-mëtë>	[**mo**métʰe]	/**mɔ** = emetʰe/	'in the trees'	(Simbiti)
	c.	<ku iriina>	[**kʰu**ɾíːna]	/**kʰɔ** = iɾiːna/	'by the name'	(Simbiti)
	d.	<kö bhëënyu>	[**kʰó**βeːɲu]	/**kʰɔ** = βeːɲu/	'as for you'	(Simbiti)
	e.	<ko bhoora>	[**kʰ**ɔβɔ́ːɾa]	/**kʰɔ** = βɔːɾa/	'for the reason'	(Simbiti)

3.4.4 Word order complications

Some exceptional cases occur when an additional word intervenes between the host and clitic, disrupting the usual word order and sometimes creating problems for the usual orthographic conventions. An example of this is in Kabwa, where question enclitics (e.g., /=k^{h}i/ 'what?', /=ha/ 'where?') are usually separated from the word they relate to by a hyphen.[10] The question clitics occur with nouns (56a, b) as well as other classes of word, such as verbs (56c, d).

(56)	a.	<ering'ana-ki?>	[ɛ́ɾíŋánák^{h}**i**]	/ɛɾiŋana=**k^{h}i**/	'what issue?'	(Kabwa)
	b.	<ensonga-ki?>	[ɛnsɔ́ː^{ŋ}gák^{h}**i**]	/ɛnsɔ^{ŋ}ga=**k^{h}i**/	'what meaning?'	(Kabwa)
	c.	<okoreri-ki?>	[ɔk^{h}ɔɾɛ́ɾí**k^{h}í**]	/ɔk^{h}ɔɾɛɾi=**k^{h}i**/	'what have you done?'	(Kabwa)
	d.	<bharingi-ha?>	[βaɾíː^{ŋ}gí**ha**]	/βaɾi^{ŋ}gi=**ha**/	'where are they?'	(Kabwa)

However, in rare instances an additional word can occur between the host and the clitic, as in (57).[11] These contexts were discovered later on in the orthography development process, when the usual practice of hyphenating the question clitic was well established. L1 speakers were confused about how to write the clitic, wanting to hyphenate it as usual, but finding that strange since doing so would attach the clitic to the intervening word rather than the verb, when it is the verb to which the clitic is most closely related. Some experimented with writing the clitic disjunctively in these exceptional cases but they did not like the result. They therefore decided that, even though the clitic is not strictly related to the immediately preceding word, it should be hyphenated onto the previous word.

(57) <Murahakaanan'ya nabho-ki?> (Kabwa)

[muɾahak^{h}aːnánjá náβɔ́**k^{h}i**]

/mu-ɾa-hak^{h}aːn-an-i-a	na=βɔ=**k^{h}i**/
SP2PL-PRS-oppose-RECP-CAUS-FV	CNJ=2.PRO=**what**

'What are you arguing about with them?'

---

[10] Sometimes the question clitic is not hyphenated. This is because the word is very short and perceived as a single unit. L1 speakers found it very unnatural to split these words with a hyphen, for example: <niki> 'is what?', <egaki> 'how?', <kwaki> 'why?'.

[11] Although this example of a verbal clitic goes beyond the scope of this chapter, the word boundary issue under discussion is relevant to noun contexts as well.

3.5 Aesthetic factors affecting orthography decisions

This section considers four areas where aesthetic factors have played a role in the orthography development of the sample languages: influence from Swahili (§ 3.5.1), capitalisation (§ 3.5.2), short words (§ 3.5.3), and words with multiple clitics (§ 3.5.4). These factors all relate to how an L1 speaker perceives the visual result when a spelling rule is applied, particularly in comparison with a perceived norm as found in other languages or elsewhere in the language in question.

3.5.1 Influence from Swahili

As mentioned in the introduction to this chapter, the most important LWC in Tanzania is Swahili, and most Tanzanians have learned this language in school. English, while also taught in school, is much less widely understood and used. Research in the 1980s states that approximately fifteen percent of the population in Tanzania have some knowledge of English, with as little as one percent of the students in secondary school having a level adequate for English-medium education (Petzell 2012:141–142). The author also states, "English and Swahili have separate roles in society [...] Swahili denotes traditional ideals, while English is related to technological modernism and external ideals." Swahili therefore has a much greater influence on the development of orthographies in local languages, both by being more familiar and by being closer linguistically and culturally to them.

This influence of Swahili can be illustrated well through the case of copula-noun combinations in Jita. Originally, a rule was made to write the copula followed by a hyphen and then the noun, as in the phrase *<unu ni-mutegi> 'this is a fisherman'. This is in contrast to Swahili, where a similar construction is written disjunctively, as in <huyu ni mvuvi> 'this is a fisherman'. Over time Jita writers forgot to follow the proposed spelling rule and no longer used the hyphen, writing the copula and noun disjunctively as <unu ni mutegi>. The Jita spelling rule has since been changed to match the Swahili, in line with speaker preferences.

3.5.2 Capitalisation

Another area that influences orthography development is capitalisation. Since Swahili only has capitalisation at the beginning of a word, sociolinguistic reasons lead to a preference for word-initial capitalisation in the local languages, and some L1 speakers can be resistant to word-medial capitalisation in their language. However, in many of these languages, capitalising the word-initial letter presents a challenge for preserving a constant word image. In Bungu, for instance, the vocative form of nouns appears without an augment vowel (58a), thus word-initial capitalisation would require a different letter to be capitalised than when the same noun appears as the subject of a sentence. The decision was instead made to capitalise the first letter after the augment (which is either the noun prefix consonant or, when there is no prefix, the first letter of the root) and thus preserve a constant word image (58b).

(58) a. <Daudi, iza!> (Bungu)

[da^{w}údi íza]

/da^{w}udi	iz-a/
1A.David	come-FV

'David, come!'

b. <Pɨne ʉDaudi wíza.> (Bungu)

(not *<Pɨne Ʉdaudi wíza>)

[penɛ oda^{w}údi wizâ]

/penɛ	o-da^{w}udi	a-a-iz-a/
then	AUG-1a.David	SP1-ANT-come-FV

'Then David came.'

Informal orthography consultations for many of the languages in southern Tanzania (i.e., from the Mbeya, Songwe and Njombe regions) show that naive L1 speakers have overcome their resistance to writing word-medial capitals in order to preserve a more constant word image.

In contrast to this situation, some language communities have strongly opposed writing word-medial capitals because it was considered undesirable in comparison with what was familiar from Swahili and English. In Kabwa, for example, the lack of augments on proper nouns means that the situation shown for Bungu in (58) does not apply and therefore maintaining a word-initial capitalisation approach created fewer problems for the constant word image principle. Word-medial capitals were rejected for Kabwa even though allowing them would avoid conflicts with other spelling rules in this language. For instance, Kabwa locatives are normally written conjunctively (<CVNoun>, [59a]). However, when a locative clitic occurs with a proper noun, L1 speakers consider the capitalisation rule to be incompatible with conjunctive spelling of the locative and so an exception to one of the two spelling rules is needed. Kabwa writers chose to break the rule of writing the locative conjunctively in order to avoid either a word-medial capital or capitalised clitic (59b).

(59) a. <kumurimi> (Kabwa)

[**kú**múɾimi]

/**ku** = mu-ɾimi/

LOC**17** = 1-farmer

'at the farmer's place'

b. <ku Masige> (Kabwa)

not *<kuMasige> or *<Kumasige>

[**k^{h}u**másigɛ]

/**k^{h}u** = masigɛ/

LOC**17** = 1A.Masige

'at Masige's place'

3.5.3 Short words

For Ndali speakers, the desire to avoid writing a monosyllabic content word was a factor in the decision to create an exception to the rule of writing the surface form of a noun after a clitic. The regular spelling rule in Ndali states that after a connective, locative clitic or the coordinating conjunction, a noun (which occurs without an augment) is written according to its pronunciation (60a) (<CV Noun, CA Noun>). However, when a monosyllabic noun appears after one of these clitics, Ndali orthography stakeholders preferred to include the augment vowel in the orthographic form even though it is not pronounced (60b), feeling that such a short word does not seem complete without its augment in the written form.

(60) a. <icha likokwe> [**itʃa**lik^{h}ók^{hw}e] /**itʃa** = lik^{h}ok^{hw}e/ 'of the tree' (Ndali)

b. <icha iswi> [**itʃǎː**s^{w}i] /**itʃa** = s^{w}i/ 'of the fish' (Ndali)

(not *<icha swi>)

3.5.4 Words with multiple clitics

One final area that deserves treatment here is the case where two clitics are combined on a single noun. This is especially interesting when both of the clitics would normally be hyphenated, since this would be unusual compared to hyphen practices in Swahili and English. Hyphen use is uncommon in Swahili and having more than one hyphen in a word is possible but unusual in English.

In Simbiti, a phrase that combines a copula with a locative followed by a noun is possible. When each of these clitics combines individually with a noun, they are followed by a hyphen and so one would expect to see a form like *<n-ko-kebhara> 'is on earth'. However, readers had difficulty with two hyphens so close together and so the rule is to write it as <nko-kebhara> (61).

(61) <nko-kebhara> (Simbiti)
(not *<n-ko-kebhara>)
[^{ŋ}k^{h}ɔk^{h}ɛ́βaɾa]
/**N** = **k^{h}ɔ** = k^{h}ɛ-βaɾa/
COP = LOC**17** = 7-earth
'is on earth'

Conversely, in Kabwa where two enclitics are included on a verbal word (62), writers have become accustomed to more than one hyphen in a single word.

(62) <Mmutuura-mo-ki?> (Kabwa)
[m:ut^{h}u:ɾa**mɔk^{h}i**]
/m-mu-t^{h}u:r-a = **mɔ** = **k^{h}i**/
FOC-2PL-put-IND = LOC**18** = **what**
'What do you put in it?'

At first, using two hyphens in these situations seemed wrong to Kabwa writers and so they wrote the question clitic <ki> disjunctively (e.g., <Mmutuura-mo ki?>). However, after time they decided that leaving <ki> hanging by itself at the end of the question also seemed incorrect. As they became accustomed to writing more than one hyphen on a single word, they realised they preferred this to writing a clitic like <ki> in isolation.

3.6 Conclusion

As the examples discussed all involve morphemes analysed as clitics, a clash of word boundary principles is inherent in every case. Broadly, the phonological behaviour of the clitics argues for attaching them to nouns and their grammatical status argues for writing them as independent words. This is a far too simplistic description of the conflict though, as the data have shown.

The principle of maintaining a constant word image argues for separating clitics from their hosts in writing, but the phonological changes at the boundary between clitic and host may mean that doing so is not simple and may be counterintuitive to L1 speakers. Using a punctuation mark, such as a hyphen, at the boundary can be an effective compromise, but then decisions may still remain concerning which vowels are written, with what orthographic depth, and whether they are written as part of the clitic or as part of the host. Sometimes writing something akin to the underlying structure of a clitic and noun combination is acceptable to L1 orthography stakeholders, but sometimes a surface form is preferred, or a compromise which is neither one nor the other. The sample languages which have vowel-final proclitics and vowel-initial nouns due to the presence of an augment exhibit particular complexity in this respect. The presence of the augment on a noun tends to increase the weight of phonological factors in favour of conjunctive spelling. Conversely, the possibility of certain clitics occurring before proper nouns or nouns which are capitalised for other reasons can sway the intuitions of L1 speakers towards disjunctive spelling.

In some cases, the phonological behaviour of the clitics is complex and varies according to the class of the following noun. When such exceptional examples come to light, an originally preferred orthography decision may need to be rejected completely or additional spelling rules added to account for them. In the sample languages the latter alternative has been followed. This allows the majority of cases to follow a preferred decision, but has the drawback of complicating the spelling rule for L1 speakers learning to write their language. It can also result in mixed messages for readers as well as for the writer. That is, the association of a particular clitic and host combination with an orthographic representation is weakened if other orthographic representations are also possible in certain contexts. Similarly, even when different decisions for different clitics are made for good reasons, the result may be that across the language as a whole an orthographic pattern such as < ...CV VC... > is sometimes pronounced with a short vowel, sometimes with a long vowel and sometimes with two separate vowels.

The complexity and interrelatedness of the behaviour of nouns with different clitics can mean that it is not possible to make a good word boundary decision about a single phenomenon in isolation. A thorough understanding of the grammar is needed so that orthography developers can see the implications of a decision to write one particular grammatical phenomenon in a certain way. This is often either because the decision in question needs to match another one for the sake of consistency and learnability or, conversely, because it is beneficial if the decision in question differs from another in order to disambiguate two phenomena and help readers. For example, the existence of affixes which are formally similar to the clitics may argue for disjunctive spelling of the clitics for the sake of disambiguation. Making an orthographic word boundary decision for a particular phenomenon without considering the wider system runs the risk of creating unforeseen and unwelcome consequences for other spelling rules.

Table 3.2 shows at a glance how languages can differ from one another in the decisions which are eventually made regarding clitics. In each case, the regular spelling rule is shown first, with examples of exceptions to this rule shown in brackets underneath. As seen in Bena and Safwa, a language can have one spelling rule for all clitics, in this case disjunctive spelling, with exceptions for some or all of the clitics.

Table 3.2. Examples of word boundary decisions from three of the sample languages

Boundary	Bena	Safwa	Kabwa
Connective	<CV Noun> <ga mukoga> 'of the river' (<CVNoun> <ikyakuliya> 'food; lit., of eating')	<CV2 Noun> <ɨshɨ m'bɨlɨ> 'of the body' (<CA-ANoun> <ɨshi-ibooma> 'of the town')	<CV ANoun> <kya abharimi> 'of farmers'
Coordinating conjunction	<CA Noun> <nu mukoga> 'and the river'	<CA Noun> <nʉ m'bɨlɨ> 'and the body' (<CA-ANoun> <ni-ibooma> 'and the town')	<CV ANoun> <na abharimi> 'and farmers'
Locative	<CV Noun> <pa mukoga> 'at the river' (<CVNoun> <paanyi> 'below')	<CV Noun> <mu m'bɨlɨ> 'in the body' (<CA-ANoun> <mwi-ibooma> 'in the town')	<CVNoun> <kubharimi> 'at the farmers' place' (<CV Noun> <ku Sara> 'at Sarah's place')
Copula	-	-	<C-Noun> <m-barimi> 'are farmers'

The exceptions in Bena are all semantically driven, and are thus limited in number, whereas the Safwa exceptions are grammatical, and much more extensive. Conversely, a language can have a different spelling rule for nearly every clitic, as seen in Kabwa, which exhibits disjunctive spelling, conjunctive spelling and hyphenation. The decisions made in each language had to take into account all the factors mentioned in this chapter, with orthography stakeholders settling on very different solutions once they were weighed.

The examples presented in this chapter illustrate a great variety of spelling rules for dealing with the boundary of a clitic and its host. Some of these are based on morphophonological or grammatical differences and are therefore well motivated linguistically. Others do not result from different linguistic phenomena, but from language community representatives choosing a compromise solution when no clear decision was forthcoming. Often such a compromise satisfies neither the linguist's desire to fully reflect morphophonological behaviour in the orthography nor the literacy specialist's aspiration for a constant word image. However, it is ultimately up to the L1 speakers to determine which solution is preferred. Then, as they gain experience in reading and writing the preferred solution, it will become clear whether it is deemed suitable and becomes established in the orthography, or whether an alternative solution needs to be found in the second generation of language development.

Orthography development in most of the sample languages has been ongoing only since 2003 or later. Even in such a relatively short time, word boundary orthography decisions relating to nouns and clitics have been changed. As L1 speakers have become more experienced as readers and writers, and more aware of grammatical processes in their languages, the acceptability of disjunctive spelling has sometimes increased. A willingness to break up in writing what is joined in speech can come with time, once the benefits for readers of doing so can be seen. Experience in reading and writing can also help L1 orthography users to feel freer to accept solutions, such as using a hyphen, which differ from English and Swahili, the languages with established orthographies most widely known in Tanzania. As feelings about orthography decisions may therefore change over time, it is important not only to test initial orthography decisions, but to retest the same decisions after some years to see if changes should be made.

References

Dixon, R. M. W. 2010. *Basic linguistic theory. Vol. 2: Grammatical topics.* Oxford: Oxford University Press.

Eaton, Helen, and Leila Schroeder. 2012. Word break conflicts in Bantu languages: Skirmishes on many fronts. *Writing Systems Research* 4(2):229–241.

Eberhard, David M., Gary F. Simons, and Charles D. Fennig, eds. 2024. *Ethnologue: Languages of the world.* Twenty-seventh edition. Dallas, TX: SIL International. www.ethnologue.com.

Gibson, Hannah, Rozenn Guérois, and Lutz Marten. 2019. Variation in Bantu copula constructions. In María J. Arche, Antonio Fábregas, and Rafael Marín (eds.), *The grammar of copulas across languages*, 213–242. Oxford: Oxford University Press.

Haspelmath, Martin. 2011. The indeterminacy of word segmentation and the nature of morphology and syntax. *Folia Linguistica* 45(1):31–80.

Jordan, Timothy R., Sharon M. Thomas, Geoffrey R. Patching, and Kenneth C. Scott-Brown. 2003. Assessing the importance of letter pairs in initial, exterior and interior positions in reading. *Journal of Experimental Psychology: Learning, Memory and Cognition* 29(5):883–893.

Kutsch Lojenga, Constance. 2014. Basic principles for establishing word boundaries. In Michael Cahill and Keren Rice (eds.), *Developing orthographies for unwritten languages*, 73–106. Publications in Language Use and Education 6. Dallas, TX: SIL International.

Meeussen, A. E. 1967. Bantu grammatical reconstructions. *Africana Linguistica* 3:79–121.

Nurse, Derek, and Gérard Philippson. 2003. Introduction. In Derek Nurse and Gérard Philippson (eds.), *The Bantu languages*, 1–12. First edition. London: Routledge.

Petzell, Malin. 2012 The linguistic situation in Tanzania. *Moderna Språk* 1:136–144.

Robinson, Holly, and Hazel Gray. 2016. Ikizu-Sizaki orthography statement. Ms. Tanzania: SIL International. www.sil.org/resources/archives/67805.

Schadeberg, Thilo C., and Koen Bostoen. 2019. Word formation. In Mark Van de Velde, Koen Bostoen, Derek Nurse, and Gérard Philippson (eds.), *The Bantu languages*, 172–203. Second edition. London: Routledge.

Schroeder, Leila. 2010. *Bantu orthography manual*. SIL e-Books 09. Dallas, TX: SIL International.

Van de Velde, Mark. 2013. The Bantu connective construction. In Anne Carlier and Jean-Christophe Verstraete (eds.), *The genitive*, 217–252. Amsterdam: John Benjamins.

Van de Velde, Mark. 2019. Nominal morphology and syntax. In Mark Van de Velde, Koen Bostoen, Derek Nurse, and Gérard Philippson (eds.), *The Bantu languages*, 237–269. Second edition. London: Routledge.

Van Dyken, Julia R., and Constance Kutsch Lojenga. 1993. Word boundaries: Key factors in orthography development. In Rhonda L. Hartell (ed.), *Alphabets of Africa*, 3–22. Dakar: UNESCO and SIL.

Venezky, Richard L. 1977. Principles for the design of practical writing systems. In Joshua A. Fishman (ed.), *Advances in the creation and revision of writing systems*, 37–54. The Hague: Mouton.

Data Sources

Aunio, Lotta, Holly Robinson, Tim Roth, Oliver Stegen, and John B. Walker. 2019. The Mara languages JE40. In Mark Van de Velde, Koen Bostoen, Derek Nurse, and Gérard Philippson (eds.), *The Bantu languages*, 501–532. Second edition. London: Routledge.

Eaton, Helen. 2019a. Kinga orthography statement. Ms.

Eaton, Helen. 2019b. Malila orthography statement. Ms.

Eaton, Helen. 2019c. Vwanji G66. In Mark Van de Velde, Koen Bostoen, Derek Nurse, and Gérard Philippson (eds.), *The Bantu languages*, 615–644. Second edition. London: Routledge.

Eaton, Helen. 2019d. Vwanji orthography statement. Ms.

Eaton, Helen. 2020a. Ndali orthography statement. Ms.

Eaton, Helen. 2020b. Sangu orthography statement. Ms.

Eaton, Helen. 2021. Nyiha orthography statement. Ms.

Gray, Hazel. 2018. Kisi phonology and morphophonology. *SIL Language and Culture Documentation and Description* 38. Dallas, TX: SIL International. www.sil.org/resources/publications/entry/76667.

Gray, Hazel. 2020. Bungu phonology and morphophonology. *SIL Electronic Working Papers* 131. Dallas, TX: SIL International. www.sil.org/resources/archives/86711.

Odom, Shannon Ronit. 2015. Zinza orthography statement. Ms. www.sil.org/resources/archives/67537.

Odom, Shannon Ronit. 2016a. Jita orthography statement. Ms. www.sil.org/resources/archives/67807.

Odom, Shannon Ronit. 2016b. Kwaya orthography statement. Ms. www.sil.org/resources/archives/67806.

Odom, Shannon Ronit. 2016c. The grammar basics of Kwaya. Ms. www.sil.org/resources/archives/67534.

Odom, Shannon Ronit. 2016d. The grammar basics of Zinza. Ms. www.sil.org/resources/archives/68080.

Odom, Shannon Ronit, and Holly Robinson. 2016. The grammar basics of Jita. Ms. www.sil.org/resources/archives/67533.

Overton, Rebekah, and John B. Walker. 2016. Kabwa orthography statement. Ms. www.sil.org/resources/archives/73084.

Overton, Rebekah, and John B. Walker. 2017. The grammar basics of Kabwa. Ms. www.sil.org/resources/archives/73083.

Overton, Rebekah, and John B. Walker. 2018. Suba-Simbiti orthography statement: Approved orthography edition. Ms. www.sil.org/resources/archives/76907.

Robinson, Holly. 2015. The grammar basics of Ikoma. Ms. www.sil.org/resources/archives/64348.

Robinson, Holly. 2018. Ikoma orthography statement. Ms. www.sil.org/resources/archives/76919.

Robinson, Holly, and Hazel Gray. 2019. Zanaki orthography statement. Ms. www.sil.org/resources/archives/86851.

Robinson, Holly, and Michelle Sandeen. 2015. The grammar basics of Ikizu. Ms. www.sil.org/resources/archives/64878.

Walker, John B., and Rebekah M. Overton. 2018. The grammar basics of Simbiti. Ms. www.sil.org/resources/archives/80843.

4
The Orthographic Treatment of Clitics in Musey

James Roberts and Soulokadi Albert Camus

Abstract

Musey, a Chadic language of Chad, has several clitics which pose a challenge to developers of its orthography. In this chapter we start with a detailed consideration of the two that occur most frequently, examining them from both morphophonological and syntactic standpoints. Then we compare what we have learned of their linguistic status to the way that they have been rendered in two traditions of writing over the past sixty years. There is uniform tacit agreement that these two clitics should be attached orthographically to the preceding word, and spelled according to their pronunciation. However, when we examine two other particles which are also clearly clitics in the language, we find that there is more variation in their orthographic treatment, and they are often written as separate words. We conclude by reflecting on the reasons for the diversity in the way these clitics have been written and with a subjective evaluation.

4.1 Introduction

Clitics are a curious hybrid, and a conundrum to linguistic theory, so it is no surprise that their treatment in a practical orthography should pose a number of uncertainties. Haspelmath (2023:1) echoes this ambivalence when he defines a clitic by what it is *not*: “a bound morph that is neither an affix nor a root.” It has been said that clitics form part of the phonological word, yet they are not part of the syntactic word (Zwicky 1977, Klavans 1995). So should the orthographic word correspond to the syntactic word? In that case clitics would be separated off by a space from the surrounding words. Or should the orthographic word correspond to the phonological word? According to that scenario, a clitic would be joined with no separation to its “host,” the word with which it is pronounced. The present study examines several clitics in the Musey language and compares their linguistic status with the way they have been treated in the extant literature in the language, specifically the Musey Bible (*Boy Lonana*) and a few other booklets.

Musey [mse] is the language of more than 400,000 speakers in the Mayo Kebbi region of Chad and in neighboring Cameroon, according to estimates from the *Ethnologue* (Eberhard et al. 2024) and extrapolations from figures given by the Bureau Central du Recensement (1993). It is a Chadic language, classified as a member of the Masa branch of the family, specifically of the north Masa group (Barreteau and Newman 1978, Shryock 1997). There have been several linguistic studies of the language, but to date there is no comprehensive description with any significant detail. The research already undertaken concerns the phonetics and phonology of Musey, including tone (Platiel 1967, Duncanson 1972, Shryock 1995, 1996); the verb phrase (Dassidi 2015); a dictionary (Shryock 2010); and a few other articles (e.g., Roberts and Soulokadi 2019 and some unpublished papers by Aaron Shryock).

The most recurring clitics in Musey are the particles /na/ and /ra/, which mark the masculine or feminine gender, respectively, of the noun with which they are associated. The following section of the present chapter is devoted to a detailed examination of these two clitics from a morphophonological and syntactic standpoint. Section 4.3 looks at the ways in which these particles have been rendered orthographically in the Musey Bible, and also in other written documents in the language. From an understanding of the status of the gender markers and their orthographic treatment, we turn in § 4.4 to two other clitics in the language, those whose behavior resembles that of the gender markers. The chapter closes with a synthesis of the orthographic practices observed in Musey and some evaluative comments thereon.

4.2 The grammatical status of the gender markers /na/ and /ra/

Together with almost all Chadic languages in Chad, Musey recognizes a distinction of grammatical gender in the nominal system. Each noun in the singular is categorized as either masculine or feminine, signaled by the morphemes /na/ (masculine) or /ra/ (feminine). In the languages of the world, grammatical gender is an inflectional property of nouns, as established by Bickel and Nichols (2007) and Corbett (1991, 2007).

To the casual observer, the gender markers of Musey appear to be suffixed onto their nouns. For one thing, they are always included in the citation form of the noun in (1) and (2), and that is the way they appear in the dictionary (Shryock et al. 1998, Shryock 2010).[1]

(1) Masculine

a	sānà	'man'
b.	kéénā	'belt'
c.	bàràwnà	'cotton'

(2) Feminine

a.	zìrà	'house'
b.	ŋgāzāārā	'hernia'
c.	dàýrā	'water lily'

Indeed, in several Eastern Chadic languages of the Guéra region in Chad, all singular nouns carry suffixes which encode either masculine or feminine gender. In Mukulu [moz] (Jungraithmayr 1990), for example, masculine nouns end in one of the following: /-e/, /–u/, /-(u)su/, as in (3). Feminine nouns, on the other hand, end in a distinct set, such as those shown in (4): /-a/, /-sa/, /-awa/, /-o/. All of these singular suffixes, whether masculine or feminine, are replaced in the plural form by a separate suffix.

(3) Masculine nouns in Mukulu

a.	/dàŋg-é/	'crowned crane'	PL /dàŋg-àgí/
b.	/kóríndè-è/	'goatskin'	PL /kórínd-àgí/
c.	/bùrk-ú/	'peanut field'	PL /bùrk-ìyàgí/
d.	/mòŋg-ùsú/	'old man'	PL /mòŋg-àgí/

(4) Feminine nouns in Mukulu

a.	/kúw-à/	'plain'	PL /kúw-ìyàgí/
b.	/áwìl-sá/	'red monkey (sp.)'	PL /áwìl-ɗí/
c.	/dàŋg-àwá/	'crowned crane'	PL /dàŋg-ìyàgí/
d.	/búmm-ò/	'large cricket'	PL /búmm-àgí/

[1] Throughout this chapter, /y/ represents the palatal glide, /j/ represents the palatal stop/affricate, and the doubling of a symbol indicates length.

4.2.1 Assimilation and fusion

Like Mukulu, Musey nouns display a variety of endings which are gender-specific. However, the diversity in Musey can be shown to be the result of a complex set of assimilations which fuse the noun root to the gender marker. In their abstract underlying shape, there are only two markers: /na/ (for the masculine) and /ra/ (for the feminine), the two morphemes which appear as such on the surface in (1) and (2). The surface manifestation of these two markers is always masked when the noun root ends in a consonant, a situation which characterizes the vast majority of Musey nouns. The contact of the final consonant of the root with the initial /n/ or /r/ of the gender marker triggers one or another of these phonological interactions, as described in Shryock (1996).

If the noun root ends in a nasal, the initial /n/ of the masculine morpheme assimilates completely to it, creating a geminate, as in (5):

(5)	a.	[kūlùmmà]	<	/kūlùm-na/	'horse'
	b.	[ɓālàŋŋà]	<	/ɓālàŋ-na/	'iron'
	c.	[gìvìnnà]	<	/gìvìn-na/	'hearth'

In the same context of a nasal consonant, the /r/ of the feminine marker undergoes a surprising transformation, becoming a voiced plosive of the same place of articulation as the nasal, seen in (6):

(6)	a.	[cēlémbā]	<	/cēlém-ra/	'bird (sp.)'
	b.	[kōlóŋgā]	<	/kōlóŋ-ra/	'pipe'
	c.	[cīndà]	<	/cīn-ra/	'tamarind tree'

The resulting complex of nasal plus voiced plosive is indistinguishable from the series of prenasalized plosives which exist as units with phonemic status in the language (Platiel 1967, Shryock 1995), in contrast with the voiceless and voiced series of plosives.

For noun roots which end in a plosive (always voiceless), the initial /n/ of the masculine marker assimilates to the point of articulation of the plosive, shown in (7):

(7)	a.	[gàlápmā]	<	/gàláp-na/	'tree (sp.)'
	b.	[bākŋā]	<	/bāk-na/	'vulture'
	c.	[ɲjētná]	<	/ɲjēt-na/	'axe'

Noun roots ending in continuants – that is, fricatives and /l/ – trigger a fusion of the /n/ and /a/ of the masculine marker, creating the nasalized [ã]. It should be noted that nasalized vowels do not exist as core phonemes of the language. Examples of this phenomenon are found in (8).

(8) a. [kūlùfã̀] < /kūlùf-na/ ‘fish’
b. [ŋgě̄ɬã̄] < /ŋgě̄ɬ-na/ ‘sand’
c. [mūlã̀ < /mūl-na/ ‘chief’

Feminine nouns which end in an obstruent or /l/ all trigger a complete assimilation of the /r/ of the marker to the preceding consonant. As we saw in (5), a geminate is created across the morpheme boundary.

(9) a. [sāppā] < /sap-ra/ ‘spear’
b. [bàkkà] < /bàk-ra/ ‘skin’
c. [kūffá] < /kūf-ra/ ‘yeast’
d. [mbássā] < /mbás-ra/ ‘country’
e. [hūllā] < /hūl-ra/ ‘turtle’

As a result of all these interactions, the only place where the /na/ and /ra/ morphemes appear in that form is after a vowel or glide, as seen in (1) and (2). Also, the /na/ morpheme after root-final /r/ is unaffected, as in (10).

(10) [kērnā] < /kēr-na/ ‘drought’

It will be noted that in all of these phonological interactions, the final consonant of the root remains intact, and only the gender marker is affected. The assimilations in Musey are all progressive, a fact which has been recognized as a problem for theorists who hypothesize that such effects should always be regressive (see Lamont 2016:7–8, reacting to the data from Shryock 1996).

4.2.2 Tone patterns

A second phonological phenomenon that serves to bind the gender marker to the noun root is tone. Noun roots in Musey are characterized by a limited number of contrastive tone patterns (Soulokadi 2016, cf. Snider 2018); the principal ones are shown in (11) to (15). Note that consonant-tone interaction in Musey (Duncanson 1972, Shryock 1995) increases the complexity of the surface patterns observed in the language. However, the data chosen here have been restricted to allow the underlying patterns to show clearly.

(11) Pattern Low
a. /vìinà/ ‘monkey’
b. /bùzùnà/ ‘blood’
c. /gàwlàŋgà/ ‘prostitute’

(12) Pattern Mid
a. /ndāārā/ 'louse'
b. /sīmīnā/ 'tear (in the eye)'
c. /sēlgēwnā/ 'distilled liquor'

(13) Pattern Mid-High
a. /ŋgōōná/ 'back side'
b. /kūnūrá/ 'in-law family'
c. /tēwgēttá/ 'ostrich'

(14) Pattern High-Mid
a. /mbíírā/ 'milk'
b. /bázínā/ 'old age'
c. /kúrvúkkā/ 'gluttony'

(15) Pattern Low-High-Mid
a. /gùúrā/ 'gourd'
b. /ŋgùzúnā/ 'grass'
c. /ndìrvíndā/ 'whirlwind'

The tones of these patterns are distributed over the entire word, regardless of the number of syllables in it. They are distinctive, as shown in the contrasting pair of (16):

(16) a. /búbúrā/ 'melon' Pattern High-Mid
b. /bùbùrà/ 'width' Pattern Low

Although each noun root carries a distinctive tone pattern, we claim that the morphemes /na/ and /ra/ are underlyingly toneless; the surface tone on which they are realized is always predictable, usually as the result of spreading of the tone from a neighboring morpheme. What is remarkable about (11) to (15) is that the gender markers participate in the realization of the tone pattern that is the property of the noun root that precedes. In examples like (17) and (18), the last tone of the noun's tone pattern falls on the gender morpheme, and not on the noun root at all:

(17) Pattern Mid-High
/tēwgēt-tá/ 'ostrich'

(18) Pattern High-Mid
/gónók-kā/ 'hatred'

4.2.3 Gender markers as clitics

At this point, the data seem to converge on a conclusion which would attach the gender markers onto noun roots by suffixation. However, a consideration of the syntax of the Musey noun phrase shows that this cannot be the case.

When a possessive, adjective, or relative clause is associated with a noun, the modifier intervenes between the noun root and its gender marker, as in (19), where the modifier is set off with bracketing:

(19) a. /kūlùm [māgí] rā/ '[your (PL)] mare'
b. /dī [wár] nā/ 'the [black] dog'
c. /sāà [ci ɮó-nā] nā/ 'the man [who killed the lion]'

Because of the mobile nature of the gender markers seen in examples such as these, we must admit that they are enclitics, not suffixes. And the examples of (19) bring out another important function exercised by /na/ and /ra/: in addition to the lexical function of marking the gender (masculine or feminine) of the noun with which they are associated, they also serve to mark the end of the noun phrase in which they occur. A third function of these clitics is to encode a certain type of definiteness, or at least the individuated nature of the nouns with which they are associated.

If we must recognize that /na/ and /ra/ are not suffixes, then, what are we to make of the facts adduced earlier about the attachment of the gender markers to the noun root?

In general, clitics are "weak" morphemes that are not phonologically independent; they are always pronounced together with another word which serves as their host. The gender markers of Musey are no exception, and until now we have seen them pronounced together with a preceding noun root. When the clitic is separated from the noun, however, as in the examples of (19), the noun can no longer serve as its phonological host, even though these clitics still mark the gender of the noun which is the head of the phrase. Instead, the new host of the gender clitic is simply the word that precedes it, regardless of its nature.

In the noun phrases of (20), the gender marker is separated from its noun. A striking feature of these examples is the fact that the gender marker assimilates to any word that precedes it, and not just to the noun whose gender it specifies. The assimilations follow the same patterns presented in (5) to (9).[2]

[2] Haspelmath (2023:16) would call the gender markers of Musey "welded clitics." He also indicates that the fact that these clitics interact phonologically with their host is remarkable for some linguists. Zwicky and Pullum (1983:504), for example, claim that phonological interactions of a morpheme with a lexical root is symptomatic of an affix, and not of a clitic with its host. The Musey data can thus be added to Haspelmath's examples of clitic welding in Bulgarian [bul], Turkish [tur], and Russian [rus], showing that such welding phenomena must not be excluded for clitics.

(20) a. [zì[-ñ] = dá] < /zi-n = ra/ '[my] house'
b. [mbūɬ [háp] = pā] < /háp = ra/ 'the [white] cow'
c. [zóŋ [gédéŋ] = ŋā] < /gédéŋ = na/ 'the [short] boy'
d. [mbàlá [yúlúm] = bā] < /yúlúm = ra/ 'the [delicious] sauce'
e. [lūm [mā ɬīgī] = nā] < /ɬīgī = na/ 'the river [which overflowed]'
f. [fūū [àmí tām kārám] = mā] < /kārám = na/ 'the food [that we ate today]'
g. [sàā [cī ɮó = nā] = nā] < /ɮó = nā = na/ 'the man [who killed the lion]'

In (20a) the gender marker is separated from its noun by a possessive pronoun suffix; in (20b–d) by an adjective; and in (20e–g) by a relative clause. The new hosts for the clitic are now a noun with the possessive suffix /–n/ in (20a), an adjective in (20b–d), the verb /līgī/ 'overflow' in (20e), the adverb /kārám/ 'today' in (20f), and another unrelated noun phrase /ɮó = nā/ 'the lion' in (20g).

One last issue that must be addressed is tone. We claim that the gender clitics are underlyingly toneless, and in (11) to (15) the clitic bore part of the tone pattern that belonged to the noun root. What happens now if the gender marker is separated from the noun? Does it continue to bear the final element of the noun's tone pattern, even at a distance? Or does it share its tone with its new host?

The first observations show that a gender marker does not continue to bear the tone of its noun if it is separated from it. Consider (21) and (22):

(21) a. /gàrì = nà/ 'guinea fowl'
b. /gàrì ɬāw = nā/ 'the red guinea fowl'

(22) a. /tēwgēt = tá/ 'ostrich'
b. /tēwgēt ɬāw = rā/ 'the red ostrich'
c. */tēwgét ɬāw = rā/

In (21a), the tone pattern of the noun root /gàrì/ is Low, and a Low tone characterizes all syllables, even the clitic /na/. When the gender marker is separated from the noun, as in (21b), it no longer bears a Low tone, but rather a Mid tone, presumably because its new host /ɬāw/ 'red' has Mid tone.

Example (22) is even more instructive, for the tone pattern Mid-High of the noun root needs the contact with the gender marker in order for the final High tone to be realized, as in (22a). When the gender marker is separated, as in (22b), though, the High tone element of the pattern is simply lost. Even though there are two syllables in the root, the High tone is not realized on the second syllable, as might have been imagined in the unacceptable (22c).

We propose the following representation in (23) to account for the patterns observed in (22). In the tone pattern Mid-High of noun roots like /tewget/, the High is a floating tone. When the toneless clitic /ra/ is available, it attaches to it and is realized, as in (23a). But when there is no toneless morpheme available, as in (23b), it does not interact with the tones on either side, and is simply deleted.

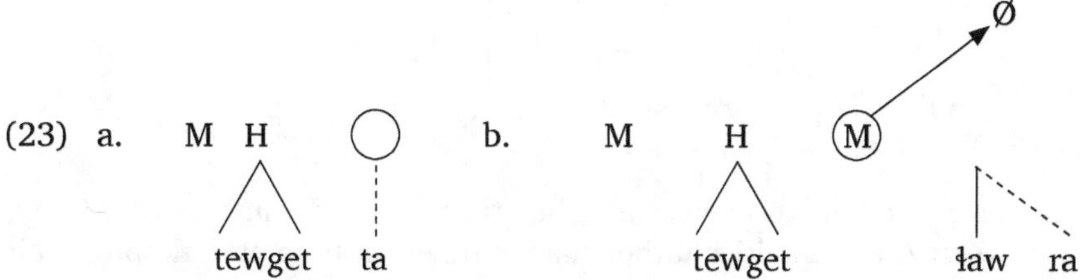

Let us consider further the tone assigned to a gender marker which is separated from its noun root. The examples of (24) show new hosts for the clitic which display three different tone levels: a Low tone in (24a), a Mid tone in (24b), and a High tone in (24c).

(24) a. /ɓú mbà = rà/ 'the clan father'
b. /gàrì ɬāw = nā/ 'the red guinea fowl'
c. /mbūɬ háp = pā/ 'the white cow'

The tonal behavior in (24a) and (24b) is not surprising: the gender marker simply repeats the (final) tone of the host that precedes it. We account for that as a simple case of spreading from the host, as shown in the previous representation of (23b). But when the clitic's host ends in a High tone, as in (24c), the clitic always takes a Mid tone. It seems that the High tone in Musey is not capable of spreading. The High tone has not been observed to spread in any other context, either, and we have already observed the limited options for a floating High tone in (23b). If the gender marker cannot receive a High tone by spreading, then, we propose that the Mid tone is the default tone in Musey, and that it is inserted in (24c) in order to provide the morpheme with a tone on the surface.[3] The representations of (25) show the spreading of Low and Mid tone from the host to the gender clitics, and that of (26) shows the insertion of the default Mid when the host ends in a High tone which cannot spread.

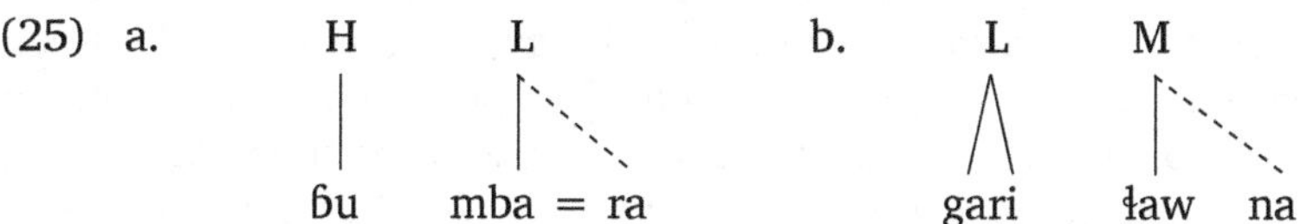

[3] These facts imply that we should revise our understanding of the five tone patterns presented in (11) to (15) to the following: Low, Mid, Mid (High), High, and Low High. The two patterns High and Low High, which end a nonfloating High, will be followed by an inserted Mid tone on the gender marker when it follows immediately.

(26)

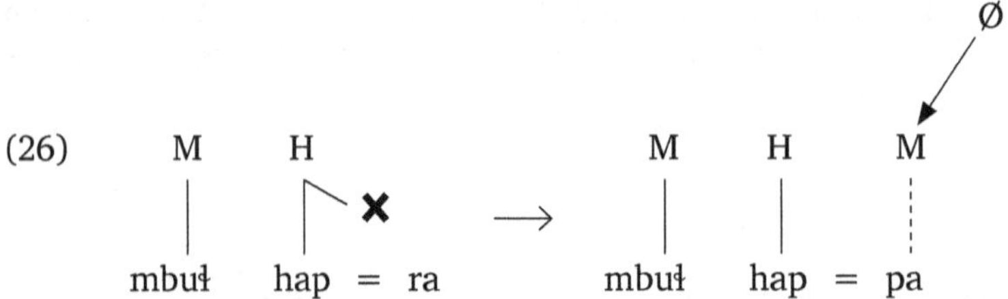

In conclusion, it has been established that the gender markers of Musey, /na/ and /ra/, are enclitics rather than suffixes on the noun, despite their grammatical link to the noun whose gender they specify. Occurring at the end of the noun phrase, these markers make the noun definite, and attach to the preceding word in the phrase, of whatever category it may be. This preceding word is the host of the clitic; it determines the tone of the clitic, and triggers a remarkable array of assimilations which serve to fuse the clitic phonologically to it.

4.3 Orthographic treatment of the gender markers

The Musey language has been written since the arrival of Protestant and Catholic missionaries more than sixty years ago. Despite some linguistic input, as seen in Duncanson (1972), the present writing systems seem to reflect a naïve yet intuitive understanding of the structure of the language by its speakers. In this section, we propose to examine how the gender markers have been written in published documents, according to both the Protestant and Catholic traditions.

The Protestant tradition of writing the language has culminated in the publication of the complete Bible (*Boy Lonana*, Alliance Biblique du Tchad 2002). Literacy materials have also been produced over the years, and a number of individual booklets as well, all following the same writing conventions. No official orthography guide has been produced for the language, so we must infer orthographic conventions from the written record. We refer to the Bible as representing the main exponent of the Protestant tradition.

Catholic writing may have evolved somewhat separately from the Protestant tradition, and there are some orthographic differences between the two systems. We will refer to two booklets produced by the Mission Catholique in Gounou Gaya (henceforth MC): *Deuxième parcours* (MC 1994), prepared for the use of catechists, and *Sadawra* (MC 1999), a prayer book. These reflect the Catholic writing system in use to the present day.

Table 4.1 displays the graphemes used in the Musey orthography as they correspond to the consonantal phonemes of the language.

Table 4.1. Consonant graphemes used in Protestant and Catholic orthographies

Consonant type	**Protestant orthography**	**Catholic orthography**
Plosives	p, b, t, d, c, j, k, g	p, b, t, d, c, j, k, g
Prenasalized plosives	mb, nd, nj, ŋg	mb, nd, nj, ng
Implosives	ɓ, ɗ	ɓ, ɗ
Fricatives	f, v, s, z, h, ɦ	f, v, s, z, h, ɦ
Lateral fricatives	tl, dl	tl~sl, dl~zl[a]
Nasals[b]	m, n, ŋ	m, n, ŋ
Liquids	l, r	l, r
Glides	y, w	y, w

[a] In the earlier booklet (MC 1994) we find <tl> and <dl>, but in the later one (MC 1999) the graphemes had been changed to <sl> and <zl>.

[b] Musey also has a phonemic /ɲ/, but it is underrepresented in both Protestant and Catholic orthographies as <y>, its nasality being ignored.

Note that the principal difference in the representation of Musey consonants is for the lateral fricatives, and in both systems digraphs are used. The other minor difference concerns the representation of the prenasalized /ŋg/.

The Musey language has five phonemic vowels, which are universally represented with the five graphemes <a, e, i, o, u>. Further discussion of the graphemes used in writing Musey can be found in Soulokadi (2021). Tone is not marked in any of the Musey writing systems, so it will not be marked in this and the following sections.

The presentation of the previous section points us to two specific aspects of the Musey orthography to which we give particular attention. (a) Are the gender markers written as separate syntactic words surrounded with spaces, or are they joined in some manner to their host? (b) Concerning the assimilations that the gender markers undergo, does the orthography reflect the underlying forms of /na/ and /ra/, or the surface results of the assimilations?

As to the first question, both Protestant and Catholic traditions write the gender markers fully attached to their host. It was stated earlier that this is the practice in the dictionary (Shryock et al. 1998), where the gender marker is joined directly to a noun root, without a space or any mark of separation whatsoever, as in (1) and (2).

We find the same practice used in the Bible, as is expected. In (27) and (28) we find the gender markers (in bold) attached to both common and proper nouns.[4]

[4] Examples shown without slashes from this point on are transcribed orthographically.

(27) Boy**na** ay ni eg Lo**na**, Boy**na** ni Lo**na**. (John 1:2),
boy = na 'word', Lo = na 'God'
'The Word was with God, and the Word was God.'

(28) Suu Israel**na** cuk zi**na** ni vok ƒiini**ra** Sinay**ra** na gay. (Exodus 19:2),
zi = na 'city', ƒiini = ra 'mount'
'Israel set up camp before Mount Sinai.'

And when the gender marker is separated from its noun, it is still attached, this time to another host, but never separated off as a separate word, as in (29). The noun and its marker are in bold.

(29) a. **boy cona** (Proverbs 15:1), < boy = na 'word'
'bad word'
b. **Musuk** Lona**ra** (Matthew 1:18), < musuk = ra, 'spirit'
'Spirit of God'
c. **sa** ma ka vi vunum u suu li dla coraɗi**na** (Psalm 1:1),
< sa = na, 'person'
'the person who does not go along with evildoers'

In (29a), the gender marker is separated by an adjective, which now serves as the clitic's host. In (29b) it is a noun complement which comes between, and in (29c) it is a full relative clause. These examples illustrate the patterns already shown in (20).

It is even possible to find two of these clitics attached to the same host. In that case each one is associated with a different noun, as in (20g). Examples (30–32) are from the Bible; the structure of each one is shown in (30b), (31b) and (32b), respectively. The final clitic in the string always refers to the first noun in the overall noun phrase.

(30) a. bege mul**nara** (Ezra 6:8)
'the king's goods'
b. [bege [mul = na] = ra], < bege = ra 'goods', mul = na 'king'

(31) a. zi ma ŋgolo**nana** (1 Kings 20:14)
'the big cities'
b. [zi [ma ŋgolo = na] = na], < zi = na 'city, village', ŋgolo = na 'importance'

(32) a. ti ma vi ku**rana** (Isaiah 9:4)
'food for the fire'
b. [ti ma vi [ku = ra] = na], < ti = na 'food', ku = ra 'fire'

Catholic writings (MC 1994, 1999) show the same practice of attaching the gender markers to their host. Just as we saw in the Protestant orthography in (30) to (32), two clitics can attach to the same host.

(33) a. Sene magi ma mbii**rana** (MC 1994:35)
'your fertile fields'
b. [sene magi ma [mbii=ra] =na], < sene=na 'field', mbii=ra 'fertility'

The second question concerns the orthographic treatment of the assimilations. In the Bible, we find that the result of the assimilation is generally followed in the writing. After nasals, we find the consonant doubled when the masculine marker follows, as in (34), and combined with a homorganic plosive when the feminine marker follows, as in (35). In each example, the relevant word is in bold.

(34) a. kona ni u kona may, **semma** ni u **semma** may. (Exodus 21:24), < sem=na 'foot'
'hand for hand, foot for foot'
b. ami u **goozoŋŋa** tuɗ ta ta tana a goɓ Lona (Genesis 22:5), < goozoŋ=na 'boy'
'I and the boy will go over there and worship God'

(35) a. Nowa cuk hu **lumba** (Genesis 7:7), < lum=ra 'boat, canoe'
'Noah went into the boat'
b. Asi tayaɗ tuɗuɗ ha hu **taraŋga** vi mulna. (Genesis 12:15), < taraŋ=ra 'courtyard'
'They took her into the courtyard of the king.'

Doubled consonants are also used to reflect the geminates created by the feminine marker after fricatives, /l/, and /k/, as in (36). In the case of the digraph <tl>, though, no doubling is implemented. The geminate is written as though it were a single consonant, seen in (37):

(36) a. Jonas li buuna hu **kuluffa** hindi. (Jonah 2:1), < kuluf=ra 'fish'
'Jonah spent three days in the fish'
b. **Della** ni a del Yakob (Genesis 27:22), < del=ra 'voice'
'The voice is Jacob's voice'
c. ko **tlekka** tok goryoɗ (Matthew 23:37), < tlek=ra 'hen'
'As a hen gathers her chicks'

(37) Do **mbutla** u ŋguuna hin ti ni ko tasi dew (Isaiah 11:7), <mbuɬ=ra 'cow', for [mbuɬɬa][5]
'The cow and the bear shall graze together'

The geminates [pp] and [tt] are evidently perceived as involving the implosive consonants /ɓ/ and /ɗ/, which are also letters in the Musey

[5] In the dictionary (Shryock 2010) we find this entry written as <mbutltla> which confirms that there is gemination in this word. However, such a complex sequence <tltl> is never found in the Bible, nor in any other literature that we have seen.

alphabet, and this results in the writing seen in (38). This practice contrasts with the writing of geminate [kk], shown in (36c).

(38) a. Ko oora u **heɓpa** ka u agi cocoo. (1 Peter 1:2),
< hep=ra 'peace', for [heppa]
'Grace unto you, and peace, be multiplied.'
b. **Faɗta** ndi ga ndini (Genesis 15:12),
< fat=ra 'sun', for [fatta]
'As the sun was going down'

After plosives, the nasal of the masculine marker assumes the point of articulation of the plosive, seen in (39). As in (38), the plosive in syllable-final position is evidently interpreted as an implosive because it is not released phonetically. However, Musey has no velar implosive, so the plosive <k> is written in the velar position in (39c).

(39) a. An mbuɗ **mbutluɓma** (Exodus 29:44),
< mbutluɓ=na 'tent', for [mbuɬup˺ma]
'I will consecrate the tent'
b. anni ndaŋgara u **buɗna** ɦawaa. (Genesis 18:27),
< buɗ=na 'ashes', for [but˺na]
'I am but dust and ashes.'
c. **tlekŋa** hel gaw (Matthew 26:74),
< tlek=na 'cock, rooster', for [ɬek˺ŋa]
'immediately the rooster crowed'

In the Catholic writings, the syllable-final plosives are always written as the voiceless <p, t, k> rather than with the mixed approach used in the Protestant Bible. Contrast (40) with (38a), and (41) with (38b):

(40) a. ɓivunna maŋ Bu-Suuna kay **heppa** (MC 1994:30),
< hep=ra 'peace'
'sacrifice to God for peace'
b. hu zi **mbudlupma** (MC 1994:38), < mbudlup=na 'tent'
'in the tent'

(41) a. yoo ma bay **zozotta** (MC 1994:48), < zozot=ra 'dirt'
'water without dirt'
b. Yezu Goroŋ ma bay **mitna** (MC 1999:26), < mit=na 'death'
'without the death of Jesus your son'

Among the phonetic changes that result from the cliticization of the gender markers, there is one case which clearly deviates from the pattern of writing the surface pronunciation. This is the case of the nasalized vowel [ã] which is the fused realization of the masculine marker /na/ after fricatives and /l/. The Musey Bible regularly writes the clitic in its basic form <na>, and for a very appropriate reason. Musey does not have phonemic nasalized vowels, and to represent them for this purpose would be to introduce a new letter not used in any other place in the language.[6] Examples of this are seen in (42).

(42) a. **Mulna** u suu mamsina tuɗ hu Yerusalem (2 Kings 5:6),
<mul=na 'king', for [mullã]
'The king and his men went to Jerusalem'
b. Hinira Sinayra ɗus kini **ndoosna** bel bel. (Exodus 19:18),
<ndoos=na 'smoke', for [ndoossã]
'Mount Sinai was wrapped in smoke'

It should be noted that in the Catholic literature (MC 1994, 1999), a separate grapheme <ã> is actually used to represent these cases, following the phonetic pronunciation very closely, but introducing a letter used nowhere else in the writing system:

(43) a. **Mullã** David ki ni tini a **mullã** voo Yerusalem. (MC 1994:38)
'King David is installed as king in Jerusalem.'
b. **Ndossã** ɗus kay ɓinira Sinayra (MC 1994:29, from Exodus 19:18)
'Smoke proceeds from Mt. Sinai'

It will be noted that alongside the new grapheme, the final consonant of the root word is also doubled. It is not clear at this point whether the consonant in these cases is actually geminated in the pronunciation.

4.4 Other clitics

Although /na/ and /ra/ are the most commonly occurring clitics in Musey, there are others. The language possesses quite a number of small particles with various functions, and it is sometimes difficult to gauge whether or not they should be considered clitics, because the extent to which each one "leans" on a neighboring word may vary. There is also lack of consensus by

[6] This practice follows the recommendation of the Lexical Orthography Hypothesis (LOH, Snider 2014). According to that principle, the results of applying lexical rules should be represented in the orthography, but not the results of postlexical rules. The assimilations described up to this point are considered to be produced by lexical rules; they never apply across the word boundary, but only within the phonological word, of which a clitic now forms a part. In these cases, the orthography reflects the surface pronunciation. However, [ã] is not a phoneme of Musey, and the coalescence process that produces it is a postlexical rule. Here the LOH proposes that the input, not the output, be represented in the orthography, and that is the practice observed in the Musey Bible.

linguists as to precise criteria for identifying clitics, for they do not form a coherent group on grammatical grounds.

In any case, we begin here by listing in (44) to (47) the particles that occur with some frequency in written materials. For each one, we give a tentative indication of its function:

(44) su question marker

(45) ka presentative, existential copula

(46) ha itive, motion away from the deictic center

(47) ay ventive, motion toward the deictic center

In both Catholic and Protestant traditions, all these particles are treated orthographically as separate words, i.e., written with a space on each side of the particle. The examples of (48) to (51) illustrate each of the preceding particles, taken from the Musey Bible; the word in question is written in bold.

(48) Va ma su kay saɓakŋa vi Yawe ka **su**? (Genesis 18:14)
'Is anything too hard for the Lord?'

(49) yona **ka** ŋgolo (Genesis 13:10)
'There is water in abundance'

(50) Ɓorow dukuŋ **ha** ki u an ɗaŋ (Genesis 13:9)
'Separate yourself from me'

(51) Mbaagi **ay** egenu (Matthew 11:28)
'Come unto me'

We note one variation in the writing of the interrogative particle /su/ in the Catholic documents we have examined. It is always written as a separate word, as we have already noted. However, when it follows a word ending in a vowel, it is usually written <zu>, as in (52). This writing reflects a pronunciation reminiscent of a word-internal process which operates across the board in Musey, the voicing of intervocalic obstruents. This may be taken as evidence that /su/ is actually an enclitic and is pronounced together with its host.

(52) Va ma dum Bu-Suunana ka **zu**? (MC 1994:10, from Genesis 18:14)
'Is anything too hard for the Lord?'

Whether or not the preceding particles should be considered clitics, there are two other morphemes that behave phonologically like the gender markers /na/ and /ra/, and which we will specifically identify as clitics in Musey. However, their orthographic treatment is different from what we have observed for the gender markers.

4.4.1 The negative marker /ɗi/

The first of these is /ɗi/, the marker of negation which occurs at the right margin of the verb phrase (Shryock 1996:165). This particle can be identified as a welded enclitic (Haspelmath 2023), undergoing assimilation to the preceding word in a way reminiscent of the feminine marker /ra/. The following examples are taken from Shryock (1996:165). When the host of the clitic ends in a vowel, glide, or /r/, the initial /ɗ/ is unchanged, as seen in (53).

(53)	a.	[ka=ɗi]	<	/ka=ɗi/	COPULA
	b.	[dew=ɗi]	<	/dew=ɗi/	'one'
	c.	[durdur=ɗi]	<	/durdur=ɗi/	'earthen roof'

When the host ends in a nasal consonant, the initial /ɗ/ is changed to a voiced plosive at the same point of articulation as the nasal, as seen in (54):

(54)	a.	[kulum=bi]	<	/kulum=ɗi/	'horse'
	b.	[sun=di]	<	/sun=ɗi/	'work'
	c.	[eŋ=gi]	<	/eŋ=ɗi/	'strength'

In all other cases, the initial /ɗ/ of the negative clitic forms a geminate with the final consonant of its host, as in (55):

(55)	a.	[salap=pi]	<	/salap=ɗi/	'weave'
	b.	[ndat=ti]	<	/ndat=ɗi/	'she'
	c.	[suk=ki]	<	/suk=ɗi/	'strength'
	d.	[kuluf=fi]	<	/kuluf=ɗi/	'fish'
	e.	[mbus=si]	<	/mbus=ɗi/	'wash'
	f.	[mbuɬ=ɬi]	<	/mbuɬ=ɗi/	'cattle'
	g.	[kul=li]	<	/kul=ɗi/	'steal'

These examples demonstrate that the host preceding the negative marker can belong to a variety of grammatical categories: nouns, verbs, numerals, pronouns, etc.

So how is this particle written in actual practice? The Catholic tradition always writes /ɗi/ as a separate word, and always in its base form <ɗi>, i.e., without reflecting its assimilation in the pronunciation to the final consonant of the host word which precedes it.

(56) Aŋ kul **ɗi**. (MC 1994:30, from Exodus 20:15)
'You shall not steal.'

(57) Aŋ li yowmus ek ndaraŋ kay vaam **ɗi** (MC 1994:30, from Exodus 20:17)
'You shall not covet any of these things'

This particle may even accept the attachment of a gender marker, as demonstrated in (58):

(58) Yezu ma li zla co ka **ɗina** (MC 1999:20), < zla = na 'thing'
'Jesus who did not do a bad thing'

In the Protestant tradition as reflected in the Bible, however, we find that this particle is always attached to its host, and the assimilations that it undergoes are reflected in a few instances in the orthography. After a nasal consonant, the assimilated form is written as such, as in (59–60). Curiously, though, after /n/, the base form <ɗi> is retained as in (61), rather than an assimilated form *<di> with the simple plosive grapheme.

(59) Aŋ vi u lo man **daŋgi** ni kan anu. (Exodus 20:3), < daŋ = ɗi, 'other NEG'
'You shall have no other gods before me.'

(60) ka Lona ɓakami ay **nambi** (Exodus 20:19), < nam = ɗi, 'he NEG'
'do not let God speak with us himself'

(61) agi ka li **sunɗi** (Deuteronomy 16:8), < sun = ɗi, 'work NEG'
'you shall do no work'

The base form <ɗi>, as seen in (61), is how this clitic is written everywhere else. The interaction with other consonants produces geminates, as we saw in (55), but the negative particle is written invariably as <ɗi>, even though it is always attached to its host. Examples (62) to (65) show this pattern, where the orthography does not reflect the pronunciation directly:

(62) Aŋ **kulɗi**. (Exodus 20:15)
'You shall not steal.'

(63) Aŋ yi sem Yawe, Lo maŋŋa, ɦawa na **gorɗi.** (Exodus 20:7)
'You shall not take the name of the Lord in vain.'

(64) Suu li kumuna suu Egiptena ka ndak a col fok **Moizɗi.** (Exodus 9:11)
'They could not stand before Moses.'

(65) Aŋ ci **maɗɗi**. (Exodus 20:13), pronounced [matti] or [mat:i]
'You shall not kill.'

The final example (65) is interesting, because the orthography diverges from the practice we observed with the feminine marker in (38b), although the pronunciation is identical. Phonetically we have a geminate [tt] in both cases. In (38b) it was written <ɗt>, but here it is written <ɗɗ>, in respect of the identity of the initial consonant of the clitic.

Finally, we note that /ɗi/ may attach to the same host as a gender marker, as in (66):

(66) Li co maŋ sa mba ka balna **koŋŋaɗi**. (Matthew 5:42),
< ko-ŋ = na = ɗi 'hand-2POSS = MASC = NEG'
'Do not refuse the one who would borrow from you.'

4.4.2 The particle /ki/

The last clitic to be considered is /ki/. This particle seems to have more than one function, and in fact we may have to recognize two homophonic clitics rather than just one. On the one hand, /ki/ expresses a completed action, and occurs at the right margin of the verb phrase (Shryock 1996:165). When it is clause-final, the particle appears in the long form /kiyo/; both forms are illustrated in (67):

(67) a. asi tuɗ **ki** ŋgoo bagiya (Genesis 4:8)
'they went to the wilderness'
b. irisi mal **kiyo** (Genesis 3:7)
'their eyes were opened'

The other function of /ki/ is as a copula which introduces predicate adjectives, as in (68):

(68) Irim **ki** cooriya.
'His eyes are red.'

Despite the diversity of function, the behavior of /ki/ is uniform with respect to its phonological behavior and its treatment in both of the orthographic traditions that we have examined. Like /ɗi/, this particle fuses with its host, the preceding word, by undergoing the same types of assimilations that we have already observed. In this case, it is the initial /k/ which submits to the influence of the last consonant of the host. After nasal consonants, /k/ becomes a voiced plosive at the point of articulation of the nasal, seen in (69); after plosives, fricatives and /l/, the /k/ assimilates completely and a geminate is formed, as in (70). After vowels, glides, and /r/, rather than remaining unchanged, the /k/ voices to [g], shown in (71). In this way, the clitic completely integrates into the preceding word, for Musey allows only voiced consonants intervocalically. (Example (70d) is from our own data; the others are all taken from Shryock 1996:166.)

(69)	a.	[hum = biyo]	<	/hum = kiyo/	'hear'
	b.	[fen = diyo]	<	/fen = kiyo/	'blow one's nose'
	c.	[galaŋ = giyo]	<	/galaŋ = kiyo/	'shake'

(70) a. [lop = piyo] < /lop = kiyo/ 'fatigue'
b. [dut = tiyo] < /dut = kiyo/ 'pick fruit'
c. [cok = kiyo] < /tʃok = kiyo/ 'stab'
d. [ŋguruf = fiyo] < /ŋguruf = kiyo/ 'agonize'
e. [gus = siyo] < /gus = kiyo/ 'sell'
f. [eɬ = ɬiyo] < /eɬ = kiyo/ 'hatch'
g. [col = liyo] < /tʃol = kiyo/ 'stand'

(71) a. [too = giyo] < /too = kiyo/ 'sweep'
b. [haw = giyo] < /haw = kiyo/ 'roast'
c. [bar = giyo] < /bar = kiyo/ 'chaff'

Following are a few examples from the Musey Bible which show the invariant <ki> or <kiyo> after a host with a final nasal in (72a), a final obstruent in (72b), and a final liquid in (72c).

(72) a. an hin paɗ vunun **ki** kaŋu (Genesis 12:2),
pronounced [...vunun = **di**...]
'I will bless you'
b. agi hin mbuɗ **ki** ko namma (Genesis 3:5),
pronounced [...mbut = **ti**...]
'you will become like him'
c. irisi mal **kiyo** (Genesis 3:7), pronounced [...mal = **liyo**]
'their eyes were opened'

In the Catholic literature as well, we find this particle always written the same way, as a separate word; consider (73) as just one example.

(73) Yakob dlit **ki** kolo (MC 1994:14), pronounced [...ɮit = **ti**...]
'Jacob awoke'

There is one minor variation that we have seen in the Catholic booklets. In the *Deuxième parcours* (MC 1994) the long form of this particle is written <kio>, but five years later (MC 1999) the same particle is written <kiyo>.

4.5 Conclusion

Table 4.2 summarizes the practices observed in the writing of the Musey clitics:

Table 4.2. Orthographic treatment of the clitics in Musey

Clitic	Joined or separate?	Surface pronunciation written?
<na>	joined	Protestant: yes, with one exception Catholic: yes, always
<ra>	joined	yes, always
<di>	Protestant: joined Catholic: separate	Protestant: sometimes Catholic: no, always <di>
<ki>	separate	no, always <ki>

The present survey of the orthographic practices with respect to clitics in Musey reveals several generalizations of interest. First, despite the differences in the two written traditions that we have examined, there is a good amount of commonality in approach. For example, everyone tacitly agrees that the gender markers should be written attached to the host word. And everyone agrees that /ki/ should be written as a separate word, and always as <ki>, even though the initial /k/ is often not pronounced as such in connected speech. Another common ideal that we perceive is the wish to imitate in writing the way the language is spoken phonetically. We have noted deviations from this ideal in actual practice, and this fact pushes us to reflect on the various levels of intuition that drive native speakers to write the way they do.

But yes, despite a certain commonality, there are differences between writers. It was stated at the outset that the Protestant and Catholic writing systems evolved somewhat independently, and to our knowledge there has not been a concerted effort to bring the two groups together to agree on a single orthographic standard for the language they all have in common. The fact that neither group has produced an orthography guide means that writers may not even be aware of the language questions that lead to divergent practices in the writing. A close examination of both the Protestant and the Catholic practices also reveals that the writers are not always consistent in following the patterns that we present in this study, even within the same system. Again, this is not surprising when there are no formulated orthographic conventions to follow. Beyond these issues, there may also be dialectal differences that ought to be reconciled, in order to produce a single writing system for all speakers to use.

It is interesting to note that even the desire to follow the pronunciation has yielded differing results. Plosives in syllable-final position are unreleased and without voicing; this pronunciation represents a three-way neutralization of voiced plosives, voiceless plosives, and implosives at the same point of articulation. In the Catholic literature, writers spell these consistently as <p, t, k>, as we see in (40) and (41). However, in the Musey Bible, we find a mixed approach to the question, with <ɓ, ɗ, k>, as seen in (38) and (36c). The perception of unreleased plosives as implosives is undoubtedly the reason that we find them written as <ɓ, ɗ> where the alphabet affords such graphemes, but as a voiceless plosive <k> when it does not. A second example is the treatment of the nonphonemic [ã]. The use of the novel grapheme <ã> in the Catholic literature is evidently an attempt to follow the pronunciation closely. However, the Bible writes this as <na>. It is not clear whether speakers perceive that the latter spelling still reflects the pronunciation, or whether they prefer to suspend the principle of following the pronunciation in this case.

Finally, we take note of the differences in grammatical function of the four clitics that we have examined in detail. The gender markers are always written together with the host, yet /ki/ is always separated off. And there is some ambivalence in the way the negative marker /ɗi/ is written. Does that suggest that there are degrees of cliticization in Musey? The clitics /na/ and /ra/ provide a cohesiveness to the noun phrase by marking its right margin, whereas */ki/* and */ɗi/* operate on the level of the verb phrase or of the clause. In any case, it seems that the function of the clitic plays a role in the way it is written intuitively. This may be an ongoing question as the written language is standardized. For each one, should it be completely joined to its host, completely separated, or partially joined with a mark to separate the parts?

To an outsider, it is not surprising to see /ki/ and /ɗi/ written as separate words, probably because of their clause-level function. On the other hand, it seems odd to join other clitics like /na/ and /ra/ onto hosts that are completely unrelated to them. It is clear that this practice follows the pronunciation, but one wonders whether the chaining of clitics as in (30) to (33) or (29c) might hinder the reader from extracting the meaning from the written text, especially for those who are able to read silently. Kutsch Lojenga (2014:83–84) suggests that an "intermediate" solution might be appropriate for clitics such as those of Musey, wherein a hyphen or apostrophe is used to join the clitic to its host, without separating it altogether. Further experimentation with the writing system and testing of such alternatives would undoubtedly be helpful. Ultimately though, the final decisions will rest with the speakers of the language, and so the widest possible participation from members of the community who actually use the language in written form is to be encouraged.[7]

---

[7] An earlier version of §§ 4.1–4.2 of this chapter was presented (Roberts and Soulokadi 2022) at the Chadic workshop (Theme: Words in Chadic languages: phonology and morphosyntax), held in conjunction with the CALL conference 2022.

References

Alliance Biblique du Tchad. 2002. *Boy Lonana: La Bible en langue musey.* N'Djaména: Alliance Biblique du Tchad.

Barreteau, Daniel, and Paul Newman. 1978. Les langues tchadiques. In Daniel Barreteau (ed.), *Inventaire des études linguistiques sur les pays d'Afrique noire d'expression française et sur Madagascar,* 291–330. Paris: Conseil International de la Langue Française.

Bickel, Balthasar, and Johanna Nichols. 2007. Inflectional morphology. In Timothy Shopen (ed.), *Language typology and syntactic description. Vol. 3: Grammatical categories and the lexicon,* 169–240. Cambridge: Cambridge University Press.

Bureau Central du Recensement. 1993. *Recensement général de la population et de l'habitat, 1993: Résultats provisoires.* N'Djaména: Ministère de l'Intérieur et de la Sécurité.

Corbett, Greville. 1991. *Gender.* Cambridge: Cambridge University Press.

Corbett, Greville. 2007. Gender and noun classes. In Timothy Shopen (ed.), *Language typology and syntactic description. Vol. 3: Grammatical categories and the lexicon,* 241–279. Cambridge: Cambridge University Press.

Dassidi Ezéchiel. 2015. The morpho-phonological structure of Musej verbs. MA thesis. University of Yaoundé.

Duncanson, Robert. 1972. Interpreting tone in the Musey language. *Work Papers of the Summer Institute of Linguistics, University of North Dakota Session.* Vol. 16, Article 3. Doi:10.31356/silwp.vol16.03.

Eberhard, David M., Gary F. Simons, and Charles D. Fennig, eds. 2024. *Ethnologue: Languages of the world.* Twenty-seventh edition. Dallas, TX: SIL International.

Haspelmath, Martin. 2023. Types of clitics in the world's languages. *Linguistic Typology at the Crossroads* 3-2(2023):1-59. https://www.academia.edu/83478708/.

Jungraithmayr, Herrmann. 1990. *Lexique mokilko.* Berlin: Dietrich Reimer.

Klavans, Judith. 1995. The independence of syntax and phonology in cliticization. *Language* 61(1):95–120. Doi:10.2307/413422.

Kutsch Lojenga, Constance. 2014. Basic principles for establishing word boundaries. In Michael Cahill and Keren Rice (eds.), *Developing orthographies for unwritten languages,* 73–106. Publications in Language Use and Education 6. Dallas, TX: SIL International.

Lamont, Andrew. 2016. Directionality and the coda condition. *Proceedings of the 2014 Annual Meeting on Phonology.* Doi:10.3765/amp.v2i0.3766.

Mission Catholique (MC). 1994. Deuxième parcours: Boy ma vi Lonna hu somora basira. Ms.

Mission Catholique (MC). 1999. Saɗawra. Ms.

Platiel, Suzy. 1967. *Esquisse d'une étude sur le musey.* Paris: SELAF.

Roberts, James, and Soulokadi Albert Camus. 2019. On ideophones in Musey. In Henry Tourneux and Yvonne Treis (eds.), *Topics in Chadic linguistics X: Papers from the 9th Biennial International Colloquium on the Chadic Languages*, Villejuif, September 7–8, 2017, 215–226. Chadic Linguistics 11. Köln: Rüdiger Köppe.

Roberts, James, and Soulokadi Albert Camus. 2022. Le statut des marqueurs de genre *na* et *ra* en musey. Paper presented at the 52nd Colloquium on African Languages and Linguistics, Leiden, August 29–31, 2022.

Shryock, Aaron. 1995. Investigating laryngeal contrasts: An acoustic study of the consonants of Musey. PhD dissertation. UCLA.

Shryock, Aaron. 1996. The representation of stricture: Evidence from Musey. In Chai-Shune Hsu (ed.), *UCLA working papers in phonology 1*, 162–182. Los Angeles, CA: UCLA Linguistics Department.

Shryock, Aaron. 1997. The classification of the Masa group of languages. *Studies in African Linguistics* 26:29–62.

Shryock, Aaron. 2010. A dictionary of Musey. Ms.

Shryock, Aaron, Mindy Palomo, and Colleen Martin. 1998. Dictionnaire pratique du musey. Ms.

Snider, Keith. 2014. Orthography and phonological depth. In Michael Cahill and Keren Rice (eds.), *Developing orthographies for unwritten languages*, 27–48. Publications in Language Use and Education 6. Dallas, TX: SIL International.

Snider, Keith. 2018. *Tone analysis for field linguists*. Dallas, TX: SIL International.

Soulokadi Albert Camus. 2016. Esquisse du système tonal de la langue moussey. Ms.

Soulokadi Albert Camus. 2021. Harmonisation du système d'écriture du musey. Mémoire de Master. Université de N'Djaména.

Zwicky, Arnold. 1977. *On clitics*. Bloomington: Indiana University Linguistics Club.

Zwicky, Arnold, and Geoffrey Pullum. 1983. Cliticization vs. inflection: English n't. *Language* 59(3):502–513.

5
Participatory Word Spacing in Acheron Preverbal and Prenominal Inflection

Russell Norton

Abstract

A participatory word spacing method is developed in which a group of research participants assess a potential word boundary in preverbal inflections of Acheron [acz] by four test questions derived from word boundary criteria of pausing, bridging, isolability, and separability. The participants' answers support the conclusion that one preverbal inflection /ɔga/ (progressive) is a separate helping verb, but three others /əga-/ (inceptive), /əd̪a-/ (negative), and /ɪja-/ (future) are prefixed to the following verb stem. Additional formal analysis confirms that only /ɔga/ (progressive) is a verb stem. For prenominal locative inflections, /ɪ/ (concealment) and /nɔ/ (contact), the same four criteria give more ambivalent answers. Some locative marking is prefixed to certain nouns and adverbs, aligning well with participants' perceptions of the unity of some locative-marked words. Other locative markers are preposition words identifiable by their morphological behaviour as stems, despite being largely syntactically dependent on noun, pronoun, or anaphoric environments. The full locative paradigm attests adverb prefixes (/ɪ-, n-/), noun prefixes (/ɪ-, nɔ-/), noun prepositions (/ɪ, nɔ/), pronoun prepositions (/ɪga, nana/), and anaphoric prepositions (/jik, naŋ/). The study supports the use of participatory research to determine word boundaries in developing languages by testing oral sentences; it also supports a role for formal stem analysis, at least in synthetic languages.

Abbreviations

=	clitic
+	test boundary
÷	syntactic dependence
1	1st person
2	2nd person
AGR	agreement marker
CL	noun class marker
FUT	future
INCEP	inceptive
INCPL	incompletive
NEG	negative
PL	plural
PST	past
SG	singular

5.1 Introduction

Acheron [acz] is a Niger-Congo language of the Talodi language cluster. It is spoken in hills above Saraf Al-Jaamous in the Nuba Mountains region of the Republic of Sudan. There were 9,830 Acheron speakers in the area as of 2006, many of whom also speak some Arabic, and who have frequent contact with other languages spoken in the neighbouring hills, Moro [mor], Lumun [lmd], and Tocho [taz]. There are also Acheron diaspora populations in several towns of Sudan, where there is language shift to Arabic in young people.

Acheron has SVO word order, and modifiers always occur after the noun, as in (1).[1] Acheron is a noun class language, with consonant class prefixes on most nouns that distinguish singular and plural. Modifiers agree with their nouns, and verbs agree with their subject noun, by agreement

[1] Tone marks are omitted because lexical tones are extremely rare in Acheron (Norton 2013:205).

prefixes that are usually identical to the noun's class prefix. In (1), this is shown for /j-ɔk, n-ɔk/ 'well, wells' and the mass noun /ŋ-ɪr/ 'water'. Thus, one of the characteristics of words in Acheron, and other languages of this type, is that successive words in a sentence after a noun are demarcated by repetition of the same word-initial consonant, that is, by alliteration.

(1) <Yok yäre yonu ngïr ngorïng.>
/j-ɔk j-ərɛ j-ɔnʊ ŋ-ɪr ŋ-ɔrɪŋ/
CL.SG-well AGR-that AGR-have CL-water AGR-good
'That well has good water.'

Like many other Niger-Congo languages, Acheron also has regular verbal inflections that appear before the verb stem and nominal inflections that appear before the noun stem. The preverbal inflections include /ɔga/ (progressive), /əga/ (inceptive), /əd̪a/ (negative), and /ɪja/ (future). Prenominal marking includes /ɪ/ (concealment) and /nɔ/ (contact). It is not automatically clear whether these are prefixed to verbs and nouns, or are separate words. In English, a major language known to Acheron writers and from which the Acheron orthography has been adapted, the equivalent morphemes are helping verbs or prepositions encoded by separate words, but this may or may not be an appropriate analysis of word boundaries in the Acheron language. Therefore, this chapter aims to settle their word or affix status.

A participatory research method for determining word boundaries is used. A participatory approach is chosen for its ability to produce reliable findings based on consensus input by a group of mother-tongue participants, and for the ability to apply the findings immediately to the writing of the language (Kutsch Lojenga 1996, Norton 2013). This method has previously been used to find phonemic distinctions in developing languages, but here it is extended to cover word boundaries as well. Formal analysis of words by their stems and affixes is also used.

5.2 Methodology

This section introduces participatory linguistic research in § 5.2.1, proposes a participatory method of word spacing in § 5.2.2, and also notes a role for stem analysis in identifying words in § 5.2.3.

5.2.1 Participatory linguistic research

Participatory linguistic research (Kutsch Lojenga 1996, 2010) involves a linguist and mother-tongue participants working together to produce findings on a language. Such research systematically draws on collective emic perceptions of the participants to generate consensus data for the language that avoids idiosyncrasies from any one speaker or mis-transcriptions by a linguist from outside the community. As a result, Kutsch Lojenga (1996:10) claims that participatory linguistic research leads quickly to better quality linguistic analyses, and she emphasises the benefits of participatory research in immediately applying linguistic insights directly to language development. Both of these claimed advantages were also witnessed in previous participatory research on the Acheron vowel inventory (Norton 2013).

Kutsch Lojenga (1996:9) envisages that research in any linguistic domain can be conducted using a participatory approach. So far, however, much of the focus of this kind of research has been on phonemic analysis. In participatory research on phonemes, words of given shapes are classified according to their perceived phonemic distinctions, and these distinctions are immediately represented by orthographic choices during the research process. This blending of phonemic analysis with alphabet design suggests the possibility of extending participatory linguistic research to include a similar blend between word boundary analysis and practical word-spacing conventions.

5.2.2 Participatory word spacing

A participatory approach to the study of word spacing will involve a linguist and a group of mother-tongue participants investigating word boundaries together. Such an approach needs to provide an adequate response to two problems, inconsistency and interference, that pioneer writers face when deciding how to space words during the development of the orthographies of their languages.

Inconsistency affects word spacing in newly written languages when pioneer writers are uncertain where to divide a stream of speech into words (Williamson 1984:9). In English, the orthography is inconsistent even in the alphabetic representation of phonemes, for example <tell, head, said> all contain the vowel /ɛ/. In many African languages, however, where phonemic orthographies have been designed in recent decades, competent writers may be consistent in spelling words phonemically, but some words may be spaced consistently and others inconsistently. Involving language developers in analysis of problematic cases could provide the clarity needed to insert spaces, or otherwise, accurately and consistently.

Interference from another language can also affect word spacing in newly written languages. Experience in minority language development shows that speakers of minority languages may import word spacing practices from a developed major language into writing their own language and may defend their spacing practices by appeal to the major language. Interference from major languages affects writing of symbols as well as spaces: for example, Ngiti speakers initially assumed their language should be written with five vowels like Swahili, but when they found nine phonemic vowels through participatory research, they chose to represent all nine in their alphabet (Kutsch Lojenga 1996:6).[2] A similar research process for word boundaries could enable writers to space words accurately for their own language.

Since interference from word boundaries in major languages arises in written language, I propose that participatory research on word boundaries should investigate oral language, by identifying emically acceptable pauses in sentences as they are spoken. Acceptable pauses in oral sentences is the first criterion for assessing word boundaries (Haspelmath 2011:38), and since it directly investigates emic judgements of word boundaries, it is central to group participatory research on the matter. It shifts the focus of research away from written language, where the risk of interference from the orthography of the dominant language comes into play, to the oral language that native speakers use independently of the dominant language. The representative nature of orthographies is well established when it comes to studying the relation between oral phonemes and written graphemes. Likewise, the word boundaries of the oral language can be represented by spaces. The practice of speaking sentences during research in order to decide where to add spaces in writing is analogous to the practice of reading a series of words aloud in participatory research on phonemes to test whether the words contain the same vowel, or the same consonant, or the same tone (Norton 2013:198). This adapts the participatory approach to the problem of word boundaries.

In addition, I propose that the linguist should guide the other research participants in investigating several word boundary criteria applied to a particular word boundary problem in order to obtain cumulative evidence from multiple criteria for either word or affix status. This is what Haspelmath (2011:59) calls a "test battery". Test batteries expose mother-tongue writers to a range of evidence concerning a debatable boundary so that they can have confidence in choosing whether to use a space or not, especially in cases that were previously unclear.

I am arguing, moreover, for the inclusion of both of these responses in word boundary research: both identifying emically acceptable pauses, which are direct judgments on the placement of boundaries in oral sentences, and exposing participants to a wider range of test evidence from other criteria as well. If linguistics is to progress, it needs methods that produce results that match consensus intuitions among speakers of the language, in order that those results are both cognitively plausible and applicable in practice. In word boundary analysis, this means finding other criteria whose predictions coincide with emically acceptable pauses.

---

[2] I am grateful to a reviewer for drawing my attention to the relevance of the Ngiti example.

5.2.3 Stem analysis

When seeking to determine whether a nominal or verbal inflection is a WORD or an AFFIX, it is worth remembering that an affix is added to a STEM. A stem, once identified, forms a word either with an affix, or affixes, or simply on its own. Analysing stems can be a detailed formal exercise, with internal morphology contributing to the formation of the stem as well as external morphology added to the stem (Spencer 2012). This approach complements the testing of word boundaries with community participants, for whereas word boundary criteria identify words by their margins, stem analysis identifies words from within.

5.3 Acheron preverbal inflections

The test questions used with Acheron participants to determine word boundaries in oral versions of preverbal inflections are presented in § 5.3.1. The results for Acheron preverbal inflections are given in § 5.3.2, and then some additional formal analysis of Acheron verbs by the author that corroborates the results is presented in § 5.3.3.

5.3.1 Word boundary test questions for preverbal inflections

Four test questions were designed for identifying word boundaries in Acheron preverbal inflections, as presented in (2) and discussed below. Word boundary criteria that are assessed by these questions are given at the end of each question in square brackets. The wording here refers generally to "the inflection" and "the stem", but in practice these questions were asked about specific expressions containing progressive, inceptive, negative, or future inflections with the verb "eat", as shown in § 5.3.2.

(2) Test questions for Acheron preverbal inflections
1. Do you say the inflection and the stem as two words or one word? [pausing]
2. Does the first vowel of the stem stay or disappear? [bridging]
3. Can you say the inflection alone without the stem? [isolability]
4. Can you add something to the inflection, before the stem? [separability]

The particular criteria of pausing, bridging, isolability, and separability were chosen because they can be answered relatively directly by native speaker participants without requiring lengthy analysis or argumentation, except to the extent that native speaker participants discuss realistic contexts in which they would find the utterances natural. They combine two initial questions about the test utterance itself with two final questions about possible alternative utterances with particular differences from the test utterance. They cover both phonology and syntax.

The first test question assesses emic perception of word boundaries by inviting research participants to consider the naturalness of pausing between the inflection and the verb stem. Asking directly about saying one word or two in the first question establishes the priority of the oral sentence over its written rendering, because the research aims to achieve a representation of the internalised language system shared by its users, rather than more shallow research on mere preferences as to the external appearance of the written language.

The second question examines a vowel hiatus at the boundary being tested, because the inflections all end in a vowel and the verb stem begins in a vowel, as in /b-ɔga+ɔrəgɔ/ 'I am eating' where the test boundary is indicated by "+". Prior observation of the language indicates that the initial stem vowel /ɔ/ is not always pronounced, hence it is this vowel that is the subject of question 2. In lexical phonology theory, invariable vowel deletion would imply a lexical process between stem and affix,[3] whereas variable vowel deletion would imply a postlexical process between two adjacent words (Kiparsky 1985:86). Kutsch Lojenga (2014:97) describes the postlexical processes that occur across word boundaries as "bridging" between two adjacent words.

Whereas the first two questions are about the phonology of the test clause itself, the last two questions ask participants to consider possible alternative clauses pertinent to grammatical analysis. With an omitted subject pronoun /ɔɪŋ/ 'I' in test sentences, the verb takes a default singular subject concord prefix /b-/ (Norton 2000:32). This verbal concord prefix attaches in front of the inflections being tested, as in /b-ɔga+ɔrəgɔ/, therefore either the inflection is a verb or the whole complex is a verb. The third question therefore examines whether the inflection can occur alone without the verb stem /ɔrəgɔ/. If the inflection is a helping verb in its own right, we predict that it will satisfy isolability (Bloomfield 1933:159, Kutsch Lojenga 2014:95), which is to say it can occur alone in the language without the following verb stem, as only a bound inflection would require the following verb stem.[4]

[3] Invariable absence of the vowel could also happen if the vowel is a prefix that is not used in the inflection being tested (see § 5.3.3); this too would be a lexical operation within a word.

[4] A reviewer asks how the author kept the participants from misinterpreting question 3 to include being able to say the inflectional form alone as a meaningless exercise, not just as a meaningful well-formed sentence. In practice, we discussed whether the forms could be used in real situations, in particular participants were asked to consider whether the inflections could be said without the stem as a reduced answer to a question containing the stem, as is possible in English: <Are you eating? I am. Will you eat? I will.> etc. In this way, the option of meaningless forms did not occur to participants.

Finally, if the inflection is a verb in its own right and not prefixed to the following stem, then we also predict that it will satisfy separability by morphemes that occur immediately after verb stems, such as the Acheron past tense suffix /-k/ or the positional adverb /naŋ/ 'on it', that would be inadmissible between a prefix and a root (question 4). If Kutsch Lojenga (2014:92) and Haspelmath (2011:32) are right about the primacy of grammatically oriented criteria in word boundary research, then the latter two test questions, testing for isolability and separability of the inflection, should enable the research to end on a decisive note.

5.3.2 Results

The test questions were put collectively to a group of three native speaker-writer participants for each of the four preverbal inflections /ɔga/ (progressive), /əga/ (inceptive), /əd̪a/ (negative), /ɪja/ (future) with a following verb stem /ɔrəgɔ/ 'eat'. All the questions produced clear answers almost immediately. The results are presented in tables 5.1–5.4. The data is transcribed phonetically, representing oral utterance data, as is necessary to produce findings about the language internalised by native speakers.

Table 5.1. Test results for /ɔga/ (progressive)

/bɔga + ɔrəgɔ/ '(I) am eating.'	**Responses**
1. Do you say it as two words or one word?	***Two.***
2. Does the first /ɔ/ of /ɔrəgɔ/ stay or disappear?	***Can stay or not.***
3. Can you say /bɔga/ 'I am' alone?	***Yes:*** [ɔʊŋ bɔga ɔrəgɔa] 'Are you eating?' [bɔga] '(I) am.' [bɔga bɔrɪŋa] 'Are (you) well?' [bɔga] '(I) am.'
4. Can you add something to /bɔga/ before the main verb /ɔrəgɔ/?	***Yes:*** [ɔɪŋ bɔgak ɔrəgɔ] 'I was eating.' [ɔɪŋ bɔga naŋ ɔrəgɔ] 'I am eating on it.'

Table 5.2. Test Results for /əga/ (inceptive[5])

/bəga + ɔrəgɔ/ '(I) have started eating.'	**Responses**
1. Do you say it as two words or one word?	***One.***
2. Does the first /ɔ/ of /ɔrəgɔ/ stay or disappear?	***Disappears.***
3. Can you say /bəga/ 'I have started' alone?	***No:*** [ɔʊŋ bəgarəgɔa] 'Have you started eating?' [ɔɪŋ bəgarəgɔ] (*[bəga]) 'I have started eating.'
4. Can you add something to /bəga/ before the main verb /ɔrəgɔ/?	***No:*** [bəgarəgɔ naŋ] '(I) have started to eat on it.'

Table 5.3. Test Results for /əd̪a/ (negative)

/bəd̪a + ɔrəgɔ/ '(I) do not eat.'	**Responses**
1. Do you say it as two words or one word?	***One.***
2. Does the first /ɔ/ of /ɔrəgɔ/ stay or disappear?	***Disappears.***
3. Can you say /bəd̪a/ 'I do not' alone?	***No:*** [ɔʊŋ bəd̪arəgɔa] 'Do you not eat?' [ɔɪŋ bəd̪arəgɔ] (*[bəd̪a]) 'I do not eat.'
4. Can you add something to /bəd̪a/ before the main verb /ɔrəgɔ/?	***No:*** [bəd̪arəgɔk naŋ] '(I) did not eat on it.'

[5] Strictly speaking, perfect inceptive. It means not only that the subject started doing something, but also that the subject has been doing it during the interval between the start time and the present time.

Table 5.4. Test Results for /ɪja/ (future)

/bɪja + ɔrəgɔ/ 'I will eat.'	**Responses**
1. Do you say it as two words or one word?	***One.***
2. Does the first /ɔ/ of /ɔrəgɔ/ stay or disappear?	***Disappears.***
3. Can you say /bɪja/ 'I will' alone?	***No:*** [ɔʊŋ bɪjarəgɔa] 'Will you eat?' [ɔɪŋ bɪjarəgɔ] (*[bɪja]) 'I will eat.'
4. Can you add something to /bɪja/ before the main verb /ɔrəgɔ/?	***No:*** [bɪjarəgɔ naŋ] '(I) will eat on it.'

The results for the progressive construction with /ɔga/ in table 5.1 consistently differ from the last three constructions in tables 5.2–5.4. Only the progressive structure /b-ɔga ɔrəgɔ/ is emically perceived by participants as two words that can be said with a pause between them, and the loss of initial /ɔ/ of /ɔrəgɔ/ is variable only after /b-ɔga/ implying a postlexical process bridging the two words. Furthermore, only /b-ɔga/ can be said alone in a clause without a further verb stem, and only /b-ɔga/ can be immediately followed by the past tense suffix /-k/ or the positional adverb /naŋ/ 'on it'. All of these findings indicate that /ɔga/ is a helping verb in its own right before the main verb stem, whereas the other three inflections /əga-/ (inceptive), /əd̪a-/ (negative), and /ɪja-/ (future) are bound to the following verb stem.

5.3.3 Additional analysis of preverbal inflections

The above participatory research findings, of a distinction between the behaviour of /ɔga/ (progressive) as a verb in its own right and the other three inflections as verbal affixes, can be corroborated by additional detailed analysis of verbs. First of all, the verb /ɔga/ is a productive copula in Acheron that can take a variety of complements as in (3). This data provides additional supporting evidence for the word boundary in /b-ɔga ɔrəgɔ/ by the nonselectivity criterion (Haspelmath 2011:45), because /ɔga/ does not select only verbs. After /ɔga/, a verb such as /ɔrəgɔ/ can be replaced by words of four other categories, so /ɔga/ is not a verbal prefix.

(3) Uses of the Acheron copula verb /ɔga/ (Norton 2018)

a.	/b-ɔga ɔrəgɔ/	'is eating'	(verb complement)
b.	/b-ɔga b-ɔbɔrɔk/	'is strong'	(adjective complement)
c.	/b-ɔga babɪɟɛk/	'is a blind man'	(noun complement)
d.	/b-ɔga b-ɪbɪŋ/	'is mine'	(possessive pronoun complement)
e.	/b-ɔga ɪppɔŋ/	'is in the fields'	(locative adverb complement)

We can also relate the findings to the internal form of verbs. Acheron verb stems are minimally of the shape VCV, as in table 5.5. The initial V is most often /ɔ-/, a stem formative which is absent in the imperative form ("eat", "sit") except when the verb stem is of minimal size ("say", "be", "have"). The final V is always one of the non-high vowels /ɛ, ɔ, a/ which determine the formation of imperatives. The form /ɔga/ used in the progressive construction is again confirmed as a verb with an imperative form /ɔgawʊ/ 'be!' determined by its final stem class vowel /-a/.

Table 5.5. Acheron verb classes

Final vowel	Stem	Imperative	Gloss
ɛ	/ʈəmɛ/	/ʈəmɪ/	'see'
	/uttɛ/	/utti/	'vomit'
ɔ	/ɔmɔ/	/ɔmʊ/	'say'
	/ɔrəgɔ/	/rəgʊ/	'eat'
	/ɔrəŋɔ-k sɪk/	/rəŋʊ-d̪ɛ sɪk/	'sit down'
	/akkɔ-k/	/akkʊ-d̪ɛ/	'cook'
a	/ɔga/	/ɔgawʊ/	'be'
	/ɔna/	/ɔnawʊ/	'have'
	/ɪnna/	/ɪnnawʊ/	'know'

The other three preverbal inflections that were found by the four test questions to be prefixed to the verb, /əga-/ (inceptive), /əd̪a-/ (negative), /ɪja-/ (future), all have a VCV shape and are still like /ɔga/ in having /a/ as the last vowel, so they cannot automatically be ruled out as verbs based on shape alone. However, their final /a/ vowel is not a stem-final vowel like it is in /ɔga/, because it does not determine an imperative form. Instead, their /a-/ is attached to the following verb root and can be identified as an incompletive prefix, as shown in (4). The incompletive prefix gives a habitual reading when used alone (4a), but is also present in the inceptive, negative and future inflections, as in the interlinear analyses in (4b–d). This distinguishes the inceptive, negative and future from the progressive

/ɔga/ whose final stem class vowel /-a/ determines the imperative inflection /ɔgawʊ/ ‘be!’.[6]

(4) Incompletive verb forms in Acheron

a. Habitual /b-a-rəgɔ/
SG-INCPL-eat
‘eats’

b. Inceptive /b-əg-a-rəgɔ/
SG-INCEP-INCPL-eat
‘has started eating’

c. Negative /b-əd̪-a-rəgɔ/
SG-NEG-INCPL-eat
‘is not eating’

d. Future /b-ɪj-a-rəgɔ/
SG-FUT-INCPL-eat
‘will eat’

5.4 Acheron prenominal inflections

Following the clear results obtained for preverbal inflections, we now examine whether similar answers can be achieved for oral prenominal inflections in Acheron as well, in particular for the locative forms /ɪ/ and /nɔ/. These locative forms commonly translate as “in” and “on”, although as shown in (5), their semantic ranges extend to “concealment” and “contact”, a distinction previously identified for the related language Lumun (Smits 2007). As before, the symbol “ + ” indicates the test boundary.

(5) Locative markers for concealment and contact

a. /ɪ + ɲasənd̪a/ ‘in, under the bag’

b. /nɔ + ɲasənd̪a/ ‘on, at, with, touching the bag’

The four tests used for preverbal inflection are considered again for these prenominal inflections in § 5.4.1. This is followed by evidence that

6 Incompletive /a-/ is a feature of several languages of the same language cluster (Smits 2017:343, Norton 2018:11). The additional inflectional prefixes before /a-/ also reduce to single phonemes accompanied by epenthesis: inceptive /g-/ and negative /d̪-/ preceded by epenthetic schwas, and future /ɪ-/ followed by a transitional approximant.

locative markers occur as prefixes in § 5.4.2, and also evidence that they occur as prepositional stems in § 5.4.3, and finally an overall locative paradigm in § 5.4.4.

5.4.1 The four previous word boundary tests applied to prenominal inflections

The grammatical tests of isolability or separability from the noun provide no indications that /ɪ/ and /nɔ/ are free word forms. Neither form is free to occur in isolation from a noun because when the noun is absent, other anaphoric forms /jik/ 'in it' and /naŋ/ 'on it' are used instead as shown in (6). Also, /ɪ/ and /nɔ/ are not separable from the noun in Acheron, because all noun modifiers come after the noun, and no words occur between locative and noun (Norton 2018:30).

(6) Anaphoric locatives of concealment and contact

a. /g-aja g-ɔnʊ ŋuzi jik/
CL.SG-cup AGR-have milk in
'The cup has milk in it.'

b. /ɔʊŋ b-ɔḍʊŋɔ-k naŋ/
2SG SG-climb-PST on
'You climbed on it.'

As to pausing, however, participants gave more ambivalent answers than with preverbal inflections on whether locative markers are said as words in their own right before nouns. In particular, they considered that some frequent locative expressions such as /ɪ-jɔk/ 'in the well', /i-zəŋki/ '(in) daylight' and /nɔ-bɪja/ 'on the tree', are spoken as single words, but that other combinations are spoken as two words, /ɪ jazɔ/ 'in the grass', /nɔ bʊməŋ/ 'with the Lumun person' and /nɔ ɔʊŋ/ 'with you (SG)'.

As to whether such judgements can be corroborated phonologically by bridging effects between two words, or by lexically conditioned effects that show phonological unity between two parts of a word, there are some pieces of evidence in the language that align with these judgements. For example, with a pronoun, /nɔ ɔʊŋ/ 'with you (SG)', both vowels in hiatus can be pronounced, so deletion of one vowel is not obligatory and is therefore a postlexical phenomenon that bridges between the two words, as also found earlier between a progressive helping verb and a main verb, */bɔga ɔrəgɔ/* 'is eating'.

It is not clear at present whether there is similar bridging with a following noun (as opposed to a pronoun). A plausible candidate for a bridging effect before nouns may be prosodic vowel lengthening. Lengthening seems to enhance a small prosodically independent locative before a noun in [|ɪː| |jaːzɔ|] 'in the grass', but not the prosodically dependent locative in [ɪ|jɔk|] 'in the well' where the vowel is clearly short and where there is a consensus among participants that the locative marker is bound. This faces a methodological challenge, however, that since vowel length is not contrastive in Acheron (Norton 1995:22, 29), it is only open to etic rather than emic observation, unlike other evidence considered in this chapter, so vowel lengthening has not been systematically verified on more examples.

On the other hand, we also find processes that show unity between locative markers and some nouns. There is one word-medial process j→s seen in /jʊwɛ/ 'river', /ɪ-sʊwɛ/ 'in the river', /jɔd̪ɔk/ '(village name)', /ɪ-sɔd̪ɔk/ 'in (village name)', but not in /ɪ jɪt̪t̪rʊk/ 'in the pig' or /ɪ jazɔ/ 'in the grass'. More surprisingly, j→s is blocked in /ɪ-jɔk/ 'in the well', which Acheron participants have repeatedly identified as a single word, and which like /ɪ-sʊwɛ/ 'in the river' has a root with a place semantics suitable for a lexicalised locative expression. Perhaps j→s is disfavoured in a shorter monosyllabic noun /ɪ-jɔk/, and/or perhaps /ɪ-jɔk/ is a more successful dialect form that has spread at the expense of a hypothetical ?/ɪ-sɔk/. Whatever the case, the result is that j→s is lexically conditioned to occur in /ɪ-sʊwɛ/ but not /ɪ-jɔk/, and lexical conditioning is also diagnostic of a word-internal process. Therefore, it supports the analysis that /ɪ-/ forms a word morphophonologically with at least some /j/-initial nouns.[7]

There is also occasional dropping of noun class consonant prefixes altogether as in /i-zəŋki/, /i-ŋki/ 'in daylight' from /zəŋki, məŋki/ 'sun, suns', although not all participants accepted classless forms like /i-ŋki/. The form /i-ŋki/ shows phonological unity through ATR harmony of the locative vowel ɪ→i with the ATR root vowel /i/. Also, internal pausing is not possible after the initial locative vowel, [iŋ.gi], nor can the stem be pronounced in isolation, *[ŋgi]. Again, these tests are in line with the participants' judgement that this particular example /i-zə-ŋki/, /i-ŋki/ is one word.

In summary, the four tests that gave clear results with preverbal inflection do not provide the same clarity for prenominal inflections. There is no grammatical support for locative words from isolability or separability tests, but there is an emic perception that nouns vary as to whether the locative marking is joined to it or not, and there is some phonological evidence that supports this variation. We have phonological evidence not

[7] Word-medial j→s is also seen in /ən-s-awwaŋ/ 'from up at home' from /j-awwaŋ/ 'up at home'. Another case mentioned in § 5.4.2 is the contrast /j-ɛ-s-i/ 'up there' versus /d̪-ɛ-d̪-i/ 'down there'. Languages closely related to Acheron show other intervocalic processes of voicing and flapping, as in Lumun [lmd] /pɪra/ 'tree', / nɔ-[b]ɪra/ 'in the tree', /tɔk/ 'well', /ɪ-[ɾ]ɔk/ 'in the well'. Unfortunately, however, voicing and flapping are not diagnostic of words in Acheron because they do not occur, thus Acheron /bɪja/ 'tree', /nɔ-bɪja/ 'on the tree', /jɔk/ 'well', /ɪ-jɔk/ 'in the well'.

only for bridged word sequences like /nɔ ɔʊŋ/ 'with you (SG)' with vowels only variably dropped in hiatus, but also for unified words like /ɪ-sʊwɛ/ 'in the river' with the lexically conditioned process j→s.

5.4.2 Locatives as prefixes

A further test discussed in a public participatory research setting is the occurrence of /ɪ/ and /nɔ/ before bound stems. Acheron has some irregular locative expressions shown in (7), in which locative markers are found with a special stem created by gemination of the first root consonant. Geminates only occur word-medially in Acheron (Norton 1995:30), so /ɪ-/ and /nɔ-/ form a phonological word with the geminated stems. The first example (7a) is an adjective-to-adverb transposition 'good' → 'well', but the same gemination is used in certain expressions describing frequent locations (7b–e). As to how well established /ɪ-/ and /nɔ-/ are in this context, the /ɪ-/ is attested in multiple forms (7a–d), whereas /nɔ-/ has only been found once (7e. /nɔ-t̪t̪ɔk/), although it does occur in a direct paradigmatic opposition, /ɪ-t̪t̪ɔk, nɔ-t̪t̪ɔk/ (7d–e). It is thus evident to speakers and linguists alike that both /ɪ-/ and /nɔ-/ are joined in the words in (7), and participants consistently write them this way.

(7) Locative words with special geminated stem

				Underlying adjective or noun (SG, PL)	
a.	<ïrrïng>	/ɪ-rrɪŋ/	'well'	/b-ɔ-rɪŋ, w-/	'good'
b.	<ïttäk>	/ɪ-ttək/	'in the house field'	/g-ə-ɾək, n-/	'house field'
c.	<ïppong>	/ɪ-ppɔŋ/	'in the far field'	/g-ə-bɔŋ, n-/	'far field'
d.	<ïddok>	/ɪ-t̪t̪ɔk/	'in the settlement'	/b-ə-d̪ɔk, m-/	'stone/nation/town'
e.	<noddok>	/nɔ-t̪t̪ɔk/	'at the settlement'[8]	/b-ə-d̪ɔk, m-/	'stone/nation/town'

While the diagnosis that these are single words is phonological, because geminates only occur word-medially in Acheron, the geminated stems are thereby bound stems morphologically as well, because they always require a prefix in front of the geminate. There is one other example of /nɔ-/ with a bound stem in /nɔ-ɽɪrək/ 'sky', from an older proto-stem **tɪḷɔk* 'sky' (Norton and Alaki 2015:92). In Acheron, this stem no longer occurs without /nɔ-/, hence it is another bound stem that requires /nɔ-/ in addition to (7e) /nɔ-t̪t̪ɔk/.

[8] This expression also translates naturally as 'in the country' or 'in the town'.

Locative affixation is also seen on certain other words. The concealment prefix /ɪ-/ is used in (7a) /ɪ-rrɪŋ/ 'well' from /b-ɔ-rɪŋ/ 'good', and the contact prefix /n-/, which would be unpronounceable in isolation, is seen in the anaphoric preposition /n-əŋəŋ/ 'with it' from /əŋ/ 'with', and in time adverbs /nə-ŋkɔra/ 'at night', /nə-ŋɔrrɔk/ 'tomorrow'. Contact locative marking in adverbials is the minimal consonantal form /n-/ (or /nə-/), whereas in nouns we have a back vowel /nɔ-/. The back vowel in nouns is a morphological linking vowel, also seen in alliterative genitive inflection as in /ŋəgʊr ŋɔ-wumik/ 'young of goat', or /zarək zɔ-ttək/ 'village, lit., belly of the house fields' which has the bound geminated stem /-ttək/ also seen in (7b) /ɪ-ttək/.

More evidence for locative affixation comes from two height locative prefixes on nouns, /jɔ-/ 'up at' and /d̪ɔ-/ 'down at'. These prefixes are used in toponyms for local settled communities marked as either up in the hills or down below the hills. Thus, /jɔ-rəmɛ/ 'Acheron hills', /d̪ɔ-rəmɛ/ 'the plain to the south of the Acheron hills', /jɔ-məŋ/ 'Lumun hills', /jɔ-sɔ/ 'Tocho hills', /d̪ɔ-ʈɔnɔ/ 'Torona village (below the hills)', /d̪ɔ-jɛd̪ɪ/ 'Talodi town (on the plain)'. The contact locative /nɔ-/ thus constitutes a further locative prefix along with /jɔ-, d̪ɔ-/. Certain place adverbs also have up/down marking, /j-əgək/ 'far up there', /d̪-əgək/ 'far down there', and /j-ɛ-s-i/ 'up there', /d̪-ɛ-d̪-i/ 'down there', where like other adverbs the linking vowel /ɔ/ is not used.

5.4.3 Locatives as prepositional stems

Another test discussed with native speakers is whether /ɪ/ and /nɔ/ are used before a following pronoun as well as a following noun, for if they were found before pronouns as well, they would not be noun prefixes. We find that /ɪ-/ is replaced by a preposition /ɪgɑ/ before a pronoun as in (8a). Likewise, the contact locative /nɔ-/ is replaced by a preposition /nana/ before a pronoun as in (8b), although the form /nɔ/ itself also occurs before a pronoun as in (8c). Not all participants accept (8c), however, hence it is marked with a "?".

(8) Locative prepositions before pronouns

a.		/bɔga	ɪga	gɛnɔŋ/	'He is in you.' (concealment)
b.		/bɔga	nana	gɛnɔŋ/	'He is with you.' (contact)
c.	?	/bɔga	nɔ	ɔnɔŋ/	'He is with you.' (contact)

However, if the formative /ɪ-/ is present within the preposition /ɪga/, then it is not only bound to nouns but also to /-ga/. Also, /nɔ/ is not reliably bound to nouns either, given its presence before pronouns in (8c), at least for some speakers, and even the other contact preposition /nana/

used before pronouns contains the alveolar nasal /n/ found in all contact locative marking.

Further data bears out the idea that we have locative prepositions before nouns and pronouns. First of all, additional evidence for /nɔ/ as a preposition comes from its use with the verb /bamɔ/ 'tell' before a demonstrative pronoun in (9b). The lack of acceptability of /nɔ/ as a preposition among a wider consensus of participants suggests it is a dialect-specific form, as both sentences (8c) and (9b) were given by a speaker of the less numerous eastern dialect.[9]

(9) Locative preposition before demonstrative pronoun

a. /ɔɪŋ bam-ɔŋ irri/
1SG tell-2PL this
'I tell you this.'

b. /ɔɪŋ bam-ɔŋ nɔ irri/
1SG tell-2PL on this
'I tell you of this.' [eastern dialect]

Next, a comparison of locative prepositions with comitative prepositions reveals the internal morphology of prepositional stems. The locative prepositions /ɪga/, /nana/, /nɔ/ shown earlier in (8a–c) are repeated in (10a–c) followed by the comitative prepositions /ŋa/, /əŋa/, /əŋɔ/ (10d–f). The preposition /ŋa/ (10d) is used in adjuncts, and the prepositions /əŋa/, /əŋɔ/ (10e–f) are used in predicates. The comitative prepositions are semantically similar to the contact prepositions, with four sentences (10b–c, e–f) all provisionally translated 'he is with you'. The prepositions in (10) all share a formal property that prepositions ending in /-a/ govern a /g/-initial pronoun (10a–b, d–e), whereas prepositions ending in /-ɔ/ govern an /ɔ/-initial pronoun (10c, f). The full pronoun sets are listed in table 5.6 and represented in the examples in (10) by 2PL pronouns /gɛnɔŋ/ or /ɔnɔŋ/.

(10) Locative prepositions and comitative prepositions before pronouns

a. /bɔga ɪga gɛnɔŋ/ 'He is in you.' (concealment)
b. /bɔga nana gɛnɔŋ/ 'He is with you.' (contact)
c. /bɔga nɔ ɔnɔŋ/ 'He is with you.' [eastern dialect] (contact)
d. /bajagɔ ŋa gɛnɔŋ/ 'He is going with you.' (adjunct comitative)
e. /bɔga əŋa gɛnɔŋ/ 'He is with you.' (predicate comitative)
f. /bɔga əŋɔ ɔnɔŋ/ 'He is with you.' [eastern dialect] (predicate comitative)

[9] The eastern and western dialects are distinguished by other differences in phonology (Norton 1995) and grammar (Norton 2018:32).

Table 5.6. Pronoun sets governed by prepositional suffixes

/g/-initial	/ɔ/-initial	Gloss
/gɪŋ/	/ɔɪŋ/	'I'
/gʊŋ/	/ɔʊŋ/	'you (SG)'
/gɛssɪk/	/ɔssɪk/	'you (SG) and I'
/gɔk/	/ɔŋɔk/	'he/she'
/gɛniŋ/	/ɔniŋ/	'we'
/gɛnɔŋ/	/ɔnɔŋ/	'you (PL)'
/gɛssɔŋ/	/ɔssɔŋ/	'you (PL) and I'
/gɛŋ/	/ɔgɛŋ/	'they'

The result is that the less widely acceptable /nɔ/ preposition in (10c) consists of a contact locative formative /n-/ combined with the pronoun-selecting suffix /-ɔ/, in contrast to /nana/ which, in reduplicated form, consists of the contact locative formative /n-/ combined with the alternative pronoun-selecting suffix /-a/. Similarly for /ɪga/ in (10a), we can now say the concealment locative formative /ɪ-/ is combined with the pronoun-selecting suffix /-a/, albeit with an intervening velar plosive giving the allomorph /-ga/.[10]

The locative forms /ɪ/ and /nɔ/ thus occur promiscuously before pronouns as well as nouns. We might try to understand this as cliticisation, in which the formatives /ɪ-/ and /n-/ form extended prepositional stems /ɪga/, /nana/ or /nɔ/ before pronouns, but cliticise onto certain place noun stems such as /ɪ=sʊwɛ/ or /n-ɔ=t̪t̪ɔk/. Their grammatical status as prepositions could then provide a linguistic rationale (in the Acheron language, not just inferred from equivalent prepositions in English) for spacing out locative words <ï> and <no> for /ɪ/ and /nɔ/ before the noun, as Acheron writers tend to do, except in specific adverbs and irregular locative nouns mentioned in § 5.4.1 and § 5.4.2. The weakness of a cliticisation analysis, however, is that it views the dependence of locatives on nouns as phonological, whereas the evidence in § 5.4.1 and § 5.4.2 is that it is also morphological, because it occurs irregularly on certain bound stems, and even syntactic as well, because locative markers fail isolability and separability tests. Furthermore, the different prepositional forms are bound to different syntactic contexts, particularly in the western dialect where /ɪ/ and /nɔ/ occur before nouns but /ɪga/ and /nana/ occur before pronouns, although /nɔ/ is freer syntactically in the eastern dialect because it can occur before either nouns or /ɔ/-initial pronouns.

---

10 The analysis predicts the existence of another preposition /ɪgɔ/ that selects an /ɔ/-initial pronoun, although this has not been observed.

More evidence of the syntactic dependence of /nɔ/ comes from comparative sentences as shown in (11). The comparative sentence in (11a) strikingly contains two successive contact locative forms, /naŋ/ and /nɔ/. The first form /naŋ/ was previously used anaphorically ('on it') in (7b), but here it precedes and governs a standard-of-comparison noun (11a) or pronoun (11c), and thus it is functioning as a comparative preposition, analogous to the alternative comparative preposition /ɔkkɔ/ in (11b).[11] Either /naŋ/ or /nɔ/ can in fact be dropped in sentence (11a) leaving either one as the sole contact locative marker, just as they are also used alone in (11c) and (11d). Crucially, however, /nɔ/ cannot precede the preposition /naŋ/, but rather always occurs immediately next to the standard-of-comparison noun. Since the preceding comparative preposition /naŋ/ is also optional, /nɔ/ is specifically dependent on the following noun. This syntactic dependence is indicated here by the symbol " ÷ " to distinguish it from cliticisation " = ".

(11) Contact locatives as pivots of comparative sentences

a.

<Yok	icci	yoga	yüccek	nang	no	nok	inni.>
/j-ɔk	issi	j-ɔga	j-ussɛk	naŋ	nɔ	÷ n-ɔk	inni/
CL.SG-well	AGR:this	AGR-is	AGR-long	on	on	÷ CL.PL-well	AGR:this

'This well is deeper than these wells.'

b.

<Yok	icci	yoga	yüccek	okko	no	yok	yäre.>
/j-ɔk	issi	j-ɔga	j-ussɛk	ɔkkɔ	nɔ	÷ j-ɔk	j-ərɛ/
CL.SG-well	AGR:this	AGR-is	AGR-long	than	on	÷ CL.SG-well	AGR-that

'This well is deeper than that well.'

c.

<Yok	yäre	yoga	yüccek	nang	icci.>
/j-ɔk	j-ərɛ	j-ɔga	j-ussɛk	naŋ	issi/
CL.SG-well	AGR-that	AGR-is	AGR-long	on	AGR:this

'That well is deeper than this one.'

d.

<Yok	yäre	yoga	yüccek	no	yerek.>
/j-ɔk	j-ərɛ	j-ɔga	j-ussɛk	nɔ	÷ j-ɛrɛk/
CL.SG-well	AGR-that	AGR-is	AGR-long	on	÷ AGR-other

'That well is deeper than the other.'

[11] It follows that the earlier anaphoric usage of /naŋ/ postverbally in (7b) should be understood as an intransitive preposition. Payne, Huddleston and Pullum (2010:39–40) perform a similar analysis of intransitive use of prepositions in English such as <outside>.

The syntactic dependence of /nɔ÷/ on the standard-of-comparison noun is more reminiscent of incorporation than cliticisation as considered above. It is incorporation-like because the function of /nɔ÷/ with respect to the noun 'well' is schematic rather than literal. It does not locate something at or on the well, but rather links the well to a scale of depth, on which it is surpassed by another well. In fact, Acheron writers are disinclined to join <no> to the standard-of-comparison noun <yok>, so they do not count the schematic expression <no yok yäre> /nɔ÷j-ɔk j-ərɛ/ 'than that well' in the same class as lexicalised locative expressions that are joined as one word such as <ïyok> /ɪ-jɔk/ 'in the well' or <noˈrïräk> /nɔ-ʈɪrək/ 'sky'.[12]

The picture that emerges is that locative marking in Acheron tends to be dependent on the following noun stem, phonologically, morphologically, and syntactically, so that word boundary criteria tend not to support an analysis of locative markers as words. And yet, locatives also function as morphologically independent stems taking the pronoun-selecting suffixes /-ɔ/ and -/a/. It is this latter finding, of their morphological independence as stems, which are able to select different complements, that aligns with participants' emic perception of locative markers as distinct words.

5.4.4 Locative paradigms

The resulting paradigms for concealment and contact locatives are given in table 5.7. Most locative marking is built from the formatives /ɪ-/ and /n-/, which enter into both morphologically dependent prefixes and morphologically independent preposition words. Only the anaphoric prepositions /jik/ and /naŋ/ are not built from these formatives, but instead are derived from older symmetrical forms **tit* and **nan* by regular consonant changes (Norton and Alaki 2015:156).[13]

A similar paradigm arises for the comitative preposition /əŋ/ 'with' mentioned in § 5.4.2 and § 5.4.3. The stem /əŋ/ can take additional morphology before pronouns (/əŋa/, /əŋɔ/) and in anaphoric use (/nəŋəŋ/), so it is also a separate word morphologically. When before a noun, it tends to assimilate as in /əŋ=bəbu/ [əŋbəbu]~[əmbəbu] 'with the thing', but participants are aware that the nasal is phonemically velar and write it as velar as in <äng bäbü> for /əŋ=bəbu/. From this we infer that /əŋ/ is also a separate word phonologically, showing bridging to the next word by variable nasal assimilation.[14]

[12] The argument here is not as watertight, because oral versions of the comparative sentences have not been tested for emically acceptable pauses.

[13] Similar patterns of locative marking are found in other Talodi languages (Smits 2017:585, Norton 2018:14, 22–24).

[14] The comitative preposition /əŋ/ was prematurely suggested to be a prefix in Norton (2013:200), based on a lack of other VC words in Acheron. It cannot be a prefix, however, because it takes suffixes and is therefore a stem. Though not a prefix, it is a proclitic in its bare VC form, as it assimilates to a following noun.

Table 5.7. Acheron locative paradigms

Locatives	Concealment	Contact
Adverb prefixes	/ɪ-/	/n(ə)-/
Noun prefixes (irregular)	/ɪ-/	/nɔ-/
Noun prepositions	/ɪ/	/nɔ/
Pronoun prepositions	/ɪga/	/nana, nɔ/
Anaphoric prepositions	/jik/	/naŋ/

The most subtle distinction in the paradigm is between the homophonous prefixes and prepositions before nouns (/ɪ/ and /ɪ-/, /nɔ/ and /nɔ-/). Acheron participants claimed to be aware of the difference between locative markers that are spoken with a noun as one word, and locatives and nouns that are spoken as two words,[15] and both sides of this distinction were found here to be supportable by analogies to other structures of the language. The interpretation that there are locative noun prefixes is possible because some bound stems require /ɪ-/ or /nɔ-/, because there are other locative noun prefixes /jɔ-/ 'up at' and /d̪ɔ-/ 'down at', and because locative prefixes also occur in adverbs. Similarly, the interpretation that there are locative prepositions before nouns is possible, because locative prepositions also occur before pronouns. This interpretation is not well supported by word boundary criteria, because each preposition form is bound to a different syntactic context (noun/pronoun/anaphoric), except that in the eastern dialect /nɔ/ occurs before both nouns and pronouns. Rather, their word status is established by their morphological independence as stems. There may also be phonological support for word status from vowel lengthening [ɪː][nɔː] in phonologically independent locative prepositions, but this noncontrastive vowel length is in need of more investigation.

5.5 Conclusion

For Acheron preverbal inflection, collective agreement was obtained among participants on the answers to the four word-boundary tests based on pausing, bridging, isolability and separability. These produced consistent answers supporting an analysis of /ɔga/ (progressive) as a preceding helping verb, and /əga-/ (inceptive), /əd̪a-/ (negative) and /ɪja-/ (future) as verbal prefixation. Additional formal analysis likewise confirms that only /ɔga/ is a verb stem, capable of taking five different complements as a copula verb,

[15] This subtle difference of perception appears to be analogous to phonetically subtle contrasts in phonology that are within speakers' awareness but difficult for outsiders to detect, such as the Acheron rhotic contrast in [zɔrɔŋ] 'wing', [zɔɽɔŋ] 'mountain'.

taking past (/ɔga-k/) and imperative (/ɔga-wʊ/) suffixes, and including within itself the verb stem formatives /ɔ-/ and /-a/.

It is notable that the participatory word spacing method applied to preverbal inflections was not undermined by interference from spacing practices for the equivalent English auxiliaries. In particular, the testing of oral sentences in the language enabled participants to access their emic intuitions about word boundaries independently of written English. Neither were participants' judgements of word boundaries in oral sentences inconsistent or arbitrary. Rather, the intuitions about pauses were consistent with the results of other word boundary tests and other language-internal evidence. I conclude that the Acheron participants were able to access emic perceptions of word boundaries in oral sentences in their own language, and that this work converges on word boundaries in verb inflection that are cognitively plausible for the Acheron language.

For prenominal inflections /ɪ/ (concealment) and /nɔ/ (contact), the complexity of the problem was greater and the test results harder to interpret. Participants judge that locative inflection is joined to some nouns but not to others. Correspondingly, a locative paradigm for Acheron was described in which the locative formatives /ɪ-/ and /n-/ are employed in both prefixes and prepositional stems. The locative prefixes /ɪ-/ and /n-/ occur in some locative nouns and adverbs, which are judged and written as single words. On the other hand, the emic perception of independent locative preposition words, though not well supported by word boundary criteria, is nevertheless correlated with their morphological behaviour as stems, with pronoun-selecting suffixes /-ɔ/ and /-a/ and irregular reduplication in the preposition /nana/. This calls for a stem-based approach in which words are identified from within, at least in synthetic languages, as well as participatory oral sentence testing in which words are identified from their margins.

References

Bloomfield, Leonard. 1933. *Language*. New York: Holt.

Haspelmath, Martin. 2011. The indeterminacy of word segmentation and the nature of morphology and syntax. *Folia Linguistica* 45(1):31–80.

Kiparsky, Paul. 1985. Some consequences of Lexical Phonology. *Phonology Yearbook* 2:85–138.

Kutsch Lojenga, Constance. 1996. Participatory research in linguistics. *Notes on Linguistics* 73:13–27. www.sil.org/sites/default/files/kutschlojcommuninvolv1996.pdf.

Kutsch Lojenga, Constance. 2010. Participatory research in linguistics. Paper presented at the SIL Global Linguistics Forum, Vajta, Hungary, August 16–20, 2010.

Kutsch Lojenga, Constance. 2014. Basic principles for establishing word boundaries. In Michael Cahill and Keren Rice (eds.), *Developing orthographies for unwritten languages*, 73–106. Publications in Language Use and Education 6. Dallas, TX: SIL International.

Norton, Russell. 1995. Variation and change in the phonology of Asheron. MA thesis. University of Essex.

Norton, Russell. 2000. The noun classes of Asheron. *Occasional Papers in the study of Sudanese Languages* 8:23–55. www.sil.org/resources/archives/35940.

Norton, Russell. 2013. The Acheron vowel system: A participatory approach. In Roger Blench and Thilo Schadeberg (eds.), *Nuba Mountain language studies*, 195–218. Cologne: Rüdiger Köppe. Also available through SIL archives.

Norton, Russell. 2018. Parallel grammar documentation in four Talodi languages. *Afrikanistik-Aegyptologie-Online*. Vol. 2018. https://journals.ub.uni-koeln.de/index.php/AAeo/article/view/3457.

Norton, Russell, and Thomas Kuku Alaki. 2015. The Talodi languages: A comparative-historical analysis. *Occasional Papers in the study of Sudanese Languages* 11:47–161. www.sil.org/resources/archives/63566.

Payne, John, Rodney Huddleston, and Geoffrey K. Pullum. 2010. The distribution and category status of adjectives and adverbs. *Word Structure* 3.1:31–81.

Smits, Heleen. 2007. Notes on the description of topological scenes in Lumun. Term paper. Leiden University.

Smits, Heleen. 2017. *A grammar of Lumun: A Kordofanian language of Sudan.* Leiden: Netherlands Graduate School of Linguistics.

Spencer, Andrew. 2012. Identifying stems. *Word Structure* 5.1:88–108

Williamson, Kay. 1984. *Practical orthography in Nigeria*. Ibadan: Heinemann.

6
Orthographic Word Difficulties in Central Chadic Languages

Shannon Yee and Ginger Boyd

Abstract

While best practice in orthography development generally prefers a consistent word image, the mutability of vowels and words in Chadic languages, typically based on their position in an utterance, complicates this task. In this chapter, we look at how speakers and orthography developers of four Central Chadic languages of Cameroon – Mafa [maf], Zulgo [gnd], Guɗe [gde], and Jimjimən [jim] – have tackled the problems of vowel mutability and word divisions, particularly with respect to how noun phrase elements such as the plural, possessive, and demonstrative markers, the verbal subject/mood complex, and the interrogative clause marker are analysed and orthographically encoded in these four languages. Ultimately, even though the mutability of vowels is a major complication in determining how to write these languages, it is not the best indicator of the status of morphemes as affixes or clitics, and therefore of where word breaks should be written. The more effective indicators for word divisions are whether the formative is cohesive or noncohesive, and whether it is restricted or unrestricted as to the syntactic category to which it can attach.

Abbreviations

-	affix	IPFV	imperfective aspect
=	clitic	LINK	linker
1	1st person	LOC	locative marker
2	2nd person	M	masculine
3	3rd person	NEG	negative
ADL	adlative	PFV	perfective aspect
ANT	anterior	PL	plural
AOR	aorist aspect	PLUR	pluractional
DEM	demonstrative	POSS	possessive
DEST	destinative case	PREP	preposition marker
DIR	directional	PST	past tense
DO	direct object marker	PUR	purpose marker
ERG	ergative	Q	interrogative marker, question
F	feminine	REM	remote
FOC	focus	RESTR	restrictive focus (“only”; “just”)
FUT	future	S	singular
GEN	genitive	SBJ	subject marker
HORT	hortative	SUB	subordinate
INCL	inclusive	SFX	suffix
INDEF	indefinite	VOL	volitional
IO	indirect object		

6.1 The conflict between linguistic analysis and orthography development

While good linguistic research, especially in the domains of phonology and morphosyntax, is essential to good orthography development, there are points where linguistics in and of itself does not go far enough. A good orthography essentially needs to be “(a) linguistically sound, (b) acceptable to all stakeholders, (c) teachable, and (d) easy to reproduce” (Cahill and Karan 2008:3). Too often the linguist analyses the language well but does not consider the other aspects to be equally as important as good linguistic analysis. Unfortunately, what is acceptable to the stakeholders may not be at all linguistically sound, and what is linguistically sound may not be so easy to teach or reproduce. Many of these conflicts are found in trying to develop good orthographies in Chadic languages, such as when words are pronounced differently in isolation than in the context of natural speech. "Those making orthography decisions need to consider how to symbolize these words – as they occur in isolation or as they are pronounced in context" (Cahill and Karan 2008:5). However, it is generally held that keeping a consistent word image is preferable for ease of both reading and writing. Cahill and Karan (2008:5) illustrate this challenge with an example from Kɔnni [kma], a Gur (Niger-Congo) language of Ghana, (1). They state that both /ɪ/ and /ʊ/ are independent phonemes, and that the alteration for the verb *give* is phonologically conditioned.

(1) Kɔnni[1] (Cahill and Karan 2008:5)

[yɪ́	bà]	'give them'
give	3PL	
[yʊ́	wà]	'give him'
give	3S	

They further write: "A strictly phonemic orthography would write *give* in two different ways. However, for spelling, the better option is to keep an invariant <yɪ> in both cases. Keeping the form of a word constant when an underlying phoneme changes to another phoneme is what has been termed a 'lexical' representation" (Cahill and Karan 2008:5). We refer to this here as keeping a consistent word image.

Many, if not most, Chadic languages exhibit vowel/word mutability. Many words vary according to their position in the sentence. In isolation or in phrase-final position, they have a fuller form than when the same word is in phrase-medial position. So, vowel mutability is not as much a phonological conditioning caused by an adjacent phoneme as it is a characteristic of Chadic vowels in general.

6.2 The problem of vowel mutability in Chadic orthography

The orthography of many Chadic languages is rendered difficult due to the mutability of vowels which is caused by a variety of factors such as palatalisation, labialisation, or the position in the sentence, whether they occur before a pause or not. This mutability of vowels occurs in the following

[1] In cited material, we are using the exact representation given by the author(s), even when this does not follow IPA but rather an Africanist variety of IPA. For example, in Africanist tradition, the semivowel<y> is often written phonetically as [y] rather than [j]. In our own data, the IPA symbols are used. Likewise, tone markings are included where they are part of the source material.

contexts: (1) when a suffix is added; (2) when an enclitic is added, and even (3) between full lexical words. The discussion about what a word is, therefore, is complicated and "[t]here is no algorithm for the segmentation of a stretch of speech into words" (Pike and Pike 1982:98).

The mutability of vowels cannot inform what is or is not a phonological word in many Chadic languages, so decisions on how to segment speech orthographically vary from language to language. For Chadic languages, trying to keep a consistent word image often means writing words as they occur in isolation regardless of the changes that occur when the word is put in context in a sentence. For this language family, "isolation forms" are those which occur before a pause, and vowels before a pause are always fully realised. In contrast, vowels found in "nonpausal" positions, in context, are weakened to a close vowel at the same point of articulation (Barreteau and Le Bléis 1990:21). However, there are exceptions, including the question of what to do with clitics.

Clitics are complicated because they may have elements of a grammatical word, but often are dependent on a host word phonologically. "[They] may sometimes form part of a host phonological word for purposes of assignment of prosodic features (such as stress and vowel harmony) ... More often, they are simply added – as an extra, unstressed syllable – to a fully articulated phonological word after all processes and rules have applied" (Dixon and Aikhenvald 2002:25). We find both tendencies in the clitics of Chadic languages studied here.

The following subsections look at how four Central Chadic languages handle the mutability of vowels in the orthography: Mafa, Zulgo, Guɗe, and Jimjimən. Some of these decisions are based on how the linguists involved analysed the languages. The four languages discussed here come from two subgroups of Central Chadic: 1) Mafa and Zulgo are both of the Afro-Asiatic, Chadic, Biu-Mandara, A.A5[2] language group, and 2) Guɗe and Jimjimən are both of the Afro-Asiatic, Chadic, Biu-Mandara, A.A8 language group. Mafa, Zulgo, and Guɗe have had orthographies[3] for many decades; the fourth, Jimjimən, is in the process of making these orthographic word decisions.

6.2.1 A synopsis of Central Chadic phonology

Chadic (196 languages) is the largest of the six families found in the Afro-Asiatic phylum (381 languages). Within the Chadic family there are four branches: West Chadic, East Chadic, Masa and Central Chadic, also known as Biu-Mandara (79 languages). The Central Chadic languages are spoken

[2] This is the manner of language classification for Afro-Asiatic languages.

[3] Linguistic work dates back to the 1970s for Zulgo and Guɗe, and even earlier for Mafa. All three languages have a published New Testament.

in northeastern Nigeria, northern Cameroon, and the western part of Chad (Eberhard et al. 2024; Gravina 2014:8–9).

Central Chadic languages tend to have approximately thirty consonants and two or three phonemic vowels, /a/, /ə/, and /i/, along with two additional phonological features, commonly referred to as “prosodies”: palatalisation and labialisation. These prosodies may produce six or eight surface, phonetic vowels. The term “prosody” in Chadic linguistics refers to suprasegmental features involving secondary articulation which are the property of the entire phonological word, affecting both vowels and consonants depending on the specifics of the language (Bow 1999; Gravina 2014).

These prosodies of palatalisation and labialisation may affect vowels (causing a system of vowel harmony), consonants (causing a complex system of labialised and palatalised consonants), or both vowels and consonants, with elements of both vowel prosody and consonant prosody combined in a mixed prosody system. Example (2) illustrates a prototypical Chadic prosody system with data from Moloko [mlw], a Biu-Mandara A.A5 language with a mixed prosody system, affecting both consonants and vowels. These examples come from personal research on this language, but the first three examples are also found in Bow 1999.

(2) Moloko (adapted from Bow 1999:19; Boyd personal data)

No prosody	/kra/	[kəra]	‘dog’
Palatalisation	/kra^{y}/	[kirɛ]	‘stake/post’
Labialisation	/kra^{w}/	[k^{w}urɔ]	‘ten’
Palatalisation	/slak^{y}/	[silek]	‘jealousy’
Palatalisation with a labialised consonant	/slak^{wy}/	[silœkw]	‘broom’

The palatalisation prosody on vowels means that an epenthetic vowel is pronounced as [i] and /a/ is pronounced as [ɛ] or [e]. The labialisation prosody results in consonants with a secondary articulation of [^{w}] and in rounding of vowels to [u]. These prosodies can interact, such that the phoneme /a/ is manifested as [œ] when the environment contains a prosody of palatalisation in connection with /w/ or labialised consonants.

6.2.2 Mafa

Mafa is spoken by between 500,000 (Kosack 2001) and 1,000,000 (Perevet 2008) people. The Protestant Church has a seventy-year history of writing Mafa and published a New Testament in 1965. The Catholic Church published their version of the New Testament in 1994.[4] The Catholic orthography writes phonetically, representing all vowels in their surface form depending on their position in the word, and all with surface tone, whereas the Protestant orthography, developed by an SIL linguist,[5] recommends maintaining a consistent word image with respect to vowels and does not write tone, as illustrated by the following quote from the Protestant/SIL orthography guide (Gravina et al. 2006):

> *In the middle of a sentence, there are often changes in pronunciation of the vowels of a word. But in the writing system, we don't write these changes.* We always write the form of the word used when pronounced in isolation. [emphasis added][6]

However, in practice the recommendation for a consistent word image for vowels is not always followed, as users of both orthographies, as well as the primers developed in collaboration with SIL and the Protestant Church, write words as they sound in context so that, depending on the position of a word in the sentence, the majority[7] of Mafa words will have two different spellings. The orthographic ideal of preserving a consistent word image is unfortunately lost in both Mafa orthographies, as seen in example (3)[8] taken from a Mafa primer. In this example, the verb has two different spellings

---

[4] "In fact, the work of Barreteau that the Catholics used was published in 1990 in a document called 'Lexique Mafa'. But well before that date, some smaller documents were published. Research on Mafa goes back to 1948 with a Protestant pastor, Eichenberger Hans, who was leading the Protestant side of the New Testament Bible translation. Authors, like Barreteau and Le Bléis, began in the 1970s" (p.c. Dadak Ndokobaï, 04/09/2021).

[5] Mafa has never been an SIL project, but some SIL linguists have helped the community when approached. This orthography is a revision of the orthography used by Hans Eichenberger and in the 1965 New Testament translation.

[6] « Au milieu d'une phrase, il y a souvent des changements de prononciation des voyelles d'un mot. Mais dans l'orthographe on n'écrit pas ces changements. On écrit toujours la forme du mot utilisée quand on prononce le mot seul » (Gravina et al. 2006:8, translation by Shannon Yee).

[7] Barreteau and Le Bléis (1990:24) write: « les noms variables sont de loin les plus fréquents ». "Variable nouns are by far the most common" (translation by Shannon Yee).

[8] While this example comes from the Protestant/SIL orthography, the same is true for the Catholic orthography. The Mafa community is working at harmonising the two Mafa orthographies.

based on its position in the sentence,[9] <ɓora> before a pause, or in isolation (3a), and <ɓorə> in the middle of the sentence or utterance (3b) and (3c).

(3) Mafa (COLACMA and SIL 2014:27)

a.	<A Mala a m **ɓora.**>	'And Mala (proper name) **aims at** it.'
b.	<Mala a **ɓorə** me?>	'What does Mala **aim at**?'
c.	<A **ɓorə** mangayak.>	'He **aims at** a big bird.'

Figure 6.1 and example (4) from a second Mafa primer, show that a single noun is written <fakaway> as the isolation form but <fakawiy> within a sentence, following pronunciation.

Figure 6.1. Mafa (COLACMA and SIL 2018:19, 23).
(Mafa figure used with permission)

(4) From Mafa (COLACMA and SIL 2018:19, 23)

a.	<**fakaway**>	'elephant' (in isolation)
b.	<**fakawiy**>	'elephant' (in context)
c.	<A viya, **fakawiy** a ndiy nyiy waf.>	'The elephant eats fruits in rainy season.'

6.2.3 Zulgo

Like Mafa, Zulgo, a language of 26,000 speakers (Eberhard et al. 2024), has been written for several decades. The New Testament was first published in 1988. Zulgo is combined with Gemzek in the *Ethnologue* (Eberhard et al. 2024),

[9] One of the challenges faced in our area and context, is the need for greater collaboration between literacy consultants and linguists. Linguists could have more involvement in the development of literacy materials and literacy specialists could provide more feedback concerning areas of difficulty in proposed orthographies.

but more recent work on Gemzek indicates that although closely related, there are differences between the two speech varieties, especially in the vowel system (Gravina et al. 2005:1).

With respect to the orthographic representation of vowel mutability, in his earlier work on Zulgo, Haller (1984:49–50) comments:

> Is neutralization of the low vowel /a/ to be written or not? There is one case where people react strongly against writing it, and that is between two major phonological words. For instance, /sā yām/ 'drink water' is phonetically realized as [sīām], *has to be spelled <sa yam> and not <si yam>. So, for writing major phonological words, we always write the "basic" form.* The problem is more complicated for minor phonological words, since they are phonologically bound to the major phonological word, and yet often they are grammatically free (clitics). Whenever major and minor phonological words are written as one word, which is the case for affixes, then of course neutralization has to be signalled. [emphasis added]

However, this policy has changed and later, Haller (2020:11) writes:

> In the proposed orthography, we always write words as they appear in the middle of a sentence. But before a pause, the close vowels in a final syllable are pronounced differently, that is, with the corresponding open vowels.
>
> Examples:
> <sik> 'foot' before a pause is pronounced with [e]
> <gər> 'head' before a pause is pronounced with [a]
> <bur> 'grinding stone' before a pause is pronounced [o]
> <gus> 'thigh' before a pause is pronounced with [wa]
> <kur> 'stone' before a pause is pronounced with [wa], etc.[10]

---

[10] Dans l'orthographe proposée, nous écrivons les mots toujours tels qu'ils se présentent au milieu d'une phrase. Mais avant une pause, les voyelles fermées dans une syllabe finale sont prononcées différemment, c'est-à-dire avec des voyelles ouvertes correspondants.

Exemples:
<sik> « pied » avant une pause est prononce avec [e]
<gər> « tête » avant une pause est prononce avec [a]
<bur> « pierre à écraser » avant une pause est prononcé [o]
<gus> « cuisse » avant une pause est prononcé avec [wa]
<kur> « pierre » avant une pause est prononcé avec [wa], etc. (translation by Shannon Yee).

6.2.4 Guɗe

Guɗe is spoken by 68,000 people in Nigeria and 20,000 in Cameroon (Eberhard et al. 2024). Guɗe is more agglutinating than the languages discussed above. Although there are other important differences between the A.A5 and the A.A8 languages, they both have word-division issues. As Menetrey and Perrin (2006:8) state in their orthography statement, certain grammatical words are written together "... where the conjunction implies phenomena of elision and/or a change in the quality of the vowel."[11]

These forms include prepositions such as "and", "with", "for", and certain grammatical elements such as the markers of the possessive or imperative or the marker of the direct object. These elements join with the first and second person plural pronouns and are written together with the pronoun. Example (5) shows the direct object marker <tə> as well as the preposition <ka> 'for' in their joint forms with the first and second person plural pronouns.

(5) Guɗe conjunctive writing of grammatical elements (Menetrey and Perrin 2006:8)

a. <taamə>
/tə amə/
DO 1PL.INCL
'us'

b. <koonə>
/ka wənə/
for 2PL
'for you'

The pausal and nonpausal phonetic effect in Guɗe is slightly different from the effects illustrated for Zulgo and Mafa. Hoskison (1983:23) identifies two classes of nouns in Guɗe as "free" and "captive", where the captive nouns have a required nasal suffix that the free nouns do not. Lengthening of the final /a/ in pausal position occurs in the free nouns, but this is not represented in the orthography. However, some free nouns vary the final vowel /ə ~ a/, and for those nouns, both forms are represented in the orthography, including when /ə/ is labialised to [u] or palatalised to [i], as illustrated in table 6.1.

[11] « ...dont la conjonction implique des phénomènes d'élision et/ou un changement dans la qualité de la voyelle. » (Menetrey and Perrin 2006:8, translation by Ginger Boyd).

Table 6.1. Guɗe free nouns (Hoskison 1983)

Orthographic	Pausal	Nonpausal	Example
<zəma ~ zəmə> 'food'	/zəma:/	/zəmə/	<see waatə zəmə cii kəya ka tii> 'it was only food he was bringing to them' (Hoskison 1983:135–136)
<kuzəna ~ kuzənə> 'grass'	/kə^{w}zəna:/	/kə^{w}zənə/	<kə ndzaa rəhunəagi kuzəna> 'the snake is in the grass' (Hoskison 1983:81)
<nwanwa ~ nwanwu> 'chief'	/n^{w}an^{w}a:/	/n^{w}anə^{w}/	<iirə makinə nga nwanwu bəra'i> 'two old wives of the chief' (Hoskison 1983:51)

Captive nouns have a semantically empty suffix /-nə/ added to the noun in nonpausal position. This nonpausal form is treated by Hoskison (1983:24–25) as the word root. In the pausal form, the final vowel of this suffix is not pronounced, but the /n/ remains. The Guɗe orthography recommends writing the full nonpausal form of the suffix as part of the word even though the final vowel is not pronounced before a pause, see table 6.2. The final example also shows that before another suffix, such as the demonstrative /-ta/, this /-nə/ suffix is deleted entirely (Hoskison 1983:24) and the root-final vowel lengthened.

Table 6.2. Guɗe captive nouns (Hoskison 1983)

Position	Form	Example
Pausal	[min] /m^{y}ə-nə/	<gusə nə **minə**> 'woman is short' (Hoskison 1983:16–17, 54)
Nonpausal	[minə] /m^{y}ə-nə/	<...pooshi **minə** ca luuvəka kya dzə ka ndzaanə də maɗəfənə> '...there was no woman who would agree to go live with hunger' (Hoskison 1983:140–141).
With suffix (e.g., /-ta/)	[mi:ta] /m^{y}ə-ta/	<**miita**>[a] 'that woman' (Hoskison 1983:24)

[a] Menetrey and Perrin (2006:4) have this word written as <meeta> /ma^{y}ə-ta/.

6.2.5 Jimjimən

Jimjimən is a language spoken by approximately 10,000 people in Cameroon along the border with Nigeria (Eberhard et al. 2024). At the end of 2017, participatory phonological research with members of the Jimjimən community was started. More intensive participatory research has been done more recently in 2020 and 2021, which has led to the writing of a draft phonology/orthography statement for Jimjimən (Boyd 2021). This collaborative phonological work is still ongoing.

Jimjimən, like many other Chadic languages, also has two nominal phonological forms, pausal and nonpausal, which can create difficulties with maintaining a consistent word image. Jimjimən has a large class of nouns with a semantically empty nasal suffix /-ə́n/ somewhat similar to Hoskison’s (1983:23) captive nouns in Guɗe. The Jimjimən suffix differs from Guɗe phonologically; in Guɗe, the suffix is /-nə/ and the vowel is elided before a pause, while in Jimjimən, the suffix is /ə́n/ and the nasal consonant is elided in nonpausal positions. In example (6), [d͡ʒə̀xún] /d͡ʒə̀xʷ-ə́n/ ‘horse’ retains its /-ə́n/ suffix since it is in pausal position, but [báʔí] /báʔʲə́n/ ‘back’ is in nonpausal position and so has no nasal suffix pronounced. The nasal is written in both pausal and nonpausal positions in the proposed orthography.

(6) Jimjimən (adapted from Gnintedem and Viljoen 2020:2; Boyd 2021:34)

<a ba’in jəhun>

[à	báʔí	d͡ʒə̀xún]
/à	báʔʲ-ə́n	dzʲə̀xʷ-ə́n/
LOC	back-SFX	horse-SFX

‘on the horse’

The proposal in the Jimjimən orthography guide to always write the noun with the full semantically empty suffix is similar to the choice made in the Guɗe orthography. However, there are modifications to the noun itself or the noun phrase, such as plural markers, possessive adjectives, and demonstratives, as well as pronouns and the use of prepositional phrases with pronouns, that can pose bigger orthographic challenges in each of these languages.

6.3 Clitics or affixes: One word or two?

Clitics are a particular challenge when it comes to a definition of the word, especially in terms of orthographic representation.

> In one sense, clitics are simply PHONOLOGICALLY BOUND WORDS, [that] are phonologically dependent on their objects. In the other, [...] clitics are CATEGORIALLY UNRESTRICTED BOUND FORMATIVES, i.e., formatives that are unrestricted as to the syntactic category of the word they attach to. In this they contrast with AFFIXES, which are usually more selective in what host they take. (Bickel and Nichols 2007:174–175)

Orthographies treat clitics differently. In French, the object pronoun clitic is written as a separate word from a following auxiliary verb even though it forms an indissoluble phonological and grammatical unit with the auxiliary verb. For example, in the sentence: <il les a vus> ‘he saw them’, the direct object <les> ‘them’, and the auxiliary verb <a> ‘have’, cannot be syntactically interrupted by an adverb (Anderson 1985:154). However, because the object pronoun can correspond to a full phrase, e.g., <(il a vu) les gens dont j’ai parlé> ‘(he saw) the people that I talked about’, intuition is that <les> ought to be a separate word.

In contrast with French, in the Papuan language Kâte [kmg], the case marker clitic attaches to whichever word (bolded) ends a noun phrase (in brackets) in example (7). From the information provided,[12] presumably the clitic is written attached to its host in Kâte.

(7) Kâte (Pilhofer 1933 cited in Bickel and Nichols 2007:175)

a.	[$_{NP}$ e=le	**fiʔ**]=**ko**	mi	fe-naŋ!	
	3S=DEST	house=ADL	NEG	climb-1PL.HORT	
	‘Let’s not climb into HIS house!’ (Pilhofer 1933:113)				
b.	[$_{NP}$ ŋiʔ	**moʔ-moʔ=sawa**]=**tsi**		e-mbiŋ	
	man	INDEF-INDEF=RESTR=ERG		do-3PL.REM.PST	
	‘Only some of the men did it.’ (Pilhofer 1933:110)				
c.	[$_{NP}$ ŋiʔ	wiaʔ	**e-weʔ**]=**tsi**	dzika	ki-steyeʔ
	man	thing	do-3S.REM.PST=ERG	sword	bite-3S.REM.VOL
	‘The man who did these things should be killed (lit., should bite the sword)’ (Pilhofer 1933:142)				

[12] While we might be comparing apples with oranges with this example, very little orthographic description of Kâte has been found. Only one clear reference to orthographic word breaks has been found in Litteral (1979:101), where she states: “Decisions made concerning word breaks [in the dictionary being reviewed] also seem inconsistent. For instance, the verbalizer *ezo* is sometimes connected and at other times separated from the verb root…” She then gives as examples five entries from page 191 of the dictionary, of which four have the verbalizer attached to the verb, and in one the verbalizer is written separately.

Given the complexity of defining a word linguistically, and the conflicts among the defining criteria, is it any surprise that encoding the word orthographically would be likewise complex and messy, especially as it concerns morphemes such as clitics?

In this survey of four Central Chadic orthographies, five grammatical contexts will be discussed: (1) the subject/mood complex in verb conjugations, (2) nominal plural markers, (3) possessives, (4) demonstratives on nouns, and (5) interrogatives. While possessives, demonstratives and interrogatives are often considered to be clitics, the subject/mood complex and the nominal plural markers are variously analysed as either affixes or clitics, and the decisions concerning how to write them vary as well. Generally, where the grammatical element is analysed as an affix, it is written conjunctively; where it is analysed as a clitic, it is written as a separate word.

6.3.1 Subject/mood complex

The subject/mood complex in many Chadic languages is affected by the spread of a prosody (either palatalisation or labialisation or both, depending on the language).[13] Viljoen (2013:110) notes for the Buwal language [bhs] (Afro-Asiatic, Chadic, Biu-Mandara, A.A7):

> There are not many morphophonemic processes in Buwal which can aid in determining word breaks, so at times the choices in this area are somewhat arbitrary. However, there are a number of principles that have been identified that contribute to developing conventions in this area. These are: (i) palatalisation spread, (ii) tonal changes and (iii) morphological independence.

Others, such as Haller (1984:49) for Zulgo, see the subject/mood complexes as "minor phonological words", "...since they are phonologically bound to the major phonological word, and yet often they are grammatically free (clitics)..." While Haller identifies the subject/mood complexes as clitics, he also indicates that

> there are a few exceptions to this rule, for instance in the case of the subject-mood pronouns. It is a delicate question of whether or not these should be written as separate words. Whereas the subject-mood pronouns of highlighted events can be defined as clitics, the subject-mood pronouns of

[13] In Chadic linguistics, tense, aspect, mood, or a combination of these are sometimes marked on the "weak subject pronoun" through prosodic patterns, tone, vowel length modifications, or other not easily segmented markers. Thus, the convention is to treat the subject pronoun and the TAM marker as a fused subject/mood complex, as it is often an agreement marker rather than a true subject pronoun (Newman 2009:628).

> general and specific events occur in one grammatical slot only, namely preceding the verb stem. (Haller 1984:49)

He does not give a clear rationale as to why the "subject-mood pronouns of general and specific events" should be considered as clitics rather than as prefixes. If, as it seems, they do assimilate to the palatalisation of the verb as well as fill only "one grammatical slot", they may act more like prefixes, see example (8).

(8) Zulgo subject/mood complex (bolded) and verb prosody (adapted from Haller 1980:15–16)

a.	[**ạ́**ṿ́l̪ár pɛ́tɛ́k]	/**á**-vəlár ^{y}pá^{y}ták/	'He gave her a dress.'
b.	[**ɛ̄**hŕa x̣ə́^{n}d̪áv]	/**ā**-^{y}hər-á hə́^{n}dáv/	'He is skinning the hare.'
c.	[**ḳú**ḳūr̄s fɛ́t]	/**ká**-^{w}kārə̄s ^{y}fə́t/	'He gathered it all.'

Despite the fact that these subject/mood complexes must always be present even when there is a full subject noun (thus acting more as subject agreement prefixes than pronouns), speakers of Central Chadic languages see these as independent pronouns and want to write them disjunctively as a result.[14] This is possibly influenced by the French grammar they learned at school.

For instance, Mafa people prefer to write these subject/mood complexes as separate words even though they co-occur with full subject nouns and assimilate phonologically, as would a prefix. This is seen from the imperfective verb form (Gravina et al. 2006:7) and results in different vowel realisations within the subject/mood complex, as shown in table 6.3.

Table 6.3. Mafa subject/mood complex and verb palatalisation /par/ 'gather'

Person	Imperfective		Perfective	
1s	<yi pere>	[yípere]	<yi pora>	[yipora]
2s	<ka pere>	[képere]	<ka pora>	[kapora]
3s	<a pere>	[épere]	<m pora>	[mpora]
1PL	<nga pere>	[ᵑgépere]	<nga pora>	[ᵑgapora]
2PL	<kine pere>	[kinépere]	<kine pora>	[kinepora]
3PL	<ta pere>	[tépere]	<ta pora>	[tapora]

When there is a full subject noun present in Mafa, the subject/mood complex is still obligatory. The noun phrases in (9) are bolded, including

[14] This is the case for Hausa [hau] in West Chadic as well (Newman 2000), where the "subject agree prefixes" are written as separate words.

the subject/mood complex, while the verbs along with the subject/mood complex are underlined.

(9) Mafa full subject nouns and subject/mood complex (adapted from COLACMA and SIL 2018:19)

a. <**Kuza** a ficə cam cam.>

Kuza	a	ficə	cam cam.
grass	3s	grow	rapidly

'The grass grows rapidly.'

b. <**Nda Mbəlama a mesə nə Ngelew** ta de a civiɗ tə hesekeɗ.>

Nda Mbəlama a mesə nə Ngelew	ta	de	a civiɗ tə hesekeɗ.
Mbelama and his father-in-law Ngelew	3PL	walk	along path in bush

'Mbelama and his father-in-law, Ngelew, walk along the path in the bush.'

In Zulgo, as in Mafa, the subject/mood complex takes on the prosody of the host and is required even with full subject nouns. Being both cohesive and syntactically restricted, the subject/mood complex acts more like a prefix, but the community preferred to write it disjunctively from the verb.

(10) Zulgo full subject nouns and subject/mood complex (adapted from Haller 2020:16)

a. <**Awis** a zəm hinne.> 'The knife is very sharp.'

b. <**Gàmburma** tə da a Tokombéré.> 'The people went to Tokombere.'

Haller (1984:49–50) states that for Zulgo, "affixes are always spelled in their modified form together with the major phonological word, whereas clitics are written in their basic form,[15] as separate words." However, the Zulgo stakeholders at the time "preferred the neutralized instead of the basic form in the orthography." Therefore, the decision was made to write <tə da> instead of <ta da> 'they went'.

In Guɗe, the subject/mood complex is not required with full subject nouns and the subject morphemes are written as separate words from the tense, aspect, and mood morphemes, with one exception. The aorist marker /-a-/ is written attached to the subject morpheme (Menetrey and Perrin 2006:9). This marker phonologically merges with the subject morpheme, as evidenced by the elision of the intervening vowel, and the decision was to write it merged with the subject morpheme, as in (11).

[15] Haller's (1984) term, "basic form" refers to how the word is pronounced (and by extension written) in isolation, as in a dictionary entry.

(11) Guɗe aorist verb form (adapted from Menetrey and Perrin 1992:8–9)

<Ca palə.>
[t͡ʃapalə]
/ t͡səʲ-a-palə/
3S-AOR-leave
'He leaves.'

Subject clitics "are categorially unrestricted bound formatives" (Bickel and Nichols 2007:174–175) and can attach to a number of different types of words. In Jimjimən, the subject formatives often form part of the preverbal subject/mood complex that indicates some part of the tense, aspect, and/or mood (TAM) as well as person, gender, and number of the subject, but can also occur separately. Due to being cohesive but grammatically unrestricted, they are analysed as subject clitics. Morphophonologically, preverbal subject clitics and TAM markers combine with either the verb root or other TAM markers, such as the anterior marker <wa>, but subject clitics can also follow the verb in certain verbal forms in Jimjimən. These subject clitics are phonologically attached to that word as exhibited by the spread of palatalisation from the host word to the clitic. In example (12), the subject clitic attaches to the TAM marker to make a subject/mood complex; the anterior is formed of a discontinuous morpheme /wa = SBJ-kə-/ which attaches to a perfective palatalised verb. It is also possible for the subject clitic to attach to the verb itself in the case of the perfective, as shown in (13). The subject clitics are bolded.

(12) Jimjimən subject clitic attached to preverbal TAM marker

<Wa**c** kəzhim ɗafan.>

[wa**t͡ʃ**kəʒim	ɗafan]
/wa = **tsəʲ**-kə- zəmʲ	ɗafan/
ANT = **3S.M**-ANT-eat.PFV	dinner

'He ate dinner.'

(13) Jimjimən subject clitic attached to verb (adapted from Boyd 2021:45)

<Zhimi**c** ɗafan.>

[ʒimi**t͡ʃ**	ɗafan]
/zəmʲ = **tsəʲ**	ɗafan/
eat.PFV = **3S.M**	dinner

'He ate dinner.'

In Jimjimən, the subject clitic is not obligatory and does not co-occur with a fully expressed subject noun phrase, as in (14), where, as also seen in the previous examples, the anterior marker /wa/ combines with the subject clitic to form the anterior subject/mood complex when the noun is not explicitly stated.

(14) Jimjimən (adapted from Boyd 2021:46)

a. <Wa hun kəfuyk.>

[wa	xún	kəfyk]
/wa	xún	kə- fəʷkʲ/
ANT	goat	ANT-fall.PFV

'The goat fell.'

b. <Wa**c** kəfuyk.>

[wat͡ʃkəfyk]

/wa=**tsəʲ**-kə-fəʷkʲ/

ANT=**3S.M**-ANT-fall.PFV

'He/it fell.'

The subject clitic also combines phonologically with negative marker /paʔ/ and is written conjunctively, (15).

(15) Jimjimən negative with subject morpheme (Yee 2021:87)

<**Pa**h ɗir pwaan nga fun.>

[**pa**xɗir pʷaːnᵑgafun]

/**paʔ**=x	ɗərʲ	pʷaːn	ᵑga	fəʷn/
NEG=2S	buy.PFV	fruit	GEN	tree

'You shouldn't have bought fruit.'

This subject clitic is phonologically similar to the subject pronoun, but forms a phonological unit with the anterior marker, as shown by the elision in (16). The first person singular subject clitic [=ɲə] may undergo an additional contraction where even the subject clitic is elided and the vowel of the anterior marker /wa/ is palatalised before a palatalised verb root, resulting in [we]. Some community members prefer to write /wa=ɲə-kəʲ-/ with its contracted subject clitic as a single word <wek>, and others want to write it as two words. The subject/mood complex is bolded in example (16).

(16) Jimjimən subject clitic orthography options (Yee 2021:18)

<**Wek** zhim ɗafan.> / <**Wany kəzhim** ɗafan.>

[**wek**ʒim ɗafan]

/**wa = ɲə-kə**-zəmʲ ɗafan/

ANT = 1S-ANT-eat.PFV dinner

'I ate dinner.'

Some linguistically informed members of the community prefer to write subject clitics as well as the TAM markers as separate from the verb stem. Even so, some aspectual information, such as the above-mentioned anterior /kə-/, the aorist /a-/, and the imperfective /ka-/, is being written with the verb stem.

The Jimjimən aorist form consists of a vowel marker /a-/ between the subject and the verb root with elision of the final vowel of the subject clitic in the subject/mood complex. Due to the position of the aorist marker /a-/ being after the subject, and native speaker intuition which connects it more closely to the verb root than to the subject, the language community prefers to write the subject clitic as a separate word, keeping the aorist marker attached to the verb and not to the subject pronoun, see examples (17) and (18). This decision is different than that which the Guɗe community took with a similar verbal marker as shown in example (11).

(17) Jimjimən (Yee 2021:20)

<Nyə **a**zəm ɗafan.>

[ɲ**a**zəm ɗafan]

/ɲə = **a**-zəm ɗafan/

1S = **AOR**-eat dinner

'I eat dinner.'

(18) Jimjimən (Yee 2021:21)

<Hən **a**titiwu.>

[xən**a**titiwu]

/xən-**a**-təʲtəʲwə/

3PL-**AOR**-cry.PLUR

'They cry and cry.'

In the imperfective aspect, the subject/mood complex and the verb are contracted, making a single phonological word, as in examples (19) and (20). Like with the anterior marker /wa/ the community members prefer to write the imperfective /ka-/ conjunctively with the element to which it attaches, (20).

(19) Jimjimən imperfective attached to subject morpheme clitic (Yee 2021:16)

< **Ka**ny afuk. >

[**ka**ɲafuk]

/**ka** = ɲə-a-fəʷk/

IPFV = 1S-AOR-fall

'I'm falling.'

(20) Jimjimən imperfective attached to verb (Yee 2021:60)

< Shendiin **ka**həd zuukun. >

[ʃendi:n	**ka**xəd	zu:kun]
/sʲand-i:n	**ka**-xəd	zə:ʷkəʷn/
girl-PL	IPFV-grind	millet

'The girls are grinding millet.'

Writing the imperfective marker /ka-/ attached to the verb also helps to differentiate it from the homophonous purposive conjunction, <ka>, which is written disjunctively, (21).

(21) Jimjimən purposive conjunction (adapted from Gnintedem and Viljoen 2020:38)

< Hən ashə **ka** kavurən ɗə vəra nga məzərin. >

[xənaʃə	**ka**	kavurən	ɗə	vəra	ᵑga	məzərin]
/xən-a-sʲə	**ka**	kavəʷrən	ɗə	vəra	ᵑga	məzərin/
3PL-AOR-come	PUR	yell	LINK	village	GEN	Bana

'They came to warn the village of Bana.'

Several of the Central Chadic languages situated along the border with Nigeria have two basic word orders, SVO and VSO (Newman 2006).[16] In Guɗe and Jimjimən, unlike in Zulgo and Mafa, word order is often Verb – Subject – Object (VSO), although with some exceptions (Menetrey and Perrin 1992). This inverted word order provides yet another context in which a decision has to be made about the orthographic form of the subject morpheme.

[16] Mafa is an exception to this statement, having only SVO word order.

(22) Guɗe imperfective inverted word order (adapted from Menetrey and Perrin, 1992:5)

<Ka	shinə	**nəci**	doorə.>
IPFV.FUT	come	SBJ.3S	tomorrow

'He will come tomorrow.'

In Jimjimən, the subject (bolded in the examples below) follows the verb in the perfective aspect and in subordinate clauses. The subject as a fully expressed noun is always a separate word, see example (23), but when the subject is a pronoun, it functions as a clitic and is phonologically attached to the verb, (24).

(23) Jimjimən inverted word order with full subject noun (Yee 2021:22)

<Kəghiny **Manassa** sa'in.>

[kəɣiɲ	**manasa**	saʔin]
/kə-ɣən^{j}	**manasa**	saʔ^{j}-ən/
ANT-build.PFV	**Manassa**	house-SFX

'Manassa built a house.'

(24) Jimjimən inverted word order with subject clitic (Yee 2021:22)

<Yiayiah vreli**c** kwalan.>

[jiajiax	vreli**t͡ʃ**	k^{w}alan]
/jə^{j}ajə^{j}ax	vrələ^{j} = **tsə^{j}**	k^{w}alan/
slowly	write.PFV = **3S.M**	word

'He wrote the letter slowly.'

When the verb contains derivational suffixes, like the directional, /-gin/ 'towards the interior', the subject morpheme follows the other verbal suffixes, as seen in (25).

(25) Jimjimən subject clitic following the directional suffix (adapted from Gnintedem and Viljoen 2020:42)

<Mak **shə**gin**hən**…>

[mak	ʃəginx**ən**]
/mak	s^{j}ə-gə^{j}n = **xən**/
SUB	come-DIR = **3PL**

'When they entered…'

Another common example of word-order inversion, shown in (26), is found with the invariable quotative verb <mic>. In collaboration with the members of the community, we, the authors, proposed to write the subject morphemes conjunctively following this verb. This rule covers even the third person plural <hən> [xən], even though it does not undergo any morphological changes.

(26) Jimjimən quotative with attached subject morphemes (adapted from Gnintedem and Viljoen 2020:43)

<Micic: « Aa-aa, ənta kahuy ba'in nga minj gakan shəc a'u ? »>

[mit͡ʃit͡ʃ	aːaː	ənta	kahuj	baʔi	ᵑga	minʒ	gakan	ʃət͡ʃaʔu]
/mətseʲ=tsəʲ	aːaː	ənta	ka-həʲj	baʔʲ	ᵑga	mənzʲ	gakan	sʲə-tseʲ=aʔəʷ/
say.PFV=3S.M	no	right	IPFV-flee	back	GEN	people	3S.M.POSS	PFV.come=3S=Q

'He said: "Isn't he coming to help the people too?"'

When the subject is in focus, it will come at the end of the sentence. In this case, the direct object follows the verb, and the subject morpheme is in the final position. The focused subject morpheme does not cliticise or form a phonological word with the verb or object; it is pronounced in the full pausal form. So, it is written as a separate word, as in example (27).

(27) Jimjimən imperfective subject-focused sentence (Yee 2021:31)

<Kaɗa slinaht **kyə**>

[kaɗa	ɬinaxt	**kʲə**]
/ka-ɗa	ɬʲən-axt	**kʲə**/
IPFV-do	work-3S.F.POSS	3S.F.SBJ

'She is doing her work.'

The situation in Jimjimən is very similar to the other Central Chadic languages with a variety of factors playing into the decision of what constitutes an orthographic word. In Mafa, Zulgo, and Guɗe, the subject/mood complex is written as separate from the verb. However, in Guɗe the TAM marker, in particular the aorist /-a-/, attaches to the pronoun. In Jimjimən, the subject/mood complex is orthographically divided with the subject morpheme as a separate word from the TAM markers (the aorist /a-/, the imperfective /ka-/, and the anterior /kə-/) which are in turn written conjunctively with the verb stem. The subject clitic is written attached to the verb and the verb phrase-initial markers, such as negative /paʔ/, anterior /wa/, and imperfective /ka/.

In the verb phrase, it is desirable to have language-specific word-division strategies that align with the morphological changes that are evident in it and with the community preference. However, the more complicated clitics for orthography development are not the subject/verb agreement forms, but the noun-final morphemes, such as the plural marker and the possessive and demonstrative adjectives, among others. Generally, all three (plural, possessives and demonstratives) are written as separate words in Central Chadic languages. The attitudes and preferences of the speakers and the recommendations based on linguistic analysis do not always align. In these languages, because of the nature of clitics as well as the mutability of vowels, there are allowances for diverse decisions regarding word divisions specific to each language.

6.3.2 Noun and noun phrase elements

6.3.2.1 Plural markers

The plural marker is often a clitic in Chadic languages, attaching phonologically to the beginning or the end of the noun phrase rather than simply to the noun head. In Mafa, plural markers always combine with the nonpausal form, regardless of the position of the noun in the phrase. In the orthography, the plural marker is always a separate word as seen in table 6.4.

Table 6.4. Mafa plural nouns (Barreteau and Le Bléis 1990:26–27, 52, 320)

Pausal singular		**Nonpausal singular**		**Nonpausal plural**	
<**bay**>	'chief'	<**biy** dalay>	'marriageable girl' (chief + girl)	<**biy** hay>	'chiefs'
<**gay**>	'house'	<baba **giy** ray>	'thumb' (father + house + hand)	<**giy** hay>	'houses'
<**sak**>	'leg'	<**sakə** ɗiyak>	'type of coiffure characterised by vertical stripes at the temples' (leg + bird)	<**sakə** hay>	'legs'

The plural in Zulgo is formed by the clitic /ga=/ which precedes the noun. While the plural marker undergoes some morphophonemic variations depending on the vowel or prosody of the noun, the plural marker is always written as a separate word, (28).

(28) Zulgo plural nouns (Haller 1980:81)

a. <ga bay> [gə̀:bāi] /gà=ə̀bāy/ 'chiefs'

b. <ga dak> [gà:dák] /gà=ādák/ 'thorns'

c. <ga dər> [gɛ̀:dɛ́r] /gà=ā^{y}də́r/ 'peanuts'

Phonologically, Guɗe shows a different pattern for nominal plural formation, in that the plural is expressed by a palatalised suffix rather than a clitic. Hoskison (1983) describes how the plural suffix attaches directly to the noun stem, except in instances of compound nouns, where it attaches to the end of the final noun. In all cases for plural nouns, the palatalised plural suffix (bolded) comes between the noun and the semantically empty captive suffix /-nə/. Some examples are as given in table 6.5. Neither Hoskinson (1983) nor Menetrey and Perrin (2006) really discuss *how* plurals should be written.

Table 6.5. Guɗe plural noun forms (adapted from Hoskison 1983:30, 35)

Nominal stem	**Singular**	**Gloss**	**Plural <nyi>**	**Alternate plural <ii> /əyə/**
	/gəʷ-**nə**/	fire	/gəʷ-**ɲʸə-nə**/	-
captive /-nə/	/tsa-**nə**/	fence	/tsa-**ɲʸə-nə**/	-
	/bʸəbʸə-**nə**/	feather	/bʸəbʸə-**ɲʸə-nə**/	-
compound with /nə/	/gəʷva-manzaːvəʸ-**nə**/ friend-children-SFX	monkey	/gəʷva-mazaːvəʸ-ɲʸə-nə/ friend-children-PL-SFX	-
	/la/	cow	/la-**ɲʸə-nə**/	[liːnə] /la-**əyə-nə**/
free /-ə/	/ɗəvə/	basket	/ɗəvə-**ɲʸə-nə**/	[ɗəviːnə] /ɗəvə-**əyə-nə**/
	/gʷanda/	frog	/gʷanda-**ɲʸə-nə**/	[gʷandiːnə] /gʷanda-**əyə-nə**/

Jimjimən follows the same pattern as Guɗe, distinct from that of Mafa and Zulgo. The plural marker in Jimjimən is the suffix /-jín/, and it attaches directly to the noun stem. So, orthographically the plural marker <yin> is attached to the noun, (29).

(29) Jimjimən plural nouns (adpated from Boyd 2021:8, 35 and Yee 2021:60)

a.	<jəhun>			'horse'
	<jəhu**nyin**>	[d͡ʒə̀xú**ɲín**]	/dzʲə̀xʷə́n-**jín**/	'horses'
b.	<kəvun>			'room'
	<kəvu**nyin**>	[kə̀vú**ɲín**]	/kə̀vʷə́n-**jín**/	'rooms'
c.	<shandan>			'girl'
	<shend**iin**>	[ʃè^{n}**díːn**]	/sʲà^{n}d-**jín**/	'girls'

6.3.2.2 Possessive adjectives

Possessive adjectives, like the plural marker, may function as clitics or as suffixes in Chadic languages. In Mafa and Zulgo, the analysis of the possessive adjective as a clitic leads to writing it as a separate word, as in tables 6.6 and 6.7. The possessive adjectives are bolded in these tables.

Table 6.6. Mafa possessives (Barreteau and Le Bléis 1990:27, 42–46, 82; COLACMA and SIL 2014:43, 53, 321)

Noun		**With possessive**		**Gloss**
<bay>	[báy]	<biy **ga**>	[bí**gā**]	'my chief'
<kəra>	[kə́rá]	<kəra **na**>	[kə́rá**nā**]	'his child'
<sukway>	[sùkwày]	<sukwiy **nga**>	[sùkwì**ŋgā**]	'our thing'

Table 6.7. Zulgo possessives (Haller 1984:40, 44)

Noun		**With possessive**		**Gloss**
<məkəs>	[mə̀kə́s]	<məkəs **ga**>	[mə̀kə́s**gà**]	'my wife'
<dam>	[dàm]	<dam **mər**>	[də̀m**mə̀r**]	'our daughter'

However, in Gude and Jimjimən, the possessive adjectives follow the pattern of the plural suffix and are analysed as nominal suffixes with the result that they are written conjunctively. In Gude, the possessive is attached as a suffix of the noun, with the exception of the first and second person plural possessives as these forms require a preposition /ga-/ to which the possessives are attached. In these instances, /ga-/ (underlined) combines with the possessive adjective suffix (bolded) and the ensemble is written separately from the noun, table 6.8.

Table 6.8. Gude possessives (adapted from Menetrey and Perrin 2006:9)

Noun		**With possessive**		**Gloss**
<tsənə>	[tsənə]	<tsən**aaku**>	[tsən**aːku**]	'your bowstring'
		<tsənə **gaamə**>	[tsənə **gaːmə**]	'our bowstring'

In Jimjimən, both the plural suffix and possessive adjective suffix occur in a fixed order: noun stem - plural - possessive, and form a single phonological word, as shown in table 6.9.

Table 6.9. Jimjimən possessives (Boyd 2021:56)

Noun		**With possessive**		**Gloss**
<kəvun>	[kə̀vún]	<kəvw**akan**>	[kə̀v^{w}**ákán**]	'his room'
<kəvunyin>	[kə̀vúɲín]	<kəvuny**akan**>	[kə̀vúɲ**ákán**]	'his rooms'
<jəhun>	[d͡ʒə̀xún]	<jəhu**ni**>	[d͡ʒə̀xú**ní**]	'my horse'
<jəhunyin>	[d͡ʒə̀xúɲín]	<jəhunyi**ni**>	[d͡ə̀xúɲí**ní**]	'my horses'

There is an alternate way to indicate possession, which is always used when additional modifiers are added to the noun. Rather than a possessive suffix which attaches to the noun, the possessive attaches to the preposition /ga-/ (not dissimilar to the Guɗe forms for the first and second person plural possessives, see table 6.8). This preposition and possessive suffix are written separately from the noun as other words, like the demonstrative, can intervene between the noun and the prepositional phrase, (30).

(30) Jimjimən prepositional possessive phrase (Boyd 2021:36)

<kəvun əcə gakan>

[kə̀və́t͡s gákán]

/kə̀və́tsə̀ gákán/

room.DEM PREP.3S.POSS

'that room of his'

6.3.2.3 Demonstrative adjectives

Consistent with the generalisation of writing modifying clitics separately from their nouns, Mafa and Zulgo write demonstratives, shown bolded, as separate words, (31) and (32).

(31) Mafa noun with demonstrative (adapted from Barreteau and Le Bleis 1990:30, tone markings excluded)

<mavər **nana**> 'this ball'

(32) Zulgo noun with demonstrative (adapted from Haller 1980:81)

<bə **aaha**> 'this body'

The Guɗe community writes their noun plus demonstrative combinations differently than how they are written in Mafa and Zulgo. The way that Guɗe vowels elide according to clear phonological rules and the set order of the elements supports the analysis of the demonstrative as a suffix (similar to the plural marker and possessive markers) rather than a clitic (like Zulgo demonstratives) (Hoskison 1983:40, 42). This makes conjunctive writing the best option, as shown in (33).

(33) Guɗe noun with demonstratives (adapted from Menetrey and Perrin 2006:9)

<tsənə> 'bowstring'
<tsə**ənə**> /tsənə **ənə**/ 'this bowstring (here)'
<tsə**ətsə**> /tsənə **ətsə**/ 'this bowstring'
<tsə**ətə**> /tsənə **ətə**/ 'that bowstring'

In Jimjimən, there are three demonstratives: distal [ə́t͡sə̀], proximal [ə́nə̀], and anaphoric [ə́tə̀]. These demonstratives attach phonologically to the nonpausal form of the noun with the deletion of the root-final vowel and nasal; see example (34).

(34) Jimjimən demonstratives (Boyd 2021:39)

<kəvun> [kə̀vún] 'room'
<kəvun əcə> [kə̀v**ə́t͡s**] /kə̀vʷə́n **ə́tsə̀**/ 'that room'
<kəvun ənə> [kə̀vún**ə̀**] /kə̀vʷə́n **ə́nə̀**/ 'this room'
<kəvun ətə> [kə̀v**ə́tə̀**] /kə̀vʷə́n **ə́tə̀**/ 'the room (already mentioned)'

While the demonstratives in Jimjimən show some phonological merging with the noun, they differ from possessives and plurals in a significant way; namely, a full word can be inserted between the demonstrative and the noun. Example (35) shows that numbers, like <bik> 'two', come between the noun, with its suffixes, and the demonstrative.

(35) Jimjimən demonstrative separability (adapted from Boyd (2021:36)

<jəhunyini bik ətə>
[d͡ʒə̀xúɲíní bík ə́tə̀]
/dzʲə̀xʷə́n-jín-ní bík ə́tə̀/
horse-PL-1S.POSS two DEM
'my two horses (those previously mentioned)'

In Jimjimən, it is also possible for the number to follow the demonstrative, such that both <jəhunyini ətə bik> and, as in (35), <jəhunyini bik ətə> are grammatical, but with a difference in focus. The focus for <jəhunyini ətə bik> is on the number <bik> 'two' but in (35), the focus is on the noun <jəhunyini>.

Whereas the possessive must attach to something, either the noun or a preposition, the demonstrative can occur on its own, see table 6.10. The fact that something else can come between the demonstrative and the noun shows that it is noncohesive (Dixon and Aikhenvald 2002:19). While there may be no criterion by itself that necessitates and is sufficient to indicate "wordhood" (Haspelmath 2011:33), the noncohesiveness of the demonstrative provides good reason to posit that the demonstrative is not a suffix, but that it constitutes a separate grammatical and orthographic word in Jimjimən.

Table 6.10. Jimjimən demonstratives and possessives (Boyd 2021:36–37, 39, 58)

With demonstrative		**With plural + demonstrative**		**With possessive adjective + demonstrative**	
<jəhun əcə>		<jəhunyin əcə>		<jəhunyi**ni** əcə>	
[d͡ʒə̀xə́**t͡sə̀**]		[d͡ʒə̀xuɲə́**t͡s**ə̀]		[d͡ʒə̀xúɲí**ní**	ə́**t͡s**ə̀]
/dzʲə̀xʷə́n	ə́**ts**ə̀/	/dzʲə̀xʷə́n-jín ə́**ts**ə̀/		/dzʲə̀xʷə́n-jín-**ní**	ə́**ts**ə̀/
horse	DEM	horse-PL	DEM	horse-PL-1S.POSS	DEM
'that horse'		'those horses'		'my horses there'	

Morphophonological processes occur in the context of both affixes and clitics as well as between full words, so are ineffective as an indication of the difference between an affix and a clitic. For Jimjimən, one of the better indications for orthographic word breaks is whether the element is cohesive or noncohesive. The plural and possessive are cohesive because nothing else can come between them and their host, while the demonstrative is noncohesive because another word may come between the demonstrative and its host.

6.3.3 Interrogatives

Having looked at the word boundary challenges in the verb phrase and noun phrase, we now turn to the clause. A common syntactic feature in Central Chadic languages for indicating questions is a clause-final interrogative marker. Each of the languages examined here includes such a marker and the ways to write it vary between these four languages. In Mafa, question markers have minimal phonological interaction and are always written separately (Barreteau and Le Bléis 1990:53), examples (36)–(38).

(36) Mafa yes/no question (adapted from Barreteau and Le Bléis 1990:129)

<Ka pə́za ɗə ?>
2S.PFV cultivate Q
'Have you finished cultivating?'

(37) Mafa how question (adapted from Barreteau and Le Bléis 1990:186)

<Ngwázə ngayí kə́ ?>
wife 2S.POSS Q
'How is your wife doing?'

(38) Mafa what question (adapted from Barreteau and Le Bléis 1990:186)

<á ndíy mə́ ?>
3S eat Q
'What is he eating?'

Zulgo has several question words, such as <weké> 'who', that co-occur with a clause-final <ya> or <a>. For yes/no questions the question word <wana> also co-occurs with a clause-final <ya/a>. In both cases, the question-final marker is pronounced [à] and written as <a> following a consonant but as [yà] <yà> after vowels (Haller 2018).

(39) Zulgo question (adapted from Haller and Watters 1984:29)

<Weké ná á-zlá síŋgwè yà ?>
who FOC 3S-took money Q
'Who took the money?'

Hoskison (1983:122) lists six question-final markers but specifies that only two, <a> and <kwa>, can be used for both yes/no and wh-questions in Guɗe. Interestingly, the first is written conjunctively, but the second marker <kwa> is written disjunctively, as in (40) where it follows a noun and (41) following a verb. We see that the question marker <a> attaches to the final word of the sentence, whether a noun as in (42) or a verb, (43).

(40) Guɗe yes/no question <kwa> (Hoskison 1983:122)

<Kə gi Musa a luuma kwa ?>
ANT go.PFV Musa to market Q
'Did Musa go to market?'

(41) Guɗe wh-question <kwa> (Hoskison 1983:122)

<Acii	mi	nə	tiia	panə	kwa ?>
because	why	SBJ	3PL.AOR	fight	Q

'Why do they fight?'

(42) Guɗe yes/no question <-a> (Hoskison 1983:122)

<Tə'i	mbusaakua ?>
exists	pumpkin.2S.POSS.Q

'Do you have a pumpkin?'

(43) Guɗe wh-question <-a> (Hoskison 1983:126)

<Yitə	ɗankia ?>
how	do.1S.FUT.Q

'What will I do?'

Questions in Jimjimən are marked by the clause-final clitic, [áʔú], which is sometimes reduced to [á].[17] Clause-final question morphemes are considered clitics because they are "unrestricted as to the syntactic category of the word they attach to" (Bickel and Nichols 2007:174–175). In Jimjimən, the interrogative clitic may attach to a noun, pronoun, infinite verb or a conjugated verb.

The following examples, predominantly sourced from a narrative story, show how the interrogative element attaches to the end of the clause, and to words of various syntactic categories.

(44) Jimjimən question marker with noun (Yee 2021:69)

<Wah kəzhim **ɗafan a'u** ?>

[wax	kəʒim	**ɗafanaʔu**]
/wa=x	kə-zəm^{j}	**ɗafan=aʔə^{w}**/
ANT=2S	ANT-eat.PFV	**food**=Q

'Did you eat?'

[17] While there may be an interrogative word at the beginning of the interrogative clause, these are not discussed in this study since they are independent words, being neither affixes nor clitics.

(45) Jimjimən tag question with pronoun (adapted from Gnintedem and Viljoen 2020:27)

<Maɗaam wushbilən aɓələbi **tən a** ?>

[maɗa:m	wuʃbilən	aɓələbi	**təna**]
/maɗa:m	wuʃbilən	a-ɓəl-əbi	**tən** = **a**/
if.not	wild.animal	AOR-kill-VOL	**1s.do** = Q

'Otherwise a wild animal will kill me, right?'

(46) Jimjimən yes/no question with infinitive verb (adapted from Gnintedem and Viljoen 2020:30)

<[…]« Yenna zana wah kəwudy **hədən a'u** ? »>

[jenna	zana	wax	kəwud^{j}	**xədənaʔu**]
/jenna	zana	wa = x	kə-wəd^{j}	**xədən** = **aʔə^{w}**/
how	such	ANT = 2s	ANT-end	**grind** = Q

'[…] "Did you already finish grinding?"'

(47) Jimjimən why question marker with conjugated verbs (adapted from Gnintedem and Viljoen 2020:26)

<Mic hən kaky : « Misa hə **katuwun a**, hə akwala ma hə **atuw a** ? »>

[mit͡ʃ	xən kak^{j}	misa	xə	**katuwuna**	xə	ak^{w}alama	xə	**atuwa**]
/mətsə^{j}	xən ka = k^{j}	m^{j}əsa	xə	**ka-təwən** = **a**	xə	a-k^{w}ala = ma	xə	**a-təw** = **a**/
say.PFV	3PL io = 3S.F	what	2S	IPFV-**cry** = Q	2S	AOR-speak = SUB	2S	AOR-**cry** = Q

'They said to her: "Why are you crying? (Why) do you cry while you speak?"'

The clause-final question element appears in a variety of different question contexts and attaches to nominal and verbal hosts, but it is always in the final position of the clause. Since the criterion of cohesiveness cannot be applied to an element that is always clause-final, Bickel and Nichols (2007:174–175) note whether an element is "restricted" or "nonrestricted" as another way to help determine word boundaries. Affixes tend to be restricted and will only attach to one syntactic category. Clitics, like the clause-final interrogative in Jimjimən, are nonrestricted since they can attach to several syntactic categories, provided that they are the last element in the clause. Due to its unrestrictedness, the Jimjimən orthography guide proposes that the interrogative clitic be written as a separate word, like the demonstrative. This proposal adheres to the general idea of writing clitics as separate words and affixes attached to their hosts.

6.4 Conclusion

The mutability of vowels is a major problem for the orthographic ideal of maintaining a consistent word image in Central Chadic languages. However, this mutability plays little role in determining what is or is not an affix or a clitic or, in other words, whether words should be written conjunctively or disjunctively. The more effective indicators are whether the formative is cohesive or noncohesive, and restricted or unrestricted as to the syntactic category to which it can attach.

- Where the formative is cohesive and restricted, it functions as an affix and is written attached to its host (**e.g., the plural and the possessives** in Guɗe and Jimjimən).
- Where the formative is cohesive, but less restricted (i.e., it can attach to any element of the verb complex), it is treated as an affix even though it has some characteristics of a clitic and is written attached to its host (**e.g., the subject morpheme in the verb complex** in Jimjimən).
- Where the formative is noncohesive (i.e., another word can come between it and its host), it is treated as a clitic and is written as a separate word (**e.g., the demonstratives** in Jimjimən).
- Where the formative is unrestricted (i.e., it can attach to many different syntactic categories), it functions as a clitic and is written as a separate word (**e.g., the interrogatives** in Jimjimən).

Table 6.11. Pausal and nonpausal orthographic decisions

Language	Nonpausal	Pausal
Mafa	Write surface form[a] <ɓorə> [ɓorə] /ɓora/ 'aim at'	Write surface form <ɓora> [ɓora] /ɓora/ 'aim at'
Zulgo	Write surface form <sik> [sik] /səʲk/ 'foot'	Write as nonpausal form <sik> [sek] /səʲk/ 'foot'
Guɗe	Captive: /-nə/ Write surface form <minə> [minə] /mʸə-nə/ 'woman'	Captive: /-nə/ Write as nonpausal form <minə> [min] /mʸə-nə/ 'woman'
	Free: /-ə/ Write surface form <zəmə> [zəmə] /zəma/ 'food'	Free: /-ə/ Write surface form, but without final vowel length <zəma> [zəma:] /zəma/ 'food'
Jimjimən	Captive: /-ən/ added Write as pausal form <ba'in> [báʔí] /báʔʲ-ə́n/ 'back'	Captive: /-ən/ added Write surface form <ba'in> [báʔín] /báʔʲ-ə́n/ 'back'
	Free: /-ə/ Write pausal form <kwalan> [kʷalanə] /kʷalan/ 'word'	Free: /-ə/ Write surface form <kwalan> [kʷalan] /kʷalan/ 'word'

[a] The official orthography recommends writing all nouns as they occur in pausal form.

The subjects are bold, the subject and TAM morphemes are underlined, and the verbs are italicised in the examples in table 6.12, which summarises the various orthographic decisions taken in the verb phrase and specifically regarding the subject/mood complex.

Table 6.12. Subject/mood complex orthographic decisions

Language	Subject pronoun morpheme	Example
Mafa	Written as a subject/mood complex disjunctively from verb	<**yi** *pere*> 'I gather'
Zulgo	Written as a subject/mood complex disjunctively from verb	<**Awis** a *zəm* hinne.> 'The knife is very sharp.'
Guɗe	Written as a subject pronoun disjunctively from verb and TAM markers	<Kə *shi* **Musa**.> 'Musa came.'
	Exception: SBJ-AOR verb	<**Ca** *palə*.> 'He leaves.'
Jimjimən	SVO order: Written as a subject/mood complex conjunctively with IPFV /ka/, ANT /wa/, NEG /paʔ/, disjunctively from verb	<Wa**c** kə*fuyk*.> 'He fell.'
	SVO order: Written as a subject pronoun disjunctively before AOR /a/, IPFV /ka-/, ANT /kə-/, and verb	<**Hən** a*titiwu*.> 'They are crying and crying.'
	VSO order: written as subject/mood complex conjunctively with verb (and other suffixes)	<*Zhimic* ɗafan.> 'He ate dinner.'
	VOS order: written as a subject pronoun disjunctively from verb and TAM markers	<Ka*ɗa* slinaht **kyə**> 'She is doing her work.'

Table 6.13. Nominal affixes/clitics orthographic decisions

Language	Plural	Possessives	Demonstratives
Mafa	Disjunctive <biy **hay**> 'chiefs'	Disjunctive <biy **ga**> 'my chief'	Disjunctive <mayər **nana**> 'this ball'
Zulgo	Disjunctive <**ga** bay> 'chiefs'	Disjunctive <məkəs **ga**> 'my wife'	Disjunctive <bə **aaha**> 'this body'
Guɗe	Conjunctive (takes -nə suffix) <tsanyi**nə** > 'fences'	Conjunctive <tsən**aaku**> 'your bowstring'	Conjunctive <tsə**ənə**> 'this bowstring (here)'
		Exception: possessive attaches to /ga/ preposition < tsənə **gaamə** > 'our bowstring'	
Jimjimən	Conjunctive <jəhun**yin**> 'horses'	Conjunctive <jəhunyi**ni**> 'my horses'	Disjunctive <jəhun **əcə**> 'that horse'
		Exception: possessive attaches to /ga/ preposition <kəvun əcə ga**kan**> 'that room of his'	

Table 6.14. Clause-final interrogatives orthographic decisions

Language	Interrogative	Example
Mafa	All disjunctive	<Ka pə́za **ɗə** ?> 'Have you finished cultivating?'
Zulgo	All disjunctive	<Wekéná á-zlá síŋgwè **yà** ?> 'Who took the money?'
Guɗe	/kwa/ disjunctive	<Kə gi Musa a luuma **kwa** ?> 'Did Musa go to market?'
	/-a/ conjunctive	<Tə'i mbusaaku**a** ?> 'Do you have a pumpkin?'
Jimjimən	All disjunctive	<Wah kəzhim ɗafan **a'u** ?> 'Did you eat?' <Misa hə katuwun **a** ?> 'Why are you crying?'

This survey of four Central Chadic languages discusses plural, possessive, and demonstrative markers on nouns as well as the verbal subject/mood complex and interrogative clause marker and underlines that there is not a uniform approach to orthographic word divisions across Central Chadic languages. The separability of the subject morpheme and the status of the TAM marker as an affix may indicate a recommendation to write the TAM marker conjunctively with the verb. While the tendency in Chadic languages is to analyse the plural and possessive as clitics and thus write them as independent words, as shown in this chapter, the input of the community, as well as the status of these modifiers as clitics or suffixes, needs to be considered for each individual language before an orthographic decision is reached.

References

Anderson, Stephen R. 1985. Inflectional morphology. In Timothy Shopen (ed.), *Language typology and syntactic description. Vol. 3: Grammatical Categories and the Lexicon,* 150–201 First edition. Cambridge: Cambridge University Press.

Barreteau, Daniel, and Yves Le Bléis. 1990. *Lexique mafa : Langue de la famille tchadique parlée au Cameroun.* Paris: Librairie Orientaliste Paul Geuthner; Orstom.

Bickel, Balthasar, and Joanna Nichols. 2007. Inflectional morphology. In Timothy Shopen (ed.), *Language typology and syntactic description. Vol. 3: Grammatical categories and the lexicon*, 169–240. Second edition. Cambridge: Cambridge University Press.

Bow, Catherine. 1999. The vowel system of Moloko. MA thesis. University of Melbourne.

Boyd, Ginger. 2021. Esquisse de phonologie jimjimən. Ms.

Cahill, Michael, and Elke Karan. 2008. Factors in designing effective orthographies for unwritten languages. *SIL Electronic Working Papers 2008-001*. Dallas, TX: SIL International. www.sil.org/resources/archives/7830.

COLACMA and SIL Cameroon. 2014. *Nga sləbiy dayi mafa I.* Titre en français : Nous apprenons la langue mafa; et nous la lisons et nous l'écrivons, I. Second edition. Cameroon: SIL Cameroon.

COLACMA and SIL Cameroon. 2018. *Nga sləbiy dayi mafa II.* Titre en français : Nous apprenons la langue mafa; et nous la lisons et nous l'écrivons, II. Second edition. Cameroon: SIL Cameroon.

Dixon, R. M. W., and Alexandra Y. Aikhenvald. 2002. Word: A typological framework. In R. M. W. Dixon and Alexandra Y. Aikhenvald (eds.), *Word: A cross-linguistic typology*, 1–41. Cambridge: Cambridge University Press.

Eberhard, David M., Gary F. Simons, and Charles D. Fennig, eds. 2024. *Ethnologue: Languages of the world.* Twenty-seventh edition. Dallas, TX: SIL International. www.ethnologue.com.

Gnintedem, Jean-Claude, and Melanie Viljoen. 2020. Résumé de caractéristiques des textes narratifs jimi. Ms.

Gravina, Richard C. 2014. The phonology of Proto-Central Chadic: The reconstruction of the phonology and lexicon of Proto-Central Chadic, and the linguistic history of the Central Chadic languages. PhD dissertation. Leiden University.

Gravina, Richard, Martin Guissata, Marti Giger, Ndzenguere Wandala, and Takoslam Joseph. 2006. Précis d'orthographe, de grammaire et de vocabulaire en langue mafa. Ms.

Gravina, Richard, Thomas Golamadang, and Timothée Sabataï. 2005. L'orthographe de la langue guemzek : Esquisse préliminaire. Ms.

Haller, Beat. 1980. Phonology of Zulgo. Ms.

Haller, Beat. 1984. Problems in attempting to write the Zulgo language. *Cahiers Du Départment Des Langues Africaines et Linguistique* 3:38–53. Yaoundé, Cameroon: University of Yaoundé.

Haller, Beat. 2018. Zulgo – French – Fulfulde Dictionary. SIL International. www.webonary.org/zulgo/overview/?lang = en.

Haller, Beat. 2020. Wetsekwa àhəm zulgwa [Proposition d'orthographe zulgo]. Édition provisoire. Ms.

Haller, Beat, and John Watters. 1984. Topic in Zulgo. *Studies in African Linguistics* 15(1):27–46.

Haspelmath, Martin. 2011. The indeterminacy of word segmentation and the nature of morphology and syntax. *Folia Linguistica* 45(1):31–80.

Hoskison, James T. 1983. A grammar and dictionary of the Gude language (Nigeria, Cameroon, Chadic). PhD dissertation. The Ohio State University, Columbus.

Kosack, Godula. 2001. *Die Mafa im Spiegel ihrer oralen Literatur : eine Monographie aus der Sicht von Frauen.* Cologne: Köppe.

Litteral, Shirley. 1979. Review of *Kâte dictionary* by W. Flierl and H. Strauss (eds.). *Kivung: Journal of the Linguistic Society of Papua New Guinea* 12(1):99–101. www.langlxmelanesia.com/llm-archive.

Menetrey, Catherine, and Mona Perrin. 1992. L'usage des temps et aspects dans le discours narratif guɗe. Ms.

Menetrey, Catherine, and Mona Perrin. 2006. Présentation de l'orthographe du guɗe. Ms. www.silcam.org/resources/archives/47439.

Newman, Paul. 2000. *The Hausa language: An encyclopedic reference grammar.* New Haven, CT: Yale University Press.

Newman, Paul. 2006. Comparative Chadic revisited. *Studies in African Linguistics* 35:188–202. doi.org/10.32473/sal.v35i0.107325.

Newman, Paul. 2009. Hausa and the Chadic languages. In Bernard Comrie (ed.), *The world's major languages*, 618-634. Second edition. Oxford: Oxford University Press.

Perevet, Zacharie. 2008. *Les mafa : Un peuple, une culture.* Yaoundé, Cameroon: Éditions CLÉ.

Pike, Kenneth. L., and Evelyn G. Pike. 1982. *Grammatical analysis*. Second edition. Summer Institute of Linguistics Publications in Linguistics 53. Dallas, TX: Summer Institute of Linguistics and University of Texas at Arlington.

Viljoen, Melanie. 2013. A grammatical description of the Buwal language. PhD dissertation. La Trobe University, Melbourne.

Yee, Shannon. 2021. Linkers and the Jimi verb phrase. MA thesis. Wayne State University, Detroit.

7
Different Types of Nasality as Orthographic Word Issues: The Case of the Samogo Languages in Burkina Faso and Mali

Paul Solomiac

Abstract

This chapter deals less with decisions about orthographic word boundaries than with what happens at the boundaries of orthographic words. Nasality is a phonological feature for both vowels and consonants that is shared by a vast majority of our world languages. What is less common is the special nasality feature shared by the Samogo languages spoken in Mali and Burkina Faso, West Africa. In these languages, nasalization of oral vowels and oral consonants unexpectedly occurs at the right boundary of some words. In this chapter, we look at a variety of morpheme alternation cases from both the orthographic perspective and the morphophonological one.

Abbreviations

DAT dative
DEF definite
GEN genitive
PL plural
PRF perfect

7.1 Introduction

In the large Niger-Congo language family, the Mande group located in West Africa presents several instances of languages with peculiar nasality features combined with interesting alternation processes that demand careful consideration when it comes to writing what happens at word boundaries.

At the border of Burkina Faso and Mali, in what is traditionally called the Kenedugu province, there is a cluster of four languages; from west to east, they are Duun [dux] and Jowulu [jow], on the Malian side of the border, and Dzùùngoo [dnn] and Seenku [sos], on the Burkina Faso side. Genetically they have all been classified as West Mande, Northwest branch, Duun-Bobo, Duun-Jo, Duun-Seenku. Raimund Kastenholz (2002) offers the following classification which we adapted with his kind permission (limited to the Duun-Seenku sub branch).

- WEST MANDE
  - Northwest
    - Duun-Bɔbɔ
      - Duun-Jɔ
        - Duun-Seenku
          - Duun cluster
            - Duun (or Duungo elsewhere in the literature)
            - Dzuun-Yiri (corresponds to Dzùùngoo)
            - Kpan (corresponds to a northern variant of Dzùùngoo)
          - Banka (in Mali)
        - Seeku (corresponds to Seenku)
      - Jɔ (corresponds to Jowulu)
    - Bɔbɔ

The present chapter will first look at the orthographic issues caused by different types of nasality in Dzùùngoo, one of these four languages. It will then consider how the other three languages deal with the same issues from both a phonological and orthographic perspective. It is hoped that the case of the Samogo languages will help orthography designers deal with nasality issues in Francophone countries where nasality already has orthographic standards at a national level.

The peculiar feature these four languages have in common is two types of nasality that have different effects on phonological processes at the right boundary of the phonological word. We will use data[1] from these languages to assess the complexity and relevance for readers to recognize the two types of nasality in their orthography. Phonological analysis in all four languages considers nasality as a suprasegmental property that exhibits two types of processes, one which associates nasality to vowels and one which assumes the existence of a floating nasal. Associated vowel nasality presents a distinctive articulatory lowering of the soft palate (the velum) causing vowels to be perceived as nasal vowels. However, language data shows that some nasal vowels and some oral or weakly nasalized vowels are associated with a variety of alternations on some adjacent morphemes.

Thus, in Dzùùngoo, [rè:] is the definite plural morpheme[2] whether the preceding vowel is nasal or oral:

(1) [kú][3] 'plant' → [kúrè:] 'the plants'

(2) [tȁ̃ã̄] 'woman' → [tȁ̃ã̄rè:] 'the women'

The definite plural morpheme has the alternate form [nè:] after some other nouns, whether its final vowel is nasal or oral:

(3) [cɛ́] 'breast' → [cɛ̃́nè:] 'the breasts'

(4) [dzĩ́] 'child' → [dzĩ́nè:] 'the children'

Phonological analysis in all four languages posits the existence in the structure of a nasal autosegment designated as N that is responsible for such processes, as for instance the nasalization of morpheme-initial [r-] resulting in [n-].

Analysts refer to this feature as a floating nasal (Solomiac 2014, for Dzùùngoo; Djilla et al. 2004, for Jowulu), a hidden nasal (Eenkhoorn-Pilon 2018, for Duun) or a latent nasal (McPherson 2020a and 2020b, for Seenku and others).

[1] The Dzùùngoo data comes from my own research on the language, and data for the other three languages comes from published and unpublished material.

[2] There is a separate morpheme for definite singular and another one for indefinite plural. The relevance of the definite morpheme for this present work is addressed later in the chapter.

[3] Though in Dzùùngoo, disyllabic words are more numerous than monosyllabic ones, the variety of distributions with monosyllabic words is more convenient for the purpose of illustration here. The processes are exactly the same for monosyllabic and disyllabic words. Regarding tone transcription, Dzùùngoo is a three-tone language: High, Mid and Low.

The question we have to deal with here is whether the contrast between the two types of nasality calls for special treatment in the orthography or whether less specific orthography rules will allow for a unified writing system with no ambiguity when reading or writing words with these particular features.

Three of the four languages already have a set orthography; one, Seenku, does not. In their current orthography, Dzùùngoo and Duun users transcribe both types of nasality with a syllable-final <n>. The Jowulu community decided to transcribe only segmental nasality with a syllable-final <n>; words with a floating nasal are recognized in their written form with a syllable-final <ŋ>. One needs to note that the syllable-final <n> is the conventional orthographic feature for vowel nasality in French, the official language in Burkina Faso and Mali, as it is in Jula [dyu] and Bambara [bam], which are both national languages, used in basic education and literacy in both countries.

In order to assess the orthography decisions for Dzùùngoo, Jowulu and Duun, I will refer to Van Dyken and Kutsch Lojenga (1993). Among the twelve key factors proposed by Van Dyken and Kutsch Lojenga, criterion number 9 "phonological bridging" deals with what happens at phonological word boundaries. It states (1993:14):

> Phonological bridging concerns the phonological phrase and what happens when one semantically defined word blends with others across word boundaries within that phrase... Should the written word change shape according to the predictable changes in pronunciation? Or should it maintain a stable appearance? Phonological bridging becomes a criterion not so much for deciding the boundaries as for knowing how to write them.

It is exactly at the phonological phrase level that this autosegment N operates in these four languages: it belongs to the noun or verb stem and its effects are not limited to the form of the noun or verb, but may be more visible on the next adjacent morpheme-initial consonant and especially on sonorant consonants.

The definite plural is such a morpheme and it will serve in the next section as an illustration of the processes involved. Though phonologically it behaves more as a clitic, it is written as a separate word in its orthographic form because it functions both at the noun phrase level and at the noun level. It does not belong to the noun alone but occurs after the last item of the noun phrase, which could be, for example, a demonstrative, an adjective or a relative marker. Thus, as such, it is written separately in conformity to the criterion of separability, which states, "A functor is also written separately from the word with which it usually occurs when other words can come between them" (Van Dyken and Kutsch Lojenga 1993:9).

(5) <ku>[4] ‘plant’ → <ku rèè> ‘the plants’ → <ku blà rèè> ‘the big plants’

We will try in what follows to understand the processes involved in the words that present these nasality features. We will look at the data we have access to in Dzùùngoo and in the other three languages and at what orthographic forms were chosen for Dzùùngoo, Jowulu and Duun for the processes involved. This overview should allow us to assess their validity for future orthography design for languages that share the same particular nasality features.

7.2 Dzùùngoo

Dzùùngoo is spoken in the area around the prefecture town of Samogohiri in about six villages. There is a variant of the language, Kpankagooma, in a second area around the other prefecture town of Samogogouan in a small cluster of villages. They represent a population of 13,400 inhabitants (Eberhard et al. 2024). What follows will tentatively answer the question “why did the Dzùùn community in Samogohiri decide to write both nasal vowels *and* the floating nasal (N) with a final <n> (as in [7]–[9]) *and* the alternant forms of morphemes caused by the floating nasal (N) with an initial <n> (as in [8]–[9])?”

(6) /kú/ <ku> ‘plant’ <ku rèè> ‘the plants’

(7) /tã̀ã̄/ <tàan> ‘woman’ <tàan rèè> ‘the women’

(8) /cɛ́(N)/ <cɛn> ‘breast’ <cɛn nèè> ‘the breasts’

(9) /dzĩ́(N)/ <dzin> ‘child’ <dzin nèè> ‘the children’

We will look at the phonological processes associated with nasality (vocalic and nonvocalic) in Dzùùngoo first through the definite plural operation in the noun phrase and then through other types of operations. Next we will consider how to interpret this data and what the implications are for orthography matters. For this present work, we will use a limited database of 2,163 noun and verb items. Out of these lexical items, we count 777 (36%) with at least one of the two types of nasality in word-final position.

[4] In the Dzùùngoo orthography, High and Mid tones are not marked and Low tone is represented with a grave accent.

7.2.1 Definite plural

Dzùùngoo has seven oral vowels /i, e, ɛ, a, ɔ, o, u/ and five nasal vowels /ĩ, ɛ̃, ã, ɔ̃, ũ/. We will consider the phonological processes from the perspective of the noun-final vowel since it is at this word boundary that alternations occur.

The close nasal vowels [ĩ] and [ũ] are clearly perceived as nasalized, and all nouns and verbs that have these vowels in word-final position also have a structural floating nasal (N). We count 338 such items, representing forty-three percent of the 777 items. All such nouns have the effect of nasalizing the initial consonant of the plural morpheme. No noun or verb with a close oral vowel has the (N) in its structure, with the exceptions of the diphthongs [ou], [ɛi] and [ei]:

(10)	[dzĩ́](N)	'child'	→	[dzĩ́nè:]	'the children'
(11)	[fũ̄](N)	'vine'	→	[fũ̄nè:]	'the vines'
(12)	[dzí:]	'mouth'	→	[dzí:rè:]	'the mouths'
(13)	[kú]	'plant'	→	[kúrè:]	'the plants'

Among these 338 items, we count 103 diphthongs, 1 [ou](N), 3 [ãũ](N), 6 [ɔ̃ũ](N), 35 [ɛ̃ĩ](N) 27 [ɛi](N) and 31 [ei](N).

(14)	[kpɛ̃́ĩ́](N)	'pocket'	→	[kpɛ̃́ĩ́nè:]	'the pockets'
(15)	[tã́ũ̄](N)	'squirrel'	→	[tã́ũ̄nê:]	'the squirrels'
(16)	[ɲɔ̃́ṹ](N)	'dance'	→	[ɲɔ̃́ṹnè:]	'the dances'
(17)	[dóù](N)	'inside'	→	[dṍũ̀nè:]	'the intestines'
(18)	[kɛ̀ì](N)	'bird'	→	[kɛ̃̀ĩ̀nê:]	'the birds'
(19)	[tséí](N)	'cadet'	→	[tsẽ́ĩ́nè:]	'the cadets'

It should be also noted that the diphthongs [ou](N), [ei](N) and [ɛi](N) present a very weak nasalization in citation form, which is therefore not marked as nasal. While there are many items with the diphthong [ei] that can minimally contrast with the 31 items with the "nasalized" diphthong [ei](N), there is no item with a non-nasalized diphthong [ou] that will contrast with the one item with [ou](N).

We count 80 items, representing ten percent of 777 items, with close-mid vowels [e] and [o] having very weak nasalization; these items also have a structural floating nasal (N). All such nouns have the effect of nasalizing the initial consonant of the plural morpheme, and in return, the plural morpheme-initial nasal has the effect of more strongly nasalizing the final vowel of the noun:

(20) [fé](N) 'night' → [fẽ́nè:] 'the nights'

(21) [bò](N) 'gourd' → [bõ̀nè:] 'the gourds'

(22) [gè] 'thing' → [gèrè:] 'the things'

(23) [dô:] 'lie' → [dô:rè:] 'the lies'

The open and open mid vowels [a, ɛ, ɔ] belong to words that associate the two types of nasality differently. There are words ending in [a, ɛ, ɔ] with no nasalization at all, either segmental or autosegmental.

(24) [gbà] 'house' → [gbàrè:] 'the houses'

(25) [dzwɛ́] 'blessing' → [dzwɛ́rè:] 'the blessings'

(26) [kɔ̀:] 'hole' → [kɔ̀:rè:] 'the holes'

There are also words ending in [ã, ɛ̃, ɔ̃] with no floating nasal (N) in the underlying structure. These vowels are unmistakably nasalized, and no nasalization process follows them on the adjacent morpheme-initial sonorant consonant. There are 40 such nouns in our database, representing five percent of 777 items.

(27) [ɲã́] 'enemy' → [ɲã́rè:] 'the enemies'

(28) [mjɛ̃̀:] 'trap' → [mjɛ̃̀:rè:] 'the traps'

(29) [ʃɔ̃́] 'thief' → [ʃɔ̃́rè:] 'the thieves'

Third, there are words ending in [a, ɛ, ɔ] with a structural floating nasal (N). Some speakers of the language nasalize these vowels more than others, but all associate them with the nasalized alternant form of the plural morpheme, which in return nasalizes the noun-final vowel.

(30) [ká](N) 'flower' → [kã́nè:] 'the flowers'

(31) [cɛ́](N) 'breast' → [cɛ̃́nè:] 'the breasts'

(32) [dɔ́](N) 'nape' → [dɔ̃́nè:] 'the napes'

Finally, there are words ending in [ã, ɛ̃, ɔ̃] with a floating nasal in the underlying structure (N).

(33) [mã̀:kã̄](N) 'noise' → [mã̀:kã̄nê:] 'the noises'

(34) [nɛ̃̀kɛ̃́](N) 'brain' → [nɛ̃̀kɛ̃́nè:] 'the brains'

(35) [tɔ̃́](N) 'side' → [tɔ̃́nè:] 'the sides'

Adding them all together, we count 319 items with a final [a, ã, ɛ, ɛ̃, ɔ, ɔ̃] and a structural floating nasal, representing forty-one percent of 777 items. Added to the forty-three percent of items with [ĩ, ũ] and the ten percent of items with [e, o] and the floating nasal, in total 737 (94%) of the 777 nouns and verbs in the database have a floating nasal. Only 40 items present only segmental nasality. The morphophonological processes at work on the definite plural morpheme have revealed the existence of a structural nasal element attached to the noun, a floating nasal, that is not linked to vowel nasality but that causes the nasalization of the adjacent morpheme-initial sonorant consonant. Considering the above data, one may say that in terms of frequency, there are more floating nasals than nasal vowels in Dzùùngoo. Given the implications the above processes may have on the orthography, it is important to determine whether such a floating nasal may cause other processes, and what such processes might be.

7.2.2 Other processes

In the noun phrase, other morphemes may undergo the same processes as the definite plural, indicating the presence or absence of a floating nasal. For instance, sonorant-initial postpositions are nasalized after a floating nasal.

(36) [sí: rɔ̃̀] 'to the market'

(37) [dzɔ̃̄(N) nɔ̃̀] 'to the ground'

Among the noun phrase operators, the definite determiner is also subject to different processes. One must note here that in Dzùùngoo, the definite morpheme for the noun and the imperfective morpheme for the verb have the same form. They have many different allomorphs, which are all phonologically conditioned variants of a posited canonical form /-rà/. As with the plural morpheme, the initial consonant of the definite morpheme is also subject to nasalization by the floating nasal. However, there is only one context where the floating nasal will have an impact on the definite and imperfective morphemes forms: polysyllabic items, nouns and verbs alike, ending with the extra short vowel structures [CV̆rV̆] or [CV̆rV̆](N) or [CV̆nV̆](N) that mark their definite/imperfective form with [-rà].

(38) [CV̆rV̆] structure : [mɛ̄rɛ̄] 'deer' + [-rà] DEF → [mɛ̄llà] 'the deer'

(39) [CV̆rV̆](N) structure : [kàrã̀](N) 'study' + [-rà] DEF → [kã̀nnà] 'the study'

(40) [CV̆nV̆](N) structure : [bɔ̃̀nɔ̃̀](N) 'fine' + [-rà] DEF → [bɔ̃̀nnà] 'the fine'

Other structural contexts call for a vocalic form of the definite morpheme:

(41) [CV] structure : [wɔ̀] 'town' + -V̀ DEF → [wɔ̀ɔ̀] 'the town'

(42) [CV](N) structure : [ká](N) 'flower' + -V̀ DEF → [káà] 'the flower'

Considering the definite forms of nouns (and the imperfective forms of verbs, which behave the same), we can confirm the limited influence of the floating nasal on the adjacent morpheme-initial sonorant. The above definite noun form [káà] 'the flower' shows that the floating nasal disappears before a vowel-initial morpheme variant.

Nominal compounding is another morphological operation where the floating nasal may initiate other phonological processes. First, the oral vowel is nasalized by the floating nasal when followed by a fricative consonant in the compounding operation as in the following example.

(43) [bɔ̄ː](N) 'cheek' # [súː] 'hair' → [bɔ̄̃ːsúː] 'beard'

Second, if the following consonant is a plosive, the floating nasal surfaces as a homorganic nasal stop.

(44) [dó](N) 'stream' # [kɔ̀ː] 'hole' → [dɔ̄̃ŋkɔ̄ː] 'backwater'

7.2.3 A tentative analysis

The variety of processes outlined above can be summarized using a formalism inspired by the autosegmental model (Clements 1985, Goldsmith 1989, Snider 1999). Just as a floating tone belongs to a tonal tier, in such a formalism, what we have called the floating nasal belongs to a nasality tier which hosts a suprasegmental element N responsible for various nasalization processes.

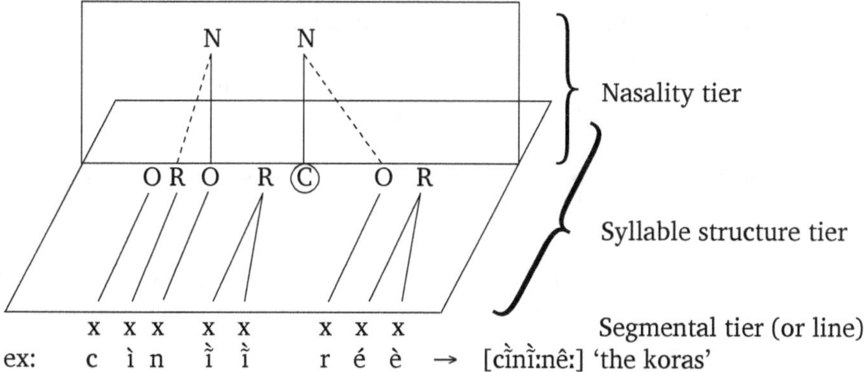

Figure 7.1. A geometrical representation of nasalization processes.

N can associate to a position on the syllable structure, either the onset (O) or coda (C) position. This position in the syllable structure is either a nasal consonant that nasalizes the vowels to its left within the phonological word boundaries or a free or floating coda (represented as a circled C) that is associated with no element on the segmental tier but has several nasalization effects on adjacent segments, as illustrated in figure 7.1.

The autosegmental theory model allows us to formalize these processes. The N element on the nasality tier is associated through solid lines to different positions on the syllable structure tier. The dotted lines represent the assimilation processes, the spreading of the nasality feature to adjacent elements on the syllable structure tier.

Two regressive assimilation processes:

There is first a very general one where any oral vowel (short or long, corresponding to the syllable rime) within the phonological word boundaries is nasalized by a following nasal consonant (onset), neutralizing the oral/nasal contrast for vowels before a nasal consonant.

(45) /ma:mã́/ = [mã̄:mã́] 'corn'

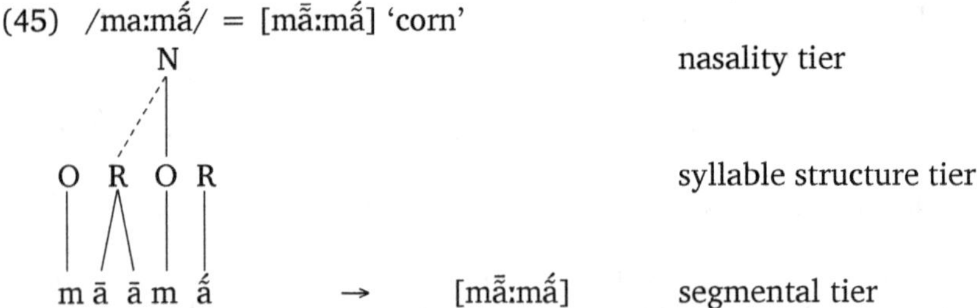

A second process happens in the morphological compounding operation when the word-final oral vowel (short or long) is nasalized by a following floating nasal (N) when followed by a second word-initial fricative consonant.

(46) /bɔ̄:/(N) # /sú:/ → [bɔ̃̄:sú:] 'beard'
cheek hair

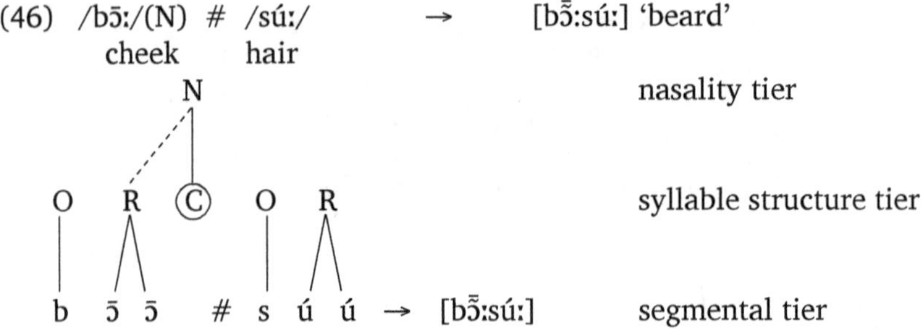

N docking process on adjacent sonorant [r]:

The floating nasal materializes as nasalization on the adjacent morpheme-initial oral sonorant:

(47) /ká/(N) + /rè:/ → [kã́nè:] 'the flowers'
flower PL

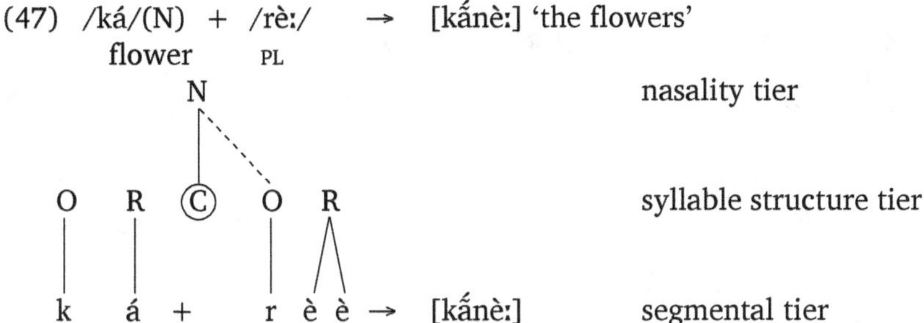

In this process, the stem-final oral vowel is nasalized by the adjacent nasalized sonorant according to the first general regressive assimilation rule above.

If there is no sonorant consonant onset next to it, then there is no linking possible and the floating nasal deletes.

N deleting process with adjacent empty onset:

(48) /ká/(N) + /V̀/ → [kâ:] 'the flower'
flower DEF

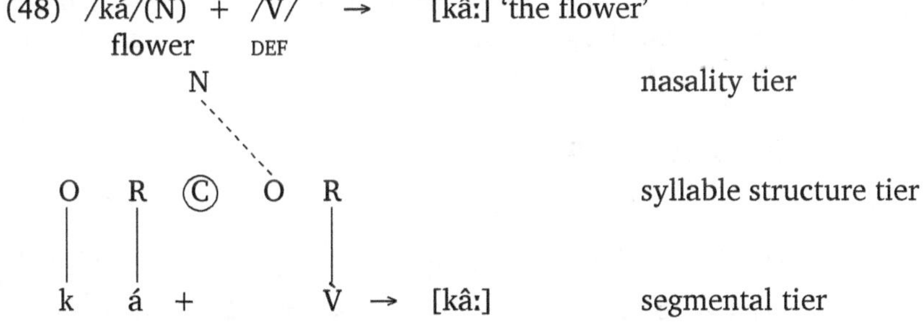

Segmental Nasal Epenthesis:

In the noun-compounding morphological operation, the floating nasal surfaces as a syllable coda in the form of a nasal consonant that shares the word-initial plosive point of articulation of the second word.

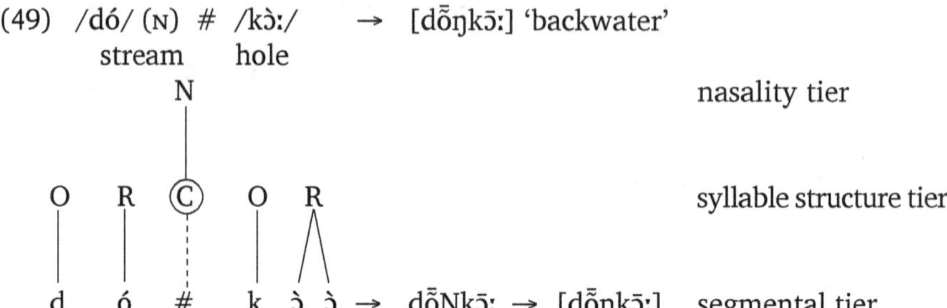

7.2.4 Implications for orthography

The previous sections showed how the floating nasal (N) has a formal impact on both the N-bearing stem and the adjacent morpheme.

Considering first the orthography of the N-bearing stem, Dzùùngoo writers represent both types of nasality with a final <n>. This means that the orthography in Dzùùngoo does not discriminate between the two types of nasality on the noun, as both are transcribed with a final <n>, but a difference can be seen on the alternant form of the adjacent morpheme, such as the definite plural.

Dzùùngoo definite plural orthography

(50) /dzíː/ <dzii> 'mouth' → /dzíːrèː/ <dzii rèè> 'the mouths'

(51) /tà̰ã̄/ <tàan> 'woman' → /tà̰ã̄rèː/ <tàan rèè> 'the women'

(52) /cɛ́/(N) <cɛn> 'breast' → /cɛ̃́nèː/ <cɛn nèè> 'the breasts'

(53) /dzí/(N) <dzin> 'child' → /dzĩ́nèː/ <dzin nèè> 'the children'

Van Dyken and Kutsch Lojenga's phonological bridging criterion asks, "Should the written word change shape according to the predictable changes in pronunciation? Or should it maintain a stable appearance?" (1993:14). Considering these four examples, it appears at first sight that the plural morpheme's alternate forms are not predictable; they are determined by the presence or absence of the autosegment N that belongs to the word's underlying structure. In itself this seems to be a good enough reason for the plural morpheme not to maintain a stable appearance in its written form.

However, there may be another issue to consider; looking at the four written noun plural forms, there seems to be some redundancy in a noun with a final oral vowel (with very weak nasalization though) and a floating nasal (N) (as in [52]). The orthographic representation of a nasal feature is present on both the noun and the plural alternant form: <cɛn nèè> 'the breasts', just as on a noun with a final nasal vowel and a floating nasal (N): <dzin nèè> 'the children' (as in [53]). For this third example, one could argue that, since the nasalization of the initial consonant of the plural is caused by the floating nasal (N) and not by a preceding nasal vowel, one orthographic representation of a nasal feature should be enough to signal there is a floating nasal (N) involved in this alternant form and therefore <cɛ nèè> 'the breasts' should be written.

If a final <n> signals both types of nasality, it is the reader's lexical knowledge that should allow him/her to resolve any ambiguity about how to interpret it either as marking a nasalized vowel or as a floating nasal that will nasalize the following plural morpheme. Dzùùn people have been writing their language for more than twenty years and some recognize that to transcribe nasality on both the plural morpheme and the noun is somewhat redundant if the noun-final vowel is not nasalized. Some even started to write some of these nouns without a final <n>, considering the fact that, as in example (47), the definite form of these nouns in certain structural contexts goes through the N deletion process that leaves no trace of nasality on them.

The current Dzùùngoo lexical database has 777 nouns and verbs with at least one of the two types of nasalization in word-final position. Of these 777 lexical items, we counted 737 (94%) that manifest the presence of a floating nasal through adjacent initial sonorant nasalization; and 40 of these 777 items exhibit just segmental nasality with no assimilation process at the righthand boundary. From a psychological point of view and considering the above statistical data, one may say that for Dzùùngoo speakers, nasality is more associated with phonological processes than with vowel quality. Therefore, for orthography users, the final <n> is at least as relevant for assimilation processes as for vowel nasalization. The polysyllabic items, nouns and verbs alike, ending with extra short vowel structures, namely, [CV̌rV̌] and [CV̌rV̌](N), illustrate the case where writing the floating nasal may be crucial in differentiating between indefinite nouns and between infinitive verb forms, just as it is for differentiating between definite nouns and between imperfective verb forms, as shown in (54) to (57).

(54) [kéré] <kere> 'a turtledove' [kél:à] <ker'là> 'the turtledove'

(55) [kērē](N) <keren> 'a rafter' [kēn:á] <ker'na> 'the rafter'

(56) [kòrò] <kòrò> 'to meet' [kòl:á] <kòr'la> 'is meeting'

(57) [kōrō](N) <koron> 'to discipline' [kōn:á] <kor'na> 'is disciplining'

There are not that many such pairs, but they certainly contribute to a feeling of necessity for such "redundant" orthography.

7.3 Jowulu

7.3.1 The data

Jowulu is spoken by 10,000 people (McPherson 2020b), mostly in Mali. The data we are using here come from two documents, one published (Djilla et al. 2004) and one unpublished (Djilla and Eenkhoorn-Pilon 2018). The language has also been analysed as having a floating nasal (Djilla et al. 2004), which has been described as part of a CV^{N}[5] syllable structure. In isolation, it is realized as a "weak [i]" after the final vowel.

(58) /do(N)/ [do^{i}] 'partridge'

(59) /kã(N)/ [kã^{i}] 'leg'

As in Dzùùngoo, one can detect the existence of the floating nasal in Jowulu in several phonological processes at the level of word boundaries in morphological operations such as compounding or in phrase structure operations with noun phrase operators.

For instance, the definite article /ki/ is realized [ŋi] following a floating nasal and [ki] in the absence of a floating nasal, whether the final vowel is oral or nasal.

(60)	/fu/ [fu]	'a house'	→	[fuki]	'the house'
(61)	/ʃɛ̃/ [ʃɛ̃]	'meat'	→	[ʃɛ̃ki]	'the meat'
(62)	/do(N)/ [do^{i}]	'a partridge'	→	[doŋi]	'the partridge'

As in Dzùùngoo, before a plosive, the Jowulu floating nasal is realized as a homorganic nasal consonant:

(63) /ko(N)/ 'man' + /fɔa(N)/ 'whitish' → [kõmvɔai]
'European (white person)'

As part of this process, the oral vowel before the nasal consonant is also realized as nasal.

The floating nasal in Jowulu causes several other consonant changes:

---

[5] This formalism CV^{N} corresponds to the formalism CV(N) used previously and which will be used in what follows.

Voiced palatals, both the plosive /ɟ/ and the glide /j/, become the palatal nasal [ɲ]:

(64) /ɲã(N)/ 'chicken' + /jɛ/ 'neck' → [ɲãɲɛ] 'chicken's neck'

Voiceless fricatives [f, s, ʃ] become voiced:

(65) /ɲã(N)/ 'chicken' + /fɔ́/[6] 'white' → [ɲãvɔ́] 'white chicken'

The floating nasal also triggers gemination of a following /l/:

(66) /ɲã(N)/ 'chicken' + /lú/ 'share' → [ɲãl:ú] 'share a chicken'

As these examples show, Jowulu has phonemic nasal vowels in addition to a floating nasal. In other words, vowel nasality is independent of the presence or not of a floating nasal, as illustrated by table 7.1.

Table 7.1. The floating nasal in Jowulu

Nasal	**/CV/**	**/CV(N)/**
/V/	ta 'go'	ka(N) 'here'
/Ṽ/	tã́ 'build'	tã́(N) 'squirrel'

As in Dzùùngoo, the initial oral sonorant consonant of such morphemes as /ri/ 'PL' or /ru/ 'in' is nasalized after the floating nasal. However, unlike Dzùùngoo, in Jowulu, the nasalization of the initial /r/ to [n] happens following any sort of nasality, i.e., a nasalized vowel (68), the floating nasal (69) or any syllable with any nasal feature (70):

(67) /ba:/ 'goat' + /-rì/ 'PL' → [ba:ri] 'goats'

(68) /nã:/ 'cow' + /-rì/ 'PL' → [nã:ni] 'cows'

(69) /do(N)/ 'partridge' + /-rì/ 'PL' → [doni] 'partridges'

(70) /bjɛni/ 'web' + /-ru/ 'in' → [bjɛninu] 'in a web'

Unlike Dzùùngoo, in Jowulu the CV^{N} syllable may contain any of the fourteen vowels (seven oral and seven nasal) in the language's phonemic inventory.

[6] Though Jowulu is a tonal language the data I had access to had little tone marking and there is no orthographic form for tone.

7.3.2 Jowulu orthography

Unlike Dzùùngoo, the Jowulu orthography represents vocalic nasality with an <n> and the floating nasal with an <ŋ>. As we mentioned in the previous section, the floating nasal causes several phonological assimilation processes on adjacent morpheme-initial consonants: the definite article /ki/ is realized [ŋi], the floating nasal is realized as a homorganic nasal consonant before a plosive and the stem vowel is nasalized, /ɟ/ and /j/ are realized as [ɲ], voiceless fricatives /f, s, ʃ/ become voiced, and /l/ is geminated. However, the result of most of these processes does not appear in the words' orthographic forms. Orthography rule #6 states that any consonant change caused by the floating nasal is *not* written (Djilla and Eenkhoorn-Pilon 2018:25).

Thus, the definite article has only one orthographic form:

(71) [fu] <fu> 'a house' → [fuki] <fu ki> 'the house'

(72) [ʃɛ̃] <shɛn> 'meat' → [ʃɛ̃ki] <shɛn ki> 'the meat'

(73) [doi](N) <doŋ> 'a partridge' → [do^{i}ŋi] <doŋ ki> 'the partridge'

Phrase structure and syntactic operations also trigger such processes during which the adjacent morpheme-initial consonant remains stable in its orthographic form.

(74) /ɲã(N)/ 'chicken' + /jɛ/ 'neck' → [ɲãɲɛ] <ɲanŋ yɛ> 'chicken's neck'

(75) /ɲã(N)/ 'chicken' + /fɔ́/ 'white' → [ɲãvɔ́] < ɲanŋ fɔ> 'white chicken'

(76) /ɲã(N)/ 'chicken' + /lú/ 'share' → [ɲãl:ú] < ɲanŋ lu> 'share a chicken'

A homorganic nasal consonant which surfaces during a morphological compounding operation is not written in the orthography, but the nasalization of the stem vowel before the nasal consonant is shown by a following <n>.

(77) /ko(N)/ 'man' + /fɔa(N)/ 'whitish' → [kõmvɔai] <konfɔaŋ> 'European (white person)'

However, orthography rule #6 is limited in its application to the main lexical categories and does not apply to noun phrase operators and postpositions that have an initial /r/, like /ri/ 'PL' or /ru/ 'in'.

(78) /ba:/ 'goat' + /-rì/ 'PL' → [ba:ri] < baa ri> 'goats'

(79) /nã:/ 'cow' + /-rì/ 'PL' → [nã:ni] < naan ni> 'cows'

(80) /do(N)/ 'partridge' + /-rì/ 'PL' → [doni] < doŋ ni > 'partridges'

(81) /bjɛni/ 'web' + /-ru/ 'in' → [bjɛninu] < byɛni nu> 'in a web'

7.4 Duun

7.4.1 The data

There are between 130,000 and 160,000 speakers (Eenkhoorn-Pilon 2018) of the Duun language, living in more than forty villages in Mali. The data we are using here come from two documents, one unpublished (Eenkhoorn and Eenkhoorn-Pilon 2005) and one published (Eenkhoorn-Pilon 2018). The language has twelve vowels, seven oral and five nasal. It also has two types of nasality, one segmental with nasal vowels, and one autosegmental which the authors call a "hidden" nasal and corresponds to the floating nasal in Dzùùngoo and Jowulu. For consistency reasons, I will continue to use the term "floating". The floating nasal is a feature of some nouns and verbs. The following pairs of nouns sound the same, with the same final oral vowel.

(82) /ka/[7] 'yam' ≠ /ka(N)/ 'flower'

(83) /ɟe/ 'thing' ≠ /ɟe(N)/ 'thigh'

The form of the definite article varies according to the noun it modifies.

(84) [ka rɔ] 'the yam' ≠ [ka nɔ] 'the flower'

(85) [ɟe rɔ] 'the thing' ≠ [ɟe nɔ] 'the thigh'

As in Dzùùngoo and Jowulu, the nasalized variant of the definite article is not conditioned by the nasal quality of the preceding vowel.

(86) [blã rɔ] 'the support' ≠ [bla nɔ] 'the in-law'
/blã/ 'support' ≠ /bla(N)/ 'in-law'

(87) [mɔ̃ rɔ] 'the millet' ≠ [mɔ nɔ] 'the shea'
/mɔ̃/ 'millet' ≠ /mɔ(N)/ 'shea'

(88) [ʃɛ̃ rɔ] 'the pot' ≠ [cɛ nɔ] 'the breast'
/ʃɛ̃/ 'pot' ≠ /cɛ/ 'breast'

[7] The data I had access to in Duun had no tone marking, and there is no tone representation in the orthography of the language except for a limited number of grammatical words.

In verbs, the floating nasal gets revealed through inflectional operations; pairs of verbs with the same final oral vowel have different perfective inflected forms.

(89) /to/ 'stay' ≠ /to(N)/ 'dip' [toː] 'stayed' ≠ [toũ] 'dipped'

(90) /ba/ 'lay' ≠ /ba(N)/ 'beat' [ba:] 'laid' ≠ [baũ] 'beaten'

Unlike in Dzùùngoo, autosegmental nasality in Duun goes together with strong segmental vowel nasality with only the close vowels [ĩ, ũ]. In contrast, words with strongly nasalized open vowels [ɛ̃, ã, ɔ̃] are *not* associated with the floating nasal. The final vowel of words with the floating nasal is either a nasalized close vowel [ĩ, ũ] or an oral or weakly nasalized open vowel [e, ɛ, a, ɔ, o] as shown in table 7.2, third column.

Table 7.2. Association of Duun vowels with the floating nasal

	Definite article	
Nasalization:	**rɔ**	**nɔ**
Strong without / with floating N	ɛ̃, ɔ̃, ã	ĩ, ũ
Weak with floating N		e, ɛ, a, ɔ, o
None without floating N	i, e, ɛ, a, ɔ, o, u	

7.4.2 Duun orthography

Like in Dzùùngoo, and unlike in Jowulu, in the Duun orthography both types of nasality are written with a final <n>. However, the difference between the two types is clear in the orthography when a following morpheme is one which has an alternant form, such as the definite article.

(91) <blan rɔ> [blã rɔ] 'the support' ≠ [bla nɔ] 'the in-law' <blan nɔ>

(92) <mɔn rɔ> [mɔ̃ rɔ] 'the millet' ≠ [mɔ nɔ] 'the shea' <mɔn nɔ>

(93) <shɛn rɔ> [ʃɛ̃ rɔ] 'the pot' ≠ [cɛ nɔ] 'the breast' <cɛn nɔ>

Looking at the Duun orthography guide (Eenkhoorn-Pilon 2018), we also learn that this orthography rule applies only to free morphemes and not to clitics or suffixes. Though phonologically, we could argue the definite article functions more like a clitic than like a free morpheme, it is written as a separate word with a space preceding it. The understandable reason is that, as with the definite plural morpheme in Dzùùngoo, it functions at the noun phrase level rather than at the noun level. As a clitic, it does not modify the noun alone but occurs after the last item of the noun phrase.

Thus, it is written separately in conformity to the criterion of separability[8] (Van Dyken and Kutsch Lojenga 1993:9).

7.5 Seenku

7.5.1 The data

There are approximately 15,000 speakers of Seenku (McPherson 2020b), which is the easternmost Duun-Seenku cluster language. The limited data we are using here come from one published article (McPherson 2020b). As with the other three languages discussed here, the author describes two types of nasality. She also posits a perceivable three-way contrast in isolation between purely oral vowels (/kâ/[9] 'griot'), purely nasal vowels (/kã̌/ 'white'), and what she calls late nasalized vowels (/kâ(N)/ 'granary', realized as [kââ̰][10]). She claims that the realization in Seenku of what was called by others a floating or hidden nasal is not simply a phonological question of [+nasal] vs. [-nasal] segments, or a docked vs. undocked floating element, but calls for more gradient considerations. She thus favors the more neutral term "latent" to the phonological term "floating". But I will continue to use the term "floating" for consistency.

As in the other Samogo languages, the floating nasal in Seenku can co-occur with both oral and nasal vowels, as illustrated in table 7.3.

Table 7.3. The floating nasal in Seenku

Nasal	/CV/	/CV(N)/
/V/	ka 'griot'	ka(N) 'granary'
/Ṽ/	kã 'white'	kɔ̃(N) 'head'

Besides the perceivable contrast in isolation, the floating nasal in Seenku can be identified through a variety of alternation processes occurring at the

[8] This criterion states that "A functor is also written separately from the word with which it usually occurs when other words can come between them."

[9] McPherson indicates that there are four contrastive tone levels in Seenku: extra-low (X, ȁ), low (L, à), high (H, á) and super-high (S, a̋), plus numerous contour tones, among which the most common are low-superhigh (LS, ǎ), high-extra-low (HX, â), and super-high-extra-low (SX, ä). Tone is a property of the syllable. Thus, a word like kâa 'fight' represents a long vowel with a HX falling tone. On sesquisyllabic words, like /bəlě/, the tone mark rests on the full tonic syllable, i.e., the second vowel.

[10] With the challenge of transcribing in IPA this unfamiliar type of nasality, McPherson explains that this sequence [aâ̰] indicates a short vowel that begins as an oral vowel and ends as a nasal one, hence the expression "late nasalized vowel".

right boundary of words. Thus, before plosives, the floating nasal is realized as a homorganic nasal stop:

(94)	/dô(N)/ child	+	/kɔ̃̀/ head	→	[dóŋ̀kɔ̃̀] 'child's head'
(95)	/kâ(N)/ granary	+	/bəlě/ big	→	[kâmbəlě] 'big granary'
(96)	/cǔe(N)/ Cuen	+	/tɛ̃́/ GEN	→	[cǔentɛ̃́] 'Cuen's'

Before fricatives, the floating nasal is realized as nasalization on the preceding vowel, though it varies between full nasalization and late nasalization. McPherson does not specify, but I suppose full nasalization and late nasalization occur as free variation.

(97)	/sâ(N)/ hare	+	/sïo/ arrive.PRF	→	[sẫ sïo] 'hare has arrived'
(98)	/ɟé(N)-ɟɛ̃́(N)/ story	+	/fĩ́/ two	→	[ɟéɲɟɛ̃́ɛ̰̃ fĩ́] 'two stories'

Sonorants /l/ and /w/ following a floating nasal can be realized as [n] and [m], which McPherson terms "nasal alternation", or the sonorants can simply be nasalized as [l̃] and [w̃] with concurrent late nasalization of the preceding vowel, which she terms "nasalization". This is also a case of free variation.

(99)	/sã́(N)/ God	+	/lɛ̃́ / DAT	→	[sã́ nɛ̃́] ~ [sã́ḁ̃ l̃ɛ̃́] 'to God'
(100)	/dô(N)/ child	+	/wɛ̃̀ / with	→	[dó` mɛ̀][11] ~ [dóõ̥̀ w̃ɛ̀] 'with a child'

The other interesting evidence McPherson presents for the floating nasal on nouns concerns plural morphology. In Seenku the plural morpheme is a suprasegmental clitic or suprafix which consists of a floating [+front] vocalic feature and a floating [+raised] tonal feature, which cause noun stem-final vowel fronting and tone raising. As we already saw with the fricative consonant, the floating nasal has the effect of nasalizing the noun stem vowel in its plural form.

11 The form [dó`] represents a HL falling tone on the short vowel; since the circumflex is already used to indicate the HX falling tone, the L tone is left to the right of the syllable, not as a floating tone, merely as part of a HL tone pattern realized on [o].

(101) /kâ(N)/ 'granary' → [kɛ̃̋] 'granaries'

There is another set of nouns, often though not exclusively with long vowels, that show a different pattern. As expected, the floating nasal in the singular noun form shows the range of effects already discussed, such as the epenthesis of a homorganic nasal stop in front of a plosive consonant.

(102) /bɔ̏ɔ̂(N)/ 'bag' → [bɔ̏ɔ̂m bəlě] 'big bag'

However, in the plural form of the noun, it is simply deleted and does not have the effect of nasalizing the noun stem vowel.

(103) /bɔ̏ɔ̂(N)/ 'bag' → [bɔ̌ɛɛ] 'bags'

McPherson suspects that the behavior in the plural is likely related to the range of variation of the floating nasal in other contexts. For instance, /bɔ̏ɔ̂(N)/ 'bag' is more likely to have its floating nasal realized as a coda (i.e., as a final [ŋ]) even in isolation or before a /w/, though it can also show the more typical pattern of nasalizing the sonorant to [w̃] in this environment. The author recognizes there is still a need for extensive analysis to account for the different free variations.

7.5.2 Seenku orthography

A team of Seenku speakers started to write their language in the context of a translation project while orthography development was still in progress. When asked to transcribe the words in table 7.4, they offered the orthographic forms shown. The table also shows the Seenku data as transcribed by McPherson (2020b), in phonemic and phonetic forms (first and fourth columns).

Table 7.4. Seenku data in tentative orthographic form

Phonemic form	English	Orthographic form	Phonetic form
/kâ/	'griot'	<ka>	[kâ]
/kǎ̃/	'white'	<kan>	[kǎ̃]
/kâ(N)/	'granary'	<kaŋ>	[kâã̯]
/kɔ̃(N)/	'head'	<kɔn>	[kɔ̃̀]
/dô(N)/	'child'	<don>	[dôõ̯]
/dô(N)/ + /kɔ̃̀(N)/	'child's head'	<don kɔn>	[dóŋ̀kɔ̃̀]
/kâ(N)/ + /bəlě/	'big granary'	<kaŋ bile / kaŋ bele>	[kâmbəlě]
/sâ(N)/ + /sïo/	'hare has arrived'	<saŋ sio>	[sẫ sïo]
/ɟé(N)-ɟẽ̋(N)/ + /fĩ̋/	'two stories'	<den-den fin>	[ɟéɲɟẽ̋ẽ̯ fĩ̋]

Table 7.4 (*continued*)

Phonemic form	English	Orthographic form	Phonetic form
/sã̋(N)/ + /lɛ̃́ /	‘to God’	<Saŋ lɛ>	[sã̋ nɛ̃́] ~ [sã̋ḁ̃ l̃ɛ̃́]
/dô(N)/ + /wɛ̃̏ /	‘with a child’	<don wɛ>	[dó̀ mɛ̀] ~ [dóȍ̥ w̃ɛ̀]
/kɛ̃̋/	‘granaries’	<kɛn>	[kɛ̃̋]
/bɔ̌ɛɛ/	‘bags’	<buɛɛ>	[bɔ̌ɛɛ]
/bɔ̏ɔ̂(N) wɛ̃̏/	‘with a bag’	<bɔŋ wɛ>	[bɔ̏ɔ́ŋ̀ wɛ̀]
/kâ(N) wɛ̃̏/	‘with a granary’	<kaŋ wɛ>	[ká̀ w̃ɛ̀] ~ [ká̀ mɛ̀]

Orthography development is still in progress and table 7.4’s third column only reflects the writers’ intuitions, but we can see that the translators transcribe what McPherson transcribed as late nasalization for the phonetic realization of the floating nasal in isolation in a variety of ways, based on their perception of the sounds. The limited data of this table shows some variations. Some words are perceived as ending with an [ŋ], like /kâ(N)/ ‘granary’ spelled <kaŋ> and pronounced by the translators [kaŋ]. Some are perceived as ending with an [n], like /dô(N)/ ‘child’ spelled <don> and pronounced by the translators [don]. Therefore the orthographic representation of the floating nasal is currently less consistent in Seenku compared to how it is in the other three Samogo languages.

7.6 Summary

As this brief overview shows, there is a great variety of processes and patterns associated with the floating nasal found in these four languages. Table 7.5 gives a synoptic view of what they have in common and where they differ.

Table 7.5. Features of the nasalization processes in Dzùùngoo, Jowulu, Duun and Seenku

Feature	Dzùùngoo	Jowulu	Duun	Seenku
Phonemic vowels	7 oral, 5 nasal	7 oral, 7 nasal	7 oral, 5 nasal	7 oral, 5 nasal
Vowel pre-N	nasal & oral with exception of [i, u]	nasal & oral	nasal limited to [ĩ, ũ] & oral with exception of [i, u]	nasal & oral
Realized in isolation	as very weak vowel nasalization	as weak final close front vowel [V i]	as very weak vowel nasalization	perceived as late nasalization [aã̰]
Docking on consonant	limited to sonorant r rV → nV (plural, postposition, DEF)	- rV → nV (plural, postposition) but same effect following Ṽ - /ki/ → [ŋi] DEF - [j, ɟ] → [ɲ] - voiceless fricative → voiced fricative - [lV] → [l:V]	limited to sonorant r rV → nV (plural, postposition, DEF)	limited to sonorants l & w l → n & w → m in free variation: l → l̃ & w → w̃
Epenthesis of homorganic nasal consonant	before plosive	before plosive	before plosive	before plosive
Nasalize V	stem V if followed by fricative C	stem V if followed by plosive	perfective inflection -V[a]	noun stem V before PL if V short
N deleted	after assimilation process followed by empty syllable onset			before PL if noun stem V long

[a] In Duun the perfective morpheme is a lengthening of the verb-final vowel.

The four languages all have in common the epenthesis of a homorganic nasal in front of a plosive consonant. In all four languages the floating nasal has a perceptible effect on the preceding vowel when a word occurs in isolation, but this effect differs between the languages and may be described accordingly as weak nasalization, late nasalization or a weak [i]. All the languages share the capacity for the floating element to dock to a following consonant, though Jowulu offers a wide variety of segments subject to such assimilation processes, whereas the other three languages limit docking to sonorants and more specifically, Seenku limits it to [l, w] and Dzùùngoo and Duun to [r]. The nasalization of stem-final oral vowels is another divergent factor. Stem vowels are nasalized before an obstruent in Dzùùngoo and before a plosive in Jowulu. In Seenku, vowel nasalization is triggered by the plural morpheme's floating vocalic feature and is conditioned by vowel length. In Duun stem vowels do not get nasalized, but the perfective inflectional suffix does undergo nasalization. The next divergent factor is the quality of the vowel which may occur preceding the floating nasal. In Jowulu and Seenku all oral and nasal vowels may precede the floating nasal (N); in Dzùùngoo, all vowels but [i, u] may precede (N) and in Duun, all oral vowels except [i, u] as well as the nasal vowels [ĩ, ũ] may precede (N).

Table 7.6 compares orthography decisions in Dzùùngoo, Jowulu and Duun.

Table 7.6. The orthography of nasalization in Dzùùngoo, Jowulu and Duun

Nasalization	**Dzùùngoo**	**Jowulu**	**Duun**
Orthographic Ṽ	Vn	Vn	Vn
Orthographic V(N)	Vn	Vŋ	Vn
Assimilation processes: pre N	not applicable (in the orthography)	compounding: oral stem vowel V → <Vn>	not applicable (in the orthography)
Assimilation processes: post N	initial sonorant <r-> → <n-> (plural, postpositions) including suffixes like DEF / imperfective on [CV̌rV̌] words	initial sonorant <r-> → <n-> (plural, postpositions) though not limited to N	initial sonorant <r-> → <n-> (plural, postpositions, def) but not suffixes like imperfective /–r/

We already invoked Van Dyken and Kutsch Lojenga's criterion of phonological bridging (1993:14) in relation to the redundancy in Dzùùngoo orthography. That is, is it necessary to write the floating nasal with a final <n> if the stem vowel is not nasalized since the effects of the floating nasal may be visible in the representation of the following orthographic word? Though psychologically, users may demonstrate a strong awareness of the morphophonological processes associated with such words, some users tend to drop the final <n>, especially on the definite form of the great majority of nouns that undergo a process of (N) deletion which clears all trace of nasality of the phonetic form, such as <kan> [ká] ‘a flower’, <kaàn> [kâː] ‘the flower’, which some write <kaà>.

Given the similarities between the Dzùùngoo and Duun orthographies and looking at the Duun data, one may wonder whether words with a floating nasal are not also subject to the same type of orthographic redundancy as in Dzùùngoo. If a Duun noun is followed by the definite morpheme <nɔ>, users will know its final vowel is necessarily [ĩ, e, ɛ, a, ɔ, o, ũ] and the floating nasal is responsible for the nasal form of the definite morpheme. Following the orthographic rules, they will write these final vowels <in, en, ɛn, an, ɔn, on, un>. If the definite is <rɔ>, the final vowel must be [i, e, ɛ, ɛ̃, a, ã, ɔ, ɔ̃, o, u] and users will write <i, e, ɛ, ɛn, a, an, ɔ, ɔn, o, u>, thus discriminating between oral vowels with no final <n> and nasalized vowels with a final <n>.

Looking at the two lists of graphemes, we realize that orthographic forms <ɛn, an, ɔn> may refer to two phonological realities: either an oral vowel followed by a floating nasal /V(N)/ or a nasal vowel /Ṽ/. However, the form of the definite (or plural or postposition) morpheme removes the apparent ambiguity. Then as in Dzùùngoo, we may ask whether it is necessary to write the floating nasal with a final <n> if the stem vowel is not nasalized itself. The question may be worth asking though we may see at least one good reason for writing the floating nasal with a final <n>:

- If users do not write the floating nasal, then the orthographic forms <e, ɛ, a, ɔ, o> become ambiguous, referring either to /V(N)/ or to /V/. If a noun is not adjacent to a definite, plural or postposition morpheme, then the reader is not able to resolve the ambiguity. Similarly, if a verb is not inflected with a perfective suffix, the ambiguity remains.

Jowulu has the most explicit orthography with a final <n> to signal nasal vowels and a final <ŋ> to signal a floating nasal. This orthography does not leave space either for ambiguity or for redundancy. Users write oral vowels <V>, oral vowels with a floating nasal <Vŋ>, nasal vowels <Vn>, and nasal vowels with a floating nasal <Vnŋ>.

7.7 Conclusion

The preceding discussion on the Dzùùngoo, Jowulu, Duun and Seenku data and their influence on orthography decisions has revealed a great variety of patterns and processes associated with what has been referred to as a floating, hidden or latent nasal. In her article on the latent nasal in Seenku, McPherson (2020b) points out that the complex nasality features found in the Samogo languages are widely shared in the larger Mande language family.

In the South Mande subfamily, initial consonant alternation processes at the right boundary of words are also well documented and are similar to what has been described here for the Samogo languages. Kpele (or Kpelle) is one of the languages of the South Mande subfamily. More than one million speakers use one of the three dialects in Guinea and Liberia (Konoshenko 2008). As with the Samogo languages, the language has oral and nasal vowels, and nasal vowels do not affect the initial consonant of the alternant forms of the adjacent morphemes. The alternant forms are instead caused by a segmental final [-ŋ]. As in the Samogo languages, the final [-ŋ] nasalizes oral sonorants and also has the effect of voicing voiceless stops. In 1976, Guinea developed a national alphabet, and Kpele, one of the larger languages in the country, adopted it. In 1989, an orthography reform resulted in some changes, including in the representation of nasalization, and more recently, linguists have worked on a modernized version of the national orthography, which again changed the representation of nasalization. Table 7.7 summarizes the evolution of the orthographic representation of nasalization in Kpele.

Table 7.7. Evolution of the orthographic representation of nasalization in Kpele

Nasalization	1976 old official orthography	1989 official orthography	Modernized orthography
Nasal vowel Ṽ	Vn	Vn	Vn
Final [ŋ]	Vnh	Vn	Vŋ

We conclude this chapter with some reflections on the challenges orthography designers may experience when dealing with such complex phonological issues as morpheme alternation caused by a floating nasal. Jowulu orthography designers responded with an explicit orthography whereas Dzùùngoo and Duun orthography designers opted for a more ambiguous yet also redundant orthography. Bible translators in Seenku had also intuitively begun to use a more ambiguous orthography. And the history shows us that, more than a thousand miles south of the Samogo languages area in Guinea, Kpele orthography designers have had to deal with a similar issue. The first official orthography in 1976 explicitly contrasted vowel nasality with alternation nasality. Then the 1989 orthography reform opted for an ambiguous representation of the two types of nasality. Though linguists tried in the 2000s to come back to a more explicit orthography, observers report that language users tend to follow the official 1989 orthography, with its ambiguity regarding nasality. It seems that for the Kpelle as well as for the Samogo orthographies, linguists have had an important role to play in orthography design, but orthography users may have a more lasting impact on long-term decisions. A thorough analysis of the processes involved at word boundaries is crucial. Nevertheless, the community of orthography users should always have the last word in the decision process.

References

Clements, George N. 1985. The geometry of phonological features. *Phonology Yearbook* 2:223–252.

Djilla, Mama, Bart Eenkhoorn, and Jacqueline Eenkhoorn-Pilon. 2004. *Phonologie du jôwulu ("samogho")*. Mande Languages and Linguistics 6. Köln: Rüdiger Köppe Verlag.

Djilla, Mama, and Jacqueline Eenkhoorn-Pilon. 2018. Grammaire fondamentale de la langue jɔ. Ms.

Eberhard, David M., Gary F. Simons, and Charles D. Fennig, eds. 2024. *Ethnologue: Languages of the world.* Twenty-seventh edition. Dallas, TX: SIL International. www.ethnologue.com.

Eenkhoorn, Bart, and Jacqueline Eenkhoorn-Pilon. 2005. Consultation sur la phonologie et l'orthographe du duungooma. Ms.

Eenkhoorn-Pilon, Jacqueline. 2018. *Grammaire fondamentale de la langue duun.* Mali: Société Internationale de Linguistique.

Goldsmith, John. 1989. *Autosegmental and metrical phonology.* Oxford: Blackwell.

Kastenholz, Raimund. 2002. "Samogo" language islands, and Mande-Senufo (Gur) interference phenomena. In Robert Nicolaï and Petr Zima (eds.), *Lexical and structural diffusion: Interplay of internal and external factors of language development in the West African Sahel,* 91–110. Nice: Université de Nice Sophia Antipolis.

Konoshenko, Maria. 2008. Tonal systems in three dialects of the Kpelle language. *Mandenkan* 44:21–42.

McPherson, Laura. 2020a. *A grammar of Seenku.* Mouton Grammar Library 83. Berlin: De Gruyter Mouton.

McPherson, Laura. 2020b. On latent nasals in Samogo. *Mandenkan* 63:68–88.

Snider, Keith. 1999. *The geometry and features of tone.* SIL International Publications in Linguistics 133. Dallas, TX: Summer Institute of Linguistics and the University of Texas at Arlington. (Second edition, 2020, also available in the SIL series Publications in Linguistics 153.)

Solomiac, Paul. 2014. *Phonologie et morphosyntaxe du dzùùngoo de Samogohiri.* Mande Languages and Linguistics / Langues et Linguistique Mandé 10. Köln: Rüdiger Köppe Verlag.

Van Dyken, Julia R., and Constance Kutsch Lojenga. 1993. Word boundaries: Key factors in orthography development. In Rhonda L. Hartell (ed.), *Alphabets of Africa,* 3–22. Dakar: UNESCO and SIL.

8
Linguistics, Politics, and Native Speaker Perception: The Analysis and Orthography of Pronominal Enclitics in Amoltepec Mixtec

Marc Schwab

Abstract

Amoltepec Mixtec has a set of pronominal enclitics which are heterogeneous in structure and in the way they attach to their host word. This chapter first presents some reasons why these enclitics can be analyzed as independent grammatical words, such as how they are not bound to a specific word class but can combine with most word classes. Then the phonological properties of the enclitics are discussed in detail with data showing how the enclitics depend on their host words in order to fulfill the requirements of a minimal phonological word in the language. The question of how to represent the enclitics orthographically is then addressed, with reference both to the relevant linguistic factors and also to the intuitions of the speakers of Amoltepec Mixtec and the orthographic guidelines which exist for Mixtec languages. A compromise solution which takes all these factors into account is then presented.

Abbreviations

1EXCL	1st person exclusive	COR	coronal
1INCL	1st person inclusive	EMPH	emphasis marker
1SG	1st person singular	FUT	future
2PL	2nd person plural	HORT	hortative
2SG	2nd person singular	INDEF	indefinite
3ANIM	3rd person animal	NAS	nasal
3F	3rd person feminine	OBJ	object (marker)
3INDEF	3rd person indefinite	POT	potential
3M	3rd person masculine	PRF	perfect
ANT	anterior	PST	past time
C	consonant	SON	sonorant
CON	continuant	V	vowel

8.1 Introduction

Clitics are an interesting category in linguistics: They are neither words nor affixes, but have properties from both these categories. Crystal (2008:80) describes them as "a form which resembles a word, but which cannot stand on its own as a normal utterance, being phonologically dependent upon a neighboring word." Dixon and Aikhenvald (2002:13) call a clitic "something which may have the status of a grammatical word but never that of a phonological word, being generally a stress-less element which attaches to some full phonological word."

In this chapter, I will present evidence for analyzing certain pronominal morphemes in Amoltepec Mixtec as clitics, and discuss how that is applied in orthography design. There are a number of factors in the analysis and decision process,[1] and they point towards different responses to the question of how to classify these morphemes. Representing them in the orthography in a form acceptable to all stakeholders formed an additional challenge.

[1] Although we did not know it at the time, our analysis is not original, but in line with other investigations into the structure of Mixtec languages. See Monica Macaulay's 1987 article which established the existence of clitics for Chalcatongo Mixtec.

When my wife and I started learning and analyzing Amoltepec Mixtec in 1997, the language had basically not been written.[2] One of the tasks in our linguistic work was the development of an orthography. I will present how not only grammatical and phonological factors had to be taken into account, but how politics and native speaker perception played a role in the development of the orthography in use today.

8.1.1 Mixtec languages and Amoltepec Mixtec

Amoltepec Mixtec is spoken in the county (*municipio*) of Santiago Amoltepec in the state of Oaxaca in Southern Mexico. It is part of the larger group of Mixtec languages. More than fifty Mixtec languages[3] are spoken in the Mexican states of Oaxaca, Guerrero, and Puebla (and in many other places where Mixtecs migrated to) by a total of more than half a million speakers. Mixtec languages are part of the Oto-Manguean language family, which today includes many languages in central and southern Mexico. Several Oto-Manguean languages which were spoken in Central America are now extinct.

Most speakers of Mixtec languages call their language *mixteco* in Spanish. In order to distinguish them, the name of a county or region (e.g., "Amoltepec Mixtec," "northern Tlaxiaco Mixtec") is usually added. For the sake of simplicity, I will use the term "Mixtec" in this chapter to refer to the variety spoken in Santiago Amoltepec [mbz], unless I specifically refer to a different variety or group of varieties.

According to the 2020 Mexican census,[4] there are roughly 14,000 inhabitants in the county of Santiago Amoltepec, and about half of them speak Mixtec. In reality, the number of speakers is higher, as indigenous languages have a low status in Mexico, and many speakers prefer to not indicate in the census that they speak an indigenous language.[5] Furthermore, many of the Mixtecs who have migrated away from the language area continue to speak their language.

---

[2] Over time, I became aware of three or four individuals who at some point had attempted to write their language. However, none of them had had any linguistic training or experience, and so they were unknowingly limited by the letters they knew from the Spanish alphabet. As a consequence, all of them were frustrated and later gave up their attempts. No effort had ever been made to promote a writing system for the language.

[3] The *Ethnologue* (Eberhard et al. 2024) lists fifty-two Mixtec languages. INALI, the Mexican government institution responsible for issues related to indigenous languages, lists eighty-one. http://www.inali.gob.mx/pdf/CLIN_completo.pdf, accessed October 27, 2022.

[4] https://en.www.inegi.org.mx/app/scitel/consultas/index#. Accessed October 27, 2022.

[5] Personal observation.

8.1.2 Phonology basics for Amoltepec Mixtec

A complete description of the phonology of Amoltepec Mixtec is beyond the scope of this chapter. Below I will present some basic information to give the reader the necessary basis for understanding the following discussion. Additional details on the phonology will be presented at appropriate places in the discussion.

Mixtec is a tonal language.[6] A monomorphemic Mixtec word is typically bimoraic[7] and has two tones.[8]

Tables 8.1 and 8.2 show the consonant and vowel phonemes in Amoltepec Mixtec. In both tables, the phonemes are shown, followed by the orthographic symbol used in the current orthography.

Table 8.1. Consonant phonemes in Amoltepec Mixtec

PHONEMES			**-cor**	**+cor**		**-cor**
			+ant		**-ant**	
- son	**- cont**		/p/ <p>	/t/ <t>		/k/ <k>
	+cont		/ɸ/[a] <f>	/s/ <s>	/ʃ/[b] <x>	/χ/ <j>
+son	**- cont**	**+nas**	/m/ <m>	/n/ <n>		/ɲ/ <ñ>
		- nas		/l/ <l>		
	+cont		/β/ <v>	/ɹ/ <r>		/j/ <y>

[a] /ɸ/ only occurs in loanwords.
[b] [s] and [ʃ] seem to have developed out of a single phoneme. In many contexts, they are either in complementary distribution, or they neutralize. However, there are enough contrasting examples to warrant having them as separate phonemes.

---

[6] For the present topic, tone is mostly not relevant. For these reasons, tone is generally not written in this chapter unless specifically mentioned, e.g., in (73–79).

[7] This is, apparently, not a unique feature of Mixtec languages. Dixon and Aikhenvald (2002:14) write: "In other languages each word must have at least two moras; thus, if a word is monosyllabic it must include a long vowel or a diphthong – this happens in Warekena (Aikhenvald 1998: 409) and in Fijian (Dixon 1988a: 25)." Since Pike (1948:79–81), this bimoraic basic word is called "couplet" (Pike called it "tonemic couplet") in much of the literature on Mixtec languages. For the most thorough more recent treatment, see Josserand (1983). Penner (2019) analyzes the couplet as foot. Trisyllabic words (and the rare longer ones) are often recognizable as the result of a historic word formation process, for example, compounding, causativization, derivation. Words that are monosyllabic either have a long vowel (and thus, two morae), or they are clitics. This chapter does not discuss all clitics in Mixtec, but focuses on the pronominal enclitics.

[8] Some words have floating tones, but this is not relevant to the issues being discussed in this chapter.

There is also a glottal stop in Mixtec, but it is not analyzed as a phoneme. It appears in two contexts. One is word-initially before vowels, where it is not distinctive, and not written in the orthography. The other is when it follows the first vowel of a bimoraic root, where it is considered a feature of the root or the vowel.[9]

Amoltepec Mixtec has six vowels, which are presented in table 8.2.

Table 8.2. Vowel phonemes in Amoltepec Mixtec

Height	**Front**	**Center**	**Back**
Close	/i/ <i>	/ɨ/ <ɨ>	/ɯ/ <u>
Open	/ɛ/ <e>	/ɐ/ <a>	/ʌ/ <o>

All of these can occur in simple form; as well as nasalized, glottalized, or lengthened, and in all possible combinations of these three features.

Nasalization, glottalization, and lengthening are all historic processes in Mixtec. The first two are considered features of the root.[10] Lengthening happens when a root only has one vowel. All three processes will be explained and illustrated in more detail in § 8.4. The following examples provide a basic introduction of the phenomena by illustrating all the possible vowel realizations for the vowel /i/.

The first two examples show the phoneme /i/ as a simple vowel in the two possible vowel slots of a monomorphemic and bimoraic root. (All examples in §§ 8.1 to 8.5 will be given in phonemic form, with a phonetic transcription in square brackets added where necessary.)

(1) /itɐ/ [ʔitɐ] 'flower' simple

(2) /kɐti/ [kɐti] 'to say' simple

Any vowel adjacent to an intervocalic nasal (/m/, /n/ or /ŋ/) is nasalized:

(3) /ʃini/ [ʃĩnĩ] 'head' nasalized

---

[9] Macaulay and Salmons (1995) describe the glottal stop (for all Mixtec languages) as a characteristic of the root. Given the distributional restrictions of the glottal stop, this is probably historically correct, and better explains the current phonology of Mixtec languages than the view that glottalization is a characteristic of a vowel. While there is no consensus whether the glottalized feature relates to the vowel or the root (or couplet, or foot), consensus does exist that the glottal stop is not a phoneme. In order to simplify what is presented here, I will treat it as a vowel feature. A detailed critique of the difference between the two approaches is beyond the scope of this chapter.

[10] For analyses of these topics in Mixtec languages in general, see Marlett (1992) on nasalization, and Macaulay and Salmons (1995) on glottalization.

Glottalization of a vowel is realized as a glottal stop [ˀ] following the vowel.

(4) /βiˀntjɐ/[11] [βiʔntjɐ] 'nopal cactus' glottalized

When a root has only one underlying vowel, this vowel is lengthened.

(5) /βi/ [βiː] 'heavy' lengthened

In cases where the single underlying vowel is glottalized, it is realized with a glottal stop, and an echo of the vowel following the glottal stop.

(6) /βiˀi/[12] [βiʔi] 'house' glottalized and lengthened

Nasalization also exists in combination with glottalization, and with lengthening:

(7) /tʃiˀni/ [tʃĩʔnĩ] 'to bind' nasalized and glottalized

(8) /stni/ [stnĩː] 'nose' nasalized and lengthened

And finally, all three vowel modifications can occur together:

(9) /tʃiˀiN/[13] [tʃĩʔĩ] 'with' nasalized, glottalized, and lengthened

---

[11] Strictly speaking, a more correct phonological annotation would be /βintjɐG/ with the G indicating glottalization of the root (see Macaulay and Salmons 1995). However, this is a very abstract representation and would make understanding the data more difficult, while not being relevant to the topic under discussion. I therefore indicate the glottalization of vowels with the symbol /ˀ/, even though it is not part of the phoneme inventory.

[12] As in example (4) (see the footnote there), a more correct phonological representation would be /βiG/.

[13] The capital /N/ in phonological transcription indicates the nasalization of the preceding vowel. Theoretically, this could also be added to examples (3), (7), and (8). However, it would be redundant in those, as they contain nasal consonants which already indicate nasalization. Marlett (1992) claims that, historically, the nasalization of a root caused the production of the nasal consonants as allophones of a set of oral consonants. In fact, the oral and nasal sonorants are in complementary distribution. But these processes seem to be no longer productive today.

Each syllable has a vowel, and may have an onset of up to three consonants.[14] The different possible syllable patterns are illustrated here for the first syllable of a word:

(10) /i.sʌ/ V.CV 'rabbit'

(11) /ti.ti/ CV.CV 'avocado'

(12) /skɨ.jɨ/ CCV.CV 'blister'

(13) /skβi.tɐ/ CCCV.CV[15] 'to lose something'

Basically, all syllables in Mixtec words are open. Most loanwords are adapted to fit this pattern, either by dropping the word-final consonant, or by adding a vowel after it:

(14) /lʌni/ (Span. *lunes*) 'Monday'

(15) /χuɐ/ (Span. *Juan*) 'John'

(16) /kɯɹɯsi/ (Span. *cruz*) 'cross'

It seems that only relatively recent loanwords do not follow this pattern (e.g., /tʌtʌɹ/, Span. *doctor,* /ɐɹʌs/, Span. *arroz* 'rice').

There are only two phonetic consonant sounds which can occur in syllable-final position. One of them is the glottal stop, which occurs in syllable-final, but never word-final, position. As mentioned above, it is analyzed and treated as a feature of the vowel, not as a consonant.

The other exception is the nasal [ŋ]. This is the allophone of /n/ in word-final position, and it occurs exclusively as the pronominal enclitic /=n/. It will be presented in more detail later in this chapter.

[14] Monica Macaulay, in her grammar of Chalcatongo Mixtec [mig], claims that "[c]onsonant clusters are generally disallowed in all varieties of Mixtec" (Macaulay 1996:26). Whilst this generalization holds true for many Mixtec varieties, there are exceptions with clusters of up to three consonants. For example, Magdalena Peñasco Mixtec [xtm] has /skʊ/, /ʃtn/, /ʃtʃ/, /ʃsj/ and /ʃnd/ (Hollenbach 2013:14). For Northern Tlaxiaco Mixtec [xtn], Gittlen reports /ʃtʃ/ and /ʃtn/ (Gittlen 2016:111). Even Macaulay herself acknowledges the existence of the combination /snd/ in Chalcatongo Mixtec (26). An analysis of fewer than three consonants in a cluster would not work well for Amoltepec Mixtec as although it would reduce the number of permitted syllable patterns, it would at the same time multiply the amount of required phonemes. For the purpose of this chapter, however, such an analysis would not affect the phonological or orthographic treatment of clitics.

[15] Other existing clusters of three consonants include /stn/, /nkj/, /ntj/, and /tnj/.

8.2 The pronominal enclitics in Amoltepec Mixtec

Mixtec has two sets of pronominal morphemes. One set consists of phonological words for first and second person reference only. The second set also includes third person forms and consists of shortened versions which are historically related to the independent pronouns or other nouns, as shown in table 8.3.[16] Mixtec does not distinguish number morphologically in nouns; the pronominal enclitic morphemes are the only group of morphemes which include a distinction of number. Both sets of pronouns are listed in table 8.3:

Table 8.3. The pronominal enclitics in Amoltepec Mixtec

Full form	Gloss	Clitic	Comment
/jɯˀɯ/	I (1SG)	**=i**	-
/jʌˀʌ/ [jʌ̀ʔʌ̀]	we (1INCL)	**=ʌ**	-
-	we (1EXCL)	**=ntɨ**	-
/jʌˀʌ/ [jʌ̀ʔʌ̄]	you (2SG)	**=n [ŋ]**	-
(/jʌˀʌ stnɐˀɐ=ntʌ/)	you (2PL)	**=ntʌ**	-
(/rɐ/)	(man)	**=rɐ**	(For all third person pronouns, there is no distinction between SG and PL.)
(/ɲɐˀɐ/)	(woman)	**=ñɐ**	
(/kɨtɨ/)	(animal)	**=tɨ [dɨ]** [17]	for animals
(/ɲɐjɨβɨ/)	(people)	**=jɨ**	for unspecified or mixed groups

Many varieties of Mixtec have more distinctions for pronouns[18] than those listed above.

[16] The origin or full form of some of the pronominal enclitics is unclear.

[17] [d] is an allophone of /t/ which only occurs in enclitics. This is the only morphological context where voiced stops occur.

[18] Marlett (2017) compares seventeen varieties of Mixtec plus three additional related languages. He identifies eighteen different categories of third person pronouns (no variety has all of them), including some which refer specifically to spherical objects, wooden objects, or liquids!

As can be seen from table 8.3, most pronominal enclitics have a single syllable with a C(C)V structure.[19] The 1SG and 1INCL morphemes consist only of a vowel, whereas the 2SG morpheme consists only of a consonant.

8.3 Reasons for treating the pronominal enclitics of Amoltepec Mixtec as orthographic words: Grammatical properties

The pronominal enclitics in Amoltepec Mixtec display a number of grammatical properties which are typically considered as reasons to write them as separate words.[20] These will be considered in § 8.3.1 and § 8.3.2.

8.3.1 Substitutability

"Substitutability refers to a situation in which a lexeme can be substituted by a grammatical morpheme in the same syntactic slot" (Kutsch Lojenga 2014:94). Unlike inflectional affixes, the pronominal enclitics in Mixtec can only appear when the referent is not mentioned otherwise, that is, by means of a noun phrase, noun, or independent pronoun. Consider the following set of examples:

(17) /ni tʃiˀi χɯɐ/ 'John died.'
PST to.die John

(18) /ni tʃiˀi = rɐ/ 'He died.'
PST to.die = 3M

(19) */ni tʃiˀi = rɐ χɯɐ/ *'John died.'
PST to.die = 3M John

(20) /ki kɐtʃi jɯˀɯ ɯ stɐ/ 'I will eat two tortillas!'
FUT to.eat 1SG two tortilla

[19] Most of the evidence in phonemic analysis points toward considering the sequence <nt> [nt] as two separate phonemes. This is represented by the "C" in brackets in the syllable structure description above. An alternative analysis of this sequence as a phonological unit would not affect the topic under discussion in this chapter.

[20] There are a number of properties which are sometimes used as proof or as a test that an element should be considered an orthographic word (see, for example, Kutsch Lojenga 2014). It is not the purpose of this section to consider all possible diagnostic tests, but rather to present evidence which shows that the Mixtec enclitics have properties which lend themselves to being written as orthographic words.

(21) /ki kɐtʃɯ ɯ stɐ/ 'I will eat two tortillas!'
/kɐtʃi = i/
FUT to.eat = 1SG two tortilla

(22) */ki kɐtʃɯ jɯˀɯ ɯ stɐ/ *'I will eat two tortillas!'
FUT to.eat = 1SG 1SG two tortilla

As can be observed in these examples, the pronominal enclitic is only permitted (18, 21) when there is no noun or pronoun already indicating the subject. Examples (17) and (20) are grammatical as they contain a noun and pronoun respectively, but no pronominal enclitics. The sentences where the enclitic is combined with a noun (19) or pronoun (22) are ungrammatical. The same principle applies where enclitics are used to indicate an object or another syntactic function.

8.3.2 Nonselectivity and separability

Nonselectivity is the property of morphemes which are not bound to a specific word class, but can combine with most word classes (Haspelmath 2011:45). This applies to the pronominal enclitics in Mixtec. Here are some examples[21] which show them following nouns (23–26), verbs (27–30), adverbs (31–34), numerals (35), and prepositions (36).

Where the pronominal enclitics follow a noun, they indicate possession or relationship:

(23) /inɐ = ɲɐ/ 'her dog' (or 'their (all female) dog')
dog = 3F

(24) /βiˀi = ɹɐ/ 'his house' (or 'their (all male) house')
house = 3M

(25) /tɐkɐ = tɨ/ 'its (or their) nest' (referring to animals)
nest = 3ANIM

(26) /sʌ = ji/ 'their clothes'
cloth = 3INDEF

[21] In order to simplify the presentation of the data, the examples in this section all have syllabic clitics, that is, they are all third person forms. The use of the nonsyllabic clitics (1SG, 1INCL and 2PL) will be discussed in the section on phonology below. However, everything demonstrated here applies to all the pronominal enclitics, including the nonsyllabic ones.

When they are combined with a verb, they mark the subject:

(27) /kɐtʃi = ɹɐ/ 'he will eat' (or they, all male)
to.eat (POT) = 3M

(28) /sɐtniɲɯ = ɲɐ/ 'she is working' (or they, all female)
to.work = 3F

(29) /kiʃi = tɨ/ 'it (animal) is sleeping' (or they)
to.sleep = 3ANIM

(30) /βɐtʃi = ji/ 'they are coming'
to.come = 3INDEF

If the verb is modified by an adverb, however, the pronoun follows the adverb (31–34):

(31) /ntisʌ = ɹɐ/ 'he is carrying (something)' (or they, all male)
to.carry = 3M

(32) /ntisʌ βi = ɹɐ/ 'he is carrying (a) heavy (load)' (as above)
to.carry heavy = 3M

(33) /sʌkʌ = ɲɐ/ 'she is hungry' (or they, all female)
hunger = 3F

(34) /sʌkʌ sɐkɐ = ɲɐ/ 'She is very hungry!' (as above)
hunger very = 3F

In contrasting each pair of examples (31–32), and (33–34), we observe how the verb and the clitic can be separated by another word. This complies with Kutsch Lojenga's criterion of separability, which "refers to a situation in which a grammatical morpheme can be separated from a neighboring lexical morpheme by the insertion of another lexical morpheme" (Kutsch Lojenga 2014:93).[22] The pronominal enclitics cannot only follow nouns, verbs. and adverbs, but most word classes, including numerals (35) and prepositions (36).

(35) /**ɯ = ji** ni tʃiˀi = ji/ 'Two of them died.'
two = 3INDEF PST to.die = 3INDEF

[22] Haspelmath (2011:44) refers to that property of a morpheme as interruptibility, which he considers "a sufficient criterion for two word status."

(36) /tʃitɛ tʃiˀiN = n tʃiˀiN = ɹɐ/ 'I saw you with him.'
tʃito = i
to.see = 1SG OBJ[23] = 2SG with = 3M

As can be seen from examples (23) to (36), the pronominal enclitic is nonselective in its grammatical context. It is also separable from its host word by another grammatical word. In these respects, it has features which support writing it as an independent word.

8.4 Reasons for not treating the pronominal enclitics of Amoltepec Mixtec as orthographic words: Phonological properties

In what has been presented to far, there has been no reason to not write the pronominal enclitics as separate units in the orthography. In the following subsections, however, I will show how that would be difficult for some of them.

It is easy to see in table 8.3 that the set of pronominal enclitics in Mixtec is not uniform structurally. While most have a C(C)V structure, the 2SG clitic consists of a consonant only and the 1SG and 1INCL clitics consist of a vowel only. We will now take a closer look at the phonological properties of these clitics.

As mentioned above, the 2SG clitic /=n/ [ŋ] is the only consonant allowed to close a syllable.[24] Just like the syllabic clitics, it can be joined to any Mixtec word, as native words invariably end with a vowel.[25] This is illustrated in the following examples.

---

[23] A human object is marked by /tʃiˀiN/, which in other contexts is translated 'with' and indicates instrument ('with a stone') or accompaniment ('with his mother').

[24] In the neighboring Mixtec variety of Ixtayutla [vmj], this morpheme is realized as a nasalized /u/ (Penner 2019:59). Other ways to analyze this might be possible, but whatever the historic origin of the enclitic /=n/, it is clearly pronounced in Amoltepec Mixtec as [ŋ] and is perceived as a consonant by native speakers. Also, most Mixtecs pronounce a word-final <n> in Spanish as [ŋ], even though the proper pronunciation in Spanish would be [n]. There is general agreement among Amoltepec Mixtec speakers that the 2SG enclitic [ŋ] should be represented by the letter <n>. This is not unique: Harris and Harris (2006:12) mention the existence of word final [n] and [n?], both also results of adding a pronominal morpheme to another word, in Santiago Nuyoo Mixtec [meh].

[25] Mixtec has a strategy for forming a second person for words that do not end in a vowel, like loanwords from Spanish. 'Your rice' (from Spanish *arroz*) would be <aros yo'o>, using the independent 2SG pronoun.

(37) /βiˀi = n/ [βiʔiŋ] 'your (SG) house'
house = 2SG

(38) /sɐtniɲɯ = n/ [sɐtnĩɲɯ̃ŋ] 'you (SG) are working'
to.work = 2SG

(39) /sʌkʌ sɐkɐ = n/ [sɐkɐŋ] 'You (SG) are very hungry!'
hunger very = 2SG

8.4.1 Phonological changes in the host word

As can be seen in (23) to (34), the enclitics with a CV syllable structure do not affect the pronunciation of the phonemes in the word to which they attach. The use of the 1SG and 1INCL clitics, however, is more complex, though sometimes there are no changes to the host word, as can be seen by comparing (40a) and (40b).

(40a) /miɲɯ/ [mĩɲɯ̃] 'cat'
cat

(40b) /miɲɯ = i/ [mĩɲɯ̃ĩ] 'my cat'
cat = 1SG

However, for the 1SG = i and 1INCL = o enclitics, it is more common that they affect the final vowel of the preceding word by either replacing it (41) or fusing with it (42) and (43).

(41) /nɐ **kɐtʌ**/ 'Let's sing!'
nɐ **kɐtɐ = ʌ**
HORT to.sing = 1INCL

(42) /**sɐtɛ**/ 'I buy'
sɐtɐ = i
to buy = 1SG

(43) /ni tʃitɛ ɨN ɲɯkβi/ 'I saw a fox.'
tʃitʌ = i
PST to.see = 1SG INDEF fox

In (41), the enclitic simply elides the word-final vowel. In (42) and (43), the two vowels coalesce, with the resulting vowel maintaining the feature

[+open] from the root vowel, and the feature [+front] from the enclitic. The result is a third (and also phonemic) vowel. In (42), the result of the coalescence of the open central vowel [ɐ] with the close front vowel [i] is the open front vowel [ɛ]. In (43), the fusion of open back [ʌ] and the close front vowel [i] is, again, the open front vowel [ɛ].[26] There are also a few cases where a clitic causes dissimilation:[27]

(44) /tʃɐtʃɯ/ 'I ate'
tʃɐtʃi=i
to.eat=1SG

8.4.2 Nasalized vowels

In this section, we will see how the nasalization of a root vowel affects the realization of the vocalic enclitics.

Nasalization in Mixtec is a feature which historically spread within a word, from the end of a root until blocked by an obstruent (Marlett 1992). It does not spread across word boundaries. There is no known monomorphemic word in which the first vowel would be nasalized, but the second not.[28] Any vowel adjacent to a nasal consonant (/m/, /n/, or /ñ/) within the etymological root is pronounced nasalized.[29]

(45) /ɲɐni/ [ɲɐ̃nĩ] 'brother (of a male)'

(46) /jɯtnɯ/ [jɯtnɯ̃] 'tree'

As seen in (46), a nonnasal consonant (in this case, [t]) stops the (historic) spreading of nasalization, so the first vowel of the word remains unnasalized. That is true for all nonnasal consonants. The glottal stop, however, is not analyzed as a consonant, but a modification of the vowel.[30]

---

[26] The process in (41) could also be represented as coalescence. Since the phonetic sound [ʌ] of the enclitic remains unchanged, I prefer to consider it a replacement (elision).

[27] Neville (2010:5) explains such cases as a way to avoid homophony between the two grammatically distinct words.

[28] For a more detailed presentation and discussion of nasalization in Mixtec languages, see Marlett (1992).

[29] Marlett (1992) suggests that, historically, there were two sets of sonorant consonants, one nasal and one oral. The nasalization of the root would affect both consonants and vowels, so that consequently the nasal sonorant consonants only occur in nasalized roots, adjacent to nasalized vowels. Non-nasalized roots would only contain the corresponding oral consonants.

[30] See § 8.1.2.

For that reason, in both words of the minimal pair (47) and (48), both vowels are nasalized, whether the first one is unmodified (47) or glottalized (48). The same applies to the lengthened glottalized vowel in (49).

(47) /kɐnɯ/ [kɐ̃nɯ̃] 'long'

(48) /kɐˀnɯ/ [kɐ̃ʔnɯ̃] 'big'

(49) /tnɯˀɯ/ [tnɯ̃ʔɯ̃] 'word'

If a vocalic enclitic attaches to a word with a nasalized final vowel, whether by addition, replacement, or coalescence, the nasalization feature of the root is also applied to the enclitic in the resulting form:

(50) /jɯtnɯi/ [jɯtnɯ̃ĩ] 'my tree'
jɯtnɯ = i
tree = 1SG

(51) /jɨtnʌ/ [jɨtnʌ̃] 'our tortilla cloth'
jɨtnɨ = ʌ
tortilla.cloth = 1INCL

(52) /tnɐɲɛ/ [tnɐ̃ɲɛ̃] 'I am sweating'
tnɐɲɐ = i
to.sweat = 1SG

Attaching the 2SG enclitic /=n/, or a nasal-initial syllabic enclitic (3F/=ɲɐ/, 1EXCL /=ntɨ/, or 2PL /=ntʌ/) does not affect the nasalization status of the word-final vowel:

(53a) /kɨˀɨ/ [kɨʔɨ] 'to touch'

(53b) /kɨˀɨ=n/ [kɨʔɨŋ] 'you (SG) touch'

(53c) /kɨˀɨ=ntʌ/ [kɨʔɨntʌ] 'you (PL) touch'

(54a) /kɨˀɨN/ [kɨ̃ʔɨ̃] 'to leave'

(54b) /kɨˀɨN=n/ [kɨ̃ʔɨ̃ŋ] 'you (SG) leave'

(54c) /kɨˀɨN=ntʌ/ [kɨ̃ʔɨ̃ntʌ] 'you (PL) leave'

8.4.3 Long vowels and echo vowels

In order to understand some of the processes occurring when a vocalic enclitic is added to a word with a long vowel or echo vowel, we have to look at the basic root structure of Mixtec again.

As mentioned in § 8.1.2, each monomorphemic grammatical word in Mixtec consists of two morae. In most cases, these words have two underlying syllables, with a consonantal onset for the second syllable. See the following examples.

(55)	/ɯni/	V.CV	'three'
(56)	/ɯtʃi/	V.CCV	'ten'
(57)	/ɐntjɐ/	V.CCCV	'where?'
(58)	/sɯtɯ/	CV.CV	'father'
(59)	/ntisʌ/	CCV.CV	'to carry'
(60)	/ntjɐjɯ/	CCCV.CV	'food'

There is a sizable group of words in Mixtec, however, which does not follow this pattern. These words have only a single underlying vowel. If this vowel is plain or nasalized (but not glottalized), it is lengthened phonetically, thus complying with the requirement to be bimoraic.

(61)	/ɯ/	[ɯː]	'two'
(62)	/ɲɨ/	[ɲɨ̃ː]	'salt'
(63)	/stʌ/	[stʌː]	'uncle'
(64)	/nkjʌ/	[nkjʌː]	'god'

If there is a glottalized vowel, the glottalization is realized with a glottal stop following it, and after that, the vowel is repeated (echoed):

(65)	/ɯˀɯN/	[ɯ̃ʔɯ̃]	'five'
(66)	/sɐˀɐ/	[sɐʔɐ]	'to make'
(67)	/tʃɛˀɛ/	[tʃɛʔɛ]	'skirt'
(68)	/ntjɛˀɛ/	[ntjɛʔɛ]	'up to here'

With two exceptions,[31] all monomorphemic words with these syllable patterns have the same vowel in both syllables.

The bimoraic nature of (61) to (68) is important when considering the way the vowel-initial pronominal enclitics affect words of these types.

Amoltepec Mixtec speakers apply two ways of combining the vocalic enclitics to a root of this type. The examples below show what happens when a pronominal enclitic is added to a monosyllabic root:

(69a)	/tjɛ/	[tjɛː]	'I am writing'
	tjɐ = i		
	to.write = 1SG		
(69b)	/tjɐi/	[tjɐi]	'I am writing'
	tjɐ = i		
	to.write = 1SG		
(69c)	*/tjɐɛ/		*'I am writing'
	tjɐ = i		
	to.write = 1SG		

Both (69a) and (69b) are accepted and commonly practiced realizations of the combination of the verb /tyɐ/ and the first person enclitic / = i/, but (69c) is not. In other words, the enclitic either fuses with the one (and only) root vowel (69a), thus changing both realizations of this vowel, or it fills the second mora of the root, and no lengthening is necessary to make the root bimoraic (69b).[32] It is not acceptable, however, to fuse the enclitic with only the second vowel realization of the root (69c), as it is done in cases where the root clearly has two separate vocalic units, as in (42–43).

The same conditions apply for roots with a glottalized vowel, and consequently, an echo realization of that vowel:

[31] There are two known exceptions. The word <va'u> 'coyote', is likely to be a word of Zapotec origin (personal communication from Meinardo Hernandez, a native speaker of a Zapotec language in the area); the word <cha'un> 'fifteen', is likely a compound of which not all original components can be identified. (Mixtec has a vigesimal number system; the number 'five' is <u'un>, which appears to be present in the second part of the word <cha'un>.)

[32] It almost appears as if the speakers of the two different accepted forms have different underlying concepts of the word structure: People who pronounce it as in (69a) unconsciously consider the root vowel as one lengthened unit, which must be modified as a whole, whereas those who use (69b) seem to recognize the "auxiliary" character of the second vowel, and therefore feel no inhibition against replacing it with the vowel of the enclitic.

(70a) /**sɛˀɛ** ɨN tniɲɯ/ 'I am doing a job.'
sɐˀɐ = i
to.do = 1SG one work

(70b) /**sɐˀi** ɨN tniɲɯ/ 'I am doing a job.'
sɐˀɐ = i
to.do = 1SG one work

(70c) */**sɐˀɛ** ɨN tniɲɯ/ *'I am doing a job.'
sɐˀɐ = i
to.do = 1SG one work

Similarly, in case of replacing the root vowel, both (pronounced) vowels are replaced:

(71) /nɐ **sʌˀʌ** ɨn βikʌ kɐˀnɯ/ 'Let's have a big party!' ***sɐˀʌ**
sɐˀɐ = ʌ
HORT to.do = 1INCL INDEF party big

(72) /nɐ **kʌˀʌN**/ 'Let's go!' ***kɨˀʌN**
kɨˀɨN = ʌ
HORT to.leave = 1INCL

All of these examples above illustrate how the vocalic pronominal enclitics are phonologically dependent on the preceding word.

8.4.4 Tone

So far, I have excluded tone in the discussion of the analysis and orthography of the pronominal enclitics in Amoltepec Mixtec. For the most part, tone is not relevant to the topic of this chapter. However, there are two tonal issues that are relevant. The first has to do with the interaction of tone and the enclitics, and is therefore treated here. The second affects the orthography, and is therefore discussed in § 8.6.4.

Anderson (2011:2004) defines clitics as "prosodically deficient elements": They do not have (all) the necessary properties to qualify as a phonological word.[33] That is true for Mixtec. Curiously, not all the pronominal enclitics share the same deficiency. Some of them contribute a syllable to their host word, but lack tone. For others, the opposite is true:

[33] Similarly, Dixon and Aikhenvald (2002:25) say that the term clitic is often used to refer to "something that is a grammatical word but not a complete phonological word."

They do have a tone, but do not contribute a syllable (or mora) to permit this tone to surface. The 2SG enclitic /=n/ contributes neither tone nor a syllable to its host word.

It is beyond the scope of this chapter to give a complete and satisfying analysis of Mixtec tone. For the present topic, it is relevant to know that the syllabic enclitics (as well as the single consonant 2SG enclitic) do not carry a tone of their own. In most cases, they accept the tone of the word-final syllable of the preceding word. (In the following examples, an acute accent indicates high tone, a grave accent indicates low tone, referring to surface tones.)

(73a) /βíkʌ́/ 'cloud'
cloud

(73b) /βíkʌ́=ɹé/ 'his cloud'
cloud=3M

(74a) /βìkʌ̀/ 'fiesta'
fiesta

(74b) /βìkʌ̀=ɹè/ 'his fiesta'
fiesta=3M

As the enclitic does not have a tone of its own, the last tone of the preceding word spreads onto the enclitic.[34] The vocalic enclitics =i (1SG) and =o (1INCL) however, are different. As mentioned above, they do not normally add a syllable (or duration) to the phrase. They do, however, carry tone, and this typically replaces the final tone of the preceding word. (Again, the indicated tones are surface tones.)

(75a) /sɯ̀tɯ̀/ 'father'
father

(75b) /sɯ̀tí/ 'my father'
sɯ̀tɯ̀=í
father=1SG

(76a) /βìˀì/ 'house'
house

(76b) /βìˀí/ 'my house'[35]
βìˀì=í
house=1SG

If the last vowel of the word already carries a high tone, the change of vowel quality as described above is usually enough to distinguish the possessed form from the unpossessed form:

[34] There are examples where this seems not to be the case. More analysis is needed, but it appears that these can be explained by other tone processes, e.g. by floating tones.

[35] See § 8.6.4 on how this is represented in writing.

(77a)	/íné/	'dog'	(77b)	/ínɛ́/	'my dog'
				íné = í	
	dog			dog = 1SG	

In cases where the word ends in an /i/ with a high tone, Mixtec speakers use a disambiguation strategy: Instead of adding the pronominal enclitic /=i/, the emphatic marker /ma/ (<maa>) is added, and the enclitic attaches to this morpheme instead of the word ending in /i/. In this way, another complete (bimoraic) structure is provided for the enclitic to attach to. Compare the forming of 1SG possessive for the following minimal pair:

(78a)	/ntìʃì/	'corn cob'	(78b)	/ntìʃí/	'my corn cob'
				ntìʃì = í	
	corn cob			corn cob = 1SG	
(79a)	/ntíʃí/	'whiskey'	(79b)	*/ntíʃí/	*'my whiskey'
				ntíʃí = í	
	whiskey			whiskey = 1SG	
			(79c)	/ntíʃí mɛ̌/	'my whiskey'
				ntíʃí mè = í	
				whiskey EMPH = 1SG	

In (78), the pronunciation of the low word-final /i/ of /ntìʃì/ 'corn cob', is raised by the 1SG enclitic. In (79), however, the word-final /i/ of /ntíʃí/ 'whiskey' is already high. In other words, the form in example (79b) 'my whiskey' would be identical to the unpossessed form of (79a), 'whiskey', and the two would be indistinguishable. The introduction of the emphatic marker /ma/ solves this issue, and instead of (79b), (79c) is used.[36]

8.5 Summary of reasons for and against treating pronominal enclitics as orthographic words

Summing up the discussion so far, we have seen that the pronominal enclitics have grammatical properties typical of orthographic words, but also phonological traits typical of affixes.

In support of writing the pronominal clitics as orthographic words, they

- can substitute lexemes (or phrases) in the same syntactic slot;
- are not bound to a specific word class, but can combine with most word classes;

[36] An alternative option which is also applied sometimes is the use of the independent pronoun /jɯˀɯ/ (1SG): /ntiʃi jɯˀɯ/ 'my whiskey'.

- can be separated from the word they refer to by other grammatical words;
- have a syntactic function in the sentence.

At the same time, they do not qualify as phonological words in Mixtec, as they

- cannot occur in isolation;
- do not comply with the requirements of the (minimal) phonological word in Mixtec, to have two morae and tone;
- cause phonological processes in their host word which do not occur across (grammatical) word boundaries.

8.6 Steps towards developing an orthographic solution for representing the enclitics

This leads us to the question of how to represent these enclitics in the orthography. From here on, the presentation of the examples will include an orthographic transcription. The reader may refer to tables 8.1 and 8.2 in § 8.1.2 for a reminder of the phoneme to grapheme correspondences, but it is appropriate to explain here some features of the current Mixtec orthography which might not be immediately obvious.

The combination of the consonants [t] and [ʃ] is written as <ch> in most varieties of Mixtec, based on the orthography of this sound combination in Spanish. In this chapter, the corresponding symbol combination <tx> is used, which represents the sound combination ([t] and [ʃ]). Where glottal stops modify vowels, they are written with the symbol <’> following the vowel. Word-initial glottal stops are not contrastive, and not represented in orthography.

8.6.1 Linguistic factors

In § 8.5 I summarized the linguistic factors. We have ample evidence that the short pronominal morphemes are indeed enclitics. That alone, however, is not enough information for designing an orthography. There might be more freedom to decide on word breaks than with morphemes which are clearly affixes, or clearly independent words, but additional information is needed for the development of a useful and acceptable orthography.

Van Dyken and Kutsch Lojenga close their essay on word boundaries in orthography development with this statement: “Ultimately, decisions on word boundaries are influenced by multiple factors, including social, political, educational, psycholinguistic and general linguistic factors” (Van Dyken and Kutsch Lojenga 1993:19–20). And in fact, in the end the political and psycholinguistic factors were more influential in the shaping of the orthography of these enclitics than the linguistic ones.

8.6.2 Native speaker perception

In the first attempts at developing an orthography, the nonsyllabic pronominal morphemes =i (1SG), =o (1EXCL) and =n (2SG) were written as part of the preceding word, but the syllabic ones as separate words. The following examples illustrate the original orthographic rule for the syllabic pronominal clitics, which was later changed:

(80) <sutu ña> 'her father'
father 3F

(81) <vi'i nto> 'your (PL) house'
house 2PL

(82) <txa ni txatxi yi> 'they already ate'
PRF PST eat 3INDEF

In the early stages of developing a writing system for Mixtec, these attempts were tried out with many speakers of the language. In most cases where we presented alternative orthography options, or asked people their opinions on ways of writing their language, they had no preferences for one way of spelling over another. The only exception to this was the reaction to our writing the pronominal morphemes as separate words. Every single person we asked strongly rejected this proposed way of spelling the syllabic pronominal morphemes, and the general reaction was "I cannot even read this (if written separately)." All people who were asked said that these morphemes were part of the preceding word, and needed to be written as part of it.[37] This strong reaction was quite surprising, given the general absence

[37] Interestingly, this native speaker perception of Mixtecs goes against a recommendation made by Constance Kutsch Lojenga, an expert in orthography development in Africa: "When is a pronominal form an independent word, and when does it have to be considered a prefix? The crucial test is to look at the third person forms (he/she, they) and provide a nominal subject instead. If the pronominal form disappears and is replaced by the nominal subject, it is a pronoun indeed, and it will need to be written separately from the verb by the criterion of substitutability. If, on the other hand, the 3SG or 3PL pronominal form is not omitted when a nominal subject is introduced, then it is most likely a subject prefix which needs to be written attached to the verb since it is not a substitutable morpheme" (Kutsch Lojenga 2014:100). For Mixtec, the question is whether the pronominal morphemes are true pronouns rather than subject suffixes (not prefixes), but in other ways the recommendation regarding deciding how they should be written based on substitutability can be applied. Examples (17) to (22) clearly show that

of strong opinions on all other aspects of the developing orthography. The generally desired alternative was to write these morphemes as part of the preceding word. However, there were obstacles to this.

8.6.3 Politics

In developing an orthography for Mixtec, it was necessary to abide by some guidelines and restrictions. The writing system had to be based on the national language Spanish and the alphabet used for writing it. In addition, we were asked to follow the guidelines of the *Academia Mixteca* (Mixtec Academy), an organization formed by speakers from a variety of Mixtec languages, with the goal of unifying the way these languages are written.[38]

One complicating factor in the list of recommendations from the *Academia Mixteca* was the way to write nasalization. Two different ways were given to indicate the nasalization of vowels. Where a nasal consonant (<n>, <m>, or <ñ>) is present adjacent to a vowel, this vowel is nasalized, and no further orthographic marking is necessary (see [45] to [49] for examples of this situation). However, if there is no nasal consonant, nasalization of a vowel is indicated in orthography by a word-final grapheme <n>, as shown in (83) to (85). This <n> is not pronounced as consonant, but it is used to indicate nasalization of the preceding vowel or vowels, according to the phonological rules of the language.

(83)	<yutxan>	[jɯtʃẽ]	'dough'
(84)	<xaan>	[ʃẽ:]	'wild'
(85)	<ka'an>	[kẽʔẽ]	'to speak'

This way of representing nasalization in orthography as required by the *Academia Mixteca*, combined with the desire of the speakers to write the pronominal morphemes as part of the preceding word, caused new problems for the orthography.

In the *Academia* orthography, the grapheme <n> is the only letter which may represent either a phoneme, or the modification of the sound of another letter: Word-finally, it indicates nasalization, but it represents /n/ in all other contexts.

---

the enclitic can substitute a nominal subject, or is substituted by it, in Mixtec, yet speakers were clear in their desire to not write the enclitics as separate orthographic words.

[38] At that time, these guidelines were still being worked out, but some trends as well as some decisions were already known. They were first (to my knowledge) formalized in a document in 2000 (Ve'e Tu'un Savi: Norma de escritura para Tu'un Savi), then edited in 2007 (Ve'e Tu'un Savi), and finalized as the Norma de escritura del Tu'un Savi (2022).

This is possible because Mixtec phonological words, in basically all varieties, always end with a vowel. A consonant letter <n> at the end of the word can therefore not be mistaken as representing a consonant. But if the syllabic enclitics would be written attached to the word without a space (according to the desire of the speakers), then the nasalization symbol <n> would not be word-final any more, and therefore, it would not be recognized as indicating nasalization. It would instead be interpreted as a word-medial consonant, as in examples (88) to (90), which represent a hypothetical orthography which follows the guidelines for writing nasalization:

(86) <xaa> [ʃɐː] 'chin'

(87) <xaan> [ʃɐ̃ː] 'wild'

(88) <xaantɨ> [ʃɐ̃ːdɨ] but looks like [ʃɐːntɨ] 'it (the animal) is wild'
wild=3ANIM

(89) <xaannto> [ʃɐ̃ːntʌ] two <n>? looks like [ʃɐːnːtʌ] 'you (PL) are wild'
wild=2PL

(90) <xaanyi> [ʃɐ̃ːji] but looks like [ʃɐːnji] 'they are wild'
wild=3INDEF

Besides, as we have already seen in examples (37) to (39), Amoltepec Mixtec is one of the few varieties of Mixtec which actually does permit a phonetic word-final consonant: the [ŋ] of the 2SG pronominal enclitic, spelled with the letter <n>.[39] How could this be differentiated from the <n> symbolizing nasalization? The potential combination of nasalized and non-nasalized roots with or without the 2SG morpheme would create sets of orthographic confusion, as shown in examples (91) to (94):

(91) <xaa> [ʃɐː] 'chin'

(92) <xaan> [ʃɐ̃ː] 'wild'

(93) <xaan> *either* [ʃɐ̃ː] 'wild'
or xaa=n [ʃɐːŋ] 'your chin'

(94) <xaann> Could xaan=n be represented in this way? 'you are wild'
wild= 2SG

[39] The sound [ŋ] is the word-final allophone of the phoneme /n/, which is pronounced [n] in all other contexts (except before [k], as in [ŋkjʌː] <nkyoo>, 'god').

So the dilemma was that writing the clitics separately was unacceptable to the speakers, but writing them as part of the word was making reading much more difficult, as it would obscure the difference between a word-final <n> (indicating nasalization), and the phoneme /n/, which may also occur word-finally.

One option would have been to comply with the desires and needs of the speakers, making the enclitic a part of the preceding orthographic word. This would have required a different way of marking nasalization, because of its effect on the word-final nasalization symbol (as explained and illustrated in examples [86] to [94]). However, this option would have gone against the required spelling rules at the national level (as expressed by the orthography rules of the *Academia Mixteca*).

The other option was to follow the political requirements of using the word-final <n> for nasalization. Because of the factors presented above, this would imply the need to separate the syllabic enclitics by a space from the preceding word,[40] thus making the infant orthography useless (in the words of the native speakers and beginning readers) for the people it had been designed for in the first place.

8.6.4 The current orthography

Thankfully, it was possible to develop a middle way of writing which was both compliant with the requirements of the *Academia Mixteca*, as well as supported and accepted by the community: The syllabic clitics, as well as the consonantal 2SG =n, would be connected to the preceding word by a hyphen. This resolves the problem presented in examples (91) to (94): With the hyphen, there are different orthographic representations for different words which contain the same sequence of letters:

(95) <xaa> [ʃɐː] 'chin'

(96) <xaan> [ʃɐ̃ː] 'wild'

(97) <xaa-n> [ʃɐːŋ] 'your chin'
chin=2SG

(98) <xaan-n> [ʃɐ̃ːŋ] 'you (SG) are wild'
wild=2SG

(99) <xaan-nto> [ʃɐ̃ːntʌ] 'you (PL) are wild'
wild=2PL

---

[40] At this time, this was actually the practice in most varieties of Mixtec that were written. I do not know, however, whether the speakers of other varieties feel as strongly about the orthography of enclitics as the Mixtecs in Amoltepec.

(100) <kɨ'ɨ> [kɨˀɨ] 'to touch'

(101) <kɨ'ɨn> [kɨ̃ˀɨ̃] 'to leave'

(102) <kɨ'ɨ-n> [kɨˀɨŋ] 'you are touching'

(103) <kɨ'ɨn-n> [kɨ̃ˀɨ̃ŋ] 'you are leaving'

(104) <kɨ'ɨ-ña> [kɨˀɨɲẽ] 'she is touching'
to.touch = 3F

(105) <kɨ'ɨn-ña> [kɨ̃ˀɨ̃ɲẽ] 'she is leaving'
to.leave = 3F

This seems not to be the optimal way to orthographically represent the differences: It takes training and practice for a reader to learn to distinguish (101), (102), and (103) correctly (and much more for a writer!). But it is a solution that actually works and is acceptable to all stakeholders.

For the vocalic enclitics =i (1SG) and =o (1INCL), there is general agreement that they should be written in the orthography as they are pronounced. That means that the underlying form is often obscured by the written surface form. At the same time, the orthography represents the actual utterance, not some abstract underlying form:

(106) <satniñui> [sɐtnĩɲɯ̃ĩ] 'I am working'
satniñu = i
to.work = 1SG

(107) <txa txite txi'in-n!> [tʃɐ tʃitɛ tʃɨ̃ˀɨ̃ŋ] 'I already saw you!'
txito = i
PRF to.see = 1SG OBJ = 2SG

(108) <Na ko'on!> [kʌ̃ʔʌ̃] 'Let's go!'
kɨ'ɨn = o
HORT to.leave = 1INCL

(109) <txatxu> [tʃɐtʃɯ] 'I ate'
txatxi = i
to.eat = 1SG

A special case occurs when the clitic has the same sound as the word-final vowel. This normally changes the tone of the vowel, but not its duration. In this case, an accent above the word-final vowel indicates the presence of the enclitic:[41]

(110) <vi'í> 'my house'
vi'i=í
house= 1SG

8.7 Conclusion

The short pronominal morphemes in Amoltepec Mixtec have been classified as clitics. Semantically as well as grammatically, they would qualify as independent words. But they are clearly dependent phonologically on the preceding element in the clause.

These enclitics differ considerably in structure, and, as a consequence, in the way they connect to their host word. The vocalic ones fuse to the stem of the preceding word, and typically modify the vowel (or vowels) and/or tone of the host word; see also examples (40) to (44), (53) to (55), (70) to (73), and (76) to (80). At the same time, if the host word is nasalized, the enclitic becomes nasalized; see examples (50) to (52). In the case of the syllabic enclitics, the final tone of the host word spreads onto the enclitic.

The general desire of the language community is to write the enclitics connected to the preceding element in the sentence. This is complicated by the general tendency (as well as pressure) in Mixtec languages to use a word-final grapheme <n> to indicate nasalization. In order to accommodate all these factors, it has been decided to write the consonant-initial enclitics (including the enclitic which is a single consonant) connected to the previous word by a hyphen. (Section 8.6.4 illustrates how this appears in the current orthography.)

If the host word ends in the letter <n> (indicating nasalization of the preceding vowel(s)), this <n> remains final before the hyphen (103). In this way, confusion with the letter <n> representing the phoneme /n/ is avoided.

The orthography for Amoltepec Mixtec is still in development, and it is likely to continue to evolve and change in this process. But for the question

[41] In the orthography, tone is not generally written. The exceptions to that are cases that would be ambiguous otherwise. This includes a limited number of minimal pairs, as well as some grammatical functions. We use the accent on a word-final <i> (113) to indicate the first person pronoun, and thus to distinguish the written form from the word without enclitic (and without accent). While the first person clitic usually raises the tone, the explanation for the accent is given in terms of grammar ("first person") instead of phonology or tone ("higher tone"), and this way of handling it is generally accepted.

of how to write the pronominal enclitics, a solution has been found that all stakeholders have accepted.

References

Anderson, Stephen R. 2011. Clitics. In Marc Van Oostendorp, Colin J. Ewen, Elizabeth Hume, and Keren Rice (eds.), *The Blackwell companion to phonology*, 2002–2018. Vol. 4, 2002–2018. Malden, MA: Wiley-Blackwell.

Crystal, David. 2008. *A dictionary of linguistics and phonetics. Sixth edition.* Malden, MA: Blackwell.

Dixon, R. M. W., and Alexandra Y. Aikhenvald. 2002. Word: A typological framework. In R. M. W. Dixon and Alexandra Y. Aikhenvald (eds.), *Word: A cross-linguistic typology*, 1–41. Cambridge: Cambridge University Press.

Eberhard, David M., Gary F. Simons, and Charles D. Fennig, eds. 2024. *Ethnologue: Languages of the world.* Twenty-seventh edition. Dallas, TX: SIL International. www.ethnologue.com.

Gittlen, Laura. 2016. *Gramática popular: Mixteco del norte de Tlaxiaco.* Gramáticas de lenguas indígenas de México 14. Mexico City: Instituto Lingüístico de Verano.

Harris, Larry R., and Mary Harris. 2006. Nuyoo Mixtec phonology. Draft. *Language and Culture Archives: Bartholomew Collection of Unpublished Materials.* SIL International. www.sil.org/resources/archives/56286.

Haspelmath, Martin. 2011. The indeterminacy of word segmentation and the nature of morphology and syntax. *Folia Linguistica* 45(1):31–80.

Hollenbach, Elena Erickson de. 2013. Gramática del mixteco de Magdalena Peñasco (Sa'an ñuu savi). *Gramáticas de lenguas indígenas de México* 13. Mexico City: Instituto Lingüístico de Verano.

Josserand, J. Kathryn. 1983. Mixtec dialect history. PhD dissertation. Tulane University.

Kutsch Lojenga, Constance. 2014. Basic principles for establishing word boundaries. In Michael Cahill and Keren Rice (eds.), *Developing orthographies for unwritten languages*, 73–106. Dallas, TX: SIL International.

Macaulay, Monica. 1987. Cliticization and the morphosyntax of Mixtec. *International Journal of American Linguistics* 53(2):119–135.

Macaulay, Monica, 1996. *A grammar of Chalcatongo Mixtec*. University of California Publications in Linguistics 127. Berkeley: University of California Press.

Macaulay, Monica, and Joseph C. Salmons. 1995. The phonology of glottalization in Mixtec. *International Journal of American Linguistics* 61(1):38–61.

Marlett, Stephen A. 1992. Nasalization in Mixtec languages. *International Journal of American Linguistics* 58(4):425–435.

Marlett, Stephen A. 2017. The pronouns in Mixtecan languages: Guidelines for glossing in English and Spanish. Ms.

Neville, Andrew. 2010. Phonologically conditioned allomorph selection. Ms. www.researchgate.net/profile/Marc-Oostendorp-3/publication/237493424_Phonologically-Conditioned_Allomorph_Selection/links/5469acf00cf2f5eb1804fc95/Phonologically-Conditioned-Allomorph-Selection.pdf.

Norma de escritura del Tu'un Savi (idioma mixteco). 2022. Mexico City: Secretaría de Cultura and Instituto Nacional de Lenguas Indígenas. https://dili.inpi.gob.mx/norma-de-escritura-del-tu%EA%9E%8Cun-savi-idioma-mixteco/.

Penner, Kevin L. 2019. Prosodic structure in Ixtayutla Mixtec: Evidence for the foot. PhD dissertation. University of Alberta. www.academia.edu/38317368/Penner_2019_Prosodic_structure_in_Ixtayutla_Mixtec_Evidence_for_the_foot.

Pike, Kenneth. 1948. *Tone languages: A technique for determining the number and type of pitch contrasts in a language, with studies in tonemic substitution and fusion.* Ann Arbor, MI: University of Michigan Press.

Van Dyken, Julia R., and Constance Kutsch Lojenga. 1993. Word boundaries: Key factors in orthography development. In Rhonda L. Hartell (ed.), *Alphabets of Africa,* 3–22. Dakar: UNESCO and SIL.

Ve'e Tu'un Savi (Academia de la lengua mixteca). 2000. Norma de Escritura para Tu'un Savi. Ms.

Ve'e Tu'un Savi (Academia de la lengua mixteca). 2007. *Bases para la escritura de tu'un savi.* Oaxaca: Secretaría de Cultura del Gobierno de Oaxaca.

9
The Orthographic Word in the Tagdal Verb Phrase

Caryn Benítez and Carlos M. Benítez-Torres

Abstract

Verbs in Tagdal (Northern Songhay, Niger) are morphologically complex. This chapter aims to address several questions concerning how to write different parts of the Tagdal verb phrase: Which parts of the verb are independent orthographic words and which are bound morphemes? How should pronominal forms with differing functions and degrees of phonological independence be represented? The verb word itself is the site of numerous morphophonological processes such as assimilation, lengthening, and epenthesis. In writing the verb word, how should the results of these processes be represented? At word boundaries, how should vowel elision be represented? Decisions on orthographic representation are explored using insights from Snider's Lexical Orthography Hypothesis (2014) and semantic, grammatical, and phonological criteria from Kutsch Lojenga (2014). Throughout, the discussion areas for further study and testing are identified.

Abbreviations

-	morpheme boundary
*	reconstructed or incorrect
=	clitic boundary
ˈ	stress marker, only in phonetic transcriptions
ADJR	adjectivizer
ALL	allative
CAUS	causative
DAT	dative
DEF	definite
DO	direct object
FUT	future
GEN	genitive
IPFV	imperfective
INDEF	indefinite
INDEP	independent
IO	indirect object
LWC	language of wider communication
NEG	negation
NP	noun phrase
OBJ	object
PASS	passive
PL	plural
PFV	perfective
REC	reciprocal
SBDR	subordinator
SBJ	subject
SBJV	subjunctive
SG	singular
TAM	tense-aspect-mode
V	verb
VEN	venitive
VP	verb phrase

9.1 Introduction

The verb phrase in Tagdal [tda] is a microcosm of the grammatical, phonological, and morphological processes and structures of the language as a whole. It provides a starting point for discussion and criteria for what constitutes an orthographic word in the language. This chapter begins with a brief overview of the Tagdal language context, then progresses to focus on what constitutes the verb word and how it should be represented orthographically. The discussion includes the representation of pronominal subject clitics and allomorphs of various verbal affixes. The latter part concentrates on pronominalised forms of direct and indirect objects and validation for determining which are bound forms and which should be written independently. The framework used for determining what constitutes an orthographic word in the Tagdal verb phrase comes from Kutsch Lojenga (2014). In addition, insights gained from Snider (2014) provide support for representing the results of word-internal preverbal affixation. Throughout this chapter, the tendencies and preferences of mother-tongue speakers in writing words are considered and provide the motivation for this study.

9.1.1 Tagdal language context

Tagdal is a Northern Songhay (NS) language spoken mainly in the western regions of the modern-day Republic of Niger and in small pockets of Mali. It is one of three Northern Songhay languages spoken in the region. These languages are very different from what Nicolaï (1981:232) calls "Southern Songhay" and which we will refer to as "Mainstream Songhay". Nicolaï (1981, 1990) further subdivides the NS languages into Sedentary and Nomadic branches, as figure 9.1 from Benítez-Torres (2021:6) demonstrates.

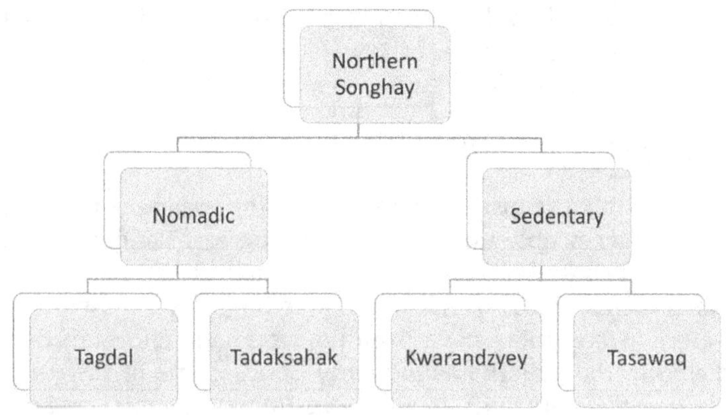

Figure 9.1. Northern Songhay languages.

In the Sedentary branch, one finds Kwarandzyey (Kora-n-dje in Christiansen-Bolli 2010; Souag 2010a, 2010b, 2012, 2015a, 2015b), spoken in southwestern Algeria, and Tasawaq, spoken in two towns in modern-day northern Niger.[1] In the Nomadic branch, one finds Tadaksahak (Christiansen-Bolli 2010), spoken mainly in Mali, and Tagdal. Due to the influence of Tuareg-Berber, Lacroix (1971, 1981) was the first to note key differences between Northern Songhay (NS) and Mainstream Songhay languages, referring to NS languages in French as "langues mixtes" (mixed languages), though it did not mean the same thing as, for example, how Thomason (2001:196) defines "mixed languages". Regardless, the idea that NS languages form a distinct unit different from Mainstream Songhay languages is not controversial (Kossmann 2008:109).

Nicolaï (1981, 1990) described various aspects of the vocabulary and phonology of NS languages, especially in comparison with Mainstream Songhay, in an effort to demonstrate that Songhay is not in the Nilo-Saharan

[1] A third language, Emghedeshie, was at one time spoken in the city of Agadez in modern-day northern Niger, but is now extinct, replaced by Hausa.

phylum.[2] The vocabulary and grammatical structures of Tagdal were recorded and analysed in the late 1990s by Harrison et al. (1999), as part of their survey of Mainstream Songhay in Niger and Mali. Later, Rueck and Christiansen (1999) did much of the preliminary work to establish an SIL team to study both Tagdal and Tadaksahak. Since the early 2000s the authors of this chapter have studied the language and worked with a handful of Tagdal speakers in translation and language development.

Benítez-Torres and Grant (2017) found that the division of NS languages in Niger and Mali into Nomadic and Sedentary is borne out grammatically. The main linguistic differences between these branches in Niger and Mali[3] have to do with degrees of Berber influence (linguistic and otherwise), with Nomadic Tadaksahak and Tagdal having, relatively speaking, more Tuareg structures and vocabulary than Sedentary Tasawaq. Tagdal and Tadaksahak speakers today are considered, especially by outsiders, to be part of the greater Tuareg-Berber socio-cultural-economic milieu in Niger and Mali.

9.1.2 History of Tagdal orthography

It could be said that the history of Tagdal writing goes back millennia, with some of the older people attempting to write short handwritten notes in the ancient Lybico-Berber script Shifinagh,[4] and more recently in Arabic script. Nevertheless, most of these attempts have been individual, and as far as we are aware, there have been no systematic efforts to develop an orthography. In the late 1990s and early 2000s, some of the surrounding Tuareg languages were written down in Roman, Arabic, and Shifinagh scripts. (See, for example, OLAC 2023.)

Language development work in Tagdal began in the early 2000s on a limited basis. Several booklets, mostly Scripture portions, have been published in trial form over the years, using both Arabic (Ajami) and Roman scripts. In the last few years, the interest of Tagdal speakers in their language has grown, and in December 2019, the National Assembly of Niger passed a law declaring Tagdal as one of eleven official languages of Niger (Ikali 2019). Since then, greater effort has been put into regularising and refining Tagdal orthography. As recently as January 2023, three SIL language consultants involved in work with the languages of Niger requested input from the authors on writing Tagdal consistently using Roman script, particularly in the context of the verb phrase. This study is an outcome of

[2] This question is beyond the scope of this study. The theory about Songhay origins can be found in Nicolaï (1990, 2003), while support for Songhay in the Nilo-Saharan phylum can be found in, for example, Dimmendaal et al. (2019.)

[3] Kwarandzyey in Algeria underwent different processes of development (Souag 2010a, 2010b).

[4] Shifinagh is sometimes written as “Tifinagh” or “Tchifinagh”.

that conversation.[5] As has been mentioned, Tagdal is sometimes written in Arabic (Ajami) script. However, this study focuses on Tagdal orthography using Roman script.

9.1.3 Linguistic preliminaries

Though it is difficult to know with any certainty, Tagdal likely originated fairly recently[6] as a bilingual mixed language (Thomason and Kaufmann 1988, Thomason 2001, Meakins 2013). A full discussion about mixed languages is beyond the scope of this study but mixed languages, including Tagdal, typically come about rather abruptly—often in the space of a single generation (Thomason 2001:196)—and, since they are not needed for external communication, they often function as vernaculars, as signs of in-group identity.[7] By looking at modern-day Tagdal structures, it can be surmised that the ancestors of modern-day Tagdal speakers were bilingual in the Songhay LWC of the time, their Tuareg vernacular, and the "new" language that probably came about by means of code-switching between them.

Among the types of mixing that have been accounted for, Velupillai (2015:68, 77) classifies Tagdal as a Form-Structure mixed language (Meakins 2013). However, Kossmann's (2010) concept of parallel system borrowing seems to come closer to describing the processes that most affect the present study. Essentially, what this means is that vocabulary of Tuareg-Berber origin tends to follow one set of prosodic and grammatical rules, while vocabulary of Songhay origin tends to follow another.[8]

Parallel systems affect the subject of this particular study in three major ways. First, vowel elision principally affects verb roots and vocabulary of Songhay origin. Verb roots of Tuareg-Berber origin do not undergo vowel elision unless they end in /a/ (Benítez-Torres 2021:31), in which case, vowel elision occurs in the same way as it does with Songhay vocabulary. Second, stress in the verb phrase, which is not represented in the orthography, typically occurs somewhere in the root. However, in roots of Tuareg origin, stress shifts, depending on the presence of certain derivational

[5] The authors serve as outside consultants and currently have no direct involvement in language development in Niger.

[6] It possibly emerged sometime in the fourteenth century CE when the Songhay Empire spread east to modern-day northern Niger. After that, Songhay became the LWC of the region until the early twentieth century CE. However, it is not known what the LWC of the region was before the Songhay conquest. Therefore, Tagdal's origins could be earlier.

[7] These types of mixed languages often arise as a sign of a newly emergent group or subgroup (Thomason 2001:198). Benítez-Torres (2009) suggests several factors that might have led to the emergence of the modern-day Tagdal.

[8] For a more complete study of this phenomenon, see Benítez-Torres and Grant 2017 and Benítez-Torres 2020, 2021.

affixes (Benítez-Torres 2021:83). Third, vowel length is important for both Songhay and Tuareg vocabulary. However, the environments conditioning long or lengthened vowels differ depending on the etymology of the word in which a vowel is realised as long.

9.1.3.1 Overview of Tagdal phonology

The variety of Tagdal chosen for writing (see Benítez-Torres 2021 for more details about Tagdal dialects) has essentially the same consonant and vowel inventories as those present in Tuareg languages in Niger and Mali.[9] Among the consonants, the stops are /b, t, ṭ, d, ḍ, k, g, q/. The fricatives are /f, s, ṣ, z, ẓ, ʃ, ʒ, x, ɣ, ħ, ʕ, h/. Glides are limited to /w/ and /j/. The laterals are /l, ḷ/, along with the taps /r, ṛ/. Finally, the nasals are /m, n, ṇ, ŋ/.[10] The vowel inventory also corresponds to both Songhay and Tuareg patterns, with the close vowels /i, u/, the mid vowels /e, ə, o/, and the near open central vowel /ɐ/, shown here as /a/.

Nomadic Northern Songhay languages have been analyzed as having long vowel counterparts to each phonemic vowel except /ə/ (Benítez-Torres 2021:21 and Christiansen-Bolli 2010:19). However, in light of various vowel-lengthening processes explained in Benítez-Torres 2021 and phonotactic constraints on long vowels in words of Songhay origin, the issue of the phonemic status of long vowels needs to be looked at more closely. Currently vowel length is underspecified in the orthography, but more study needs to be done concerning how to represent both long vowels and the results of vowel lengthening.

Tagdal shows a preference for CVC or CV_1V_1 syllables, but CV syllables are also attested. V, V_1V_1, and VC syllables are limited to the left margins of words having more than one syllable. Most words are polysyllabic, but some words of Songhay origin are monosyllabic (for example <mon> 'eye' and <ha> 'thing'). Syllable structure has implications for vowel length—there are no long vowels in closed syllables or word-finally. Furthermore, in words of Songhay origin, vowels in open syllables are realised as long and only Songhay words have initial V_1V_1 syllables, as demonstrated in (1).

(1)	[ˈiːɾi]	1PL	[ˈboːɾa]	'person'
	[ˈeːlaw]	'elephant'	[ˈkuːsu]	'cooking pot'
	[ˈaːʒiɾ]	'groundnut'	[goːˈɾa]	'to sit/stay'

[9] See, for example, Heath's (2005) and Kossmann's (2011) descriptions of Tuareg languages in Mali and Niger.

[10] The symbols /ṭ, ḍ, ṣ, ẓ, ḷ, ṛ, ṇ/ represent the pharyngealized consonants /tˤ, dˤ, sˤ, zˤ, lˤ, rˤ, nˤ/.

Like Berber languages, vowels in stressed syllables can be described as having a higher pitch contour, as well as increased airstream, compared to vowels in unstressed syllables (Christiansen-Bolli 2010:44, Benítez-Torres 2021:32). All vocabulary of Songhay origin would have likely had tone at one time, but now it has shifted to stress, though the related language, Tasawaq, still has tone (Benítez-Torres and Grant 2017). Regardless, stress is underspecified in the orthography. This does not seem to cause any problems for readers of Tagdal.

9.1.3.2 Tagdal pronouns and pronominal clitics

Tagdal has a series of pronouns and pronominal clitics, derived from Mainstream Songhay pronouns, which are referred to throughout this study. The term "clitic" is used here to refer to a form that is phonologically dependent on a neighbouring word (Crystal 2008:80) but is independent syntactically (Anderson 2005:10). Clitic pronouns in Tagdal are syntactically free and function as subjects, direct objects, and indirect objects. They can also be part of possessive forms, but this will not be discussed. Table 9.1 shows the pronominal forms in Tagdal. The pronominal clitic forms do not communicate meaning when pronounced in isolation.

Table 9.1. Pronouns and pronominal clitics

	Singular			**Plural**	
Person	**Independent**	**Clitic**	**Clitic allomorph**	**Independent**	**Clitic**
First person	/ɣa:j/ <ɣay>	/ɣa=/ <ɣa>	[aɣ=] <aɣ>	/i:ri/ <iri>	/i:ri=/ <iri>
Second person	/nin/ <nin>	/ni=/ <ni>	[in=] <in>	/anʒi/ <anji>	/anʒi=/ <anji>
Third person	/anga/ <anga>	/a=/ /=a/ <a> <-a>		/inga/ <inga>	/i=/ /=i/ <i> <-i>

As will be explained later in this study, the first person singular clitic /ɣa=/ is realised as [aɣ=] preceding the dative marker /sa/ (§ 9.2.2.3). In a similar manner, the second person singular clitic /ni=/ is realised as [in=] preceding the dative marker /sa/ (§ 9.2.2.3) and also when it precedes the future tense affix /tə-/ and the negation affix /sə-/ (§ 9.2.1.2).[11]

[11] The reasons for this are beyond the scope of this study.

9.2 Overview of the Tagdal verb phrase

The Tagdal verb phrase can be morphologically complex, with various possible verbal affixes and pronominal clitics, as table 9.2 shows. The following sections of this chapter will focus on how the many parts of the Tagdal verb phrase are represented in the Tagdal orthography – as affixes, bound clitics, or separate words. Some of the verbal affixes have allomorphs, and writing these will be discussed as well.

Table 9.2. Tagdal verb structure

Pronominal subject clitic	Negation prefix	TAM prefix	Derivational prefix	Verb root	Directional suffix	Pronominal clitic	Pronominal clitic	Dative marker	Pronominal clitic
SBJ	NEG	TAM	CAUS/ REC/PASS	V ROOT	ALL/VEN	DO	IO	DAT	DO[a]

[a] In clauses with an indirect object, the direct object occurs after the indirect object.

The required elements of the Tagdal verb phrase (shown as shaded in table 9.2) are the initial pronominal subject clitic, the tense-aspect-mode (TAM) marker,[12] and the verb root. Other possible affixes preceding the verb root include negation and derivational prefixes. Following the verb root are directional affixes and object complements. Of particular importance to this discussion will be the representation of pronominal object clitics in the orthography. Example (2) demonstrates some simple Tagdal verb phrases.

(2) a. <Ɣazuru.>
/ɣa= zuːru/
1SG= run
'I ran.'

b. <Abkoy-a.>
/a= b- koy =a/
3SG= IPFV- go =3SG
'He goes (habitually) there.'

Almost all the affixes, except the derivational affixes, are of Songhay origin. Unlike Mainstream Songhay languages (see, for example, Heath

[12] The exception is the perfective aspect, which is a zero morpheme.

1999a, 1999b), however, Tagdal is much more agglutinative, probably due to Tuareg-Berber influence, as example (3) illustrates.

(3) a. <**Iribtəwnəmsəɣray** daɣo aɣo kan.>[13]

/**i:ri**=	**b-**	**təw-**	**nəm-**	**s-**	**əɣray**	da:ɣo	a:ɣo	kan/
1PL=	IPFV-	PASS-	REC-	CAUS-	**learn**	place	that	in

'We (were forced to) learn together in that place.'

b. <**Iritəsəsəmələɣətkat-i.**>

/**i:ri**=	**tə-**	**sə-**	**sə-**	**məl:əɣət**	**kat-**	=**i**/
1PL=	FUT-	CAUS-	CAUS-	**race**	**ven-**	=**3**PL

'We're going to help organise a race (for) them toward here.'

c. <**Itəwnəmsəkərəd.**>

/**i**=	**təw-**	**nəm-**	**sə-**	**kərəd**/
3PL=	PASS-	REC-	CAUS-	**hobble**

'They were made to be tied up together.'

9.2.1 Preverbal elements

The elements of the verb preceding the verb root include pronominal subject clitics, TAM prefixes, negation prefixes, and the derivational prefixes. The status of pronominal subject markers as clitics will be discussed, as will the orthographic representation of verbal prefixes and their allomorphs.

9.2.1.1 Pronominal subject clitics

Pronominal subject clitics are a required part of the verb. They are unstressed and written attached to the verb, not as separate pronouns. Table 9.3, based on Benítez-Torres (2021:37), shows the preverbal pronominal subject clitics in Tagdal. Each of these is a bound clitic, derived from Mainstream Songhay pronouns. (See § 9.1.3.2 Tagdal pronouns and pronominal clitics.)

[13] Throughout this chapter, boldface type is used in examples to draw attention to the parts of the example that are relevant to the discussion.

Table 9.3. Pronominal subject clitics

Person	Singular		Plural	
First person	/ɣa=/	<ɣa>	/i:ri=/	<iri>
Second person	/ni/ or [in=][a]	<ni> or <in>	/anʒi=/	<anji>
Third person	/a=/	<a>	/i=/	<i>

[a] The second person singular clitic /ni=/ becomes /in=/ before the future tense affix /tə-/, the negation affix /sə-/, and the postverbal dative marker /sa/.

These pronominal clitics have a grammatical function and are, for the most part, distinct from independent pronouns, given in table 9.1.

All pronominal subject clitics are written attached to the verb root, even the ones that are identical to the independent pronouns (i.e., first and second person plural) in isolation. Pronominal subject clitics are a required element of the verb[14] and cannot be substituted by an independent noun or noun phrase (NP). Sometimes they co-occur with a full NP or an independent pronoun, as shown in (4). (4a) demonstrates an instance of the proclitic co-occurring with an independent pronoun; in (4b) the clitic co-occurs with a full NP, while in (4c), the clitic occurs without either a NP or a pronoun.

(4) a. <**Anji, anji**mfas.>

/**anʒi**	**anʒi**=	m-	fas/
2PL.INDEP	**2PL**=	SBJV-	dig

'It is you (PL) who need to dig.'

b. <**Asaməd aɣo a**yiɣšəd.>

/**as:aməd**	**a:ɣo**	**a**=	əɣʃəd/
leather.sack	**this**	**3SG**=	damage

'This leather sack is ruined.'

c. <**Ɣa**tədaykat mota əyinayan.>

/**ɣa**=	tə-	day	-kat	m:ota	əyina:yan/
1SG=	FUT-	do.commerce	-VEN	car	new

'I'm going to buy a new car.'

[14] There are some exceptions, such as in subject relative clauses (see, for example, Benítez-Torres 2021:158).

9.2.1.2 Negation, TAM, and derivational affixes

Following the pronominal clitic and preceding the verb root are various negation, TAM, and derivational affixes. The derivational affixes, as expected, are closest to the verb root. Writing these morphemes in the proper order attached to the verb root is, for the most part, not problematic. However, some of these verbal affixes have allomorphs, depending on their environments. When deciding how to orthographically represent the results of preverbal affixation within the Tagdal verb, insights from Snider's Lexical Orthography Hypothesis (Snider 2014) are helpful. Snider claims that native speakers are aware of the output of lexical processes (2014:25–26). Therefore, an orthography that "consistently represents the output of the lexical level" is preferable (Snider 2014:25). As Snider predicts, Tagdal writers are aware of changes that result from preverbal affixation and prefer to write the verb words with allomorphs as pronounced.

This is not an exhaustive description of how to write all the verbal affixes in Tagdal. Only the affixes that exhibit morphemic alternations and serve to illustrate morphophonemic processes within the verb word are presented. Some morphophonemic rules apply to verbal affixes in general. For example, many verbal affixes consist of a consonant and a schwa (/tə-/, /nə-/, /sə-/, etc.). In cases where a verb root which follows the affix begins with /ə/, only one /ə/ is pronounced and written, as in (5).

(5) <i**nə**qbəl>
[iˈ**nə**qbəl]

i=	**nə-**	əqbəl
3PL=	NEG-	accept

'they don't accept'

9.2.1.2.1 Perfective aspect

The perfective aspect of a verb is unmarked by a verbal affix, as illustrated in (6), from Benítez-Torres 2021:101.

(6) <Ɣakoy.>

/ɣa=	koy/
1SG=	go

'I left.'

If the verb root begins with a vowel (usually /ə/ for Tuareg roots), an epenthetic palatal glide [j] is inserted, and the /ə/ assimilates to the close position of the [j] to become [ɪ]. Glide epenthesis is common between morphemes to preserve the syllable structure of the word. It does not happen across word boundaries. Example (7), from Benítez-Torres 2021:101, draws attention to the difference between the surface form with the [j] inserted and the underlying form of the verb root.[15]

(7) <Šiji aɣo, iri**yidəẓ**.>
[ʃiːˈʒi aːˈɣo iːɾi**jɪdːəẓ**]
/ʃiːʒi aːɣo iːri= **ədəẓ**/
night DEF 1PL= **tired**
'That evening, we were tired.'

Tagdal speakers are aware of the results of this process of epenthesis and assimilation and prefer to write the verb as pronounced after the processes have taken place. According to Snider (2014:40), since this is a lexical process applying across morpheme boundaries, spelling the word with the changes is appropriate.

9.2.1.2.2 Negation morpheme nə- *and the future tense* tə-

In both the future tense /tə-/ and the negation morpheme /nə-/, the /ə/ changes to [u] or [i], assimilating in height and roundness to a following semivowel [w] or [j], as (8) demonstrates.

(8) a. <**Atə**koy.>
[**atə**ˈkɔj]
/a= **tə-** koy/
3SG= FUT- go
'He will go.'

b. <A**ti**yarda.>
[a**ti**ˈjaɾda]
/a= **tə-** jaɾda/
3SG= FUT- agree
'He will agree.'

[15] In related Tadaksahak, the /j/ is actually part of the root and is not inserted (Benítez-Torres 2021:79).

c. <**Atu**warɣa.>
[**atu**ˈwaɾˈɣa]
/a= **tə-** waɾɣa/
3SG= FUT- be.big
'He will be a great (man).'

d. <**Anə**koy.>
[**anə**ˈkɔj]
/a= **nə-** koy/
3SG= NEG.PFV- go
'He didn't go.'

e. <**Ani**yarda.>
[**ani**ˈjaɾda]
/a= nə- jaɾda/
3SG= NEG.PFV- agree
'He didn't agree.'

f. <**Anu**warɣa.>
[**anu**waɾˈɣa]
/a= **nə-** waɾɣa/
3SG= NEG.PFV- be.big
'He didn't become a great (man).'

The schwa assimilation process is the same as that of the perfective aspect in (7). As with the other TAM affixes, Tagdal speakers are aware of the output of vowel assimilation. Since the process is word-internal and occurs when affixes are added, according to Snider (2014:39–40), it is a lexical process, and the word should be spelled as pronounced.

9.2.1.2.3 Derivational affixes and suppletion

Tagdal has a series of three derivational affixes, each of which attaches onto verb roots of Tuareg-Berber origin: the passive /təw-/, the reciprocal /nəm-/, and the causative /s-/. The language treats them as part of the verb root, including for stress placement. Benítez-Torres (2021:84–89) discusses this in some detail. The most common causative affix is /s-/, since it has several allomorphs which assimilate to the place of articulation of a sibilant in the root, demonstrated in table 9.4. Therefore, this issue bears directly on the question of how the causative /s-/ should be written. As in the other cases of verbal affixes, Tagdal writers prefer to spell the causative affixes as pronounced, as with the assimilation processes discussed above, resulting from affixation of TAM and negation morphemes.

Table 9.4. Causative /s-/ and allomorphs

Verb Root	**Gloss**	**Causative morpheme /s-/ with allomorphs**	**Orthographic form**	**Causative gloss**
/ˈəɣrəf/	'water animals every other day'	/s-/	səɣrəf	'cause to water animals every other day'
/əktəb/	'write'	/s-/	səktəb	'cause to write'
/ˈəlːəm/	'uncover'	/s-/	sələm	'cause to uncover'
/ˈbəkːəmət/	'ambush'	[sə-]	səbəkmət	'cause to ambush'
/ˈəʃrəɣ/	'judge'	[ʃ-]	šəšrəɣ	'cause to judge'
/ˈmətʃa/	'store'	[ʃə-]	šəmətša	'cause to store'
/ˈəʒləg/	'place directly on top'	[ʒ-]	jəjləg	'cause to place directly on top'
/ˈəʒːərgən/	'be dirty'	[ʒ-]	jəjərgən	'make dirty'
/ˈəmːəzrej/	'confuse'	[z-]	zəməzray	'cause confusion'
/ˈwəzːiːwəz/	'scatter'	[zə-]	zəwəziwəz	'cause to scatter'
/zəˈdːej/	'know' (someone)	[zə-]	zəzəday	'cause to know'

Now, concerning the derivational morphemes in general, these only attach to verb roots of Tuareg-Berber origin. When verbal concepts that are usually expressed with a Songhay root take on causative, reciprocal, or passive meaning, the Songhay root is replaced by a Tuareg verb root with derivational morpheme(s) already attached.[16] In cases of suppletion, the verb stem is not separable into affix + root because the Tuareg root form without the derivational prefix(es) is not an independently meaningful verb in Tagdal. Table 9.5 demonstrates this.

[16] Benítez-Torres (2020) suggests that this process of suppletion was a means by which the language kept Songhay and Tuareg vocabulary—each with different prosodic rules—apart.

Table 9.5. Suppletion of Songhay verbal cognates in derived stems

Songhay verb roots		**Tuareg-derived stems**					
		Causative		**Reciprocal**		**Passive**	
<baɣa>	'love'	<sərat>	'cause to love'	<nəmərat>	'love one another'	<təwərat>	'loved'
<da>	'give'	<səsuga>	'cause to give'	<nəməsuga>	'give to each other'	<təwəsuga>	'given'
<dab>	'dress'	<səlsa>	'cause to dress'	<nəmməlsa>	'dress each other'	<təwəlsa>	'dressed'
<daw>	'send'	<səsoka>	'cause to send'	<nəməsoka>	'send each other'	<təwəsoka>	'sent'
<gar>	'protect'	<zəzaygəz>	'cause to protect'	<nəməzaygəz>	'protect each other'	<təwəzaygəz>	'protected'
<har>	'declare'	<səməl>	'cause to declare'	<nəməl>	'declare to each other'	<təwəməl>	'declared'

9.2.1.2.4 The verb root

Verb roots look very different and, in fact, follow different prosodic rules (which are beyond the scope of this chapter), depending on whether they are of Tuareg or Songhay origin. In general, all monosyllabic CV or CVC verb roots are of Songhay origin, as are CV_1V_1.CV(C) and CVC.CV. These typically begin with almost any consonant except /t/ or /s/. By contrast, Tuareg-Berber roots typically begin with /ə/, and always have at least two syllables, and often as many as three or four. Table 9.6 demonstrates a few common verb roots.

Table 9.6. Common Songhay- and Tuareg-origin verb roots

Songhay origin verb roots		Tuareg-origin verb roots	
/dut/	'pound (grain)'	/ˈədbaq/	'close'
/mej/	'have'	/ˈəfnəz/	'make small'
/goːˈɾa/	'sit, stay'	/ˈəfraːj/	'be sick'
/guːˈna/	'look'	/ˈəɣrəs/	'pass through'
/ˈhaŋga/	'hear'	/ˈənfa/	'win something'
/ʒiːˈda/	'walk'	/ˈəzri/	'replace'
/karˈfo/	'tie someone with rope'	/səˈlːəɣad/	'plead'
/kɔj/	'go'	/ləˈfaɣʃəd/	'be unpleasantly surprised, disappointed'
/wi/	'kill'	/ˈtəwːaːla/	'leap'
/zoq/	'fight'	/ˈtəxfər/	'rent'
/ˈzuːɾu/	'run'	/zəˈdːej/	'know' (someone)

9.2.1.2.5 Imperative form

The verb root very rarely occurs in isolation, and when it occurs without inflectional affixes, it has an imperative function. Except to denote urgency, the imperative form of the verb is rarely used since it can be considered rude or can communicate a perceived marked difference in social rank. Nevertheless, (9) shows imperative forms found in natural text.

(9) a. <**Ɜṭkəl-a!**>

/**əṭkəl** =**a**/

grab =**3SG**

'Take it!'

b. <**Zawkat** aɣs-i!>

/**zaw** **-kat** ɣa= sa =i/

carry -VEN 1SG= DAT =3PL

'Bring them to me!'

(Along with the imperative form of the verb, [9] also shows direct and indirect object pronouns, which will be discussed in § 9.2.2.2 and § 9.2.2.3 respectively.)

9.2.2 Postverbal elements

The postverbal elements include the directional affixes /-kat/ and /-nan/ and direct and indirect objects. Key questions to be considered have to do with pronominal forms and clitics and how these should be represented in the orthography, specifically whether or not they are part of the verb word. Vowel lengthening and vowel elision are processes that affect orthographic representation decisions.

9.2.2.1 Directional affixes /-kat/ and /-nan/

Immediately following the verb root are the optional directional markers /-kat/ and /-nan/. These are affixes that indicate whether the action is moving toward or away from the semantic centre. The venitive /-kat/ indicates that the action is moving toward the speaker and the allative /-nan/ away from the speaker. In limited contexts, the presence of one of these suffixes or the other in the verb stem indicates different meaning. For example, <day> 'engage in commerce' combined with the venitive <kat> creates <daykat> 'buy', whereas with the allative /-nan/ it creates <daynan> 'sell'. Another example is <koykat> 'come' and <koynan> 'go'. Since new meaning is sometimes acquired with the conjunction of a verb stem and /-kat/ or /-nan/, the semantic criterion of "conceptual unity" from Kutsch Lojenga (2014:90) is used here in support of writing these affixes conjunctively with the verb stem.

If the verb root is intransitive, this marks the limit of the verb as an orthographic word. If it is transitive, on the other hand, /-kat/ and /-nan/ may be followed by one of the third person pronominal direct object clitics /=a/ or /=i/. In this context, the vowel in /-kat/ or /-nan/ is lengthened, as in (10). This is an indication that the direct object clitic is also part of the verb since the vowel-lengthening phenomenon in Tagdal does not cross word boundaries.[17]

(10) a. <Ɣaday**nan-a.**>

[ɣaˈdej**naːna**]

/ɣa= day **-nan** **=a**/

1SG= do.commerce -ALL **=3SG**

'I sold it.'

[17] Attaching third person direct object pronouns to the end of the verb triggers vowel lengthening in the syllable preceding the direct object. See Benítez-Torres 2021:105–106 for a description of this phenomenon, which occurs with vocabulary of Songhay origin. Since Tagdal shows a preference for heavy word-internal syllables, vowel lengthening is not confined to verb morphology, but is the result of affixation. Put simply, CVC + V re-syllabifies as $CV_1V_1.CV$. This process is word-internal and does not occur across morpheme boundaries.

b. <Irizaw**kat-i**.>

[iːriˈzɔw**kaːti**]

/iːri=	zaw	**-kat**	**=i/**
1PL=	carry	**-VEN**	**=3PL**

'We brought them.'

c. <Amsəkoy**nan-a**.>

[amsəˈkoj**naːna**]

/a=	msə-[18]	koy	**-nan**	**=a/**
3SG=	NEG.SBJV-	go	**-ALL**	**=3SG**

'He shouldn't go there.'

Vowel lengthening in Songhay cognates is relatively predictable in Tagdal. The majority of the time all vowels except /ə/ are pronounced as long in word-internal open syllables. During various informal tests the authors found that Tagdal speakers did not write the vowels in /-kat/ and /-nan/ as lengthened when conjoined with pronominal direct object clitics /=a/ or /=i/, though they did produce the vowels as long, suggesting that they were not aware of the vowel-lengthening process. In accordance with guidelines in Snider (2014:40), since speakers are not aware of the process of vowel lengthening, the affixes /-kat/ and /-nan/ are consistently written in their underlying form.

9.2.2.2 Pronominal direct object clitics and pronouns

As discussed in § 9.2.2.1, the third person direct objects /=a/ and /=i/ are part of the orthographic verb since they are phonologically bound to it. All other direct object pronouns are independent, as shown in table 9.7 (cf. table 9.1. Pronouns and pronominal clitics). They are unstressed, in contrast to indirect object pronouns (as explained in § 9.2.2.3).

Table 9.7. Direct object pronouns

Person	**Singular**		**Plural**	
First person	/ɣaːj/	<ɣay>	/iːri/	<iri>
Second person	/nin/	<nin>	/anʒi/	<anji>
Third person	/=a/	<-a>	/=i/	<-i>

[18] The subjunctive negation morpheme /msə-/ and the future negation morpheme /səkoy-/ are preverbal affixes not discussed in this chapter because they are orthographically unambiguous.

In (11a) the direct object is a full NP, while (11b) to (11d) contain pronominalised forms.

(11) a. <Ɣabəbaɣa **mota ayo.**>

[ɣabəˈbːaːɣa **ˈmoːta aːˈɣo**]

/ɣa=	b-	baːɣa	**moːta**	**aːɣo/**
1SG=	IPFV-	want	**car**	**that**

'I loved that car.'

b. <Iyixfəl **iri** kasaw kan.>

[iˈjɪxfəl **ˈiːɾi** ˈkasɔw kan]

/i=	əxfəl	**iːri**	kasaw	kan/
3PL=	lock	**1PL**	prison	in

'They locked us up in prison.'

c. <Inaragan ibtekat **ɣay.**>

[iˈnaɾaːgan ibˈteːkat **ɣaːj**]

/inarːagan	i=	b-	te	-kat	**ɣaːy/**
strangers	3PL=	IPFV-	arrive	-VEN	**1SG**

'The strangers were approaching me.'

d. <Afarad-**a** ar ayidəz.>

[aˈfːaɾaːd**a** aɾ aˈjɪdːəz]

/a=	farad	**=a**	ar	a=	ədəz/
3SG=	sweep	**=3SG**	til	3SG=	tired

'She swept it until she got tired.'

In (11d), lengthening takes place on the verb /farad/ 'sweep' when the third person direct object clitic is adjoined. This is the same vowel-lengthening process that happens when the third person direct object clitic is adjoined to the directional affixes /-kat/ and /-nan/ (see § 9.2.2.1). This compensatory lengthening only happens word-internally, providing further evidence that third person pronominal direct object clitics are part of the orthographic verb word.[19]

From the beginning of the development of a working orthography in Tagdal, third person pronominal direct object clitics have been written as adjoined to the verb stem with a hyphen (11d), showing that they are phonologically bound but syntactically independent. The use of a hyphen

[19] The topic of compensatory lengthening and the orthographic word in Tagdal is beyond the scope of this chapter but is a very pertinent area for further study.

to show the close phonological connection of a clitic to a host morpheme, while at the same time keeping them separate, is suggested by Kutsch Lojenga (2014:74). Further consultation with Tagdal readers and writers should be done to determine whether the use of a hyphen is helpful or not.

Except for the third person pronominal clitic forms, all pronominal direct objects are independent pronouns and written as independent morphemes, as in (11b) and (11c). The fact that a direct object can be separated from the verb by an indirect object (§ 9.2.2.3) provides additional motivation for writing direct object independent pronouns as separate from the verb. (For more information on writing direct object pronominals, see § 9.2.3 Vowel elision.)

9.2.2.3 Indirect object with dative marker /sa/

If a clause is ditransitive and has an indirect object, the direct object follows the indirect object. The dative marker /sa/ immediately follows the indirect object and precedes the direct object. If both the direct object and the indirect object are nouns or NPs, as in (12), the dative marker /sa/ is written as an independent grammatical morpheme.

(12) a. <Anakat **an kayna sa** ha hosayan.>

/a=	na	-kat	**a=**	**n**	**kejna**	**sa**	ha	hos:a:jan/
3SG=	give	-VEN	**3SG=**	**GEN**	**younger.sibling**	**DAT**	thing	beautiful

'He gave his younger brother something nice.'

b. <Irihar **boren sa** šimi.>

/i:ɾi=	har	**bo:ɾen**	**sa**	ʃi:mi/
1PL=	declare	**people**	**DAT**	Truth

'We told the people the truth.'

The dative marker /sa/ is a grammatical function word that functions at the level of the NP. It is written separately from the indirect object NP because other elements, such as adjectives, can be placed between it and the noun, as in (13). Using this criterion of separability, whereby "...a grammatical morpheme can be separated from a neighboring lexical morpheme by the insertion of another lexical morpheme" (Kutsch Lojenga 2014:85), /sa/ is written as a separate word in the orthography.

(13) <Amasəɣri asəkna **aro janunan sa** qaran.>

[am:a'səɣri a'səkna **aː'ɾo ʒaː'nuːnan sa** 'qaːɾan]

/amasəɣri	a=	səkna	**aːro**	**ʒaːnu**	**-nan**	**sa**	qaːran/
teacher	3SG=	demonstrate	**man**	**old**	**-ADJR**	**DAT**	reading

'The teacher taught the old man how to read.'

Pronominal indirect object clitics, listed in table 9.8, have a different, though related, form to that of pronominal subject clitics (table 9.3) and pronominal direct objects (table 9.7). (See also table 9.1 for an overview of pronominal forms.) Pronominal indirect objects are always written attached to the dative marker /sa/. The first and second person plural have referential independence when pronounced in isolation, but all forms in the paradigm are written as conjoined to /sa/ for the sake of consistency.

Table 9.8. Indirect object clitic pronouns

Person	Singular		Plural	
First person	/aɣ=sa/	<aɣsa>	/iːri=sa/	<irisa>
Second person	/in=sa/	<insa>	/anʒi=sa/	<anjisa>
Third person	/a=sa/	<asa>	/i=sa/	<isa>

Even though /sa/ is written as a separate word when it is accompanied by a noun or NP, according to Kutsch Lojenga (2014:92) it is acceptable to write it as conjoined when accompanied by a pronoun. Further, when the indirect object is pronominalised, stress in the entire VP always shifts to the indirect object clitic, as (14) demonstrates.

(14) a. <Asəkna **aɣsa** boren fonen.>

[asəkna '**aɣsa** boː'ɾen foː'nen]

/a=	səkna	**ɣa=**	**sa**	boːren	foːnen/
3SG=	demonstrate	**1SG=**	**DAT**	people	2PL

'He pointed certain people out to me.'

b. <Asəkna **aɣs-i.**>[20]

[asəkna '**aɣsi**]

/a=	səkna	**ɣa=**	**sa**	**=i/**
3SG=	demonstrate	**1SG=**	**DAT**	**=3PL.OBJ**

'He pointed them out to me.'

[20] Since the final vowel in /sa/ is elided, the only vowel left is that of the enclitic.

The indirect object is written separately from the verb, even in its pronominal forms. As discussed in § 9.2.2.1 and § 9.2.2.2, there is phonological motivation for adjoining the third person pronominal direct object clitics to the verb due to a vowel-lengthening process. However, vowel lengthening does not occur when the third person indirect object pronominals /a = sa/ or /i = sa/ follow a verb stem ending in a CVC syllable, such as /-kat/ or /-nan/, as shown in (15).

(15) a. <Abəbaɣa sa intəzaw**kat as-a**.>

[abəˈbːaːɣa sintəzɔw**kat ˈasa**]

/a=	b-	baaɣa	sa	ni=	tə-	zaw	**-kat**	**a=**	**sa**	**=a/**
3SG=	IPFV-	want	SBDR[21]	2SG=	FUT-	take	**-VEN**	**3SG=**	**DAT**	**=3SG.OBJ**

'He wanted you to bring it for him.'

b. <Ɣatəzaw**nan is-a**.>

[ɣatəzɔw**nan ˈisa**]

/ɣa=	tə-	zaw	**-nan**	**i=**	**sa**	**=a/**
1SG=	FUT-	carry	**-ALL**	**3PL=**	**DAT**	**=3SG**

'I'm going to take it for them.'

In example (15), where both the direct object and the indirect object are third person pronominal clitics, both conjoin to the dative marker /sa/, forming a single unit of phrasal stress. The final vowel of /sa/ elides when conjoined with the direct object enclitic / = a/.[22]

In summary, the third person pronominal direct object clitics are phonologically bound to the verb and written attached to the verb. The pronominal indirect object clitics, however, are not written attached to the verb because they are not phonologically bound to it. Furthermore, phonologically they pattern as proclitics, conjoining with the dative marker /sa/. The pronominal direct object clitics pattern as enclitics, attaching to a preceding host—either to a verb stem or the dative marker /sa/.

9.2.3 Vowel elision

Writing verb phrases having direct and/or indirect objects in their pronominal forms poses some difficulties for Tagdal writers due the process of vowel elision at morpheme and word boundaries, whereby the final vowel of a morpheme or verb root is elided when followed by a vowel. At the end of the verb, elision is most common in verbs of Songhay origin,

---

[21] The subordinator /sa/ has no relation to the dative marker /sa/.

[22] Vowel elision will be discussed in § 9.2.3.

though it also occurs in verb roots of Berber origin that end in /a/ (Benítez-Torres 2021:30).

In table 9.9, the examples show that the final vowel of the verb root is elided when the third person pronominal direct object clitics /=a/ or /=i/ are adjoined to a verb ending in a vowel. One of the principles given by Kutsch Lojenga (2014:72) is that an orthographic word must be faithful to the syllable structure of the language. Since it has been established that third person direct object clitics pattern phonologically as part of the verb word and Tagdal does not have CVV syllables (except in the case of long vowels and then only word-internally), the verb word is spelled as it sounds after the elision process has applied, without the final vowel of the verb root.

Currently in the orthography a hyphen is being used to show the connection between third person pronominal clitics and the verb (see § 9.2.2.2), and if there is a verb-final vowel, it is left unwritten. However, it might be worthwhile to present Tagdal speakers with the option of using an apostrophe to mark elision, both verb-finally (as in table 9.9) and after the dative maker /sa/ (as in table 9.10).

Table 9.9. Vowel elision at morpheme boundaries

Underlying form	**Phonetic realisation**	**Orthographic representation**	**Suggested representation**	**Gloss**
/dumbu =i/	[dumˈbi]	<dumb-i>	<dumb'i>	'slaughter them'
/jiini =a/	[ʒiːˈna]	<jiin-a>	<jiin'a>	'seize it'
/hurru =i/	[huˈrːi]	<hurr-i>	<hurr'i>	'search for them'
/əɣra =i/	[ˈəɣri]	<əɣr-i>	<əɣr'i>	'understand them'
/səkna =i/	[ˈsəkni]	<səkn-i>	<səkn'i>	'demonstrate them'

This suggested change is motivated by Kutsch Lojenga (2014:82) who states that, "Generally, the result of the elision process is indicated by replacing the elided vowel with an apostrophe (and leaving no space between the morphemes)..." Since French is a principal[23] language of Niger (Eberhard et al. 2024), some Tagdal speakers who have gone to school may be familiar with the French orthographic process by which an elided vowel is marked with an apostrophe, in a similar way to what is suggested for Tagdal. Example (16) from French illustrates this process.

(16) <la vache> 'the cow' *<la allumette> <l'allumette> 'the matchstick'

[23] The term "principal language" comes from Eberhard et al. (2024) and refers to "[l]anguages that have been identified as having a working function at the nation-wide level." https://www.ethnologue.com/methodology/#principalLangs.

Currently in the orthography, all direct object independent pronouns are written separately from the verb (see § 9.2.2.2). However, in addition to marking elision across morpheme boundaries between a verb and clitic pronoun (as illustrated in table 9.9), it would be informative to explore the response of Tagdal speakers to the use of an apostrophe to mark vowel elision when writing all verb-initial direct object pronominals, both clitics and independent pronouns. As part of the exploration process, it would need to be determined if the vowel is truly eliminated between a vowel-final verb and a vowel-initial independent pronoun in both fast and slow speech. If the vowel can be pronounced in slow speech, that would lend strong support to writing the verb and the independent pronoun without marking elision (Kutsch Lojenga 2014:81), as is currently the practice.[24]

Example (17) from Benítez-Torres 2021:107 illustrates a vowel-final verb followed by an independent pronoun functioning as a direct object. The phonetic transcription represents a normal speed of speech. The orthographic representation currently used is given, along with a possible orthographic representation using an apostrophe to mark elision.

(17)	Example					Current representation	Representation marking elision
	[iˈ**kəmː** **ˈiːɾi** ˈtafːaːla kan]						
	/i=	**kəmːa**	**iːri**	tafːaːla	kan/	<**ikəmma iri** tafala kan>	<**ikəmm'iri** tafala kan>
	3PL=	**find**	**1PL**	hut	in		
	'They found us in the hut.'						

Elision also occurs between the final vowel of the dative marker /sa/ and a vowel-initial direct object pronominal, as table 9.10 demonstrates.

[24] In the time the authors spent in Niger, only one exception was found to the persistent practice of vowel elision between a verb and a following vowel-initial pronominal: <da insa> 'do for you' was pronounced [ˈdeĩsa]. (See Benítez-Torres 2021:26, 30 for a full explanation of everything happening phonologically in this VP.) However, it was spoken by an older man who was considered an expert; all other speakers the authors have encountered pronounced it with the elision fully intact. (See example [20].) Regardless, it left enough doubt in our minds to justify a re-evaluation of elision.

Table 9.10. Direct object pronouns and clitics following dative /sa/

Person	Underlying form	Phonetic realisation	Orthographic representation	Suggested representation
		Singular		
First person	/sa ɣ:aj/	[sa ɣa:j]	<sa ɣay>	
Second person	/sa nin/	[sa nin]	<sa nin>	
Third person	/sa=a/	[sa]	<s-a>	<s'a>
		Plural		
First person	/sa i:ri/	[si:ɾi]	<sa iri>	<s'iri>
Second person	/sa anʒi/	[sãʒi]	<sa anji>	<s'anji>
Third person	/s=i/	[si]	<s-i>	<s'i>

Since the third person direct object clitics /=a/ and /=i/ are phonologically bound to the dative marker /sa/, in the working orthography they were written as bound to /sa/ with a hyphen and the elided vowel /a/ of /sa/ left unwritten, as <s-a> and <s-i>, in the same way that they are written when bound to a verb (see § 9.2.2.2). As has been explained previously, marking the elision with an apostrophe might be tested by presenting Tagdal speakers with the option of using an apostrophe to consistently mark elision between vowel-final elements (both verbs and dative marker /sa/) and vowel-initial direct object pronominals. Once presented with the options and paradigms (as in table 9.9 and table 9.10), their reactions and preferences could be discussed, and after experimentation they could decide what would be their preferred way to represent elision in the orthography.

Example (18) shows pronominalised indirect and direct objects in context. In (18b) elision occurs across word boundaries between the dative marker and the direct object clitic, and, as has been suggested, it is marked with an apostrophe.

(18) a. <Izaw **insa ɣay.**>

/i=	zaw	**ni=**	**sa**	**ɣa:j/**
3PL=	send	**2SG=**	**DAT**	**1SG**

'They sent me to you.'

b. <Akar **as'iri.**>

/a=	kar	**a=**	**sa**	**i:ɾi/**
2SG=	strike	**3SG=**	**DAT**	**1PL**

'He attacked us for her.'

When both the indirect object and direct object are pronominalised in the same verb phrase, the final vowel of both the verb and the dative marker /sa/ are elided in normal speech, greatly reducing the phrase in its surface form.

(19) <**Na** is'i!>
[ˈ**n**isi]
/**na** i= sa =i/
give 3PL= DAT =3PL
'Give those (things) to them!'

Even though the phrase consists of four morphemes, the surface realisation of this phrase in normal speech only has two syllables. Beginning writers tend to want to write it as it sounds *<nisi>. Another short example is (20), with the verb /da/ 'to do'.

(20) <**Da** iris**'a**!>
[ˈ**di**ːɾ**isa**]
/**da** iːri= **sa** =**a**/
do 1PL= DAT =**3SG**
'Do it for us.'

In (20) the elided vowel /a/ of the dative /sa/ is the same as the first vowel of the following third person pronominal direct object clitic /=a/. Tagdal writers tend to spell the above phrase as pronounced— *<dirisa> or even *<dirsa>. The problem with writing only the surface form is that the presence of the direct object can be completely lost if it is not marked in some way, especially since in some contexts it is grammatically and semantically possible to simply end the clause with the dative marker /sa/, as in (21).

(21) a. <Ɣatəjaw **insa.**>
/ɣa= tə- jaw **ni**= **sa**/
1SG= FUT- help **2SG**= **DAT**
'I'm going to help you.'

b. <Ayingəd an iman **sa.**>
/a= əngəd a= n iman **sa**/
3SG= put.on.turban 3SG= GEN soul **DAT**
'He put his turban on by himself.'

In summary, vowel elision is a common process in Tagdal, especially across word boundaries in normal speech. It is most obvious and problematic for the orthography in the context of the verb phrase because of the prevalence of vowel-initial pronominal forms. As the preferences and practices of Tagdal readers and writers emerge and develop, it may be determined that the use of an apostrophe to mark elision is helpful.

9.3 Conclusion

The discussion above has centred on writing various elements of the Tagdal verb phrase, particularly on word boundary issues. Linguistically based conclusions were drawn, considering phonological, grammatical, and semantic criteria as outlined in Kutsch Lojenga 2014. While there are few readers and writers of Tagdal at the time of writing this chapter, their intuitions and concerns about word boundaries and morphophonemic alternations have been taken into consideration and are the motivation for delving further into the topic of the orthographic word in the Tagdal verb phrase.

Preverbal morphemes that are part of the verb word include various TAM affixes, negation affixes, and derivational affixes. Some of these affixes trigger morphophonological changes that are recognised by Tagdal speakers, who have shown a preference for representing the results of these phonological processes orthographically. The directional suffixes /-kat/ and /-nan/ follow the verb root and are written as part of the verb word because they are semantically inseparable from some of the verb roots with which they are associated.

Another important aspect of writing the Tagdal verb phrase concerns how to write the various pronominals. The subject marker pronominal morphemes are a required element of the verb phrase and do not substitute for full NPs, so they are written as proclitics bound to the verb stem. All direct object pronominal forms can be replaced by a nominal direct object. Furthermore, all but the third person direct object pronouns are independent pronouns, written separately from the verb. However, the third person singular /=a/ and plural /=i/ are enclitics, phonologically bound to the verb stem. As one-syllable morphemes they are not pronounceable in isolation. When adjoined to the directional morphemes /-kat/ and /-nan/ at the end of the verb stem, or to verb stems ending in a CVC syllable in general, they trigger vowel lengthening on the verb stem. Currently, they are written as conjoined to the verb stem with a hyphen.

When a verb is ditransitive, the indirect object comes between the verb and the direct object. Indirect object pronouns are not independent pronouns and are written as proclitics joined to the dative marker /sa/. Indirect objects follow the verb and are marked and followed by the grammatical morpheme /sa/. This marker is written as an independent morpheme when it follows a noun or noun phrase. Since other elements, such as adjectives, can come between a noun and the dative marker, /sa/ is not conjoined with an indirect object noun due to the grammatical criterion of separability (Kutsch Lojenga 2014:85). When /sa/ is bound with a proclitic indirect object, the stress of the verb shifts to the indirect object. Pronominal indirect objects are not part of the verb word and do not trigger vowel lengthening as the direct object third person pronominal clitics do. Pronominal indirect objects are written disjunctively from the verb and conjunctively with the dative marker /sa/.

One of the most challenging decisions in the orthographic representation of the verb phrase has to do with vowel elision across morpheme and word boundaries, particularly when the final vowel of a verb root is elided when followed by a vowel-initial pronominal. Currently, between a vowel-final verb and direct object clitic pronoun, the elided vowel is left unwritten and unmarked, and a hyphen is used to mark the relationship of the direct object pronominal to the preceding verb. Vowel elision across word boundaries, as between the verb and indirect object, is not marked. It is suggested that elision between a verb and direct object pronominal could be marked with the use of an apostrophe, depending on whether Tagdal speakers find it to be useful or not.

The issue of fast and slow speech must be considered when deciding whether to replace the elided vowel with an apostrophe (Kutsch Lojenga 2014:81). Specifically, testing with Tagdal speakers is needed to determine if the final vowel of a verb is always deleted, even in slow speech, before a vowel-initial direct object independent pronoun and/or before a vowel-initial indirect object pronominal. If the elided vowel is never pronounced in slow speech, the vowel can be omitted in the orthography and perhaps replaced by an apostrophe. However, if it can be pronounced in slow speech, the vowel should be written (Kutsch Lojenga 2014:81) and the pronominals should be written disjunctively from the verb. More input is needed from Tagdal readers and writers to determine when and how to mark elision.

Another area for further study and testing has to do with the phonological status of long vowels in Tagdal and how long vowels should be represented orthographically. This seems to be tied to syllable structure and compensatory lengthening which in turn affects the shape of the orthographic word.

Orthography development in Tagdal is still in the early stages and many of the suggestions represented in this chapter are tentative, a starting point for ongoing discussion and testing. As more Tagdal speakers become interested in reading and writing and their skills expand, it is hoped that they will take an active role in advancing the orthography to meet their needs and language development goals.

References

Anderson, Stephen. 2005. *Aspects of the theory of clitics.* Oxford: Oxford University Press.

Benítez-Torres, Carlos M. 2009. Inflectional vs. derivational morphology in Tagdal (Northern Songhay): A case of language mixing. In Fiona McLaughlin, Matondo Masungu, and Eric Potsdam (eds.), *Selected Proceedings of the 38*th *Annual Conference on African Linguistics: Linguistic Theory and African Language Documentation*, 69–83. University of Florida, March 22–25, 2007. Somerville, MA: Cascadilla Proceedings Project.

Benítez-Torres, Carlos M. 2020. Suppletion in Tagdal: A study of some verb root interactions between Songhay and Tuareg-Berber vocabulary in a Northern Songhay language. *Journal of Pidgin and Creole Languages* 35(2):332–359.

Benítez-Torres, Carlos M. 2021. *A grammar of Tagdal: A Northern Songhay language.* Amsterdam: LOT. doi.org/10.48273/LOT0608.

Benítez-Torres, Carlos M., and Anthony P. Grant. 2017. On the origin of some Northern Songhay mixed languages. *Journal of Pidgin and Creole Languages* 32(2):263–303.

Christiansen-Bolli, Regula. 2010. A grammar of Tadaksahak, a Northern Songhay language of Mali. PhD dissertation. University of Leiden.

Crystal, David. 2008. *A dictionary of linguistics and phonetics.* Sixth edition. Malden, MA: Blackwell.

Dimmendaal, Gerrit J., Colleen Ahland, Angelika Jakobi, and Constance Kutsch Lojenga. 2019. Linguistic features and typologies in languages commonly referred to as "Nilo-Saharan." In H. Ekkehard Wolff (ed.), *The Cambridge handbook of African linguistics*, 326–381. Cambridge: Cambridge University Press.

Eberhard, David M., Gary F. Simons, and Charles D. Fennig, eds. 2024. *Ethnologue: Languages of the world.* Twenty-seventh edition. Dallas, TX: SIL International. www.ethnologue.com.

Harrison, Byron, Annette Harrison, and Michael Rueck. 1999. Southern Songhay speech varieties in Niger: A sociolinguistic survey of the Zarma, Songhay, Kurtey, Wogo, and Dendi peoples of Niger. *SIL Electronic Survey Reports* 1999-04. Dallas, TX: SIL International. www.sil.org/resources/publications/entry/9227.

Heath, Jeffrey. 1999a. *A grammar of Koyra Chiini: the Songhay of Timbuktu.* Berlin: Mouton de Gruyter.

Heath, Jeffrey. 1999b. *Grammar of Koyraboro (Koroboro) Senni, the Songhay of Gao.* Cologne: Rüdiger Köppe.

Heath, Jeffrey. 2005. *A Grammar of Tamashek (Tuareg of Mali).* Berlin: Mouton de Gruyter.

Ikali. 2019. Nation : Le tagdal devient officiellement la 11e langue nationale du Niger. *ActuNiger*, December 10, 2019. www.actuniger.com/culture/15675-nation-le-tagdal-devient-officiellement-la-11e-langue-nationale-du-niger.html.

Kossmann, Maarten. 2008. Adjectives in Northern Songhay. *Afrika und Übersee* 90:109–132.

Kossmann, Maarten. 2010. Parallel system borrowing. Parallel morphological systems due to the borrowing of paradigms. *Diachronica* 27(3):459–488.

Kossmann, Maarten. 2011. *A grammar of Ayer Tuareg (Niger).* Cologne: Rüdiger Köppe.

Kutsch Lojenga, Constance. 2014. Basic principles for establishing word boundaries. In Michael Cahill and Keren Rice (eds.), *Developing orthographies for unwritten languages*, 73–106. Publications in Language Use and Education 6. Dallas, TX: SIL International.

Lacroix, Pierre-Francis. 1971. L'ensemble songhay-jerma : Problèmes et thèmes de travail. In *Actes du 8ème Congrès de la SLAO (Société Linguistique de l'Afrique Occidentale)*, 24–28 mars 1969, 87–100. Annales de l'Université d'Abidjan, Série H, Fasicule hors série. Abidjan: Université d'Abidjan.

Lacroix, Pierre Francis. 1981. Emghedeshie, « Songhay language of Agadez », à travers les documents de Barth. In E.R.A. 246 du CNRS "Langage et Culture en Afrique de l'Ouest" (ed.), *Itinérances – en pays peul et ailleurs : mélanges réunis par les chercheurs de l'ERA 246 du CNRS à la mémoire de Pierre Francis Lacroix*, 13–19. Paris: Société des Africanistes.

Meakins, Felicity. 2013. Mixed languages. In Peter Bakker and Yaron Matras (eds.), *Contact languages: A comprehensive guide,* 159–228. Boston: De Gruyter Mouton.

Nicolaï, Robert. 1981. Le songhay septentrional. Etudes prosodiques. In E.R.A. 246 du CNRS "Langage et Culture en Afrique de l'Ouest" (ed.), *Itinérances – en pays peul et ailleurs : mélanges réunis par les chercheurs de l'ERA 246 du CNRS à la mémoire de Pierre Francis Lacroix*, 229–256. Paris: Société des Africanistes.

Nicolaï, Robert. 1990. L'évolution 'problématique' du songhay septentrional (Analyse d'une situation de contact). *Travaux du Cercle Linguistique de Nice 10–11*, 135–148.

Nicolaï, Robert. 2003. *La force des choses ou l'épreuve 'nilo-saharienne' : Question sur les reconstructions archéologiques et l'évolution des langues.* Cologne: Rüdiger Köppe.

OLAC. 2023. OLAC resources in and about the Tawallammat Tamajaq language. Open Language Archives Community. www.language-archives.org/language.php/ttq. (Information on website updated from time to time.)

Rueck, Michael, and Niels Christiansen. 1999. Northern Songhay languages in Mali and Niger: A sociolinguistic survey. *SIL Electronic Survey Reports* 1999-008. Dallas, TX: SIL International. www.sil.org/resources/publications/entry/9124.

Snider, Keith. 2014. Orthography and phonological depth. In Michael Cahill and Keren Rice (eds.), *Developing orthographies for unwritten languages*, 23–43. Publications in Language Use and Education 6. Dallas, TX: SIL International.

Souag, Lameen. 2010a. The Western Berber stratum in Kwarandzyey. In Harry Stroomer, Maarten Kossmann, Dymitr Ibriszimow, and Rainer Vossen (eds.), *Etudes berbères V, Essais sur des variations dialectales et autres articles*, Berber Studies, 177–189. Vol. 28. Cologne: Rüdiger Köppe.

Souag, Lameen. 2010b. Grammatical contact in the Sahara: Arabic, Berber, and Songhay in Tabelbala and Siwa. PhD dissertation. SOAS, University of London. doi.org/10.25501/SOAS.00013430.

Souag, Lameen. 2012. The subclassification of Songhay and its historical implications. *Journal of African Languages and Linguistics* 33(2):181–213.

Souag, Lameen. 2015a. Explaining Korandjé: Language contact, plantations, and the trans-Saharan trade. *Journal of Pidgin and Creole Languages* 30(2):189–224.

Souag, Lameen. 2015b. Non-Tuareg Berber and the genesis of nomadic Northern Songhay. *Journal of African Languages and Linguistics* 36(1):121–143.

Thomason, Sarah G. 2001. *Language contact: An introduction*. Edinburgh: Edinburgh University Press.

Thomason, Sarah Grey, and Terrence Kaufman. 1988. *Language contact, creolization, and genetic linguistics*. Los Angeles, CA: University of California Press.

Velupillai, Viveka. 2015. *Creoles and mixed languages: An introduction*. Amsterdam: John Benjamins.

10
When Is Long Too Long? Word Length and Readability: A Case Study from Muna (Indonesia)

René van den Berg

Abstract

Studies on word length in newly written languages are rare. This chapter provides a case study from Muna, an Austronesian language of Southeast Sulawesi, Indonesia. Because of its rich morphology, Muna has a large number of long words, creating potential obstacles for reading fluency. As a result, a number of affixes and clitics are written as separate words. After providing some background on the Muna language, the first part of this chapter discusses the process by which these decisions were reached, and provides ample illustrations. In the second part, a comparison is drawn with word length in various other languages, both European and languages of Indonesia and Papua New Guinea, and how word length relates to readability. This leads to a few recommendations in the conclusion.

Abbreviations

ADV	adverbializer	LOC	locative
APPL	applicative	NMLZ	nominalizer
APPROX	approximately	OBJ	object
ART	article	PASS	passive
ART.F	feminine article	PASS.PTCP	passive participle
ART.M	masculine article	PFV	perfective
CA	class affix	PL	plural
CAUS	causative	POSS	possessive
DU	dual	PURP	purpose
EXCL	exclusive	RDUP	reduplication
FUT	future	REAL	realis
HON	honorific	RECP	reciprocal
INCL	inclusive	SG	singular
IND.OBJ	indirect object	SUDD	sudden action
INT	intensive	TR	transitivizer
IRR	irrealis		

10.1 Introduction

The conversion of a purely spoken language to one that also has a written dimension is not a straightforward process.[1] Many decisions need to be made, some of which are easier than others. Which script will be used? To what extent will the conventions of the national language(s) be followed? What symbols will be chosen to represent unusual sounds? Where are the word boundaries? How much testing needs to be done before an orthography is "official" and an item can be printed? And who actually makes those decisions? There is considerable literature on this topic, including the contributions in Cahill and Rice (2014) and Jones and Mooney (2017). But it appears that relatively little academic attention has been paid to the question of word length in the field of orthography design for unwritten languages. Eaton and Schroeder (2012) and Kutsch Lojenga (2014), both of which deal exclusively with principles for establishing word boundaries, do not even mention word length as a factor to consider.

---

[1] I would like to thank my wife Lydia for her critical input during the writing of this chapter, as well as a few German-speaking SIL colleagues. Mike Cahill and Helen Eaton also provided valuable input on a first version.

This chapter tries to address this issue by focussing exclusively on the question of word length in orthography. When is a word too long to be read? Why is the German compound *Rechtsschutzversicherungsgesellschaften*[2] hard to read at first sight, especially for non-native speakers of German? With thirty-nine letters and meaning 'insurance companies providing legal protection', the word is a formidable and intimidating obstacle to the eyes and the mind of an innocent reader, though educated native speakers admittedly have no trouble reading such words. German is famous for its extravaganza of hyperextended compounds, but it is not unique. Welsh has a famous train station of fifty-eight letters, but since "this is a Victorian contrivance for the benefit of tourists with no basis in historical usage", I disregard it.[3] A noncontrived example is the Hawaiian woman who made the news when her thirty-six-character name *Keihanaikukauakahihulihe'eka haunaele* did not fit on an identification card.[4] This may be an extreme case, but various examples of long words can also be pulled from languages that have only recently been "reduced" to writing (see § 10.6 for examples). But how long is a long word? More than ten, fifteen, or twenty characters?

The case study I present here is from Muna, a Western Austronesian language spoken in Southeast Sulawesi, Indonesia. It is meant to be a practical contribution to the question of word length and readability. The theoretical literature on word length is extensive (see Grzybek 2007 for an overview), often with detailed statistical formulae and analyses, but my concern in this chapter is practical: how long are long words in Muna, and a few other written languages? And I try to answer the central question of this chapter – how does word length affect readability, especially for new readers? Can words be too long? If so, is there (or should there be) an upper limit?

This chapter is organized as follows. After giving some background to the Muna language and its rich morphology (§ 10.2), I discuss the decisions that were made regarding writing Muna; first the process of reaching these decisions (§ 10.3), followed by five specific areas dealing with word length and word breaks (§ 10.4). In § 10.5 I briefly discuss current practices in writing Muna. This is followed by a section on word length from a comparative perspective (§ 10.6), where I compare Muna with three Germanic languages (English, German, Dutch), and with the national language Indonesian and the neighboring language Wolio. I also bring in a few languages from Papua New Guinea for an even wider perspective on long words. The next section

[2] Taken from https://www.germanpod101.com/blog/2018/11/02/the-5-longest-words-in-german-and-their-meanings/ (accessed 17 January 2023).

[3] The full (contrived) name is Llanfairpwllgwyngyllgogerychwyrndrobwllllantysiliogogogoch https://en.wikipedia.org/wiki/Llanfairpwll_railway_station (accessed 11 January 2023).

[4] https://www.npr.org/sections/thetwo-way/2013/12/31/258673819/hawaiian-woman-gets-ids-that-fit-her-36-character-last-name (accessed 11 January 2023). Thanks to Kristy Wedel for alerting me to this information.

(§ 10.7) deals with word length in the light of readability studies. In § 10.8 I offer some conclusions and recommendations.

10.2 Muna: Some background

Muna [mnb] is an Austronesian language of Southeast Sulawesi (formerly Celebes, see map 10.1), spoken by some 300,000 to 350,000 people,[5] comprising various dialects. Muna belongs to the Celebic supergroup. The main typological features of Muna, drawn from van den Berg (1989, 1996), are presented in map 10.1, representing the northern, "standard" dialect.[6]

Map 10.1. Muna Island in Indonesia

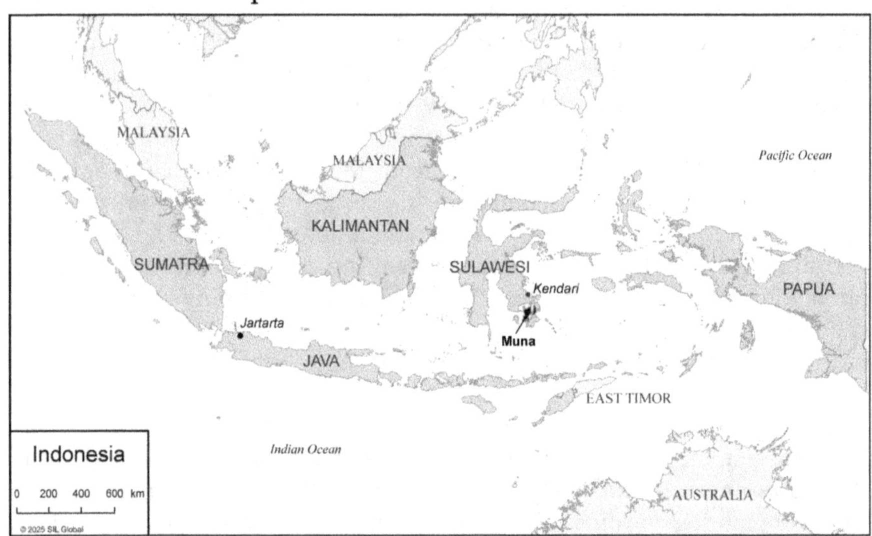

[5] The exact number of speakers of Muna is hard to determine, due to outmigration to the provincial capital Kendari, the discrepancy between administrative and linguistic boundaries, and also language shift to Indonesian among people who are ethnically Muna. The number given here is my personal estimate, and includes the large number of Muna speakers in Kendari. The *Ethnologue* (Eberhard et al. 2024) lists 266,000 speakers, based on the 2010 census.

[6] I would like to convey my heartfelt thanks to the many Muna people who have helped in my study of their beautiful and fascinating language since 1985, including Nilus Larangka, Hanafi, La Ode Abdul Fattah, La Ada, La Mokui (all deceased); as well as Lukas Atakasi for the southern dialect. More recently Mainuru Hado and Muslimin Uka have been very helpful. I consider myself very blessed for having had the opportunity to study an unwritten language and help develop it.

The phonology of Muna is moderately rich with five vowels: /i ɛ ɑ ɔ u/ and twenty-five consonants, including seven prenasalized consonants: /p t k b d g ɓ d̪ m n ŋ ^{m}p ^{m}b ^{n}t ^{n}d ^{n}s ^{ŋ}k ^{ŋ}g f s h β ʁ r l/. The orthography uses <bh> for the bilabial implosive /ɓ/, <dh> for the voiced lamino-dental plosive /d̪/, <gh> for the voiced uvular fricative /ʁ/, <ng> for /ŋ/, and <w> for /β/. There are no final consonants and no consonant clusters; V and CV are the only allowed syllable types. Primary stress falls on the penultimate syllable.

Muna morphology is rich in prefixation and suffixation, while infixation, circumfixation, and reduplication are also common. Verbal morphology is especially rich, as illustrated in the following inflectional and derivational categories (with the illustrated element bolded).[7]

- subject prefixes, e.g., ***a**-kala* (1SG-go) 'I go/went'; ***no**-kala* (3SG.REAL-go) 's/he goes/went';
- direct object suffixes, e.g., *no-wora-**kanau*** (3SG.REAL-see-1SG.OBJ) 's/he sees me'; *a-wora-**e*** (1SG-see-3SG.OBJ) 'I see him/her/it';
- indirect object suffixes, e.g., *a-basa-**angko**-e* (1SG-read-2SG.IND.OBJ-3SG.OBJ) 'I (will) read it for you';
- TAM morphology: irrealis infix *-um-*, e.g., *a-k*<***um***>*ala* (1SG-<IRR>go) 'I will go', perfective *mo,* and reduplication marking continuous action;
- valency-changing affixes, including causative *fo*$_1$- and *feka-*, reciprocal *po-*, transitivizing *Ci-*, detransitivizing *fo*$_2$-, applicative *ghoo-,* requestive *fe-*, and accidental passive *ti-*;
- various modal and adverbial notions, e.g., *manso-* 'habitually', *piki-* 'quickly, soon, early', *ta-sika-…-ha-* 'suddenly', *poka-* 'playfully, not seriously'.
- various nominalizations: *ka-* and *-ha,* as well as the circumfix *ka-…-ha* marking location, time, instrument or reason, e.g., ***ka**-lente-**ha**-no* (NMLZ-born-NMLZ-3SG.POSS) 'the place/time where s/he was born'.

Nouns are not marked for case or gender, and only marginally for number. There are five pronominal sets. Pronominals do not distinguish gender, but clusivity is distinguished for 1PL. The unmarked constituent order is VS in intransitive clauses and SVO in transitive clauses, though variations are common for pragmatic reasons. The language uses prepositions.

10.3 Muna orthography decisions: The process

Muna was traditionally not written. A few grammatical and lexical studies appeared between 1968 and 1986 (see van den Berg 1989:6 for references),

[7] Muna words used in this chapter are written in italics.

using ad hoc spellings for the "unusual" phonemes /ɓ d̪ ʁ/ which do not occur in Indonesian, but orthography was not explicitly discussed in these works. This changed in the late 1980s as a result of my own research on the Muna language. During my first research period on Muna (from June 1985 till November 1986), my wife Lydia and I considered these earlier spelling conventions, and after a detailed study of the phonology and various discussions with co-workers and teachers, we settled on the symbols <bh dh gh> for the phonemes /ɓ d̪ ʁ/ for the purposes of our own practical orthography. The three digraphs with *h* made the special character of these sounds obvious, although phonologically the three do not constitute a natural class. But the problem of word breaks was still an open question. Our intuitive tendency was to equate the grammatical with the orthographic word, and hence to write all affixes in combination with the root as one word: *noworakanau* for *no-wora-kanau* (3SG.REAL-see-1SG.OBJ) 's/he sees me'. However, several words looked very long as a result, often exceeding fifteen characters, as for example *noparintangikasami*, an eighteen-character word consisting of a root, a prefix and two suffixes: *no-parinta-ngi-kasami* (3SG.REAL-govern-TR-1PL.EXCL.OBJ), 'he governed us'. At this point it was not clear whether such long words would affect readability if the language was going to be further developed and used in education.

In early 1990, when we visited Muna again, we convened an orthography meeting with co-workers, teachers, a lecturer in linguistics from the provincial university and some government officials, most of whom had become friends. Some fifteen people attended this meeting, and we had a lively discussion on various topics, specifically the symbolization of the three "unusual" phonemes, the writing of long vowels, and the issue of word breaks and word length. In the end, agreement was reached to use the symbols <bh dh gh> for the three unusual sounds, to use double vowels for long vowels (e.g., *fumaa* /fu'ma:/ 'eat'), and to avoid overlong words by splitting off certain affixes from their roots or stems, as detailed in § 10.4. A subcommittee was formed to look at the details. As a result of their work, a spelling guide was drawn up and published (Hanafi et al. 1991). This *Pedoman ejaan bahasa daerah Muna* ("Spelling guide for the Muna language"), for which I was the advisor, is a thirty-nine-page booklet written in Indonesian, consisting of an introductory section explaining the need for standardizing the spelling of unwritten local languages in Indonesia, followed by a detailed section on orthography rules for Muna: common consonants, special consonants, vowels, long vowels and vowel sequences, syllable divisions and word breaks. The book ends with sixteen pages of illustrative texts in Muna, taken from various genres: an animal tale, a legend, some riddles, some traditional poetry, various lullabies, two formal wedding invitations, and a wedding speech.

Even though writing in Muna is still relatively rare, these rules have been mostly adhered to when people write and publish in Muna. This is true for the primary school books written by La Ode Sidu, who was a member of the spelling committee and collaborator and co-author of the two dictionaries: Muna-English (van den Berg 1996) and Muna-Indonesian (van den Berg and La Ode Sidu 2000), as well as a more recent Indonesian-Muna dictionary (Sirad Imbo 2012). However, there are also rules that people do not abide by, including the conventions for word breaks (see § 10.5 for details).

These rules were also transferred to the Bible translation project which took place in the southern Muna dialect, centered around the villages of Labasa, Lakapera and Waleale, headed by a local translation team for which I was the advisor. The segmental phonology of the southern Muna dialect is quite divergent from the "standard" northern dialect, in that the south has /h/ for northern /r/, /ʔ/ for northern /ʁ/ (and also /ʔ/ for northern /h/). The glottal stop in southern Muna is represented by <'>, illustrated by *foho'u* (southern Muna) and *foroghu* 'drink' (northern Muna). For further details on the southern Muna dialect, see van den Berg 2004. The translation team adopted the conventions for word breaks, which seemed to work to everybody's satisfaction.

In spite of these rules and conventions, several unresolved issues emerged in the course of the translation project and during efforts to publish other books in northern Muna. As a result, in early 2014, I met with La Ode Sidu (now a university professor in the provincial capital of Kendari) to discuss a number of remaining spelling issues, including word breaks, variant forms, proclitics, sequences of three identical vowels, and punctuation for introducing quotations. Of the original five members of the Spelling Committee, La Ode Sidu was the only one still alive and active, and so the two of us made a few new decisions that have been implemented since then.[8]

On reflection, it seems that even though there was a committee, my own role in this process has been considerable, possibly larger than it could or should have been. I am not aware of having "pushed" a specific spelling agenda, but neither has there been an attempt at a more participatory approach by travelling around villages with a team of people, explaining the issues and getting local input. Given the visa restrictions we worked under and considering that Muna is spoken in several hundred villages covering a large area, that might also not have been easy to accomplish. The fact that the committee decisions were well received and have never been challenged (as far as I know), was another factor in not pursuing further community involvement on orthography decisions.

[8] Unfortunately, these decisions have not yet been disseminated on a public forum or incorporated in a new version of the Muna Spelling Guide.

10.4 Word break decisions in Muna

In this section I list the various decisions that were made regarding word length and where to break up long words. This concerns pronominal suffixes (§ 10.4.1), numeral prefixes (§ 10.4.2), prepositions (§ 10.4.3), prenominal particles (§ 10.4.4), and reduplication (§ 10.4.5). In terms of the criteria listed by Kutsch Lojenga (2014), these elements are all phonologically bound to their lexical host – they cannot occur as independent words. In terms of grammatical criteria, they do not display mobility or separability, while substitutability is only possible for a subset of the pronominal suffixes (see § 10.4.1). Semantically, they range from virtually meaningless elements (the article *o* in § 10.4.4), to having distinct lexical meanings (the numeral prefixes in § 10.4.2).

10.4.1 Pronominal suffixes

The pronominal suffixes of Muna are listed in table 10.1, together with the free pronouns.[9] (Subject prefixes are excluded as they are complex and less relevant for the purposes of this chapter.)

Table 10.1. Muna pronominals

Num	**Person**	**Free**	**Possessive**	**Direct Object**	**Indirect Object**
SG	1	*inodi, idi*	*-ku*	*-kanau*	
-	2	*(i)hintu*	*-mu*	*-ko*	*-angko*
-	2 HON	*intaidi*	*-nto*	*-kaeta*	
-	3	*anoa*	*-no*	*-e*	*-ane*
DU	1 INCL	*intaidi*	*-nto*	-	
PL	1 INCL	*intaidi-imu*	*-nto-omu*	-	
-	1 EXCL	*insaidi*	*-mani*	*-kasami*	
-	2	*(i)hintu-umu*	*-Vmu*	*-ko-omu*	*-angko-omu*
-	2 HON	*intaidi-imu*	*-nto-omu*	*-kaeta-amu*	
-	3	*andoa*	*-ndo*	*-da*	*-anda*

[9] An alternative arrangement of the pronominal system is also possible (and possibly preferable), using a binary minimal-augmented division, rather than a tripartite singular-dual-plural division with a sole dual member. In a minimal-augmented system (see Dixon 2010:196–199), the first person dual inclusive (1SG + 2SG) joins the four singular forms (1SG, 2SG, 2SG.HON, 3SG) in opposition to the remaining plural forms, creating a perfectly symmetrical system in Muna of five "minimal" and five "augmented" pronouns. In this system, the terms "singular" and "plural" are no longer appropriate, as the dual in the first group is obviously not singular.

These suffixes are phonologically and grammatically part of the verb or noun. They cannot be pronounced in isolation (except in self-reference when talking about a morpheme), and can also be followed by other suffixes. However, the direct object suffixes have a special property in that they are in complementary distribution with free pronouns. Compare *a-ghondohi-ko* (1SG-look.for-2SG.OBJ) 'I look for you' with an object suffix, and *a-ghondohi ihintu* (1SG-look.for 2SG) 'I look for you', with a free pronoun. The clauses have the same meaning, though the free pronoun gives focus to the object. The combination **a-ghondohi-ko ihintu* (1SG-look.for-2SG.OBJ 2SG) is ungrammatical. Subject prefixes, on the other hand, cannot be substituted by a free pronoun and co-occur in combination with them.[10]

In order to reduce word length on verbs, the decision was made to write four object suffixes as separate words (disjunctively): *kanau* 'me', *kaeta* 'you (honorific SG)', *kaeta-amu* 'you (honorific PL)' and *kasami* 'us (EXCL)'. Because each of them has a clear meaning, there is "referential independence" (Kutsch Lojenga 2014:98) in addition to their substitutability, making it more acceptable for these suffixes to stand on their own in writing. When the Bible translation project was started, the disyllabic possessive suffix *mani* 'our (EXCL)' was added to this list by the translation team. These decisions are illustrated in tables 10.2 and 10.3, each displaying the morphological make-up of the word (with the root bolded), the rejected unary orthography (elements written together or conjunctively), and the suggested binary orthography of the word (elements written separately or disjunctively). The use of hyphens was not considered as an option for writing suffixes, as hyphens in Indonesian are used for writing reduplication (see § 10.4.5), and also for breaking off long words at the end of a line. Going against national language spelling conventions was not an appealing option.

Note in table 10.2 that *-kanau* and *-kasami* can also be followed by the perfective suffix *-mo*, as well as the plural marker *-Vmu*, where V stands for a vowel copied from the stem. This *-Vmu* suffix pluralizes either the second person subject, or the dual inclusive object. The last two examples are from the southern Muna dialect, indicated by "southern". Note that in southern Muna the object suffix *kaita* means 'the two of us' (1DU.INCL.OBJ), and does not have an honorific meaning. Also, the southern Muna equivalent of *kasami* (1PL.EXCL.OBJ) is *kainsami*.

In tables 10.2 and 10.3, the roots are shown in bold.

[10] This complementary distribution leads Kroeger (2005:327–328) to the statement that the object suffixes in Muna are more like clitic pronouns. On other tests, however, they qualify as suffixes.

Table 10.2. Object suffixes

Morphology and meaning	Rejected orthography	Suggested orthography
*no-**wora**-kanau* 3SG.REAL-see-1SG.OBJ 'he sees me'	*noworakanau*	*nowora kanau*
*ta-do-sika-**tudu**-ha-kanau-mo* JUST-3PL.REAL-SUDD-order-SUDD-1SG.OBJ-PFV 'they suddenly ordered me'	*tadosikatuduhakanaumo*	*tadosikatuduha kanaumo*
*o-meka-**mate**-kanau-umu* 2SG-IRR.CAUS-die-1SG.OBJ-PL 'you (PL) will kill me'	*omekamatekanauumu*	*omekamate kanauumu*
*ta-**faraluu**-ghi-kaeta* 1PL.EXCL-need-TR-2SG.HON.OBJ 'we need you (HON)'	*tafaraluughikaeta*	*tafaraluughi kaeta*
*ta-**mealai**-kaeta-amu* 1PL.EXCL-IRR.ask.permission-2SG.HON. OBJ-PL 'we ask your (PL) permission (to leave)'	*tamealaikaetaamu*	*tamealai kaetaamu*
*do-**angkafi**-kasami* 3PL.REAL-follow-1PL.EXCL.OBJ 'they followed us'	*doangkafikasami*	*doangkafi kasami*
*o-feka-**mate**-kasami-imu* 2SG-CAUS-die-1PL.EXCL.OBJ-PL 'you (PL) kill us'	*ofekamatekasamiimu*	*ofekamate kasamiimu*

*no-po-**bhai**-'ao-kaita-omu* (southern) 3SG.REAL-RECP-friend-APPL-1DU.INCL.OBJ-PL 'he accompanies us (all)'	*nopobhai'aokaitaomu*	*nopobhai'ao kaitaomu*
*ta-da-mo-**limba**-kainsami-mo?* (southern) JUST-3PL.IRR-IRR.CAUS-go.out-1PL.EXCL. OBJ-PFV 'will they just release us?' (Acts 16:37)	*tadamolimbakainsamimo*	*tadamolimba kainsamimo*

Table 10.3 shows examples of the 1PL.EXCL possessive suffix *-mani*, which not only marks the possessor on nouns, but also indicates the agent on passive participles.

Table 10.3. Possessive suffix *-mani*

Morphology and meaning	**Rejected orthography**	**Suggested orthography**
***lambu**-mani* house-1PL.EXCL.POSS 'our house'	*lambumani*	*lambu mani*
*kae-**late**-ha-mani* NMLZ-live-NMLZ-1PL.EXCL.POSS 'our dwelling place'	*kaelatehamani*	*kaelateha mani*
*ne-mo-**limpu**-ghoo-mani* PASS.PTCP-CA-forget-APPL-1PL.EXCL.POSS 'what we forgot'	*nemolimpughoomani*	*nemolimpughoo mani*
*kae-fo-**ere**-ha-mani-mo* NMLZ-CAUS-rise-NMLZ-1PL.EXCL.POSS-PFV 'that is the reason we built (it)'	*kaefoerehamanimo*	*kaefoereha manimo*

There are two other possessive suffixes which are also disyllabic, but these are not written separately. In the case of *-Vmu* 'your (PL)', it was felt that writing this suffix as a separate word did not make sense, as it is phonologically intimately linked to the preceding word due to the vowel harmony. Hence 'your (PL) house' (morphologically *lambu-umu*) is written as *lambuumu*, not *lambu umu*. Similarly, 'your (PL) dwelling place' (morphologically *kae-late-ha-amu*) is written as *kaelatehaamu*, not *kaelateha amu*. Writing this suffix separately also encourages people to insert a glottal stop before *umu* (or *amu*) when they read aloud (as has been observed), because such glottal insertion happens naturally in Indonesian between like vowels. But in the case of Muna, such an inserted glottal is unnatural and hampers understanding.

The other possessive suffix still concatenated to the verb is *-nto-omu* 'our (PL INCL)' or 'your (PL HON)'. The reasons for this decision were that this is a complex suffix consisting of two elements and that the simple suffix *-nto* is always written attached to the head noun. Perhaps this is not completely consistent, and as a result some rather long words with possessive suffixes are found in Muna texts, e.g., *kalambehintoomu* 'our (PL INCL) girls/daughters', morphologically *kalambe-hi-nto-omu* (girl-PL-1DU.INCL-PL).

10.4.2 Numeral prefixes

The numbers one to nine occur in three forms in Muna: as free forms (used in counting), prefixed to a classifier or a measure noun (to refer to objects), and reduplicated (to refer to humans), as shown in table 10.4. As mentioned earlier, the prefixed forms cannot occur on their own, but need a noun as a host. The various forms across the columns are historically all related, but a variety of sound changes has resulted in a large number of irregular and unpredictable forms.

Table 10.4. Numerals

Num	Free	Prefixed	Reduplicated
1	*ise*	*se-*	*se-ise*
2	*dua*	*raa-*	*ru-dua*
3	*tolu*	*tolu-*	*to-tolu*
4	*paa*	*fato-*	*po-paa*
5	*dima*	*lima-*	*di-dima*
6	*noo*	*nomo-*	*no-noo*
7	*pitu*	*fitu-*	*pi-pitu*
8	*oalu*	*alu-*	*oalu*
9	*siua*	*siua-*	*si-siua*

Since the prefixed forms are all disyllabic (including *raa-*, but with the exception of *se-* 'one'), the resulting words are again fairly long. Because these prefixed numerals have a clear lexical meaning, it was decided to write them separately, as shown in the examples in table 10.5. Note in the last example that *-fulu* 'ten' acts as a host noun for forming decades (the numbers 20–90).

Table 10.5. Prefixed numerals

Morphology and meaning	Rejected orthography	Suggested orthography
raa-wula-mo two-moon-PFV 'already two months'	*raawulamo*	*raa wulamo*
tolu-gholeo three-day 'three days'	*tolugholeo*	*tolu gholeo*
fato-ghulu four-body 'four (animals)'	*fatoghulu*	*fato ghulu*
fitu-fulu seven-ten 'seventy'	*fitufulu*	*fitu fulu*

Complications arose with three prefixes (or possibly proclitics) that are frequently found together with numerals: the future numeral *na-*, the approximate *pe-*, and the prefix *ta-* meaning 'remaining, left, another'.

It was decided that a single occurrence of any of these prefixes would be written as one word with the numeral, but combinations of two (such as *ta-na-* and *na-pe-*) would be written as separate words.[11] When all three prefixes occur together (*ta-na-pe-*), only the first two are written as one word, and the third with the following noun. The reason for this decision was that writing *tanape* as one word would possibly result in reading this word with (automatic) penultimate stress /ta'nape/, instead of the correct stress on [ta]: /'tanape/. These decision are illustrated in table 10.6. Note that even when these prefixes are added, the numeral is still separated from the noun.

[11] The approximate prefix *pe-* does not occur by itself, as it always takes the future prefix *na-*, even when referring to past or present situations.

Table 10.6. Prefixes occurring with numerals

Morphology and meaning	Rejected orthography	Suggested orthography
*na-raa-**wula*** FUT-two-moon '(it will be) two months'	*naraawula*	*naraa wula*
*ta-na-tolu-**taghu*** LEFT-FUT-three-year '(it will be) another three years'	*tanatolutaghu*	*tana tolu taghu*
*na-pe-fato-**ahadhi*** FUT-APPROX-four-week 'approximately four weeks'	*napefatoahadhi*	*nape fato ahadhi*
*ta-na-pe-lima-**gholeo*** FUT-LEFT-APPROX-five-day '(it will be) about another five days'	*tanapelimagholeo*	*tana pelima gholeo*

10.4.3 Prepositions

Muna has five monosyllabic proclitic prepositions: three locatives (*ne, we, te*), in addition to *bhe* 'with' and *so* 'for'. These prepositions are always followed by a noun, pronoun or demonstrative, and never found standing on their own.[12] They form one phonological word with the following head. In spontaneous writing, these elements are often written in combination with the next word as one word. But for the sake of readability and uniformity with Indonesian (where prepositions are written as separate words[13]), the spelling committee decided to write all prepositions as separate words. This is illustrated in table 10.7.

[12] *So* 'for' is also a future proclitic particle before verbs, a usage that is not illustrated here.

[13] This is the rule, but the general locative preposition *di* 'at, in, on, by' is often incorrectly written as a prefix, partially because it is homophonous with the passive prefix *di-*. It is not unusual to see official signs in Indonesia saying *Dilarang masuk disini* 'Entrance prohibited' with *disini* 'here' written as one word for what is correctly *Dilarang masuk di sini* (morphologically PASS-forbid enter LOC here, 'forbidden to enter here').

Table 10.7. Prepositions

Morphology and meaning	**Rejected orthography**	**Suggested orthography**
ne=ini LOC=this 'here'	*neini*	*ne ini*
we=lambu-ku LOC=house-1SG.POSS 'at/to/in my house'	*welambuku*	*we lambuku*
te=wawo-no LOC=top-3SG.POSS 'on top of it'	*tewawono*	*te wawono*
bhe=kamokula-ndo with=parent-3PL.POSS 'with their parents'	*bhekamokulando*	*bhe kamokulando*
so=moghane-no for=man-3SG.POSS 'for her husband'	*somoghaneno*	*so moghaneno*

10.4.4 Prenominal particles

Muna has several prenominal proclitic particles which are phonologically attached to the following noun. The most common of these is the proclitic article *o=*, which is elusive in meaning and usage. It does not mark definiteness or number, but it precedes bare nouns after an intonational break (see van den Berg 2011 for some discussion). Most people writing Muna tend to write the article connected to the next noun, but the spelling committee decided to write it as a separate word, partly to differentiate it from the homophonous prefix *o-* (a second person subject marker on verbs), partly because the Indonesian article *si* (which is mostly found before names and adjectives) is written separately, and partly on the analogy of articles in English and Dutch. The proclitic articles *la=* and *wa=* (before male and female names respectively, usually capitalized) are written as separate words as well, also before the nobility particles *ode* and *odhe* (normally also capitalized). These particles are usually considered to be part of a person's name and are therefore left untranslated. A final prenominal particle which is written separately is the pluralizing particle *ndo*, typically found before animate nouns and names.

While the effect of these short words (only one to four characters) on word length may appear to be minimal, the decision to write them separately is in line with the desire to keep words as short as possible, without hampering understanding. Examples are given in table 10.8.

Table 10.8. Prenominal particles

Morphology and meaning	Rejected orthography	Suggested orthography
o = robhine ART = woman 'a/the woman'	*orobhine*	*o robhine*
o = kameko ART = palm.wine 'palm wine'	*okameko*	*o kameko*
ndo = La = Eta PL = ART.M = E. 'La Eta and his friends'	*ndoLaEta,* *ndo LaEta* *ndoLa Eta*	*ndo La Eta*
Wa = Ode Ndale ART.F = NOBLE N. 'We Ode Ndale'	*WaOde Ndale*	*Wa Ode Ndale*
te = ndo = fokoamau-ku LOC = PL = uncle-1SG.POSS 'at my uncle's house'	*tendofokoamauku* *tendo fokoamauku*	*te ndo fokoamauku*

10.4.5 Reduplication

Following long-established spelling practices in Indonesian, reduplication in Muna is generally indicated by a hyphen. This is a very clear visual help in identifying the root and the reduplicant, even when they are surrounded by affixes. And it also helps to break up long words, presenting an intermediate solution between conjunctive and disjunctive writing. However, in Muna the hyphen is only used for full disyllabic reduplication. In the case of partial reduplication, where only the first syllable is repeated, no hyphen is used. In these cases the reduplicated vowel can be slightly longer than the original vowel, but it does not have the same length as a full double vowel, and the resulting element before the hyphen would not be recognized as a possible root or stem. This is exemplified in table 10.9, where the last example illustrates partial reduplication.

Table 10.9. Reduplication

Morphology and meaning	Rejected orthography	Suggested orthography
*dae-kala~**kala*** 1PL.INCL.IRR-RDUP~go 'we will walk'	*daekalakala*	*daekala-kala*
*feka-ngkoko~**ngkokoso*** ADV-RDUP~diligent '(study) diligently'	*fekangkokongkokoso*	*fekangkoko-ngkokoso*
*ka-po-gaa~**gaa**-ti-ha-ndo-mo* NMLZ-RECP-RDUP~separate-TR-NMZL-3PL.POSS-PFV 'that was the reason they (all) separated'	*kapogaagaatihandomo*	*kapogaa-gaatihandomo*
*no-mpo~**mpona*** 3SG.REAL-RDUP~long 'it is rather long (in time)'	*nompo-mpona* *nompoo-mpona* *nompoompona*	*nompompona*

Taken together, these decisions have led to a considerable reduction in overall word length, and a concomitant increase in readability.

10.5 Current writing practices

This section deals with two issues relating to the current practice of writing Muna. The first concerns deviations from the recommendations in the 1991 *Muna Spelling Guide* (Hanafi et al. 1991). The second is how Muna people actually write in spontaneous discourse, especially regarding word breaks.

In the last thirty years, the following two rules from the *Muna Spelling Guide* regarding word breaks have not been followed in various Muna publications, including the dictionaries, the translation of the New Testament, a number of school books, reading books, and the trilingual online text collection.

1. The possessive suffix *-mani* 'we (EXCL)' is written separately from its head (see § 10.4.1 and table 10.3), not combined as recommended in the *Muna Spelling Guide*.
2. The *Guide* also recommends that four prefixes are written as separate words: *piki-* 'quickly, soon, early', *paka-* 'when first (in temporal adverbial clauses)', *mansi-* 'just one or two remaining', and *manso-* 'habitually, often'. The reasons for treating these prefixes differently from other disyllabic prefixes such as *feka-* 'causative; adverbial' and *poka-* 'playfully, not seriously' have not been documented, and are no longer clear. Possibly it was felt that they have more semantic content than other disyllabic prefixes. Whatever the exact reason, it was felt (both by myself and by members of the translation team) that this decision was somewhat arbitrary, and hence it was abandoned. All four prefixes (some of which are actually fairly rare) are now written combined with their root, as one word.

As for current spelling practices regarding word breaks, obviously there is considerable variation for a language that is barely taught in schools and that has a limited written literature. On the whole it seems that people intuitively put the word breaks where they belong from a phonological word perspective, that is, with affixes and clitics attached to the root. Other issues, such as writing <b> for <bh>, not writing final long vowels, as in *wakutu* for *wakutuu* 'time', and writing <oE> for <oe>, as happens in Sirad Imbo (2012), are ignored here. But there are also various recurring issues showing consistent patterns. I have compiled a list of the most common deviations from the recommendations in the *Muna Spelling Guide* regarding word breaks. These observations are based on written Muna texts from various sources: a collection of funny stories (La Mokui 2006), a draft translation of the Qur'an in Muna (Alimuddin Silae 2015), and various recent email and WhatsApp exchanges with Muna friends. The most consistent word break issues that emerge are: 1) attached articles; 2) attached prepositions, 3) separated subject prefixes; and 4) lack of hyphens in reduplication. These are illustrated in table 10.10 (for the sake of simplicity words are given without their morphological make-up).

Table 10.10. Current spelling practices

Issue	Attested examples	Suggested improved orthography	Meaning
Attached articles	*oghuu*	*o ghuu*	'mushroom'
	oanahihi	*o anahihi*	'children'
	okalelei	*o kalelei*	'epidemic'
Attached prepositions	*naini*	*na ini, ne ini*	'here'
	nehamai	*ne hamai*	'where'
	wegaluno	*we galuno*	'in his garden'
	tedhunia ini	*te dhunia ini*	'in this world'
	sowutono	*so wutono*	'for himself/herself'
Separated subject prefixes	*no faraluughi*	*nofaraluughi*	's/he needs'
	a feolu	*afeolu*	'I take shelter'
	na koana	*nakoana*	's/he will have a child/children'
No hyphens in reduplications	*tulatula*	*tula-tula*	'story'
	segho segholeo	*segho-segholeo*	'every day'

The conjunctive writing of articles and prepositions is unsurprising, as these form clear phonological units with their nominal hosts. The lack of hyphens in reduplication is probably just a typing error or an oversight. But the disjunctive writing of subject prefixes is remarkable, as these elements are clearly phonologically bound to their verbal host. This is possibly a case of hypercorrection: writers are aware that some initial elements (such as articles and prepositions) should be written separately, and they extend this to subject prefixes.

10.6 Word length from a comparative perspective

This section looks at Muna word length from a comparative perspective. What is the average word length in Muna? How long are the longest words? And how do these facts compare to other languages? Is Muna unusual in some way?

We start with the question of average word length, taking the character (with or without diacritics) as the basic unit. There are three ways to determine average word length in a given language. The first is list-based, which calculates the length of words based on all the entries of a dictionary or a standard wordlist used for spelling checks. In such a list-based approach, frequency plays no role, and short and frequent words (such as English *a, the, in, and, of*) have the same status as long and infrequent words such as *cacophonically* or *morphophonemics*. The second approach is corpus-based, where the average is measured on the basis of actually occurring words in a large corpus, counting every word. Short high-frequency words such as *a, in, of, the* will bring the average down, even if there are also various long words. This is token frequency. The third approach is also corpus-based, but only counts types, not tokens. In other words, words such *a, in, of, the* are each counted only once. That means that *cacophonically* and *in* again have the same status, but only if they occur in the same corpus. The first and third approach obviously do less justice to a general "feel" for word length in a given language, which is typically based on the visual perusal of a text. In this chapter I therefore focus on the second approach, but also include the first and the third.

In order to compare Muna with other languages, I chose three Germanic languages with a long history of writing (English, Dutch, German) and two Austronesian languages with which Muna is in contact: Indonesian [ind], the national language of Indonesia, widely spoken on Muna, and the language of education, government and media in Indonesia, plus Wolio [wlo], a neighboring Celebic language, spoken on the island of Buton.[14]

For a research corpus, I selected a translated text to ensure that the figures are comparable and accurate, and not skewed by genre. The chosen text is Genesis chapters 37 to 50, a narrative about the life of Joseph (a.k.a. Yusuf), one of the patriarchs. This text is not huge, containing some 11,000 words in English, but sufficient for the present purposes. The data was extracted from online sources[15] and stripped of all numbers (chapters and verses), punctuation (full stops, commas, colons, semicolons, question and exclamation marks, quote marks, hyphens and dashes), as these tend to be counted either as separate "words" or as part of the preceding or following word by automated calculation apps. Contractions, such as English *it's, we've* and German *ob's, mag's* are taken as two words. Hyphens marking reduplication (in Indonesian, Wolio and Muna) were replaced by spaces, as words containing hyphens are counted as one word, thus skewing the results. Indonesian words such as *bersama-sama* 'together' were therefore split into *bersama sama* and hence counted as two words. For Muna, two text versions were used: one with the five special pronominal suffixes (see § 10.4.1) written as separate words ("free"), and one with these pronominal suffixes written connected to their host ("bound"). Table 10.11 shows the results for these six languages.[16]

[14] Thanks to Jonathan McDowell for helping me with the Wolio data.

[15] Translation and sources are as follows. English: NIV 1983, https://www.biblestudytools.com/niv/; Dutch: HSV 2010, https://herzienestatenvertaling.nl/home; German: Luther 1912, https://www.biblestudytools.com/lut/; Indonesian: Terjemahan Baru 1974, https://alkitab.me/; Wolio: Kitabi Momangkilona Wolio 2019, https://play.google.com/store/apps/details?id=org.ipsapps.indonesia.wlo.kitab.wolio&gl=US; Muna: Tula-tulano anabi Yusuf 2020, https://alkitab.bahasamuna.org/eng (All accessed 18 January 2023.)

[16] Average word length for tokens was calculated in the following way: 1) create a plain text file of the corpus; 2) use the "word count" feature in Word, which gives the number of characters and words; 3) divide characters by words. For types the

Table 10.11. Word length in six selected languages (Genesis 37–50)

Language	Characters	Words (tokens)	Average word length (tokens)	Unique words (types)	Average word length (types)
English	44,519	10,962	4.06	1,402	5.95
Dutch	50,161	11,935	4.20	1,562	6.60
German	46,753	10,338	4.52	1,671	6.35
Indonesian	58,325	10,339	5.64	1,691	7.51
Wolio	60,177	10,248	5.87	1,858	8.03
Muna (free)	56,646	9,179	6.17	2,360	8.21
Muna (bound)	56,646	9,037	6.26	2,380	8.42

The difference between the three Germanic languages and the three Austronesian languages is quite striking. Even German, renowned for its long words, scores relatively low at just 4.5 characters per word (token length). English is actually lower than usually reported. Corpus-based word length in English is generally put at around five characters per word; some studies suggest 4.9, others 5.2, depending on the genre investigated.[17] It is unclear why for biblical material this average is considerably lower, or whether it reflects the particular translation chosen (NIV). For Dutch, the average word length based on frequency is usually given as five characters. However, a list-based count for Dutch yields ten characters per word, due to the large number of compounds written as one word, a feature Dutch shares with German.[18]

For German the corpus-based average is 5.99,[19] and again it is unclear why the figure here (4.52) is considerably lower. The large number of compounds written as one word in German is responsible for these higher figures.

Of the three Austronesian languages, Muna has the highest score, even in the "free" version, with the five pronominal suffixes written separately. This confirms my intuition that Muna words tend to be long. Another interesting fact emerging from this table is that Muna has fewer words for the same content, about twenty percent less than English, and almost twenty-five percent less than

following procedure was used: 1) load the corpus in AntConc, a free concordance program available at https://www.laurenceanthony.net/software/antconc/; 2) create a wordlist in AntConc; 3) export the wordlist to Excel and sort by word length (https://trumpexcel.com/sort-by-length-excel/); 4) copy the wordlist to Word and use the word count feature to calculate the average.

17 https://www.wyliecomm.com/2021/11/whats-the-best-length-of-a-word-online/ (accessed 11 January 2023).

18 https://www.startpagina.nl/v/kunst-cultuur/taal/vraag/74831/letters-meeste-woorden-geschreven/.

19 https://www.duden.de/sprachwissen/sprachratgeber/Durchschnittliche-Lange-eines-deutschen-Wortes.

Dutch. Does this indicate that there is a correlation between number of words and word length? That would appear to be the case. Muna simply packs more meaning into a single word than English does, as illustrated by the word *a-gholi-angko-e-mo* [1SG-buy-2SG.IND.OBJ-3SG.OBJ-PFV], a multimorphemic word which corresponds to a six-word clause in English 'I already bought it for you'.[20]

It is also interesting to briefly compare these findings with the list-based technique, the first approach mentioned above. List-based approaches for the Germanic languages apparently show considerable discrepancies with the corpus-based approach, such as 8.20 for English, 9.70 for Dutch, and a staggering 11.66 for German.[21] Another source in German gives the figures 10.6 and 14.43 characters per word.[22] I do not have list-based information for word lengths in Indonesian and Wolio, but I do for Muna.

Table 10.11 shows that the average Muna word has around 6.2 characters. The list-based number is actually quite similar, but surprisingly, it is shorter: 5.9 characters per word. This figure is derived from the 7,350 entries in the 1996 Muna-English dictionary. Note, however, that this dictionary is root-based, following lexicographical conventions for Austronesian languages in Indonesia and the Philippines. As a result, inflectional and derivational forms are not counted, but only roots. For example, the root *gholi* 'to buy' is included, but longer and inflected forms such as *nogholie* 'he bought it', *negholimu* 'what you bought', *taegholiangko* 'we will buy for you' are not listed as entries in the dictionary, and hence excluded from the count. With 5.9 characters per root, it is also clear that Muna words are inherently long. There are no monosyllabic content words (only a few articles and prepositions), and the percentage of disyllabic, trisyllabic and quadrisyllabic roots is 54, 36 and 8 percent, respectively (van den Berg 1989:24–25). Examples include *la.mbu* 'house', *ro.bhi.ne* 'woman' and *to.nu.a.na* 'soul', with full stops marking the syllable breaks.

There is, however, one issue with table 10.11. These averages potentially obscure one important factor: the actual range of variation in word length. Theoretically, it is possible for a language to have many short monosyllabic words (of one to five characters), as well as a substantial number of long polysyllabic words (of ten to fifteen characters) in the same text, leading to an average of five characters. In another language, the range of variation is just between two and eight characters, without any long words, also

[20] See https://www.inter-contact.de/en/blog/text-length-languages for an interesting comparison of text length and word length in various European languages, based on a legal economic text, where Finnish scores the highest for word length and the lowest for number of words. The conclusion is that "Finnish gets the content across with the least amount of words but with the longest word length." (Accessed 18 January 2023.)

[21] http://www.ravi.io/language-word-lengths. Accessed 18 January 2023 (site no longer available).

[22] https://www.duden.de/sprachwissen/sprachratgeber/Durchschnittliche-Lange-eines-deutschen-Wortes (Accessed 25 January 2023).

resulting in an average of five. An average can therefore obscure the full range of variation. Is this the case for Muna?

In order to test this hypothesis, the actual range of variation for the six languages was calculated[23] and displayed in the following seven histograms. First, the three Germanic languages are shown: English (figure 10.1), Dutch (figure 10.2) and German (figure 10.3). In each figure, the horizontal axis shows word length in terms of the number of characters, whereas the vertical axis displays frequency.

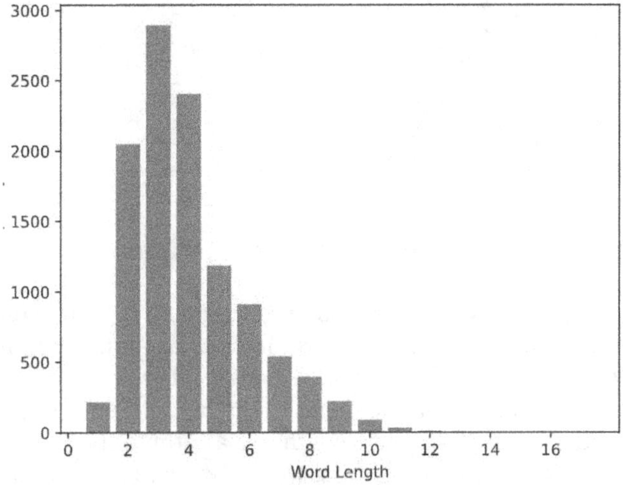

Figure 10.1. English word length.

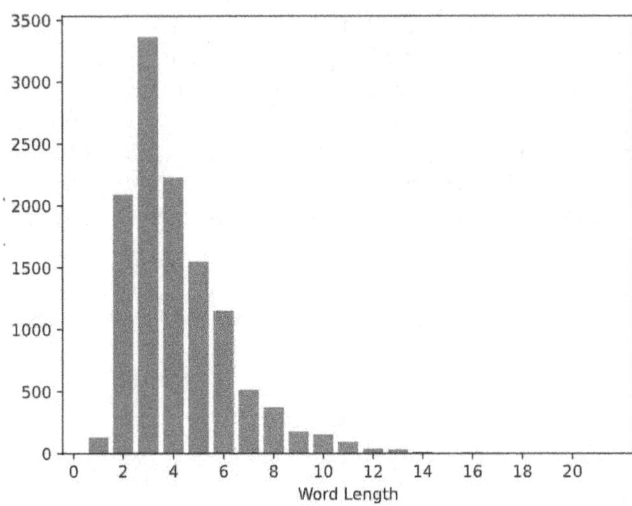

Figure 10.2. Dutch word length.

[23] Many thanks for providing technical assistance in this area to Moss Doerksen, who used a Python script with matplotlib to generate the histograms.

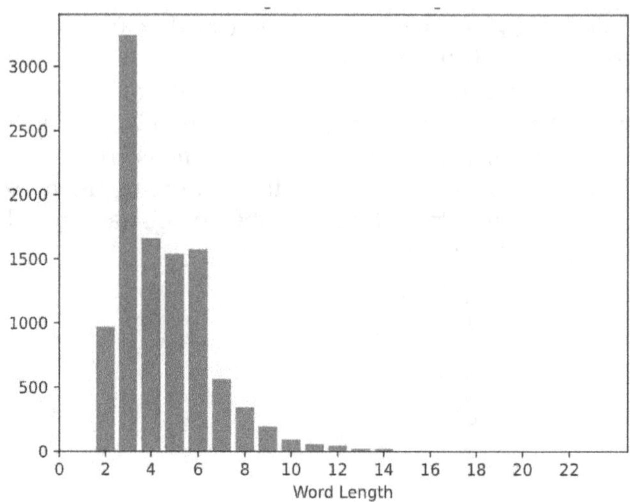

Figure 10.3. German word length.

These three figures confirm that German and Dutch words are on average slightly longer than English, as English has almost nothing beyond ten characters. It is also clear that German has the longest word, one of twenty-three characters (just one, hence invisible in the figure). Somewhat surprisingly, the most frequent length in all three languages is three characters. The actual number of long words (which I somewhat arbitrarily define as words of twelve characters or more) is rather low in all three languages, not exceeding 1%: twelve for English (0.1%), sixty-eight for German (0.7%), and seventy for Dutch (0.6%). This means that in spite of German's reputation for having long words, such instances appear to be infrequent outliers which are barely significant for the average.

Moving now to the three Austronesian languages, the following figures illustrate Indonesian (figure 10.4), Wolio (figure 10.5), and Muna in two shapes: once with the pronominal affixes written disjunctively ("free", figure 10.6), and once with those pronominal affixes written conjunctively ("bound", figure 10.7).

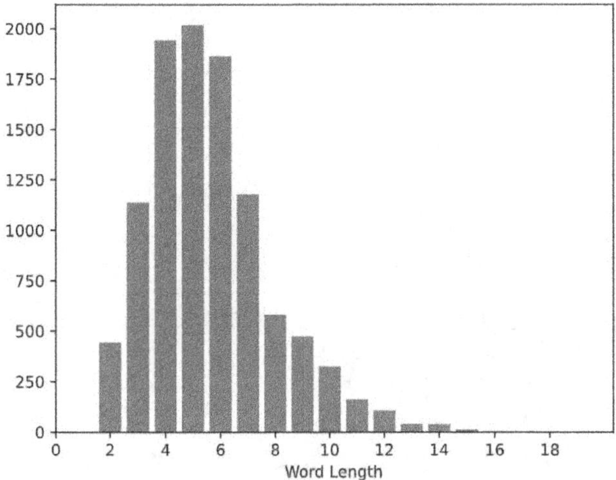

Figure 10.4. Indonesian word length.

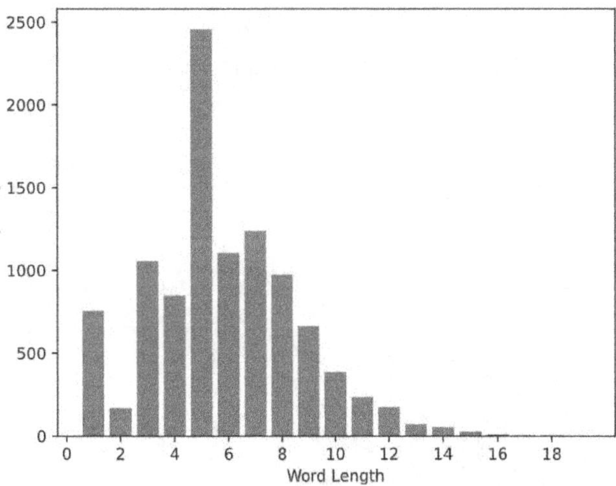

Figure 10.5. Wolio word length.

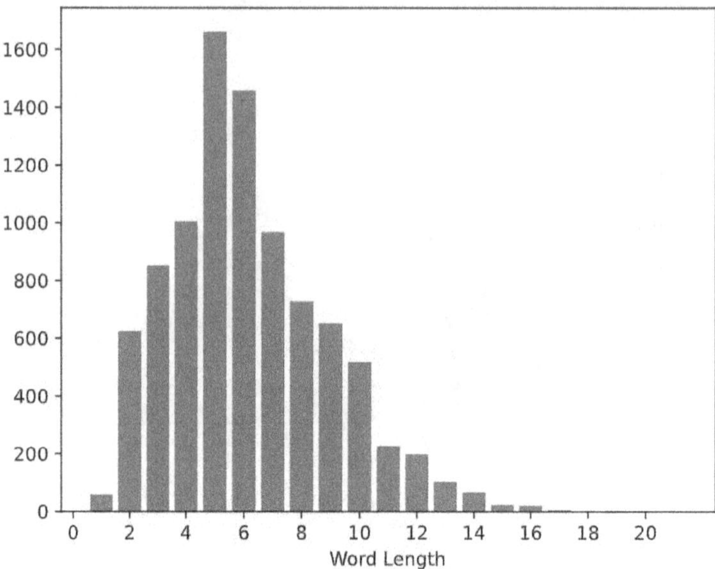

Figure 10.6. Muna word length (free).

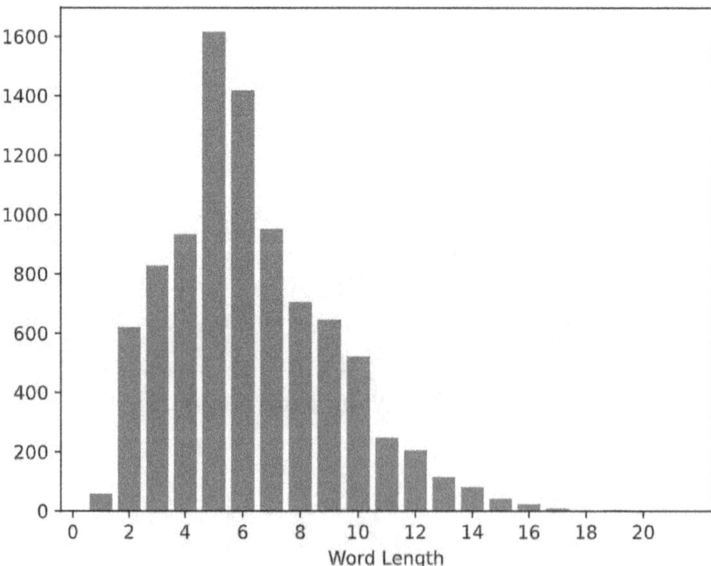

Figure 10.7. Muna word length (bound).

As expected, there are clearly many more longer words in these three languages. The largest group is five characters in all three languages, and words of twelve characters or more are not uncommon. The exact numbers of long words (twelve or more characters) in all six languages are presented in table 10.12.

Table 10.12. Number of long words in six languages (Genesis 37–50)

Characters in word	English	Dutch	German	Indonesian	Wolio	Muna (free)	Muna (bound)
12	6	30	33	61	89	137	144
13	3	22	16	30	58	79	90
14	2	7	15	23	29	45	58
15	1	2	2	10	22	21	35
16	-	5	1	5	6	19	22
17	-	1	-	4	4	6	9
18	-	1	-	3	5	1	1
19	-	1	-	4	2	2	4
20	-	-	-	-	-	1	2
21	-	1	-	-	-	1	2
22	-	-	-	-	-	-	-
23	-	-	1	-	-	-	-
total	12	70	68	140	215	312	367

As a matter of interest, here are the five longest words for each of these languages from this Genesis 37–50 corpus.

English: *grandchildren* (13 characters), *laughingstock* (13), *interpretation* (14), *granddaughters* (14), *interpretations* (15).

Dutch: *zielsbenauwdheid* (16) 'anguish of soul', *voortreffelijkste* (17) 'most excellent', *eerstgeboorterecht* (18) 'birthright', *begerenswaardigheid* (19) 'desirability', *honderdzevenenveertig* (21) 'one hundred forty seven'.

German: *wiedergekommen* (14) 'came back', *hineingefressen* (15) 'eaten in, invaded', *verschmachteten* (15) 'languished', *Schwiegertochter* (16) 'daughter-in-law', *hundertsiebenundvierzig* (23) 'one hundred forty seven.' Note that most of these are compounds.

Indonesian: *disendengkannyalah* (18) '(it) was tilted/put in a slightly slanting position', *ditanggalkannyalah* (18) '(it) was stripped off', *ditinggalkannyalah* (18) '(it) was left behind', *diperhambakannyalah* (19) '(he) was enslaved', *diperintahkannyalah* (19) '(he) was ordered'. These are all verbs containing the passive prefix *di-*, the causative or applicative suffix *-kan*, the 3SG possessive/agent suffix *-nya*, and the perfective enclitic *-lah*.

Wolio: *bheapasalaamatiaka* (18) 'he will save', *bheatomalinguakamo* (18) 'it will be forgotten', *bhekudhawuakakomiu* (18) 'I will give you (PL)', *bhekupadhaangiaakea* (19) 'I will make/create,' and *bhekupaumbaakakomiu* (19) 'I will tell you (PL).' All these verbs start with the future proclitic *bhe.*

The five longest words in Muna ("free") are shown in table 10.13, which also provides the number of syllables and the morphological make-up.

Table 10.13. Longest Muna words (Genesis 37–50)

Ltrs	Syll	Word	Morphological make-up	Meaning
18	8	*taomengkongkoraamu*	*ta-ome-ngko-**ngkora**-amu* JUST-2SG-RDUP-sit-PL	'you (PL) are just sitting'
18	9	*amaginduluangkoomu*	*a-**maghindulu**-angko-omu* 1SG-IRR.go.ahead-2SG.IND.OBJ-PL	'I will go ahead of you (PL)'
19	10	*katifopesuahantoomu*	*ka-ti-fo-**pesua**-ha-nto-omu* NMLZ-PASS-CAUS-enter-NMLZ-1PL.INCL-PL	'the reason that we were brought in'
20	10	*namopandehaoandaghoo*	*na-mo-**pande**-hao-anda-ghoo* 3SG.IRR-IRR.CAUS-know-INT-3PL.IND.OBJ-PURP	'so that he will introduce them'
21	10	*tanosikagampihaandamo*	*ta-no-sika-**gampi**-ha-anda-mo* JUST-3SG.REAL-SUDD-move-SUDD-3PL.IND.OBJ-PFV	'he suddenly moved away from them'

As shown in the rightmost column of table 10.12 ("Muna bound"), if the pronominal suffixes *-kanau, -kasami, -kaeta* and *-mani* were not written as separate words, an additional fifty-five words of more than twelve characters would have been the result. This includes another two overlong words: *tofosalamatikasamimo* (20), morphologically *to-fo-**salamati**-kasami-mo* (2SG.HON-CAUS-safe-1PL.EXCL.OBJ-PFV) 'you (HON) have saved us', and *namekaambanokanaughoo* (21), morphologically *na-meka-**ambano**-kanau-ghoo* (3SG.IRR-IRR.CAUS-ashamed-1SG.OBJ-PURP) 'in order to make me ashamed'. Writing these suffixes as separate words (*tofosalamati kasamimo* and *namekaambano kanaughoo*) has clearly decreased the number of long words, though not as drastically as expected. The number of long words in Muna is still large. Are there other options to split them?

This is not so straightforward, as three of these long words in table 10.13 involve the indirect object suffixes *-angko* or *-anda,* in combination with the plural suffix *-Vmu.* Separating these long words into two (or even three) words looks desirable, but splitting them at any point causes problems. Unlike *-kanau, -kasami* and *-kaeta,* the suffixes *-angko* and *-anda* are not intuitively identified as morphemes by native speakers. There is no hesitation to mention and discuss the object suffix *-kanau* with its meaning ('me'), but the same is not true for *-angko* ('for you'). The psychological status of the indirect object suffixes is quite different from the direct object suffixes, and it takes considerable effort to explain that *-angko*, too, is a "segment" of a word with its own meaning. Hence writing *amaghinduluangkoomu* as two words *amaghindulu angkoomu* is not an option. The second word is not independently recognisable as a separate word. It seems that Muna readers simply have to live with long words.

One question remains. Muna clearly has the longest words of the six languages compared. But how exceptional is Muna compared to other languages for which an orthography has only been recently introduced? This chapter is obviously not the place for a thorough investigation of this issue, but anecdotal evidence suggests that there are "worse" cases. I was alerted to four languages of Papua New Guinea, where there are reports of speakers who have complained about long words being an obstacle to readability, especially of the printed New Testament.[24] The languages are: 1) **Amele** [aey], a Papuan (Trans-New Guinea) language of Madang Province; 2) **Yipma** (a.k.a. Baruya) [byr], and 3) **Waffa** [waj], both Papuan (Trans-New Guinea) languages spoken in the Eastern Highlands Province; and 4) **Iduna** [viv], an Austronesian (Oceanic, Papuan Tip) language spoken in Milne Bay Province. I also include Tok Pisin [tpi], an English-based creole that is widely spoken in the country and one of the national languages of Papua New Guinea. To make the comparisons accurate and valid, I took a small sample for each of these languages (the first chapter of the Gospel of Mark, as Genesis is not available in some of these languages[25]), and calculated the average word length, for both tokens and types. As in the earlier Genesis sample, numbers and punctuation marks were removed, and the hyphen in Iduna (used to mark compounds and certain enclitics) was replaced by a space. The results are shown in table 10.14.

Table 10.14. Word length in five languages of PNG

Language	**Characters**	**Words**	**Average word length (token)**	**Average word length (type)**
Amele	5,101	1,041	4.90	5.83
Yipma (Baruya)	6,675	853	7.82	9.01
Waffa	7,174	1,055	6.80	7.84
Iduna	5,675	865	6.56	8.44
Tok Pisin	5,098	1360	3.75	4.96

[24] These reports reached me about Amele from Luke Aubrey and Jed Carter, about Yipma (Baruya) from Koen den Hartogh, and about Iduna from Kristy Wedel.

[25] The texts were taken from https://png.bible/ (accessed 4 January 2023), a site which has Scripture translations for 261 languages of PNG.

In terms of token word length, Amele still looks reasonable with 4.90, but the other three use exceptionally many long words, all clearly longer than Muna with 6.17. Especially Yipma, with an average of almost 8 characters per word (roughly twice as many as English), seems unusual. The contrast with the national languages English (4.06) and Tok Pisin (3.75) is remarkable and cause for concern.

To illustrate the point and to give the reader a visual "taste", below is the last verse of the text in question (Mark 1:45) in these five languages, unglossed and untranslated. (In Amele <c> represents a glottal stop, and <q> a labio-velar plosive. In Yipma and Iduna, the apostrophe represents a glottal stop; in Yipma <ɨ> stands for the mid-central vowel [ə].)

Amele
Dana euqa uqa nunui feei je eu cunug saadi cobon hatuhatu cunug je eu doin. Odonnu Jisas uqa camasac jobon osona lecwe qee. Uqa jobon hahagum maha danaca qee euna biloloi. Euqa dana cajaca age hatu nahanaha cunugdec uqa cemenug hoin.

Yipma (Baruya)
Sara kudaasa' a'mwei walyuna yaka yuyaba yagaala sa' wɨjɨwaakya'nei yuyaraavɨ wɨdɨvainadaa'na yɨkwaasa'. Gamɨ sara kya' "A'mwera nyanganapɨjɨ nɨmɨnyɨna nanyɨdahidɨwagamaremwaaibɨthɨka!" daka Jizaazai angeba mwɨyai yaayeba mwaalɨna yadɨsɨ gazabazabadaa'nyɨ gamɨnyawɨnna yɨkabɨna ye'.

Waffa
Tuduu rikioo hama inna kuaivaa rikioo pikioo vioo gioonna kiaapuuya mmannammanna kiaa mmiravai. Kiaa mmuuvaara iya inna suvuaivoora kiaa Yisuuva hama yoosinnaivaki kooyaa nuairavai. Ivo oro koo mmuyai gaanga yoosinnaiyauvaki hara kioo varuduu gioonna kiaapuuya vo yoosinna vo yoosinnaiyauvakidiri innasi nniravai.

Iduna
Atu kaliva gilowoga be gina yana yamumu valeyana givebutu kaliva moya'aidi agaidiya gilukahihiyena, ada au valeyana ginauna. Moya'aidi hiyo'oyo'o fa'ina, Yesu keke anafaiweya melaleya ginaluku kaliva matadiya. Au melalagaga agaidiya gimiyami. Atu kaliva melala tulina tulina agaidiya hitauya be Yesu againe hiyo'o.

Tok Pisin
Tasol dispela man i go, na em i tokim ol manmeri long olgeta dispela samting i bin kamap long em. Em i autim dispela stori long olgeta hap. Olsem na Jisas i no inap i go moa insait long wanpela taun long ai bilong ol manmeri. Nogat. Em i stap ausait tasol, long ol hap i no gat man. Na ol manmeri bilong olgeta hap ol i kam long em.

Note the relatively short words of Tok Pisin, the contrast with Iduna and especially with Yipma, which has a thirty-one-character word in line 2: *nanyidahidiwagamaremwaaibithika.* One can sympathize with Yipma readers, who feel that the presence of such words forms a real obstacle to literacy and vernacular Scripture use. In terms of word length, it also makes their language look very different from the national languages English and Tok Pisin.

To end this section on a slightly lighter note, here are the longest words from the Bible and the Quran. The longest Hebrew word in the Old Testament is וְהָאֲחַשְׁדַּרְפְּנִים (*veha'aḥashdarpením*) with eleven consonants and nine vowel signs (eighteen characters in transcription). Its meaning is 'and the satraps' (Esther 9:3).[26] The longest Greek word in the New Testament is προκεχειροτονημένοις *prokecheirotonēmenois* (twenty characters), meaning 'having been chosen beforehand' (Acts 10:41). The longest Arabic word in the Quran is فَأَسْقَيْنَاكُمُوهُ *fa'asqaynākumūhu* (eleven consonants, sixteen characters in transliteration) 'for you to drink' (Surah 15:22).[27] However, ancient manuscripts did not normally write word breaks, and since the script for Semitic languages like Hebrew and Arabic is consonant-based, one could argue that these comparisons are not really helpful. At the very least, they show that long words are not a new invention.

10.7 Word length and readability

Why is word length an issue at all? Is this not something we can conveniently ignore? I do not believe so. Based on my own experience and from talking to colleagues, word length is an issue, especially in societies where reading is uncommon, new, or both. It is linked to the notion of readability, which I briefly explore in this section.

As literacy and education spread among Western populations in the past two centuries, the notion of readability engendered considerable interest; for an excellent overview see DuBay (2004). An important question is: what makes some texts hard to read, and why are other texts so much easier? According to Gray and Leary's (1935) landmark study *What Makes a Book Readable*, readability is a combination of content (propositions, organization, coherence), style (semantic and syntactic elements), design (typography, format, illustrations) and structure (chapters, headings, navigation). Focussing on style, where it is the easiest to examine measurable features of a text, a plethora of tests was carried out to measure sentence length, percentage of easy words versus difficult or technical words, number of pronouns, percentage of monosyllables, percentage of polysyllables, and the number of prepositional phrases, among other things. Flesch (1948)

[26] https://preply.com/en/question/longest-word-in-hebrew (accessed 20 January 2023).

[27] https://arabic-for-nerds.com/longest-word-quran/ (accessed 20 January 2023).

proposed a simplified test, using just two variables for measuring readability: the number of syllables and the number of sentences for each one hundred-word sample. His work led to the Flesch Reading Ease formula, which has been widely used in readability studies, and with some modifications, is still used today.

For our particular purposes, Flesch's notion of word length is important. Flesch, however, measured word length not in characters, but in syllables. The actual reason for taking the number of syllables in a word, rather than the number of characters, as the basis for word length is unclear to me. For one thing, counting syllables is less straightforward and also less amenable to computerized calculation than counting characters (though obviously computers were not in common usage in Flesch's time). One can also wonder whether monosyllabic words such as *thoughts* and *strength* (both having eight characters) are really easier to read and process than polysyllabic words such as *anybody* and *Honolulu* (each having four syllables, and seven and eight characters respectively). Or are these words exceptional and is there a more direct relationship in English between the length of a word and the number of syllables?

Whatever the reason, table 10.15 (from Flesch 1948, quoted in DuBay 2004:22), correlates the number of syllables per one hundred words to ease of reading.

Table 10.15. Flesch Reading Ease Formula

Syllables in 100 words	Ease of reading
123 or less	very easy
131	easy
139	fairly easy
147	standard
155	fairly difficult
167	difficult
192 or more	very difficult

From the perspective of Indonesian and Muna, it is very striking that an average of two syllables per word (so 200 syllables in total) would make a text extremely difficult. (By contrast, the first one hundred English words of § 6 of this chapter have 148 syllables, making this chapter "standard" – I hope readers agree.) But subsequent readability studies for English have consistently corroborated the dual measurement of sentence length and syllables per word (e.g., Fry 1977). Fry's Readability Graph (taken from DuBay 2004:46) has an upper limit of reading ability at 182 syllables per 100 words, equivalent to seventeen or more years of education. Obviously such scores are language-specific, and these formulas need to be adapted for different languages, which has indeed been done for Spanish, French, German, Dutch, Swedish, Russian, Hebrew, Hindi [hin], Chinese, Vietnamese, and Korean [kor] (Rabin 1988). Further readability formulas (for English) are also readily available online, all of them measuring word length and sentence length.[28]

The Flesch Reading Ease formula can also be applied to Muna, but the interpretation of the various levels as "easy" or "difficult" needs to be adjusted, as words are inherently longer in Muna. On the other hand, the correlation between word length and number of syllables is much tighter in Muna than it is in English, as Muna has only open CV and V syllables, in which all the prenasalized consonants (written as digraphs or trigraphs) count as a single consonant. Written Muna syllables are therefore of four types: one character (*o, a*), two characters (*ku, ma, la, po*), three characters (*mba, mpu, ndi, nse*), and only one type has four characters (*ngka, nggu*). Long monosyllabic words such as *thoughts* and *strength* never occur. So a modified syllable-based score might actually work well for Muna.

To illustrate the different correlation between words and syllables in English and Muna, I took two 100-word samples, one from a folk story (*Karaka Bhala Wobha*, "The Big-Mouth Frog"), which had 284 syllables, and one from Genesis (chapter 37:1–6), which resulted in no fewer than 304 syllables! Compared to English, these figures are extremely high, but they confirm that measuring readability in Muna is a very different issue with its own specific challenges. Unfortunately, I am not aware of any readability studies done for Muna, and my own experience is limited to seeing or hearing people stumble over long words, as well as unknown words.

Perhaps the time has come to consider doing similar readability studies for "unwritten" or "newly written" languages. What I mean is not only the readability and acceptability of an orthography as such, but also the readability of texts, including the study of word length. Dozens of readability studies on English and other European languages are available, but what about the hundreds of languages such as Muna, where written literature is a relatively recent introduction, where the body of published literature is limited, where orthographic practices are not firmly established, where official government support may be lacking, and where researchers and language advocates have a plethora of issues to pay attention to? In such situations, the challenges of designing and implementing a workable and acceptable orthography may often mean that there is inadequate time and resources for the testing of orthography on a grand scale, and also for carrying out a readability study of texts. As a result, many languages may end up with an orthography that is not adequately thought through, with, for example, too many long words. The situation in Muna is probably not overly problematic, as many potentially long words have been "cut up", but

[28] One example is https://readabilityformulas.com/articles/readability-guidelines-to-calculate-readability-scores.php (accessed 2 January 2023).

I have the impression that there is still room for improvement. Exactly where these solutions lie is not so easy to see, given the complex morphology of Muna, but intermediate solutions such as the use of hyphens, apostrophes or half-spaces (Daams 1982) could be explored. Collaboration among local teachers and educators, native writers, as well as local researchers may move the discussion forward.

Perhaps it might also be helpful to consider establishing an upper limit of word length for new orthographies, similar to the limits imposed on sentence length for readability. The UK government, for instance, issued a statement in 2014 meant for authors in government departments that twenty-five words per sentence is the limit for any communication with the population. "Studies have shown that sentences of eleven words are considered easy to read, while those of twenty-one words are fairly difficult. At twenty-five words, sentences become difficult, and twenty-nine words or longer, very difficult." [29] Another guideline is "When you use a longer word (eight or nine letters), users are more likely to skip shorter words (three, four or five letters) that follow it. So if you use longer, more complicated words, readers will skip more. Keep it simple."[30]

It seems clear, however, that an upper limit for word length is critically dependent on the language structure, especially its morphological profile and its syllable structure. Germans may tolerate long words, because these are all compounds, the constituent parts of which are relatively easy to process, possibly helped by the complex syllable patterns of the language. Germany also has a long tradition of writing and an excellent educational system. Languages with agglutinative morphology and simple syllable structures, such as Muna, combined with a much shorter writing tradition and little or no place for local languages in formal education, face extra challenges. These situations are hardly comparable.

I would therefore like to suggest that there is a need to develop clear guidelines on word length for new orthographies for minority languages, suitable in their national contexts. In other words, based on further research on word length and readability, guidelines could be drawn up that put the upper limit of word length at, for example, fifteen for Papua New Guinea, and eighteen for Indonesia. Such guidelines would help orthography specialists, educators, translators and language activists, all of whom are (or should be) concerned with lowering the barriers of literacy and increasing reading fluency and pleasure in reading. The fact that the German government is unlikely to comply with such guidelines (which might be called *Wortlängeabschreckungsmassnahmen* 'word length deterrent measures', thirty-one characters), should not act as a deterrent to the rest of the world.

---

29 https://insidegovuk.blog.gov.uk/2014/08/04/sentence-length-why-25-words-is-our-limit/ (accessed 2 January 2023).

30 https://www.gov.uk/guidance/content-design/writing-for-gov-uk#how-people-read (accessed 2 January 2023).

10.8 Conclusions and recommendations

There is much more to say about word length and readability. I finish by presenting some conclusions, and offering a few recommendations.

- Word length is a major factor in readability. The higher the frequency of long words, the harder a text is to read.
- The intuitive choices which were made to reduce word length in the Muna orthography make good theoretical sense. But the presence of words of up to twenty-one characters means there is still room for improvement.
- In newly designed orthographies, careful attention should be paid to the issue of word length. As much as possible, long words should be avoided.
- Extensive testing needs to be done on readability in languages with a simple syllable structure and a rich morphology (agglutinative, polysynthetic or incorporating), focussing on issues of word length. Creative solutions for reducing word length should be explored and documented.
- The establishment of an upper limit of long words, taking the context of the national language(s) into account, is potentially helpful for people involved in designing new orthographies for minority languages.

References

Alimuddin Silae. 2015. Terjemahan Al Qur'an bahasa Indonesia diterjemahkan dalam bahasa Muna. Wamba Malauno Kuraani do wamba Wunaane [The Indonesian translation of the Qur'an translated into Muna]. Ms.

Cahill, Michael, and Keren Rice, eds. 2014. *Developing orthographies for unwritten languages.* Publications in Language Use and Education 6. Dallas, TX: SIL International.

Daams, Nicolaas. 1982. *A practical writing system for the language of Rennell and Bellona.* Honiara: Solomon Islands Translation Advisory Group.

Dixon, R. M. W. 2010. *Basic linguistic theory. Vol. 2: Grammatical Topics.* Oxford: Oxford University Press.

DuBay, William H. 2004. *The principles of readability.* Costa Mesa: Impact Information. www.researchgate.net/publication/228965813_The_Principles_of_Readability.

Eaton, Helen, and Leila Schroeder. 2012. Word break conflicts in Bantu languages: Skirmishes on many fronts. *Writing Systems Research* 4(2):229–241.

Eberhard, David M., Gary F. Simons, and Charles D. Fennig, eds. 2024. *Ethnologue: Languages of the world.* Twenty-seventh edition. Dallas, TX: SIL International. www.ethnologue.com.

Flesch, Rudolf. 1948. A new readability yardstick. *Journal of Applied Psychology* 32:221–233.

Fry, Edward. 1977. Fry's readability graph: Clarifications, validity, and extension to level 17. *Journal of Reading* 21(3):242–252.

Gray, William S., and Bernice E. Leary. 1935. *What makes a book readable.* Chicago, IL: Chicago University Press.

Grzybek, Peter. 2007. History and methodology of word length studies: The state of the art. In Peter Grzybek (ed.), *Contributions to the Science of Text and Languages*, 15–90. Dordrecht: Springer.

Hanafi, La Mokui, La Dame, La Kimi Batoa, and La Ode Sidu. 1991. *Pedoman ejaan bahasa daerah Muna, dan beberapa contoh sastra Muna* [Spelling guide for the Muna language, with some samples of Muna literature]. Raha: [no publisher]. www.bahasamuna.org/en/learning-muna/muna-spelling-guide.

Jones, Mari C., and Damien Mooney. 2017. *Creating orthographies for endangered languages.* Cambridge: Cambridge University Press.

Kroeger, Paul R. 2005. *Analyzing grammar. An introduction.* Cambridge: Cambridge University Press.

Kutsch Lojenga, Constance. 2014. Basic principles for establishing word boundaries. In Michael Cahill and Keren Rice (eds.), *Developing orthographies for unwritten languages*, 73–106. Publications in Language Use and Education 6. Dallas, TX: SIL International.

La Mokui. 2006. Tula-tula dhedhe [Funny stories]. Ms.

Rabin, Annette T. 1988. Determining difficulty levels of text written in languages other than English. In Beverley L. Zakaluk and S. Jay Samuels (eds.), *Readability: Its past, present, and future.* Newark: International Reading Association.

Sirad Imbo, La Ode. 2012. *Kamus Bahasa Indonesia-Muna. Wamba Malau Do Wamba-Wunaane* [Indonesian-Muna Dictionary]. Kendari, Indonesia: Universitas Halu Oleo Press.

van den Berg, René. 1989. *A grammar of the Muna language.* Dordrecht: Foris.

van den Berg, René, in collaboration with La Ode Sidu. 1996. *Muna-English dictionary.* Leiden: KITLV.

van den Berg, René, and La Ode Sidu. 2000. *Kamus Muna-Indonesia* [Muna-Indonesian dictionary]. Kupang: Artha Wacana Press.

van den Berg, René. 2004. Notes on the southern Muna dialect. In John Bowden and Nikolaus P. Himmelmann (eds.), *Papers in Austronesian subgrouping and dialectology*, 129–169. Canberra: Pacific Linguistics.

van den Berg, René. 2011. Elusive articles in Sulawesi: Between syntax and prosody. In Jan-Olof Svantesson, Niclas Burenhult, Arthur Holmer, Anastasia Karlsson and Håkan Lundström (eds.), *Language documentation and description* Vol. 10:208–227. London: School of Oriental and African Studies.

11
The Orthographic Word as a Social Construct: A Perspective from Karen Languages

Ken Manson

Blank spaces make orthographic words very salient units of written language. (Haspelmath 2011:33)

Abstract

The Karen languages have an identical grammar: clause structure is topic-comment (SVO), and noun phrase is possessor-head noun-modifiers. Multiple scripts for Karen have been used. Although the orthographic word cannot be based on linguistic principles, (Karen) linguists applying the current orthography have often tried to do so. However, the social history of orthography development also involves beauty and aesthetics. Thus, the orthographic word is better considered as a social construct.

Abbreviations

1	1st person	NOM	nominalizer
3	3rd person	OBJ	object
ADJ	adjective	PL	plural
ADV	adverb	SG	singular
CLF	classifier	SUBJ	subject
LOC	locative	TEMP	temporal noun/adverb
N	noun	TOP	topic
NEG	negation		

11.1 Introduction

In recent years, researchers have shown an increased interest in the grammatical word versus the phonological word (Dixon and Aikhenvald 2002; Taylor 2015a; Aikhenvald et al. 2020a). However, from an academic point of view, the orthographic word suffers from poor, confusing and conflicting definitions and little guidance regarding the practice of orthography development.

> It must be borne in mind, however, that word-space conventions are just that—conventions, which have emerged over the course of time and presumably in response to non-orthographic principles of wordhood. Even today, the conventions are not fully settled. (Taylor 2015b:7)

> And an orthographic "word" can be at odds with words of other kinds. The relationships between all of these, and their development throughout the history of each language are a further, fruitful field for investigation. (Aikhenvald et al. 2020b:18)

In this chapter, I argue that we, as linguists, do not have a good answer based on linguistic principles to the question: "How do linguists recognize an orthographic word?" Linguists rely on the concepts of the morphosyntactic word and/or phonological word when they argue for the orthographic word (Kutsch Lojenga 2014), but these are not uniformly applicable across languages and contexts.

Language documentation shares the challenges of segmenting the orthographic word (Ochs 1979; Himmelmann 2006; Jung and Himmelmann 2011). Himmelmann (2006:253) focuses on:

> [A] middle-sized transcription unit, delimited by empty spaces, which represents a basic unit in terms of meaning, grammatical function, or sound structure, typically a morphosyntactic or phonological word.

There are a great many differences in combining and separating the orthographic word between individual linguists and writers and different speech communities.

In a traditional structuralist/positivism sense, language is a monolithic object; but, equally important, language is not an abstract system of fixed rules. Languages are not fixed or stable objects but are continually (re)shaped (cf. historical linguistics). It is simplistic to think that a speaker uses fixed rules of grammar and speaks one (idio)lect, style, or register. A named language is essentially a group of speakers who share a cultural identity and who speak partially overlapping idiolects.

In the sociopolitical sense, language is a social practice and action performed by individuals in reflexive, relational, and complex ways. Individuals engage in complex interactions with "multiplicity, fluidity, mobility, locality and globality resources" (Bradley et al. 2020:2). They make use of the communicative resources available to them in and across multiple places and power dynamics.

Similarly, making orthographies is a social practice performed by individuals in communities in reflexive and complex ways. Mark Sebba (2009:35),[1] writing in the inaugural *Writing System Research* journal, treats "writing systems as a social practice", as does Michael Cahill (2014:§ 2.3) who states that "all orthographies are political".

Haspelmath (2011:65) addresses how linguists have grappled with the (morphosyntactic) word:

> Linguists have no good basis for identifying words across languages, and hence no good basis for a general distinction between syntax and morphology as parts of the language system.

Many orthographies based on the Latin alphabet use spaces between words. However, there are many Asian scripts that do not use spaces between words (e.g., Thai, Indic, Chinese, Japanese, and premodern Korean).

In their description of the Vietnamese-based orthography of Cado [pac], Vitrano-Wilson et al. (2018) demonstrate that authors can separate two-syllable monomorphemic words with a space or add a hyphen to join them orthographically. "The precise rules for when to use a space or a hyphen, or when to concatenate, are still being determined by Cado writers" (2018:56). Likewise, new and emergent orthographies are not rule based, they are developing conventions in communities.

---

[1] See also Sebba (2007).

In this chapter I focus on the orthographies in use in Karen language communities in Myanmar and Thailand. I consider two case studies: four-syllable elaborate expressions, and the classifier phrase, which are ubiquitous in the Mainland Southeast Asia region. Finally, I offer some concluding remarks on the idea of the orthographic word as a social construct, in the light of the data presented.

11.2 Background

There are competing orthographies in Greater Mainland Southeast Asia (MSEA) based on Indic (national languages such as Burmese [mya], Khmer [khm], Lao [lao], and Thai; regional languages like Mon [mnw], Pwo [pwo], and Sgaw Karen [ksw]), Latin (e.g., Vietnamese, Lahu [lhu], Pinyin [pny]), and indigenous Kayah Li script (Kayah, Yintale [kvy]), Leke – Karen chicken scratch script (Sgaw, Pwo) and Myainggyingu script (Sgaw, Pwo).

The orthographic white space marks sentences in Thai (1a), phrases in Burmese (1b), "words" in Kayan (1c), and, to complete the lineup, syllables in Lahu (1d).[2]

(Mark 1:35–39 Thai New Century Version) [Sentences]

(1a) ครั้นเวลาเช้ามืดพระเยซูทรงลุกขึ้นแล้วเสด็จออกจากบ้านไปยังที่สงบเงียบและอธิษฐาน ซีโมนกับเพื่อนๆ ออกตามหาพระองค์ เมื่อพบแล้วจึงร้องทูลว่า "ใครต่อใครกำลังตามหาพระองค์!" พระเยซูตรัสตอบว่า "ให้เราไปที่อื่นๆ ในละแวกใกล้เคียงกันเถิดเพื่อเราจะได้ไปเทศนาที่นั่นด้วย ที่เรามาก็เพื่อการนี้แหละ" ดังนั้น พระองค์จึงเสด็จไปทั่วแคว้นกาลิลี พระองค์ทรงเทศนาในธรรมศาลาของพวกเขาและทรงขับผีออกหลายตน

'Before daybreak the next morning, Jesus got up and went out to an isolated place to pray. Later Simon and the others went out to find him. When they found him, they said, "Everyone is looking for you." But Jesus replied, "We must go on to other towns as well, and I will preach to them, too. That is why I came." So he traveled throughout the region of Galilee, preaching in the synagogues and casting out demons.' (NLTse)

[2] In this chapter, orthographic transcriptions using Latin script are in italics. Some examples have an additional line of phonemic transcription.

Burmese (Mark 1:35–39 Modern Judson Bible 2017) [Phrases]

b) နံနက်အချိန်၊ မိုးမလင်းမီ ကိုယ်တော်သည် ထပြီးလျှင် တောအရပ်သို့ထွက်ကြွ၍ ဆုတောင်းတော်မူ၏။ ရှိမုန်နှင့် သူ၏အပေါင်းအဖော်တို့သည် လိုက်၍ရှာကြသော်၊ ကိုယ်တော်ကိုတွေ့လျှင် လူအပေါင်းတို့သည် ကိုယ်တော်ကို ရှာကြပါသည်ဟု လျှောက်ဆို၏။ ကိုယ်တော်ကလည်း ငါသည် နီးစပ်သောမြို့ရွာတို့၌ တရားဟောခြင်းငှာ သွားကြကုန်အံ့။ ထိုသို့အလို့ငှာ ငါကြွလာပြီဟု မိန့်တော်မူ၍၊ ဂါလိလဲပြည်အရပ်ရပ် တရားဇရပ်တို့၌ တရားဟောလျက် နတ်ဆိုးတို့ကို နှင်ထုတ်လျက် နေတော်မူ၏။

Kayan (Mark 1:35–39) [Words]

c) *Bă naòlaraò, mŏ̌n cŏ̌ lĭ̌ mŏ̌ khă, Jesŭ sahtaô dò lai thabă dŏ̌ kalăn bă pra cŏ̌ aò lapră lapra nulò. Naòkhă, Sĭmon dò angaòn lai kwansŏ̌n Jesŭ nulò. Dò bă a sŏ̌nlaŏ̌ Jesŭ khă anănthŭ̌ tai, “Pra ăpra kwansŏ̌n na.” Blănmè, Jesŭ taicein anănthŭ̌, “Khĭ lailan mwaĭ dŏ̌ kasailan rwaĭlan tathanaò thasaŭ arî akaĭ nulò. Thanudò, Jesŭ lai dŏ̌ kăn Galilă kalăn pŭkaŭ dò sailan rwaĭlan ta bă Jŭdaphao Tathabăthyûn kaŭ nulò. Dò khlŭswaĭhtan kaĭ tasûtana aò dŏ̌ pra akaŭ nulò.”*

Lahu (Mark 1:35–39 Lahu Bible) [Syllables]

d) *Mvuhˇ shawˉ teˇ na̰, mvuhˇ maˇ htiˇ she_ htaˇ, Ye_suˆ tu leh heh puiˉ hk’aw lo k’ai leh, oˇ ka̬ lo bon law̬ chehˇ ve yo̬. Siˉmon_ leh yawˇ geh chehˇ ve aw̬ chawˇ teˇ hpa_Ye_suˆ hta̭ g’a̭ ca ve yo̬. Yawˇ hui Ye_suˆ hta̭ maw̤ htaˇ, Chaw hk’a peu-e̬ naw̬ hta̭ ca chehˇ ve yo̬ teh̭ yawˇ hta̭ hto piˇ ve yo̬. Ye_suˆ yawˇ hui hta̭ k’oˆ piˇ ve, Aw̬ paˇ aw̬ kui lo caw̬ ve venˇ hk’aˆ teˇ hpa_ hta̭ htawˇ nga̬ bon g’a ma_ piˇ tu̬ aw̬ g’uˇ suh_ k’ai-a veu̬. Aw̬ lawn k’o, chi hk’e te tu̬ nga̬ la̬ ve yo̬ teh̰, yawˇ k’aw̭ k’oˆ piˇ ve yo̬. Ga_li_lehˇ mvuhˇmi̬ teˇ ka̬ le le yawˇ hui ve bon yeh̬ teˇ hpa_ aw̬ hk’aw lo yawˇ bon ca ma_ piˇ leh, neˇ teˇ hpa_ hta̭ g’a̭ k’o̬ ve yo̬.*

In this particular script of Lahu,[3] there is a convention of writing syllables of proper noun loanwords together with no spaces (see (1d), *Ye_suˆ* ‘Jesus’, *Siˉmon_* ‘Simon’, and *Ga_li_lehˇ* ‘Galilee’).

11.2.1 Karen languages

The Karen languages form a clearly defined branch of Trans-Himalayan with no uncertain members (Manson 2017). The speakers of Karen languages are primarily located along the eastern border of Myanmar from Shan State southwards to the southernmost tip of Myanmar, and the Irrawaddy delta. The total number of languages is unknown, but it would appear from the

[3] Lahu has seven scripts in use! These are the five Latin scripts: (1) the Pinyin script and (2) the Hmong script from China, (3) the Protestant script, (4) the Catholic script, and (5) the Matisoff script; (6) the Thai script; and (7) the Vietnamese script.

literature that there are over thirty distinct Karen languages (see Shintani 2012).[4] The figure of twenty-one given in the *Ethnologue* (Eberhard et al. 2024) is most likely underreported.

Recently, I researched the Kayan dialects[5] (Manson 2019) and found that they have super-dialect groups (Gekho, Yinbaw, Southern, Northern, Lahta/Zayein and "outliers"). When the Kayan from different villages meet together, they initially talk with their own village lect, then they adjust their pronunciation to the other person's lect, and if they do not understand each other, they switch to another dialect (Standard Pekon [pdu]) or Burmese, or Sgaw Karen if they are Baptist. Karen youths are growing up in highly complex sociolinguistic environments, which feature dynamic multilingualism and mutlidialectism that include multiple languages and dialects to which they have different exposure.

All Karen languages have SVO clause order. The change from OV (Trans-Himalayan) to VO was at the Proto-Karen level.[6] See examples (2a)[7] and (2b) for transitive clauses and (2c) for a ditransitive clause.

(2a)	*Bauf sof hpav dof*	*auf*	*klauj hpo hsiv*	*hsoof*[8]	Sgaw [ksw]
	/bau^{53}so^{53} p^{h}aʔ^{4}do^{53}	au^{53}	klau^{11} p^{h}o^{55}s^{h}iʔ^{4}	s^{h}u^{53}/	
	tiger big	eat	cow nursing	very.often	
	SUBJ	VERB	OBJ	ADV	
	'The big tiger very often eats nursing cows' (Seguinotte 2007:8)				

b)	*làqnílàqkhòq*	*nàq*	*cò kàq*	*tàq-ʔɔ̀q*	*thòqzáq*	Mobwa [jkm]
	/lə^{1}nị̤^{5}lə^{1}k^{h}o^{1}	nə^{1}	cọ̤^{1} kə^{1}	ta^{1}-ɔ^{1}	t^{h}o^{1}za^{5}/	
	one.day	TOP	Mr Crooked	want-eat	pork	
	TEMP		SUBJ	VERB	OBJ	
	'One day, Mr. Crooked wanted to eat pork.' (Jones 1961:248)					

4 According to Shintani (quoted in Kato 2019:131 fn1), the number of Karenic languages could be near fifty.

5 There are over 350 Kayan villages (Eden Phan 2005).

6 There are Austroasiatic (Proto-Palaungic) loan words in Proto-Karen (and also Proto-Kuki-Chin). The Karen human DNA (mtDNA and Y) has affinity to Proto-Palaungic and Trans-Himalayan (in contrast to Burmese speakers) (Summerer et al. 2014). The origin legend of Karen is they passed through "a river of flowing sand" (Jones 1961:224–231; Marshall 1997:5–6) to reach modern-day Myanmar, before the Burmese came.

7 Superscript numbers indicate tone: 1 low, 3 medium, 5 high.

8 See the rules of § 11.2.2.1.2 Sako (Romanized) script.

c)	/jə-	pʰí-lâɴ	ʔəwê	lái?àʊ/	Eastern Pwo [kjp]
	1SG-	give-down	3SG	book	
	SUBJ	VERB	PRIMARY.OBJ	SECONDARY.OBJ	

'I gave him/her a book.' (Kato 2017:1075)

In the noun phrase in (3), the order is the possessive (phrase) followed by the head noun followed by modifiers.

(3)	/ʔa^1	hi^{53}	ʔa^{1}li^1	do^5	su^1	Mɛ^1/	Kawyaw [kxf]
	3SG	house	red	big	3	CLF.round	
	POSS	N	ADJ	ADJ	NUM	CLF	

'her/his three big red houses' (Wai Lin Aung 2013:61)

11.2.2 Karen scripts

There is an abundance of competing scripts used in the Karen branch (Indic/ Myanmar-based, Latin-based, and Indigenous), and often multiple scripts are used for a single language.

11.2.2.1 Sgaw Karen scripts

11.2.2.1.1 Christian Missionary Sgaw script

This was created by Jonathan Wade (an American Baptist missionary) in the 1830s using consonant symbols in the Myanmar script along with unique vowel and tone graphemes created for Sgaw.

Sgaw Christian Missionary script example (Mark 1:35–39)

(4) လၢခံတဂီၤ, ဂီၤဂီၤကလဲာ်တချူးမ့ၢ်ဆ့ၣ်ထီၣ်နှၣ်, ယ့ၣ်ရှူးဂဲၤဆၢထၢၣ်ဒီးဟးထီၣ်လၢဟံၣ်ပူၤဒီး
လဲၤဝဲဆူတၢ် လီၢ်လၢပှၤတအိၣ်ဝဲနီတဂၤဘၣ်ဒီးဖဲနှၣ်ဘါထုကဖၣ်တၢ်လီၤ. စီၤရှံမိၣ်ဒီးအသကိး
တဖၣ်ဟးထီၣ်လၢအလီၢ်ခံဒီးလူၤယုကွၢ်အီၤလီၤ. တုၤအထံၣ်အီၤတစုဒီးအဝဲသ့ၣ်စံးဘၣ်အီၤ,
"ပှၤကိးဂၤဒဲးယုထံၣ်နၤလီၤ."အဝဲစံးဆၢတၢ်ဒီးစံး, "မ်ပလဲၤသကိးဆူဝ့ၢ်ဖိဝ့ၢ်ဆၣ်အဂၤ အဂၤတ
ကွၢ်. ယကဘၣ်စံၣ်တဲၤတဲလီၤတၢ်လၢတၢ်လီၢ်တဖၣ်နှၣ် အပူၤဒံး, အဂ့ၢ်ဒ်အံၤယဟဲလၢတၢ်နှၣ်
အဂီၢ်လီၤ." ဒီးလဲၤဝဲသကုၤကီၢ်ကၤလံၤလါ, စံၣ်တဲၤတဲလီၤတၢ်လၢဘူၣ်ဘျိၣ်လၢ အမ့ၢ်တၢ်ဘါ
လီၢ်တဖၣ်အပူၤဒီးဟီထီၣ်ကွံာ်တၢ်နါတဖၣ်လီၤ

11.2.2.1.2 Sako (Romanized) script

A Latin-based script (Sako) was created and developed by a "Protestant missionary who came to spread Christianity in Burma around 1930" (Seguinotte 2007:1). The script is being used for the Catholics and academics in Thailand. In his dictionary Joseph Seguinotte (2007:11–12) includes the following principles for writing words.

> Words that consist of two or more syllables can be written together, unless the syllable has a final tone marker (<v, j, x, f, z>) which adds a white space.
>
> A syllable or word that follows <k’, t’, n’, p’, m’, y’, l’, s’>[9] must always be written with no space.

(5a)	*moohkof*	*hauf hkof*[10]		Sgaw [ksw]
	/mu^{55}k^{h}o^{53}/	/hau^{53}k^{h}o^{53}/		
	‘sky’	‘land’		(Seguinotte 2007:11)

b) *htof kwaz hklef*
/t^{h}o^{53}kwa^{33}k^{h}le^{53}/
‘pink-necked green pigeon’ (*Treron vernans*) (Seguinotte 2007:11)

c) *t’hai div baf*

/tə=	hai^{55}	di?^{4}	ba^{53}/
NEG=	come	again	NEG

‘[S/he] hasn’t come yet.’ (Seguinotte 2007:246)

d) *htif wai k’buvluv*

/t^{h}i^{53}	wai^{55}	kəbu?^{4}lu?^{4}/
see	3SG	probably

‘[S/he] probably saw it/him/her.’ (Seguinotte 2007:25)

In example (5a) ‘sky’ the second syllable *hkof* is “compounded” to *moo* but ‘land’ *hkof* has just a space between the first and second syllable. The ‘pink-necked green pigeon’ (5b) has three syllables in a grammatical/semantic word. Example (5c) is a three major syllable[11] clause; and in (5d) the adverb breaks Seguinotte’s second principle. These examples illustrate the inconsistency of the orthographic word.

---

9 <’> represents [ə], which is part of a minor syllable.

10 These two elements can appear together, in what is known as an “elaborate expression” (see § 11.3.2). In that case, the meaning is ‘universe’ (heaven and earth).

11 The major syllables are tone bearing, whereas the minor syllables are not.

11.2.2.2 Pwo Karen scripts

Recently Kato (2021; 2022) has provided descriptions of the competing Pwo Karen writing systems from a linguistic perspective, namely the Buddhist Pwo Karen script (6a), the Christian Pwo Karen script (6b), the Leke script (6c) and the Myainggyingu script (6d). Examples of the scripts (Kato 2021) follow:

(6a) ဖံ့ၠဆိုဒ်ဖေါဟ်ဆုံအူးခဲို
ခဲိုယိုဝ် ဖံ့ၠဆိုဒ်ဖောဟ်ဆုံဖေါတ်ဆုံအူးဖိုင်လုံဖးကျ် မွဲဆုံဖေါတ်ဆုံအူး လုံဆုံ၏အူးယောဝ့်

b) ဖျိုၩဆၢ်ၩဖိၣ်ဆၢ်အူၣ်ခွံၩ
ခွံၩယီၩ ဖျိုၩဆၢ်ၩဖိၣ်ဆၢ်ဖိလ်ဆၢ်အူၣ်ဖၢ်ၩလဖၣ်နီၣ် မွဲဆၢ်ဖိလ်ဆၢ်အူၣ် လၢ်ဆၢ်ဘၣ်အူၣ်ရှိၢ

c) [illegible]
[illegible]

d) [illegible]
[illegible]

The Pwo Karen people who received Buddhism from the Mon at various monasteries tried to use the Mon script to write their language in the late eighteenth century. In the mid-nineteenth century, a standardized Buddhist script (6a) was developed. The Christian script (6b) is based on the Sgaw script created by Wade, Mason, and Brayton in the 1840s. According to legend, the Leke script (6c) developed in the mid-nineteenth century. A Sgaw Karen monk, U Thuzana (1947–2018), created the Myainggyingu script (6d) for Sgaw, but Pwo Karen people can also write Pwo in this script (Kato 2021).

In addition, the Northern Pwo [pww] Karen people living in Thailand have been using the Thai script (Cooke et al. 1976; Phillips 2002) and follow the Thai convention of separating sentences with spaces, as in the following example, from Luke 15:12:

(7a) Northern Pwo Karen Bible

อ พู ไป๊ะ ล แฌ้ นอ ไคล้ ดื๊ อ แพ่ บี่ อึ้ง, 'แพ่-เอ้อ, น คอง น แซยั้ พี่ อ ล้างเทะ แบ ยิ๊ แด นอ,
อางน้าง ไมวะ เอะ แย้ ค๊องเนง อึ้ง', ฌ้อง อ แพ่ อางน้าง อ คอง อ แซยั้ เอะ อ พูแคว๊ คึ๊ง แฌ้ เลา'

https://www.bible.com/bible/1736/LUK.15.12

b) Northern Pwo Karen Bible (2016)

อพูไป๊ะลแฌ้นอไคล้ดื๊อแพ่บี่อึ้ง, 'แพ่-เอ้อ นคองนแซยั้พี่อล้างเทะแบยิ๊แดนอ
อางน้างไมวะเอะแย้ค๊องเนงอึ้ง' ฌ้องอแพ่อางน้างอคองอแซยั้เอะอพูแคว๊ คึ๊งแฌ้เลา

[His younger son spoke with his father like this,] ["Father, dear,] [your stuff that comes to me] [(you) give (it) to me now."] [Then, their father gave all his stuff to his two sons.] (This is a rough translation of the N Pwo. The brackets reflect the positioning of the spaces in the text.)

11.2.2.3 Kayah Li scripts

Kayah Li has three scripts. The indigenous script was created in 1962 by Htae Bu Phae, himself a Kayah Li person. Example (8a) is an indigenous script for people outside Myanmar (the script is banned in Myanmar), (8b) is a Latin-based script for the Catholics, and (8c) is the recent Sgaw-based script for the Protestants.

Western Kayah Li [kyu] Mark 1:35

(8a) [illegible]
[illegible]

b) Bí mo̱lĭ ro̱mṹ mo̱khíó pǎpré akhěnuô, Jesŭ kahtò cuốcóbě dố khǎlẹ́ dố ŭ o tôprẹ̀~ to tôpho.

c) ဘီ မ့ၠလီး ရှိမံ မ့ၠခီအ် ပးပြ် အၢခဲးနု်, ယ်ၤဆ့ ကၢထံၤ စ့်စ်ဘဲး ဒ် ခးလ့ၠ် ဒ် အ်း အိၤ တ်ၤပြုၢ်~ တိၤ တ်ၤဖိၤ။

Example (8a) forms the basis of the computer adaption to the (8b) Latin and (8c) Sgaw Karen scripts. There is consistency throughout the scripts in Western Kayah Li with respect to word spaces (8a–c).

While the Sgaw-based and the Latin-based scripts are used for Western Kayah Li in Myanmar, more recently Eastern Kayah [eky] Li (SIL International 2022), Yintale, and Kawyaw have been using the indigenous Kayah Li-based script.

11.2.2.4 Pontifical Institute of Missionaries for the East (PIME) scripts

The first four PIME fathers (Eugenio Biffi, Rocco Tornatore, Sebastiano Carbone and Tancredi Conti) arrived in Taungoo in March 1868. They crossed Salween River to the east where the Geba, Bwe, Kayaw, Kayah, and Gekho lived (Myanmar Catholic Church n.d.). From 1869 to 1875 Goffredo, the brother of Tancredi Conti, and Sebastiano Carbone developed an orthography and literacy materials for the Geba. Later, the Geba orthography was adapted and used by Bwe, Gekho Kayan, Kayah and Kayaw (see, for example: 8b, 13, 16, 18, and 20). In 1896 Father Paolo Manna reached the Gekho region and further developed the Gekho Kayan orthography (Gheddo 2000).

11.3 Case studies

11.3.1 Latin-based Mark translation of Kayan, Kayaw, and Kayah

In the late 1990s the Karen Baptist Association felt the need to translate the Scriptures into various Karen languages, and so Saw Lar Baa (2001) created the Sgaw-based orthography and developed participatory workshops for the other Karen languages.

The Kayan Baptists adapted the Sgaw-based orthography for Kayan in the early 2000s. In 2004 Kayan from all walks of life met together in Taunggyi, the capital of Shan State, to decide on the orthography. At that meeting the Gekho Kayan orthography was considered. The Baptist leaders listened to the Kayan youths who said, "it is our own orthography," and unanimously decided on the Gekho orthography as the basis for all the Kayan literacy materials. However, the marking of five tones with the vowel markings was cumbersome, and was reduced to three tones in the late 2000s.

The Kayaw orthography created by Fr Gulio Rovagnati in the late 1940s was based on the Geba Karen (Kayaw Literature and Cultural Committee 2003). Hsar Shee (2017) highlights in her conclusion to the Kayaw orthography statement:

> There are still problems in combining and separating words. Writers do better if they are familiar with English. However there is still inconsistency in whether the third person pronoun is written attached to the verb or not, whether compound are (sic) joined or separated, and whether 4-part elaborate expressions are written as four, two or one word. Verb particles are sometimes written joined to the verb, sometimes separately. The current situation is a laissez faire situation without a great push for standardization.

11.3.2 Four-syllable elaborate expressions

Four-syllable elaborate expressions are an areal feature for Greater Mainland Southeast Asia and found in most languages in the region. They are a sonorous/poetic device, often with the pattern ABAC or ABCB. Phonologically they repeat a syllable and often they repeat the second syllable's rhyme, "making the language sound more beautiful and balanced, and less abrupt" (Jarkey 2015:233). Consider the elaborate expressions in Bwe (9) and Sgaw (10).

(9) [ɟə-mo^{3}-cə-pa^{3}] [and] [ɟə-bu^{3}-jə-wɛ^{3}] Bwe [bwe]

/ɟə-	mo	ɟə-[12]	pa/		/ɟə-	bu	ɟə-	wɛ/
3SG-	mother	3SG-	father		3SG-	young.sibling	3SG-	old.sibling
A	B	A	C		A	B	A	C
'their parents'				[and]	'their relatives'			

(Henderson 1997:vol 1: p55#110)

(10) [haʔ^{3}tʰa^{53}haʔ^{3}la^{33}] Sgaw [ksw]

/haʔ^{3}	tʰa^{53}	haʔ^{3}	la^{33}/
go	up	go	down
A	B	A	C

'walk around' (Schie 2019:55)

Elaborate expressions in Karen languages are phonological words, not grammatical words, and so there is a primary stress on the final syllable, for example Pa'O (11) and Pekon Kayan (12):

(11) [ˌpʰu^{2}ˌpo^{4}ˌwe^{2}ˈpo^{4}] Pa'O [blk]

/pʰu^{2}	po^{4}	we^{2}	po^{4}/
elder	child	younger	child
A	B	C	B

'cousin(s)' (Thanamteun 2000:50)

(12) [ˌpa̤^{1}ˌhjən^{53}ˌpa̤^{1}ˈpʰan^{5}] Pekon Kayan [pdu]

/pa̤^{1}	hjən^{53}	pa̤^{1}	pʰan^{5}/
1PL	house	1PL	paddy.store
A	B	A	C

'our house and paddy store' (Manson 2010:122)

11.3.2.1 Kayan

In Kayan spelling, word conventions are evolving regarding four-syllable elaborate expressions. The negative elaborate expressions seem to be showing a change from being written without spaces (Eden Phan 2001)

[12] In Bwe the person/number prefixes (subject and possessive) have voiced assimilation to the following syllable.

(13a, b) to being written with white spaces (13c), though this is a tendency rather than a consistent pattern:

(13a) *cô̌ceicô̌klôn* Pekon Kayan [pdu]

/sə^{5}=	sen^{53}	sə^{5}=	klən^{5}/
NEG=	stout	NEG=	stable
A	B	A	C

'not firmly set up' (Eden Phan 2004:3)

b) *cô̌sácô̌blaò* Pekon Kayan [pdu]

/sə^{5}=	s^{h}a^{1}	sə^{5}=	blau^{1}/
NEG=	sew	NEG=	mend
A	B	A	C

'not sew (nor) mend' (Mark 2:21) (Standard Kayan draft 2008)

c) *cô̌ pau cô̌ thei* Pekon Kayan [pdu]

/sə^{5}=	pə^{3}	sə^{5}=	θe^{1}/
NEG=	look	NEG=	know
A	B	A	C

'not see and understand' (Mark 8:17) (Standard Kayan draft 2008)

As can be seen when comparing (13b) and (13c) currently there is sometimes inconsistency between the two options in one piece of writing. The published Dimawso Kayan Mark (2008) takes the elaborate expression out, as in example (14):

(14) *cô̌ sáblaò* Dimawso Kayan [pdu]

/sə^{5}=	s^{h}a^{1}	blau^{1}/
NEG=	sew	mend

'not mend' (Mark 2:21) (Kayah Baptist Association 2009)

In the Baptist Dimawso Kayan publications of Mark, Luke, Acts, 1 and 2 Thessalonians, and Psalms, the negative is marked as a separate orthographic word, as in example (15):

(15) *Bwedau mwaǐ cô̌ aò dô̌ pa ŭdeǐn* Dimawso Kayan [pdu]

/bwe^{53}dọ̤^{1}	mwe^{3}	sə^{5}=	au^{53}	də^{5}	pạ̤^{1}	u^{5}den^{5}/
Lord	TOP	NEG=	exist	LOC	1PL	side

'The Lord is not at our side' (Psalm 124:1) (Kayah Baptist Association 2015)

In summary, Kayan writers are in the process of standardizing the use of white spaces in four-syllable expressions with the AB AC and AB CB patterns, but current practice still shows some inconsistency in this area (e.g., ABAC).

11.3.2.2 Kayaw

Kayaw writers took quite a long while to standardize their elaborate expressions, omitting spaces between syllables, see (16a–c):

(16a) *taritakè̌* Kayaw [kvl]

/ta³-	ri³	ta³-	kɛ⁵/
NOM-	good	NOM-	look
A	B	A	C

'news, happening' (Mark 1:45) (Kayaw Bible Translation Committee 2018)

b) *mademalû̌*

/ma³	de³	ma³	lɯ⁵/
do	can	do	save
A	B	A	C

'able to save' (Mark 1:23) (Kayaw Bible Translation Committee 2018)

c) *ghāthū ghāprā* *ghāthūghāprā*

/ga¹-θu¹	ga¹-pra¹/	/ga¹-θu¹-ga¹-pra¹/
area-miss	area-quiet	area-miss-area-quiet
A B	A C	A B A C
'desolate place' (Mark 1:35) (Kayaw Bible Translation Committee 2018)		'desolate place' Kayaw-English Dictionary

In (16c) the elaborate expression has two different forms: the Mark 1:35 is from the highly/edited revised publication of Mark (2015) (AB AC) and the Kayaw-English dictionary (ABAC) is standardized.

11.3.2.3 Kayah

Kayah writers took quite a long while to standardize their elaborate expressions, omitting spaces between syllables, see (17a–c):

(17a) *tè̤ritè̤kyǎ* Western Kayah [kyu]

/tɛ̤¹-	ri¹	tɛ̤¹-	kja³/
NOM	good	NOM	look
A	B	A	C

'news' (Mark 1:2, 4) The New Testament in the Kayah language (2014)

b) *me̤còme̤pe̤*

/me̤¹	tʃɔ⁴	me̤¹	pe̤³/
do	straight	do	level
A	B	A	C

'straighten/level' (Mark 1:3) The New Testament in the Kayah language (2014)

c) *atè̤zû́tè̤nyà̤*

/a¹-	tɛ̤¹-	zɯ̤⁴	tɛ̤¹-	ɲa̤⁴/
3	NOM-	believe	NOM-	believe
	A	B	A	C

'their faith' (Mark 2:5) The New Testament in the Kayah language (2014)

11.3.3 Classifier phrases

Classifier phrases are an areal feature for Greater Mainland Southeast Asia and found in most languages in the region (Migliazza 1996; Enfield 2018; Vittrant et al. 2019; Vittrant and Allassonnière-Tang 2021). "Classifier phrases" is a Eurocentric misnomer for the grammatical word (see Manson 2010:77–78, 81–83).

In the Karen languages, the classifier phrase has the order of numeral prefix followed by classifier base.

11.3.3.1 Kayan

In Kayan, numerals rarely occur in isolation, but are always bound to the following classifier. When reciting numbers, Kayan speakers usually include a classifier (often the human classifier <*pra*>). In rare cases where no classifier is present during the counting, there are several tonal changes occurring on the numerals "two", "four" and "five".

Kayan writers tend to concatenate the numeral prefixes and classifier base (i.e., no white space between them), see examples from Mark chapter 8 (18a, b):

(18a) *takaō* *ngaǐma* Kayan [pdu]
/təko⁵³ ŋa̤i⁵- ma⁵/
bread 5- CLF.round
'five bread rolls' (Mark 8:19) (Kayah Baptist Association 2009)

b) *pra* *ngaǐreī*
/pra̤¹ ŋa̤i⁵- ren¹/
people 5- CLF.thousand
'five thousand people' (Mark 8:19) (Kayah Baptist Association 2009)

In contrast to (18a, b), the following verse (19) has a space between the numeral and classifier:

19) *ngaǐ* *dǎn*
/ŋa̤i⁵- dan⁵/
5- CLF.basket
'five baskets' (Mark 8:20) (Kayah Baptist Association 2009)

There is a tendency toward the orthographic choice shown in (18a, b), but there is not complete consistency even within one chapter of the same publication.

11.3.3.2 Kayaw

Kayaw authors attach the numeral prefix to the classifier base, as in (20).

(20a) *thôkô* *hanu* *něma* Kayaw [kvl]
/θə³kə³ ha³nu³ nɛ⁵- ma³/
bread that 7- CLF.round
'those seven bread rolls' (Mark 8:6) (Kayaw Bible Translation Committee 2018)

b) *pra* *jĕ̌htō*
/pra^3 jɛ^5- t^{h}o^1/
people 5- CLF.thousand
'five thousand people' (Mark 8:19) (Kayaw Bible Translation Committee 2018)

11.3.3.3 Kayah

Kayah authors tend to write the numeral prefixes joined to the classifier base, as in these examples from Mark chapter 8:

(21a) *khỏ̀mŭ* *nyă̤klọ̤̀* Western Kayah [kyu]
/k^{h}ɔ^{4}Mu^3 ɲạ̤^{3}- klọ̤^{4}/
bread 5- CLF.round
'five bread rolls' (Mark 8:19) The New Testament in the Kayah language (2014)

b) *kayă* *nyă̤rí*
/ka^{1}ja^3 ɲạ̤^{3}- ri/
people 5- CLF.thousand
'five thousand people' (Mark 8:19) The New Testament in the Kayah language (2014)

11.4 Concluding remarks

When Karen authors are using Latin-based orthographies, they develop and coalesce their ideas for the orthographic word in community. The grammars of all the Karen languages are consistent with respect to the clause structure, the noun phrase, the four-syllable elaborate expression, and the classifier phrase.

The four-syllable elaborate expression is a case in point. Kayan writers use two orthographic words, whereas in Kayah, writers use only one orthographic word, and in Kayaw, writers fluctuate between one and two orthographic words.

However, in the case of the "classifier phrase", Kayan, Kayaw, and Kayah writers all use just one orthographic word. This indicates that orthography alone is a poor indicator of the morphosyntactic word in Karen languages.

Languages are social rather than linguistic objects. All orthography conventions are part of social systems, particularly script choices and orthographic word choices. These choices develop a cultural load as markers of social distinction (Edwards 2009). Karen insiders (Kayan, Kayaw, Kayah) often accept and are content to use distinct orthographic systems; however, linguistic outsiders cannot easily define the Latin-based (Kayan, Kayaw, Kayah) orthographic word. It would seem that (at the most basic level) an orthographic word can be identified by the spaces around it, and therefore the orthographic word is not really a linguistic construct.

That is, it seems that the orthographic word cannot be defined in crosslinguistic terms. It cannot be defined grammatically and/or phonologically. And if an orthographic word cannot be defined linguistically, it is not a linguistic object.

Linguists, therefore, would seem to have no theoretical basis for judging disputes about the orthographic word.

References

Aikhenvald, Alexandra Y., R. M. W. Dixon, and Nathan M. White. 2020a. *Phonological word and grammatical word: A cross-linguistic typology*. Explorations in Linguistic Typology 10. Oxford: Oxford University Press.

Aikhenvald, Alexandra Y., R. M. W. Dixon, and Nathan M. White. 2020b. The essence of "word." In Alexandra Y. Aikhenvald, R. M. W. Dixon, and Nathan M. White (eds.), *Phonological word and grammatical word: A cross-linguistic typology*, 1–24. Explorations in Linguistic Typology 10. Oxford: Oxford University Press.

Bradley, Jessica, Emilee Moore, and James Simpson. 2020. Translanguaging as transformation: The collaborative construction of new linguistic realities. In Emilee Moore, Jessica Bradley and James Simpson (eds.), *Translanguaging as transformation: The collaborative construction of new linguistic realities*, 1–12. Bristol: Multilingual Matters. Doi:10.21832/9781788928052-004.

Cahill, Michael. 2014. Non-linguistic factors in orthographies. In Michael Cahill and Keren Rice (eds.), *Developing orthographies for unwritten languages*, 9–25. Publications in Language Use and Education 6. Dallas, TX: SIL International.

Cooke, Joseph R., J. Edwin Hudspith, and James A. Morris. 1976. Phlong (Pwo Karen of Hot district). In William A. Smalley (ed.), *Phonemes and orthography: Language planning in ten minority languages of Thailand*, 187–220. Pacific Linguistics Series C–43. Canberra: Pacific Linguistics.

Dixon, R. M. W., and Alexandra Y. Aikhenvald, eds. 2002. *Word: A cross-linguistic typology*. Cambridge: Cambridge University Press.

Eberhard, David M, Gary F. Simons, and Charles D. Fennig, eds. 2024. *Ethnologue: Languages of the world*. Twenty-seventh edition. Dallas, TX: SIL International. www.ethnologue.com.

Eden Phan. 2001. ကယန်းလူမျိုးများသား၏ဆွေ့စဉ်မှတ်တမ်းဝင်များစာစောင် [The journal of the Kayan people]. Mae Hong Son, Thailand: Kayan Literacy and Culture Committee.

Eden Phan. 2004. *Kayănphao caŭcaŭhtwănhtwăn atahtŏn dò ngaǒsau ngaǒswȋ* [The narratives, beliefs and customs of the Kayan people]. Mae Hong Son, Thailand: Kayan Literacy and Culture Committee.

Eden Phan. 2005. *The narratives, beliefs and customs of the Kayan people*. Mae Hong Son, Thailand: Eden Phan.

Edwards, John. 2009. *Language and identity: An introduction*. Cambridge: Cambridge University Press.

Enfield, N. J. 2018. *Mainland Southeast Asian languages: A concise typological introduction*. Cambridge: Cambridge University Press. Doi:10.1017/9781139019552.

Gheddo, Piero. 2000. *Missione Birmania. I 140 anni del Pime in Myanmar (1867-2007)*. Bologna: Editrice Missionaria Italiana. https://atma-o-jibon.com/italiano8/gheddo_pime150anni12.htm.

Haspelmath, Martin. 2011. The indeterminacy of word segmentation and the nature of morphology and syntax. *Folia Linguistica* 45(1):31–80. Doi:10.1515/flin.2011.002.

Henderson, Eugénie J. A. 1997. *Bwe Karen dictionary: With texts and English-Karen word list*. London: School of Oriental and African Studies.

Himmelmann, Nikolaus P. 2006. The challenges of segmenting spoken language. In Jost Gippert, Nikolaus P. Himmelmann, and Ulrike Mosel (eds.), *Essentials of language documentation*, 253–274. Berlin: Mouton de Gruyter.

Hsar Shee. 2017. Kayaw orthography statement. Ms.

Jarkey, Nerida. 2015. *Serial verbs in White Hmong*. Brill's Studies in Language, Cognition and Culture 12. Leiden: Brill. Doi:10.1163/9789004292390.

Jones, Robert B. 1961. *Karen linguistic studies: Description, comparison, and texts*. University of California Publications in Linguistics 25. Berkeley: University of California Press.

Jung, Dagmar, and Nikolaus P. Himmelmann. 2011. Retelling data: Working on transcription. In Geoffrey Haig, Nicole Nau, Stefan Schnell, and Claudia Wegener (eds.), *Documenting endangered languages: Achievements and perspectives*, 201–220. Berlin: Mouton de Gruyter.

Kato, Atsuhiko. 2017. Pwo Karen. In Graham Thurgood and Randy J. LaPolla (eds.), *The Sino-Tibetan languages*, 942–958. Second edition. London: Routledge.

Kato, Atsuhiko. 2019. Pwo Karen. In Alice Vittrant and Justin Watkins (eds.), *The Mainland Southeast Asia linguistic area*, 131–175. Berlin: De Gruyter Mouton. Doi:10.1515/9783110401981-004.

Kato, Atsuhiko. 2021. Pwo Karen writing systems. Reports of the Keio Institute of Cultural and Linguistic Studies 52:23–55.

Kato, Atsuhiko. 2022. Pwo Karen writing systems 2: Western Pwo Karen. Reports of the Keio Institute of Cultural and Linguistic Studies 53:23–57.

Kayah Baptist Association. 2009. *Li Marku: Tathanaò thasaŭ arî akaĭ bakyădò Jesŭ* [Mark: The gospel of Jesus]. Dimawso, Myanmar: Kayah Baptist Association.

Kayah Baptist Association. 2015. *Li Pratadaôphao dò Li Htònhtan 120–134* [Acts and Psalms 120–134]. Dimawso, Myanmar: Kayah Baptist Association.

Kayaw Bible Translation Committee. 2018. Marko Cècǒhtǐ Kayaw Èjō [The Gospel of Mark in Kayaw]. Ms.

Kayaw Literature and Cultural Committee. 2003. The history of Kayaw. Ms.

Kutsch Lojenga, Constance. 2014. Basic principles for establishing word boundaries. In Michael Cahill and Keren Rice (eds.), *Developing orthographies for unwritten languages*, 73–106. Dallas, TX: SIL International.

Manson, Ken. 2010. A grammar of Kayan, a Tibeto-Burman language. PhD dissertation. La Trobe University, Melbourne.

Manson, Ken. 2017. The characteristics of the Karen branch of Tibeto-Burman. In Picus Shizhi Ding and Jamin Pelkey (eds.), *Sociohistorical linguistics in Southeast Asia: New horizons for Tibeto-Burman studies in honor of David Bradley*, 149–168. Leiden: Brill. Doi:10.1163/9789004350519_010.

Manson, Ken. 2019. Kayan dialects in light of Proto-Karen. Paper presented at the 52nd International Conference on Sino-Tibetan Languages and Linguistics, University of Sydney, June 24–26, 2019.

Marshall, Harry Ignatius. 1997. *The Karen of Burma: A study in anthropology and ethnology*. Bangkok: White Lotus.

Migliazza, Brian. 1996. Mainland Southeast Asia: A unique linguistic area. *Notes on Linguistics* 75:17–25.

Myanmar Catholic Church. n.d. Taunggnu diocese. http://www.catholicmyanmar.com/diocesecbcmforall.php?diocese = taungngu.

New Living Translation (NLTse). 2015. *Holy Bible, New Living Translation*. Second edition. Carol Stream, IL: Tyndale House Foundation.

The New Testament in the Kayah language. 2014. *Lisăsě Athě Kayă Ngọ̤́* [The New Testament in the Kayah language]. Loikaw, Myanmar: Wycliffe and Commission for Bible Ministry Loikaw Diocese.

Ochs, Elinor. 1979. Transcription as theory. In Elinor Ochs and Bambi B. Schieffelin (eds.), *Developmental pragmatics*, 43–72. New York: Academic Press.

Orranat Thanamteun. 2000. The phonological study of Pa-O (Taungthu) at Ban Huay Salop, Tambon Huay Pha, Muang District, Mae Hong Son. MA thesis. Mahidol University, Bangkok.

Phillips, Audra. 2002. The West-Central Thailand Pwo Karen people. In TU-SIL-LRDP Committee (eds.), *Minority language orthography in Thailand: Five case studies*, 69–83. Bangkok: TU-SIL Language Research and Development Project.

Saw Lar Baa. 2001. The phonological basis of a Northwest Karenic orthography. MA thesis. Payap University, Chiang Mai.

Schie, Anne van. 2019. *Karen Sgaw morphology: Expressing grammatical relations in Karen Sgaw*. LINCOM Studies in Asian Linguistics 90. München: LINCOM Europa.

Sebba, Mark. 2007. *Spelling and society: The culture and politics of orthography around the world*. Cambridge: Cambridge University Press.

Sebba, Mark. 2009. Sociolinguistic approaches to writing systems research. *Writing Systems Research* 1(1):35–49. Doi:10.1093/wsr/wsp002.

Seguinotte, Joseph. 2007. *Pgaz K'Nyau dictionary*. Edited by Alfonso de Juan. Bangkok: Windows on the World.

Shintani, Tadahiko. 2012. *A handbook of comparative Brakaloungic languages*. Tokyo: The Research Institute for Languages and Cultures of Asia and Africa.

SIL International. 2022. ScriptSource - Kayah Li. https://scriptsource.org/cms/scripts/page.php?item_id = script_detail&key = Kali.

Summerer, Monika, Jürgen Horst, Gertraud Erhart, Hansi Weißensteiner, Sebastian Schönherr, Dominic Pacher, Lukas Forer, David Horst, Angelika Manhart, Basil Horst, Torpong Sanguansermsri, and Anita Kloss-Brandstätter. 2014. Large-scale mitochondrial DNA analysis in Southeast Asia reveals evolutionary effects of cultural isolation in the multi-ethnic population of Myanmar. *BMC Evolutionary Biology* 14(1):17. Doi:10.1186/1471-2148-14-17.

Taylor, John R., ed. 2015a. *The Oxford handbook of the word*. Oxford Handbooks in Linguistics. Oxford: Oxford University Press.

Taylor, John R. 2015b. Introduction. In John R. Taylor (ed.), *The Oxford handbook of the word*. Oxford Handbooks in Linguistics. Oxford: Oxford University Press. Doi:10.1093/oxfordhb/9780199641604.013.43.

Vitrano-Wilson, Seth, Ryan Gehrmann, Carolyn Miller, and Cheung Xaiyavong. 2018. Tone marks as vowel diacritics in two scripts: Repurposing tone marks for non-tonal phenomena in Cado and other Southeast Asian languages. *Writing Systems Research* 10(1):43–67. Doi:10.1080/17586801.2018.1493409.

Vittrant, Alice, and Marc Allassonnière-Tang. 2021. Classsifers in Southeast Asian languages. In Paul Sidwell and Jenny Mathias (eds.), *The languages and linguistics of Mainland Southeast Asia: A comprehensive guide*, 733–771. Berlin: De Gruyter Mouton.

Vittrant, Alice, Justin Watkins, and David A. Peterson, eds. 2019. *The Mainland Southeast Asia linguistic area*. Trends in Linguistics 314. Berlin: De Gruyter Mouton.

Wai Lin Aung. 2013. A descriptive grammar of Kayah Monu. MA thesis. Payap University, Chiang Mai.

Appendix

Pike, Kenneth. L., and Evelyn G. Pike. 1982. *Grammatical analysis*. Second edition. Summer Institute of Linguistics Publications in Linguistics 53. Dallas, TX: Summer Institute of Linguistics and University of Texas at Arlington. Extract (pp. 98–101) used by permission.

Criteria for word division

There is no algorithm (a fail-safe mechanically applicable set of steps for arriving at the one correct result) for the segmentation of a stretch of speech into words. The judgment of two analysts in weighing the importance of segmentation criteria for any one language may differ. If so, then (ideally) they should be expected to publish different descriptions that are mechanically convertible into each other (i.e., by a set of rules one should be able to change the one description mechanically into the other). In such instances, practical goals of making an alphabet, or writing a grammar, or of the preparation of language lessons, may be well served by both. Usually, however, one description will be slightly more economical for one part of the description, and the other slightly more economical for another part—or for another purpose. Here, as elsewhere, the observer inevitably intrudes himself into the output of his labors. Language about language (including linguistic theory formation) is not exempt from the intrusions, inevitably, of an observer component.

Note that a disjunct definition of the term *word* is needed (Principle 2.2b[1]); one set of criteria will identify many words, but other sets of criteria

[1] Editor's note: p22 in Pike and Pike 1982.

are needed to identify other words. In this chapter, we present various criteria for identifying word boundaries.

Principle 6.1 ***Isolatability***: In normal, nonhesitant speech, the potential minimum normal unit in a reply slot of an exchange will be **no less than** a word; such constituents are isolatable. This is in direct contrast to affixes which may not be a total normal reply, and hence not isolatable. (In reply to the question *What bit you?* one might hear *That!*, but never, apart from linguistic discussion, *-ing*, *-s*, or *un-*.)

> **Comment**: Space between words is the convention for indicating word division. Thus, nothing less than a word must be bounded by spaces. In the phrase *the boys* there are two words appropriately separated by a space, but *boys* may not be separated into *boy* and *s* as two words, since *-s* is not a word; therefore, neither is *boy* a word when it occurs with a suffix such as *-s*.

Principle 6.2 ***Relative Mobility versus Rigidity***: (a) Mobility of words: Words are likely to be appropriate to more grammatical slots than are nonwords. Specifically, minimum elements which may occur both at the beginning of monologs and at the end of monologs are usually to be considered words.

> **Comment**: Note *boys* in *Boys like to play ball*, and in *I enjoyed meeting those boys*; or in *Boys will be boys*. Similarly, words may often fill various slots. (Note *manliness* in *His manliness was attractive*; *His outstanding characteristic was manliness.*)

> **Comment**: In language about language (metalanguage), it is difficult to apply this criterion. Even if one says *the ifs and ands*, it does not help to identify *if* as a word, since one finds this to be merely a **metalanguage frame** which can contain nonwords as in *the* -ings *and the* -eds *of words like singing and wanted.*

(b) Rigidity in the order of parts of words: The parts within a word (roots and affixes) are likely to maintain an **internal stability**, i.e., a constant order in relation to one another, whereas within larger units in which words are the parts, the order may be less rigid. (Note *boy-s*, but not *s-boy*, in contrast to the words in *John ran away*, *Away ran John*, *Away John ran*; or *I saw the man dead* versus *I saw the dead man.*)

> **Comment**: An utterance will never begin with a suffix and will never end with a prefix (by definition of these terms).

Principle 6.3 ***Noninterruptibility of a Word by Words***: In general, a sequence of words is normally not expected to come in the middle of a word. Thus a stretch of speech that is interrupted by a free word sequence has the probability of being composed of at least two other words—the first part and the last part. (This criterion supports the breaking of *a man* into two words, since one may also say *a very large man*, with *very* and *large* as words (potential reply forms) interrupting the word sequence *a* and *man*. Compare *if so* with *if you say so*, for *if* as a word.)

> **Comment**: Compounds with fixed combinations such as *fireplace* lose their meaning and role relationships if interrupted, as in *fire made in that place*. **Idioms** such as *Jack-in-the-pulpit* lose their unitized meaning and role relationships in a sequence such as *Jack who used to take his place in the pulpit.*

> **Comment**: Some languages, however, allow nouns to be incorporated regularly into verbs. English allows phrases to be incorporated regularly into possessives, or into nominal plurals: *(the) King-of-England's (hat)*; *(the) I-don't-want-tos (of a spoiled child)*. This inclusion of a higher-level unit in a lower-level slot is nonnormal and should not be used as a basis for setting up regular patterns.

Principle 6.4 ***Slot-Role Proportion as a Criterion for Nonisolatable Words***: When there is a filler class of elements, one of which is a word by Principle 6.1 and another of which is not, the second may be called a word by analogy with the first, if the two have the **same proportional slot-role relation** to the context. (Thus, if in reply to the question, *What bit you?* one can obtain either *That wildcat*, *That*, or *A wildcat*; then, although one does not obtain *A*, the morpheme *a* may be considered to be a word because it is in the same filler class with *that*.)

Principle 6.5 ***Phonological Words versus Grammatical Words***: We have been using **isolatability** as our most fundamental criterion for identifying a word. Not only is such a word a grammatical word, but it is also a phonological word—a stress group. (A stress group is a sequence of one or more syllables, with only one stressed—accented—syllable, and with no pauses within the sequences. Compare the single stress groups *Cóme!*, *the-bóy*, and *was-cóming*.) Segmentation criteria from the two hierarchies give the same segmentation at this point. The phonological hierarchy segments a stream of speech into sounds, syllables, stress groups, and larger units. In general, no utterance is isolatable unless it is at least a **stress group** (or else a somewhat comparable **rhythm group**) with a nucleus of at least one syllable. In the norm, grammatical segmentation coincides with phonological segmentation (*Tómmy!*, because it is isolatable and is a single stress group, is a word both grammatically and phonologically.)

It is, however, in the instance in which the two hierarchies do not coincide that problems arise in word segmentation. This is the situation in phrases such as *the man*, *the other man*, *a tree*, *a big tree*, in which the morphemes *the* and *a* are not stressed and normally are not isolatable, hence are not phonological words. In Principles 6.3 and 6.4 we have shown them to be grammatical words. Such phonologically bound but grammatically free forms are called **clitics** and are treated in the grammatical formulas as words. If they are phonologically bound to what follow they are **proclitics**; if to what precedes they are **enclitics**. (In the above phrases *the* and *a* are proclitics. In the sequence *Í'm góing!* the morpheme *m* is an enclitic as it is in *I véry certainly'm nót góing.*)

> Comment: Occasionally it is helpful, in rewriting text, to place a hyphen between a clitic and its phonological nucleus (e.g., *Í-m*; *a-big bóok*); at other times it may be more convenient to put spaces between the two, as in English normal orthography, *a big book*. If ambiguity is avoided, various alternatives may be equally useful, or vary in desirability in accordance with the spelling traditions of the geographical area or academic convention.

Principle 6.6 *Segmentation of Function Words versus Content Words*: If we call the nuclei of noun phrases, verb phrases, adjective phrases, and adverbial phrases **content** words, but call various links or relaters **function** words, then we can say that content words are more easily isolated by the above principles than are function words. Relaters are often clitics.

> Comment: It is more probable that content words, rather than function words, will be allowed to occur appropriately as total reply forms. Yet, under some circumstances, a function word does occur as a reply. *I see that you went into that high-priced store?* Reply: *So?* Similarly, content words have, in general, greater **freedom of occurrence** (occur in more slots) than do function words; hence it may be difficult to distinguish them (i.e., function words) from affixes, unless one uses the proportion criterion of Principle 6.4 carefully.

> Comment: There are deep theoretical reasons why function words are so frequently found as clitics, while content words are rarely found predominantly in clitic form. These reasons have reference to the contrastive types of efficiency of large open classes versus small closed ones; we are not yet ready to discuss these problems. (See Chapter 7, Prin. 7.5.) For the present, we merely take as a given fact that both function words (or affixes) and content words can be expected in all languages, and suggest ways to differentiate the function words from the affixes.

Contributors

Cathryn Bartram has worked in linguistics and orthography development for over 30 years. She is the Lead Tutor in Linguistics for the MA Language, Community and Development, at Moorlands College, UK. Cathryn also coordinates the Orthography Services department of SIL Global and is an orthography consultant. She holds a PhD from the School of Oriental and African Studies, University of London. Her research interests include tone, morphophonology, and orthography development.

Caryn Benítez was a member of the Northern Songhay/Tagdal translation team from 1999 until 2014. More recently she has been the training unit coordinator and director of the Linguistics Institute at Payap University in Chiang Mai, Thailand. She holds an MA degree in linguistics from the University of Texas at Arlington.

Carlos M. Benítez-Torres has been a member of the Northern Songhay/Tagdal translation team in the Republic of Niger since 1999. He has also been a member of the faculty of linguistics at Payap University in Chiang Mai, Thailand since 2014. He holds a PhD in linguistics from the University of Leiden.

Ginger (Virginia L.) Boyd has a PhD in African linguistics from the University of Leiden. She is a Senior Linguistics Consultant with SIL Global and currently lives in Yaoundé, Cameroon. She has worked in languages in Central African Republic, Gabon, Republic of Congo and Democratic Republic of Congo as well as Cameroon. Her interests include phonology, morphophonology, morphology, language typology and text analysis in Bantu, Ubangian and Chadic languages.

Soulokadi Albert Camus is a doctoral student at the Université de N'Djaména, Chad. He wrote his Master's thesis on harmonizing the orthography of Musey, which is his mother tongue. He is currently writing a comprehensive grammar of Musey for his PhD.

Helen Eaton is a Senior Linguistics Consultant with SIL Global, working in Tanzania. She received her PhD in linguistics from the University of Reading in 2002. Her early research was on the Sandawe language of Tanzania, particularly in relation to grammar and information structure. Currently her focus is on orthography development in Bantu languages. Her research interests also include Bantu grammar and discourse.

Hazel Gray received her MA in African linguistics from the University of Leiden in 2013. She specialises in Bantu linguistics and has been involved in orthography development in Tanzania since 2008.

Ken Manson has an MA and PhD in linguistics from La Trobe University. He is a lecturer and a consultant with SIL Australia. He has worked in various languages in Greater Mainland Southeast Asia. His interests include descriptive linguistics, language documentation, field methods and historical linguistics.

Rebekah M. Mészároš received her MA in Field Linguistics from Redcliffe College, University of Gloucester, in 2017, writing her dissertation on "Vowel Hiatus Resolution in Simbiti and the Orthographic Implications". She is currently training as a Linguistics Consultant, specialising in phonology. Much of her work with SIL Tanzania is focused on orthography development.

Russell Norton is an associate professor in linguistics at the Theological College of Northern Nigeria and a linguistics consultant with SIL Global. He received his PhD in linguistics from the University of Essex, UK, in 2003. His interests range across the description, history and ecology of languages of Nigeria and Sudan, interfaces between theology and linguistics, and participatory linguistic research.

James Roberts is the linguistics coordinator for SIL Chad. He received his PhD in linguistics from Georgetown University and has worked continuously in central Africa since 1990. He has taught linguistics in both North American and African universities, and has researched and written on the description of languages of the Chadic family, as well as many other languages spoken in Chad and neighbouring countries. Phonology and orthography development are among his particular concerns.

Marc Schwab and his wife Ellen have been working in a language development project in Santiago Amoltepec Mixtec [mbz] in Mexico since 1997. This work includes the investigation, learning and analysis of the language, and the development of its written form. Marc has studied theology, linguistics, and anthropology, and his special interests are the areas where these domains touch or overlap. He has an MA in Intercultural Studies from Columbia International University (South Carolina).

Paul Solomiac received his PhD from the University of Lyon in 2007. He is a Linguistics Consultant with SIL Burkina Faso. From 1982 to 1983 he was a member of a survey team which conducted research on vitality, bilingualism and mutual intelligibility in a dozen languages of Burkina Faso. He has been involved in language development in Dzùùngoo in Burkina since 1987. Since 1998 he has been contributing to the development of participatory research workshops in Burkina, which have helped dozens of national Bible translators to gain awareness of language structures and get involved in the development of their own languages.

René van den Berg is from the Netherlands and studied linguistics at the University of Leiden, from which he received his PhD in 1989. He is a Senior Linguistics Consultant with SIL Global and a specialist in Austronesian languages. He has done fieldwork in Indonesia and Papua New Guinea, and has taught at SIL schools in the UK and Australia. His publications include grammars of Muna, Balantak, and Busoa (all three in Sulawesi, Indonesia), and of Vitu and Bola (both in Papua New Guinea). He also did research on Scripture use and was involved in training and mentoring Papua New Guinean linguists.

John B. Walker is a Linguistics Consultant with SIL Tanzania and received his MA from Trinity Western University in 2013 where he wrote his thesis on "Comparative Tense and Aspect in Mara Bantu." His current focus is on lexicography and dictionary production in several Bantu languages of Tanzania. He and his teammates celebrated the publication of the trilingual Kabwa-Swahili-English dictionary in 2023. His other related interests include historical/comparative linguistics, morphosyntax, and helping minority language speakers develop practical orthographies.

Shannon Yee earned her degree in linguistics from the University of Michigan in 2000. She spent more than fifteen years teaching English as a Second Language before shifting her focus to linguistic fieldwork and earning an MA in Linguistics from Wayne State University in 2021. When possible, Shannon is pursuing her passion for training and research in language documentation and collaboration with minority language communities working out of Yaoundé, Cameroon. Her focus is on syntax with a particular interest in the influence of grammar on orthography design.

SIL Global
Publications in Language Use and Education
ISSN 1545-0074

7. **Leadership in literacy: Capacity building and the Ifè program**, by JeDene Reeder. 2017, 347 pp., ISBN 978-1-55671-389-7.
6. **Developing orthographies for unwritten languages**, edited by Michael Cahill and Keren Rice. 2015, 265 pp., ISBN 978-1-55671-347-7.
5. **The early days of sociolinguistics: Memories and reflections.** Reprint, edited by Christina Bratt Paulson and G. Richard Tucker, 2010, 259 pp., ISBN 978-1-55671-253-1.
4. **Language contact and composite structures in New Ireland**, by Rebecca Sue Jenkins, 2005, 275 pp., ISBN 1-55671-156-5.
3. **Namel Manmeri: The in-between people—language and culture maintenance and mother-tongue education in the highlands of Papua New Guinea**, by Dennis L. Malone, 2004, 263 pp., ISBN 1-55671-147-3.
2. **And I, in my turn, will pass it on: Knowledge transmission among the Kayopó**, by Isabel I. Murphy, 2004, 235 pp., ISBN 1-55671-155-7.
1. **Reading is for knowing: Literacy acquisition, retention, and usage among the Machiguenga**, by Patricia M. Davis, 2004, 343 pp., ISBN 1-55671-094-0.

SIL Global Publishing Services
7500 W Camp Wisdom Road
Dallas, TX 75236-5629
publications@sil.org

www.ingramcontent.com/pod-product-compliance
Lightning Source LLC
Chambersburg PA
CBHW061424300426
44114CB00014B/1526
* 9 7 8 1 5 5 6 7 1 5 7 5 4 *